A FEAST OF
SOUPS

A FEAST OF SOUPS

THE COOKBOOK FOR SOUP LOVERS

With Recipes for First Course, Main Course, and
Dessert Soups; Cold Soups; Kids' Soups; Fish Soups;
Crock Pot Soups—and Hundreds More

Jacqueline Hériteau

The Dial Press · New York

Published by
The Dial Press
1 Dag Hammarskjold Plaza
New York, New York 10017

Copyright © 1981, 1982 by Jacqueline Hériteau

Certain of the recipes in this book first appeared
in *Vogue* magazine January 1982.

First printing

Design by James L. McGuire

Library of Congress Cataloging in Publication Data

Hériteau, Jacqueline.
A feast of soups.

Includes index.
1. Soups.   I. Title.
TX757.H47   641.8'13   81–9888
ISBN 0-385-27196-4   AACR2

This book is for my father, Marcel Hériteau,
whose good taste in food, and achievements
as a professional chef of stature,
have been a rich heritage.

ACKNOWLEDGMENTS

A lot goes into a cookbook that isn't covered by the author's name alone. There's the agent, in this case a brilliant young woman we will all long remember, Barbara Grant. And the editor— Nancy van Itallie, who fell in love with soup. The copyeditor who pulled it all together, Sybil Pincus. The publishing house, which has faith in the work and backs it in investment dollars. There is the designer, Jim McGuire, who made the gray of a printed page bright with graphic artistry. And the illustrator, Peter Kalberkamp.

My thanks to all those who brought this work to life. And a special note of appreciation to the commercial houses that helped me to try my recipe theories. Presto, makers of pressure cookers, J.C. Penney, Sunbeam, and General Foods generously provided food processors, all very good and solid equipment. The Oregon Freeze Dry food products—shrimp, fish, and mushrooms—were delicious and helpful in the testing of the fast-food applications of the recipes here. I am especially grateful to the makers of Doxsee Clam Juice, the Doxsee Food Corporation in Baltimore, Maryland, who gave me plenty of clam juice to test the seafood recipes in Chapter 4.

CONTENTS

PREFACE

FIRE ON THE HEARTH

A soup-centered meal, like a fire on the hearth, is a great deal more than the sum of its parts. Soup is warmth and comfort, security and strength, ease and good flavor. For most of man's history hearty, meaty soups, like French pot-au-feu, New England boiled dinner, and thick fish chowders, were the mainstay of family and communal meals. In many lands, they still are. With contemporary accessories like food processors, blenders, and slow-cook electric pots, soups are beginning to qualify not only as down-home cookin', but as practical, fast foods. They're easy (almost impossible to overcook), economical (thriftier than most meat stretchers), and above all, they're creative—an invitation to cook *your* way, to *your* taste, to meet *your* needs.

Many of the recipes here are soups my family has made and loved for years. Others are the result of a soup-lover's curiosity. I have been trying soups of all sorts from all sorts of sources and many lands ever since I started homemaking. What I've learned in my quest is that there are thousands of soups, not a mere five hundred, and dozens of ways to make each. Bouillabaisse in my favorite family restaurant in New York is delicious but different from the fish soups called bouillabaisse made by my peasant friends along the shores of the Mediterranean. Different, too, from bouillabaisse I've eaten in little and big restaurants in Cannes, Marseilles, and Paris.

So—have fun!

Jacqueline Hériteau

A FEAST OF
SOUPS

One

WITH THANKS TO PAPA CHÉRI

In the late forties I rented a little stone house from the Bertrand family in southern France—the Riviera, Fitzgerald country. It was in the rolling hills just behind Cannes, one of the few working farms left among luxury villas in a walled town called Mougins. Today it belongs to the world of international movie stars, but then my beloved Bertrands and their farm belonged to the eighteenth century.

Madame Bertrand was sixty-four, an only child and not into food. Her mother had done the cooking until she died, and Madame Bertrand had always worked in the fields. The Bertrands' crops were mostly flowers, so it wasn't hard work. Even after her mother had died, Madame Bertrand preferred outdoor work with her husband and son to being indoors at the stove like the other wives and mothers in the neighborhood. So it would be late afternoon before she'd come back to the yellow stucco farmhouse to start the fire in her stove. She'd fill her mother's big, battered soup kettle with water, and the sound of the filling was my signal to exchange the great American novel I was writing for a lesson in soup making.

Madame Bertrand never made her soup twice with the same ingredients, and there wasn't a cookbook in her house. The first thing that went into the water was salt, measured in her palm, about a tablespoonful for three quarts. That was followed by five or six whole black peppercorns. Then she'd walk around the big kitchen table talking a mile a minute about the day's work and local gossip—looking for inspiration for the soup. She'd pluck onion and garlic from the braided strands of herbs hanging from the ceiling near the stove away from the sunlight. Usually there was at least one trip to the herb and kitchen gardens for a leaf from the sweet bay tree by the front steps, for thick, tightly curled sprigs of parsley, for tomatoes, ripe sweet peppers, squash. A precious sprig of wild thyme would come from her apron pocket; she'd pick herbs while gathering grasses to feed the two goats. A handful of white rice went into the pot. The broth bubbled—the fire warmed the kitchen—night inched in through the open door. As we waited for the men to come back from the fields, she took zucchini, cabbage, carrots—whatever the garden had in plentiful supply—from a big bowl in the middle of the kitchen table and sliced these into the broth. From the cool larder came leftovers saved from lunch—the midday meal, which was the main meal of the day. Sometimes there were drippings from a roast, a bit of curried beef, a tail end of fish, leftover mussels, meat sauce from a pasta meal, *pistou,* wilting salad and its dressing, bits of beef, a roasted lamb shank, or baked chicken wing tips too dried by cooking for comfortable eating. She added her selections one at a time, looking for inspiration, before adding more.

With the setting of the sun, the men returned, slow and tired, smelling of sun and soil. They washed their stiff, hard-worked hands at the sink. Madame set thick white bowls and big plates on the table's white linoleum cover. Sometimes yesterday's stale baguette of bread, sliced into rounds and buttered, or else sautéed briefly in olive oil and minced garlic, was divided among the bowls before the soup was ladled on and, wow, was it good! More often, fresh bread was cut into big chunks with Madame's pocket jackknife and piled into a basket lined with a red and white checked napkin. That, with the soup, butter, cheese, figs fresh or dried, pears, grapes, wine, and coffee made up supper. My rent was one dollar a month and a slab of chocolate; so once a month, we had semisweet Swiss chocolate to finish the meal, and a liqueur made illegally in the Bertrand still in the garage.

As I look back on it, those soup-suppers, as the stars came out in the soft Mediterranean twilight, were almost too romantic to be true. Yet that sweet lady who didn't like to cook was teaching me lessons that I have treasured all my life and which are especially timely right now. Soup is a great way to entertain and a great family food. It feeds multitudes for very little and doesn't require nearly as much attention from the cook as other main dishes.

A GREAT WAY TO ENTERTAIN

Soup as a main course is a fresh approach with all the right messages for today. The utensils for serving soup are casual, welcoming, and richly beautiful: a great big ceramic pot full of bouillabaisse; a big yellow enameled ladle; a simple wicker basket piled high with crusty bread, hot biscuits, buttered English muffins; a cutting board heaped with cheeses; butter in a crock; black and green grapes; coffee and homemade cookies. The cost is minimal, the effect maximal! Bouillabaisse looks like a million-dollar dish because it includes lobster, mussels, clams, and fish. Soups, like Chinese dishes, feed a multitude using only a few of the glamorous ingredients but lots of the less expensive items, like water, onions, potatoes, and tomato paste.

Here are some menu suggestions for entertaining elegantly and easily with soups:

Soup-Centered Menus for Dinner Parties

Avgolemono
Endive Salad with Watercress
Crackers and Blue Cheese
Lemon Sherbet with Cointreau
Café Espresso with Zest of Lemon

Lobster à la Nage
Ruby Oakleaf Lettuce with French Dressing
French Bread, Butter Curls
Homemade Apple Pie with Vanilla Ice Cream
Coffee—Tea

Favorite Mushroom Soup
Filet Mignon with Grilled Tomato Slice
Escarole and Watercress Salad
Chilled Fresh Pineapple Sticks with Homemade Cookies
Café Espresso with Zest of Lemon

Split Pea Soup with a Ham Bone
Buttered Rolls Stuffed with Hot Dogs
Mulled Cider

Sailaway Chowder (First Meal)
Scallop Broth
Whole Chicken Lobsters with Lemon Butter

Hot Butter Biscuits, Butter Curls
Apricot Sherbet
Coffee—Tea

Sailaway Chowder (Second Meal)
Fish Soup
Hot Dinner Rolls, Butter Curls
Endive Salad
Homemade Sour Cherry Pie with Vanilla Ice Cream
Coffee—Tea

Soupe à l'Oignon
French Bread, Butter Curls
Salad of Tossed Greens
Crêpes Suzette with Triple Sec
Café Espresso with Zest of Lemon

Fish Chowder Boston Style
Butter Biscuits, Butter Curls
Hearts of Iceberg Lettuce Salad
Fruit Salad with Homemade Cookies
Coffee—Tea

Cioppino
Bread Sticks, Butter Curls
Baked Lasagna
Salad of Tossed Greens with Fennel Greens
Fresh Strawberries marinated in Semisweet White Wine, a
    Graves such as Château Cadillac
Café Espresso with Zest of Lemon

SOUP TO SAVE CALORIES AND DOLLARS

When I was a reporter in Montreal I was sent to cover the
opening of the Escoffier Society. It was a bit of a coup because
Papa chéri was the founder of the Society with one Gaby Richard,
and he had told me women weren't allowed. I was going to sneak
in anyway via the fourth estate. Whee!

Well, Gaby served me sherry and canapés himself, but when
they got down to serious eating I discovered there was no place
for this reporter at the horseshoe-shaped table in the big dining
hall. Ladies really weren't allowed! The attitude of reverence
Escoffier had toward a meal can be measured by the fact that
he'd exclude anything as distracting as a female.

The Escoffier Society reenacts official turn of the century "eat-
ings" with twenty-five courses, wines to match (*Papa* used to
roll home), napkins you tie around your neck, and after each
course a guest stands and offers a critique of the last course. As
I understand it, Escoffier didn't invent the food, but he did set
down recipes and rules still valid on how to structure a great
big meal. In his day—the Edwardian era—curvacious ladies were
most appreciated. The characters played by the late Mae West
were examples—Diamond Lil and other corseted creatures. Men
had very broad chests and big bay windows! To maintain all that
avoirdupois, meals were hearty. To keep appetites keen through-
out dinner, Escoffier formalized rules that had been evolving
ever since the French Revolution deprived chefs of their patrons
(just as it deprived the aristocrats of their heads and fortunes).
Chaud followed *froid*, dry followed sweet, textured dishes followed creamy ones, harsh alcohols were not allowed to wreck the
palate's ability to appreciate the fine flavors to come, and when

there was just too much food, a *trou Norman,* a shot of apple brandy (Calvados), was downed at a gulp to make the stomach receptive to more food. The *trou Normand* was, in this country at least, translated into a mid-meal sherbet. The first course usually was soup.

The recipes you'll find in Chapter 5 are for classic soups derived from those that started off a meal like this Edwardian dinner:

Cream of Asparagus Soup
Cold Lobster with Mayonnaise
Lemon Sherbet
Saddle of Lamb with Lima Beans
Hearts of Lettuce and Palm Salad
Brie   Oka   Roquefort
Peaches Madeleine
Petits Fours
Chilled Chocolate Mints   Salted Almonds
Café Espresso with Lemon Zest
Choice of Liqueurs

The meal is meant to begin with sherry or with a "cooked wine," an aperitif such as Lillet. The first glass of dinner wine is served after the soup course—a slightly chilled Blanc de Blancs perhaps, or a nice white Bourgogne to accompany the lobster dish; a semidry rosé or a very light, dry Bordeaux to go with the lamb and cheeses; a bubbly semisweet or sweet white, such as Sauternes, to accompany the dessert.

Here are some trimmed-down modern menus for party meals that begin with soup. That makes the first course relatively inexpensive—and quite elegant.

Party Menus that Begin with Soup

Potage Bonne Femme (Potato and Green Leek Soup)
Roast Rump of Beef Baked with Garlic and Mustard
Watercress Salad with Blue Cheese Dressing
Honeydew Melon with Lime Wedges
Coffee—Tea

Vichyssoise
Baked Fillet of Sole Amandine
Tiny Fresh Spring Peas in Lettuce
Hearts of Escarole Salad
Baked Caramel Custard with Homemade Cookies
Café Espresso with Zest of Lemon

Soupe à l'Aille (Garlic Soup)
Leg of Lamb with Fresh Mint Sauce
Fresh Baby Lima Beans
Escarole Salad with Garlic Dressing
Lemon Sherbet with Cointreau
Café Espresso with Zest of Lemon

Oyster Chowder or Oyster Stew Grand Central Style
Baked Ham with Pineapple Rings and Maraschino Cherries
Baked Yams and Butter—Creamed Pearl Onions
Salad of Tossed Greens and Celery Hearts
Mincemeat Pie with Hard Sauce
Coffee—Tea

Whether you are starting a meal with soup or making soup the main course, you will be saving money and calories. When you start a meal with soup, it cuts the appetite, and that means you can save dollars and calories on the main dish that follows: the portion can be smaller, and/or the course can be lighter— eggs instead of costly meats. When soup saves calories, you can spend them on treats—desserts like homemade cookies, pies, pastries, good fruit and cheeses.

Here are some of the meals our family enjoys. The family includes two teen-agers—Holly, who is thin and perpetually wanting to be thinner, and David, who is growing rapidly and is eternally ravenous.

Soup's-On Family Menus

Thursday Night Soup
Grilled American Cheese Sandwich
Ice Cream or Sherbet with Homemade Cookies
Coffee—Tea—Milk

Two-Penny Soup with Hot Dogs
Corn Bread, Butter Curls
Cole Slaw with Diced Apples
Hot Chocolate with Whipped Cream

Duck Soup
Cream Cheese and French Bread
Iceberg Lettuce Salad with Diced Fruit
Coffee—Tea—Milk

Turkey Soup Williamsburg Style
Crackers, Butter Curls
Avocado and Grapefruit Salad
Coffee—Tea—Milk

Scotch Broth—Marcel Hériteau's Recipe
Chicory Salad with Garlic
French Bread, Butter Curls
Orange Sherbet
Coffee—Tea—Milk

Red Lentil Chowder
Brie and English Muffins
Fresh Fruit Platter
Coffee—Tea—Milk

Soup-Centered Meals for One or Two

Icy Beet Soup with *Crème Fraîche*
Hot Dinner Rolls, Butter Curls
Watercress and Blue Cheese Salad
Pineapple Sherbet with Homemade Cookies
Coffee—Tea—Milk

Manhattan Clam Chowder
Corn on the Cob
Old-Fashioned Strawberry Shortcake
Coffee—Tea—Milk

Cream of Asparagus Soup
Chef's Salad Shore Style with Lobster and Shrimp
Fresh Fruit Platter
Coffee—Tea—Milk

Cream of Tomato—Fast
Southern Fried Chicken
Salad of Tossed Greens
Chilled Applesauce with Grated Orange Rind and *Crème Fraîche*
Coffee—Tea—Milk

Corn Chowder
Reuben Sandwich
Root Beer Float

Chilled Cantaloupe and Prosciutto
Spinach and Egg Soup—Fast
Profiteroles filled with Whipped Cream
Coffee—Tea—Milk

Soup-Centered Meals for Dieting
(See also the calorie-trimming suggestions in Chapter 10.)

Gazpacho French Style
Hearts of Lettuce Salad with Lemon Juice
Honeydew Melon with Lime Wedges
Coffee—Tea

Pot-au-Feu
Escarole Salad with Garlic Dressing
Apples with Low-fat Cheese
Coffee—Tea

Fish Broth Mediterranean Style
Boston Lettuce Salad with Lemon Juice
Low-calorie Meringues with Ice Milk
Coffee—Tea

Avocado Soup—Lean
Poached Eggs on Protein Toast
Low-fat Yogurt with Diced Fresh Pineapple or Strawberries
Coffee—Tea

Cream of Chicken Soup—Lean
Mushroom Omelet
Escarole Salad with Lemon Dressing
Cider

Cream of Cauliflower Soup with Cheese—Lean
Protein Toast
Grapefruit Sections
Coffee—Tea

Soups really can save calories as well as dollars. Mother's
Vegetable Soup, as filling and delicious as it is, has fewer than
a hundred calories per serving. Fish chowders, in addition to
being loaded with proteins of the best sort, fit the leanest diet.
Fish is relatively low in calories—the very rich flavor comes from
a bit of nutmeg. The butter or fat in a soup, divided among the

many portions a soup provides, adds up to surprisingly few calories per person.

A HOSPITABLE POT—AND BIG DIVIDENDS

Years ago in the cold underpopulated stretches of Sweden it was the custom to bed and board anyone who came to your door. If you didn't, chances were the man knocking would make a meal for the wolves that night. As each guest finished his dinner, a not-too-wealthy host would request leavings be scraped into the kettle where tomorrow's hospitable pot was already simmering. To the squeamish, we say all that simmering sanitized!

But we shouldn't be squeamish about leftovers. In French and Chinese households drippings from roasts and gravies are saved; in France this gravy base is classed among *fonds de cuisine*. The literal translation is "bottoms of cooking," which I used to take to mean the scrapings of pots where roasts cooked. However, the real meaning is "foundation for cooking," and included in this category are things like stock and sauce bases. I have heard that in one famous Chinese chef's kitchen there was a *fonds de cuisine* two hundred years old. Maybe that's like the hundred-year-old eggs in China which are only a few months old! The message, however, is clear: *Don't* be squeamish. In a soup-making household no food scraps—from potato peelings to leftover salad —should go to waste.

Celery tops too green for salads are great in soups, and parsley stems or the crunchy parts of watercress added as a garnish can turn leftover *Potage Bonne Femme* into a new experience. Chicken Broth à la Supermarket (Chapter 2) and Thursday Night Soup (see Creative Cooking, Chapter 8) will warm the heart of the clever penny-pincher. Soups make evident—and teach you—the butcher's tricks. He cuts chickens up and sells you all the parts separately for more than he sells the whole per pound. You can do that, too. Save livers to make paté, wing tips, backs, necks, and bones from baked or uncooked chickens, along with drippings, to make chicken soup.

Which leftover for which soup? Almost any soup can be stretched by almost any addition when you want to say "stay for dinner" to an unexpected visitor. I recently won a pat on the back by stretching a simple chicken soup with the lamb and curried rice dish I had left over from the day before. Mother's Vegetable Soup can take any quantity of leftover tomato juice, broth, or milk and come up tasting as if it had just been picked in a garden. Rice, noodles, spaghetti, potatoes, more vegetables—

you name it—can stretch a soup to feed two to four more people with very little effort!

SOUP AS A "FAST FOOD"

Cross my heart! Soups are slow to cook—but they're fast to make. Most soups are simmered this or that, the longest job being chopping, dicing, or slicing. With food processors those chores are chores no more. The best vegetable soups begin with a chopped onion sautéed in butter—but that takes only five to ten minutes. The rest, the stove and the soup kettle combine to do. Hearty meat soups and a really good onion soup begin with the browning of bones to make a brown stock or consommé, but you can make that by the vat and freeze or can it. You don't have to make it from scratch every time. Even in the refrigerator it keeps for ages: sealed in by the fat that rises to the surface as it chills, it will keep for longer than it will take you to use it up.

Some of the best soups require a little fancy finishing just before serving, but that's the fun of them—the stove or the slow-cook electric pot, a dutch oven, or one of the other contemporary absentee-cook utensils does the rest. Topping onion soup with cheese and bringing that to a bubbly brown under the broiler really does come under the heading of "fun"—so does decorating an exquisite Oriental broth like Cucumber Soup with its last-minute lacing of egg.

EQUIPMENT THAT MAKES SOUP COOKING EASY

You can make soup in any kettle and slice the ingredients with a sharp knife. But soup making is encouraged if you have a few really good tools to work with. Here's my list of favorites:

FOOD PROCESSOR: The most expensive food processor has been copied successfully, in my opinion, by several good manufacturers. J.C. Penney, Sunbeam, and General Electric were kind enough to lend me machines to work with in the testing of recipes for this book, and I can endorse all three. The instruction booklet provided with the purchase of a processor shows the steps for chopping, mincing, slicing thin or thick, before soup making begins. You'll weep no more when handling the onions: the processor encases the gasses that bring tears to your eyes.

The machine also saves time and effort in the puréeing process so many soup recipes call for.

My Braun blender, which has three up-curved blades, minces onions, and my Braun food-chopping equipment with interchangeable parts can do anything my food processors can do. They are a little more complicated to put together and take apart, but before you leap to buy a processor, check the equipment you have.

SOUP KETTLE: Where I grew up a "kettle" is what you boil water to make tea in. Here, however, it is used to represent a large cooking pot, one that can hold four quarts of liquid, or more. A heavy, commercial-gauge aluminum kettle with a close-fitting lid is the most practical. A heavy kettle over medium heat sautés onions in the time described in the recipes; in a light-weight kettle, ingredients heat up in a less even, less controlled fashion and can brown and burn in some places when your back is turned. A heavy kettle over low heat allows you to make a smooth cream sauce effortlessly; in a lighter-weight kettle, the cream sauce is apt to lump and never smooth out.

In some recipes where a lot of sautéeing is called for, I have suggested you use a saucepan to start the soups. A saucepan is a large, shallow cooking utensil, like a skillet or frying pan, but with higher sides. A saucepan is a handy part of the *batterie de cuisine* but is not essential. A good heavy-gauge kettle can do most anything a saucepan can do.

As for enamel versus metal, good enamelware is wonderful to work with, especially when it is pretty enough to bring to the table. It has all the advantages of cast-iron cookware—cooks evenly, heats slowly, makes good cream sauce—but be aware that it doesn't brown meats as quickly as cast-iron ware. The browning of meats in many beef recipes and some chicken recipes is the key to deep, rich flavor.

When you are working with four quarts of ingredients and liquids you will need a container that can hold at least one and preferably two quarts more.

STOCK POT: A stock pot is bigger than a soup kettle by a lot— six quarts is the minimum size. It is lighter, however, and just about essential for making broths and stocks which usually include four or more quarts of water plus a lot of solid ingredients that take up space, like beef bones. Do you need both a soup kettle and a stock pot? So many soups start with the sautéeing of onions that having a heavy kettle to sauté in is practical; it saves washing both a soup kettle and a saucepan used for sautéeing. If you can afford only one of the pair, however, and plan to make broths and stocks, spend your budget on a good stock pot. Pots sold for the making of stock are not magical in any way. A big 12-quart jam kettle with a lid will do beautifully, and so will an eight-quart Dutch oven or a pressure food processor in the big canning sizes. I use a very battered soup kettle I bought at an auction twenty years ago for twenty-five cents for making my stocks—the same one I use for jam and steaming mussels and cooking lobster et al.

DUTCH OVEN: This is an enamel or cast-iron pot with handles on either side and a domed lid. It's ideal for making soups as well as slow-cooked stews that must simmer in the oven. In the 4-quart size, it's apt to be heavy to handle and a little less practical around the kitchen than a 4-quart kettle. Newer models may be lighter in weight and some are enamelled. These are a better choice for soup-making: buy the largest size, six to eight quarts.

ELECTRIC SLOW-COOK POT: Wonderfully handy for soup makers who work all day: start the soup in the morning, and it is ready by the time the family gets home. General Electric makes a handsome stainless steel all-purpose pot that slow-cooks, and it has many uses. Its big advantage over conventional slow-cook pots of ceramic is that you can turn the heat to high to sauté the first ingredients that base the soup, then turn it to low for the simmering period after the liquids are added. Its disadvantage (there's a pro and con to everything) is that the ingredients in thick creamy soups, like split-pea soup, tend to stick to the bottom and burn a little unless watched—and this never happens with a ceramic slow-cook pot.

Someday someone will invent an electric version of this in heavy metal that won't cause foods to stick and that is so pretty you can carry it right to the table.

PRESSURE COOKER: If you have a pressure canner (these come in sizes up to 22 quarts) you'll find it a good size for making broths.

LADLE: You really need a ladle to dip out soup; no spoon I've ever owned is big enough to save my impatience. There are inexpensive enameled, long-handled ladles pretty enough to bring to the table. The purely utilitarian types—stainless steel with black Bakelite handles—aren't quite right at a nicely set table with a pretty tureen.

WOODEN SPOONS: I have a collection of tall-to-small wooden spoons I use for stirring soups. They are slow to heat up, so cream sauces won't stick to them as they do to metal spoons.

SOUP SPOONS: There are two types: round bowls and oblong bowls. My family prefers the round type. The oblong type is more formal and is found in better silverware sets. Chinese soups are eaten with a large, flat-bottomed china spoon. They're inexpensive, and if you are going in for Oriental food, fun to have.

SOUP BOWLS: China table settings include soup plates and/or consommé cups. They're really essential to table settings for a formal meal that begins with soup and continues with other courses. If soup is the main course, then any of the big soup plates in china, ceramic, or enamel bakeware will set an attractive table. If you are debating the virtues of investing in soup plates versus soup bowls, my recommendation would be the plates. Soups cool off more quickly in these, and they are almost essential for serving meaty one-dish dinner soups.

To make onion soup you pretty well have to have those charming little ceramic pots that are ovenproof and can be passed under the broiler for the last few minutes of cooking. There are enamelware versions of these which I like less. You could use a ceramic soup mug instead, as long as it is ovenproof. The advantage to the mug is that you can use it to serve soups at outdoor parties.

STORAGE CONTAINERS: Producing wonderful soups quickly and effortlessly depends in part on the materials you keep available for soup making. One of the most important is broth, chicken or beef. You can buy it canned, but the best is homemade from meat parts as they become available: chicken parts saved up in the freezer, beef bones, and veal scraps. Plan to make your broths in big batches and freeze them in clearly labeled 1-cup lots. For this purpose you can use 8-ounce plastic party cups or glasses: cover their contents with plastic wrap bound in place by twist-ties or with a rubber band. Or buy 1- or 2-cup plastic freezer containers.

I store scraps, useful for my soup larder, in sandwich bags (those with Ziploc tops are the easiest to handle)—anything from herbs to the stems from scallions, which I chop and use as a substitute for a garnish of chives.

TABLE SETTINGS: In my family, we really do eat a lot of soup. Most evening meals consist of soup, salad, cheese, and fruit. Sometimes, instead of fruit, we serve a homemade dessert such as apple pie, chocolate cake, a Napoleon or a cherry tart from the great pastry maker down the block.

We set the table with soup spoons, salad fork, knife, butter knife, a large service plate under a big soup plate, a large bread and butter or salad plate, and a set of dessert plates. We serve the salad and cheese on the large bread and butter or salad plate, and often we place the fruit there, too, for cutting or peeling. If the salad plate is unusually messy or too gloriously garlicky for comfort we use a small, clean dessert plate for the fruit. If a pastry or other dessert is served, it is served on a clean dessert plate, with a fork, or a fork and spoon.

LARDER FOR THE SOUP KITCHEN

There are basic materials that come from the supermarket that should be in the kitchen where soup is a mainstay. These include:

ONIONS: Whatever onions are least expensive will do. Buy by the bag, and choose bags whose contents show no tendency to sprout. Store your onions in a cool, dry place, but not in the refrigerator. If any start to sprout new shoots—as they tend to do in early and mid-spring—use these first. The new shoot is good, so don't discard it. Scallions can be used instead.

DRIED ONIONS: These are a second choice to fresh onions. See Chapter 11 for uses. I keep a small jar on hand.

GARLIC: This appears in lots of recipes. Buy whole garlic heads from the produce department. Look for large heads with over-size cloves, and press them to make sure they are firm and fresh. Store in a cool, dry place.

CELERY: Celery and celery leaves are called for in many recipes. Choose large heads with leaves shading to golden toward the center of the head. Store in the crisper.

CARROTS: Carrots are another staple of soup making. Buy these by the bag. Choose large carrots and store them in the crisper.

DRIED MUSHROOMS: Mushrooms are an asset to almost any soup: mushrooms, onions, clam juice, and butter make one of the best soups in this book. When you can find dried mushrooms at reasonable rates, buy and store them in an airtight container. Oregon Freeze Dry Foods produce excellent dried mushrooms in big tins, and these I keep in a tall, pretty glass jar in the kitchen next to the rice and dried grains for soups. Buys in slightly aged mushrooms are worth considering; as long as the mushrooms aren't dark and gooey-looking they're fine for soup. If you can't use them right away, chop them into big chunks and freeze them in a plastic container.

POTATOES: With onions and potatoes and salt you can make a soup even if there's nothing else in the house, so keep potatoes in stock. Big, old potatoes with lots of prominent eyes and skins that look about ready to wrinkle are the best for soups. They thicken a soup in a way young, fine-grained potatoes cannot.

PARSLEY: Parsley is one of the herbs that turns up most often in soup cooking, and it also is used as a garnish for soup. Buy fresh bunches of the tightly curled variety from the produce counters. Cut the bottom half-inch from the stems, remove the rubber band, and stand the parsley in warm, fresh water. I use it as I would a vase of flowers in my kitchen and pick sprigs from it as needed in cooking. In spring and summer, when the flowers on the terrace are in bloom, I often tuck a few small bright marigolds, or miniature roses, or broken petunia blooms, in among the parsley branches. Cooking, after all, is as much about beauty as it is about filling one's stomach with palatable nourishment.

The flat, Italian parsley is considered by some to be finer than the tightly curled variety; I find the tightly curled parsley easier to chop fine—and prettier in a glass of water. That's why I buy it.

When there is lots of parsley available from your own, or another's, garden in summer, put some in the freezer for winter use. Chop it in big lots in the food processor and store it in sandwich bags. Save chopped parsley stems, too; they make a great garnish and a good flavoring.

DILL: Another wonderful herb for soups is dill. Dill weed or seed, dried, imparts lots of flavor, unlike dried parsley. To have dill available for a garnish, to dress up soups when the cooking is over, it must be fresh or fresh-frozen. Handle bunches of fresh dill as suggested for parsley, above. Dill freezes well. Don't bother to chop it; just store it in plastic bags. The fine, ferny leaves will break into tiny pieces once frozen if you just slap the bag once or twice, so there's no need to mince it before storing it. Freeze leftover fresh dill stems to use as a cooking herb in soups.

CHERVIL: This turns up in some recipes. It is available, fresh, from greengrocers most of the year. Handle as parsley.

THYME: Nice fresh, but dried thyme is almost as good. It is one of the most-used herbs in soup cooking, so keep a supply handy.

BAY LEAF: Bay and sweet bay are the same thing: a shrub or tree with long, rather leathery leaves that bring wonderful flavor to soups and stews. The size of the leaf is specified in the recipes here. You can easily have too much bay. My father brings us fresh bay from Aunt Marthe's bay tree once a year, and it is an especially fine French variety. But bay put up by herb houses in ordinary cartons or bottles is good, too. Store out of the light: bright sun bleaches the color, resulting in perfectly good bay leaves that are a funny buff color. Remove the bay before serving the soup.

WHOLE CLOVES: This is a spice basic to soup cooking. Keep a jar on your spice shelf. Remove the cloves before serving the soup: they are *awful* to eat!

WHOLE PEPPERCORNS: These impart much more flavor than ground pepper. But use ground pepper, too. It's best freshly ground in a mill. Try to remember to remove whole peppercorns from soups; I am forever crunching them up, and the flavor is a bit too strong.

SALT: I use ordinary table salt for most recipes. However, pot-au-feu and other specialties call for coarse sea salt. The only kind I find easy to get is what is called kosher salt. I think it lacks the flavor of real sea salt, but it will do.

ROSEMARY: Popular herb used in many Italian and some Spanish and Mexican soups. Keep a jar of the dried leaves handy for soups.

BASIL: Another herb popular in Italian soups. The dried herb has relatively little flavor. Place whole branches of the fresh herb in a plastic container and store in the freezer.

BUTTER: The recipes here all call for butter—lightly salted butter—except for a few that specify sweet butter—unsalted butter. I buy butter in quantity when it is on sale and store it in the freezer. A fine substitute is margarine if you prefer to use it. Or use safflower or vegetable oil. Don't use olive or sesame oil unless specified in the recipe. These are strongly flavored.

CHICKEN BROTH: I buy whole chickens and save various parts to make broth, which then is stored in the freezer in 1-cup lots for use in soups. See Chapter 2 for further explanations about this.

BOUILLON CUBES OR GRANULES: There are excellent gourmet brand bouillon cubes and granules for chicken, beef, and even veal broths. Instant broth is a fine substitute for homemade broth when you haven't any. It's worth your while to spend a little time finding a brand you really like. The very good ones are expensive. Among the inexpensive commercial types from supermarkets, Steero is my favorite.

BONES: When you are offered buys on soup bones, snap them up and store them, well wrapped, in the freezer. If you have a roast boned, claim the bones from the butcher and freeze them for future use. Any meat bone, except pork, can be used to enhance soup.

BEEF: Tough and bony cuts of beef can make great soup meats. In beef, look for flanken, flunken (short ribs), oxtails, neck bones, and neck. Don't, by the way, confuse these two. *Neck bones* are disjointed bones with a few bare scraps of meat clinging to them and are wonderful to flavor soups. *Neck*, however, is a thick slice of meat surrounding a small bone and is very good for use in soups that will be the main course—one-dish dinner soups.

LAMB: Lamb neck, neck bones, and shank pieces are the best buys of this animal. Wrap carefully and freeze for use in Scotch Broth.

VEAL: Veal makes a delicate broth. Neck and neck bones are sometimes available, as well as shank cuts. Buy and freeze for future use.

PORK: Ordinary pork bones are called for in very few soups, but pork hocks, fresh or smoked, are a wonderful ingredient to add to any dried bean soup and to split pea soup. Smoked ham hocks can be used as a substitute for a baked ham bone in split pea soup. Pigs' feet, trotters, and other economy cuts of pork appear in a number of recipes in Chapters 3 and 6. They aren't always available in supermarkets, so I buy them when they do appear and try to keep a package or two of each, well wrapped, in the freezer for future use. A smoked shoulder butt is another inexpensive pork product great in dried bean soups, split pea, and lentil soups. Slices of ham added to dried bean and pea soups improve the flavor and make them into more of a meal, so I keep these on hand in the freezer, too.

SALT PORK: Mostly whole fat, this is what our forebears used as the base for stews and soups, and it still is the tastiest base for hearty meat and dried legume soups. Corn chowder, fish and clam chowder, and a number of other classic soups are better by far when salt pork is used. Look for pieces with a creamy, fresh look and a good-sized stripe of lean meat in the center. Don't confuse salt pork with fatback, which has no lean in it; that's how you can tell the difference. And don't try to use bacon instead of salt pork—it just isn't the same.

CHORIZO AND OTHER SAUSAGES: Chorizo, Polish sausage, and other specialty sausages are the mainstay of many of the one-dish dinner soups, and I keep one of each in the freezer, well wrapped. Chorizo is a hot Spanish sausage; hot Italian sausage is a good substitute. Polish sausage is not, though it is good in other soup recipes.

RICE: Long grain, converted rice is what I use for soups. I keep a large jar of it on hand.

BARLEY: A little barley turns into a lot in a soup. I keep a small quantity of pearl barley (white rather than brown) on hand, stored in an airtight container, and add it by the tablespoonful, not the cupful, to stretch soups and to make up impromptu recipes. Lots of people think a soup that doesn't have a bit of barley in it isn't real soup. Pearl barley is husked—brown barley has the husk on, and it is tasty, but it doesn't bring that mellowness to a soup that I associate with pearl barley.

SPLIT DRIED GREEN PEAS: Dried peas can be added to soups to stretch them for another meal, but the peas will require quite a bit of cooking—an hour, at least. I always have at least one bag of these on hand to make split pea soup. When I don't have a ham bone to flavor it, or ham hocks, I use hot dogs or a slice of ham. (See PORK, above.) Yellow split peas have almost the same flavor as green split peas and are used interchangeably.

(They are pretty, layered with green peas, in a tall glass container: separate the layers with plastic wrap.)

LENTILS, BROWN OR RED: Lentils make wonderful, meaty soups with lots of flavor. I keep a bag of these on hand too, and in the winter, serve lentil soup of one type or another about every ten days. Red lentils, once cooked, look rather like the brown lentils, and I find their flavors rather similar. And, like yellow split peas, they are pretty in glass containers.

If I've suggested that soup can be all things to all people, it's intentional. For the gourmet, soup-centered meals are relatively new and can be as refined as Rouquefort mousse. For the penny-watcher, soup-centered meals save dollars and first-rate leftovers that might otherwise not be used. Soup can accommodate left-over salad (the only dish I've ever found that could!). For the health food buff, soups can provide splendid nutrition and a minimum of cholesterol, no-no meats, and other "out" foods. For those in need of warmth, comfort, and something to eat, soup does it without demanding more time and energy than working homemakers have.

Two
THE BASICS OF SOUP COOKERY

The real fun in soup making comes after you've made enough soups to know you can walk into the kitchen and turn out a soup from whatever you have on hand and without a recipe. A *good* soup.

Many of the best soups have two key ingredients. The first is onions sautéed in butter, and the second is a good broth, a clear, tasty meat stock or consommé which is used in place of plain water.

Other important ingredients in many soups are the thickeners. Then there are the garnishes to add a final fillip of flavor and touch of color and a few basic processes.

MINCED: This means reduced to the smallest size you can get. It refers to onions, garlic, and vegetables in general. To mince onions by hand, cut a checkerboard pattern from the top of the onion to within a half-inch of the base, then slice across. The last half-inch will be a little harder to mince. To mince with the food processor, peel and cut the vegetable into big chunks, then process until it is in fine little pieces.

CHOPPED: Chopped here means coarsely-chopped—cut to the size of julienne vegetables—between ⅛ and ¼ inch. I use "chopped" in place of "diced," which is what soup recipes call for, because dicing with the food processor can be tedious and isn't necessary except for a particularly formal soup. You could substitute the word "diced" almost everywhere I've recommended "chopped." To chop by hand or in a food processor, follow the procedures for mincing but make the pieces larger.

PEELING: Where possible, avoid peeling. Carrots, parsnips, zucchini—anything with a tasty or pretty skin doesn't need to be peeled. But some vegetables do need peeling. You can make a tasty soup with unpeeled potatoes, but the soup will be darker. Turnips must be peeled. Peel on cucumber slices is decorative, especially when the slices are very thin, but sometimes cucumbers are so heavily waxed they need peeling. Onions are always peeled. Peel them under running water if they make you cry. Garlic always needs peeling. Lay it on a cutting board and whack it hard with the flat of a knife first: that makes peeling easy.

THE A, B, C's OF SOUP MAKING

The first step in many soups is to sauté onions, which are the flavor base of soups all over the world. Then you simmer. Then you thicken. Then you bind and garnish.

SAUTÉ: Unless otherwise specified, the sautéed onions and/or vegetables must not brown, even lightly. Adjust the heat under the saucepan or kettle so the butter does not brown. After the onions are added, keep stirring. If browning begins, remove the kettle from the heat and keep stirring until it has cooled.

SIMMER: How rapidly soups cook is important. The cooking period is long, and unless the soup is simmering in a slow-cook pot, the liquid evaporates quickly. That's great when you are intending to strengthen a flavor by boiling down an insipid soup, but when you are making split pea soup and dried bean dishes, rapid evaporation can result in a burned soup.

The message is: Check long-cooking soups often, and add more liquid if the water level is much below the solid ingredients.

"Simmer" means the slowest bubbling possible. "Slow boil" is faster than "simmer." "Boil" is faster than "slow boil," and "rapid boil" means cooking as quickly as possible. Cover the soup with a close-fitting lid. Covered, "simmering" soups lose about three cups of liquid per hour of cooking; a soup can lose twice that much when cooking rapidly, uncovered. Adjust the heat carefully, and remember to put the lid on when you leave the soup.

If a soup begins to burn on the bottom, remove it from the heat and at once place the bottom in cold water. Then, unless it is clearly burned, stir up the soup, add water, and continue cooking. If the bottom has burned, pour the unburned soup off into another kettle, add water, and continue cooking.

PURÉE: Puréed soups, once the ingredients were very tender, were pressed through a sieve. Today we purée in a blender or a food processor. Process two cups at a time: more will spurt out the top. When I liquefy hot ingredients I lift the removable cap from the center of the blender cover as soon as I have turned the machine on low: that lets steam escape. Pour the processed soup into a bowl. When you have completed puréeing, return the soup to the kettle for reheating.

THICKENING: Some soups start out with thickeners among the ingredients—generally chopped or diced potatoes; old potatoes thicken best. Puréed vegetables will thicken a soup, with or without potatoes. Potatoes in other forms can be used to thicken soups, too. Here's a small list:

½ cup mashed potatoes thickens 4 cups of soup

1 teaspoon potato flour thickens 1 cup of soup

1 tablespoon instant mashed potato powder thickens 1 cup of soup

Potato flour looks and acts like cornstarch, clearing and thickening the hot broth.

Quick-cooking tapioca is added to some consommés to thicken them slightly.

To use any of these, just whip into the hot soup, or follow package instructions.

ROUX: A great many classic soups are thickened by the addition of a *roux*. *Roux* is a paste made of all-purpose flour stirred into melted butter. It is the basis of all cream sauces. A *béchamel* sauce is made by stirring vegetable or meat broth and milk into a *roux*. A cream sauce (*sauce blanche*) is similar, but the liquid is milk and/or cream. I understand that a measure of the Victorian/Edwardian cook's talent lay in whether the cream sauces (and there were lots of them) were lumpy. It's a fact that unless you know what you are doing when you are working the liquid into the *roux*, the soup will have lumps.

The process is really simple once you master the pitfalls. The heat must be very low, or it will scorch the flour. Overheated flour will not expand to absorb the liquid added. The result will be a thin, faintly bitter soup. We used to make cream sauces in the double boiler to avoid lumps, but they can be made right on the stove top as long as the heat is low.

Add the liquid all at once to the *roux* and stir very rapidly. Keep stirring as the liquid thickens and smooths out. Cold liquid will not thicken until it has warmed.

The steps in adding *roux* to soup are: over *very* low heat, melt the butter and stir in the flour; add all the liquid, still over low heat, and stir until the soup thickens and smooths. The soup may be simmered after the thickener has been added without harm.

VELOUTÉ: A cream soup is a purée enriched with milk or cream. A velouté is creamier and much richer, the classic Edwardian first course. It is made with chicken, beef, or veal stock thickened with *roux* and enriched with egg yolks, with or without cream.

Adding the yolks calls for as much care as making a cream sauce. Pour beaten yolks into boiling liquid, and they will cook instantly into fragments, giving a curdled effect you can't cure. Instead, pour hot broth, one-half to one cup of it, into the beaten yolks, then, with the soup removed from the heat, gradually beat this back into the soup *without ever letting the soup boil.* If the soup is to be reheated, do not let it boil.

SECRETS OF SUCCESS

To make good soups, you need more taste than skill. In our family we say that with one pound of mushrooms and two pounds of butter you can face any emergency. Where soups are concerned we say, when you have good broth or stock and heavy cream in the freezer, you can turn anything into a soup. That's almost literally true.

But even with broth and heavy cream on hand, whether or not the soup will be delicious will depend on your cultivated taste. The recipes you follow are only guides. Every bag of dried beans is different from every other. Every package of frozen peas is unique. Potatoes differ from pound to pound and season to season. One steak is divine and another tasteless. Flour from one bag absorbs more liquid than flour from another. Some salts are saltier than others. Even if you follow a recipe slavishly and it is as painstakingly detailed as Julia Child's, the soup will never be exactly the same twice. The moral of this story is you must taste what you are cooking often. The genius of the good cook is in her/his ability to adjust the dish as it is cooking to achieve just the flavor most desired. So—taste. Add more salt, pepper, spices, herbs; make the soup thicker or thinner; richer or leaner. If it is coming up bland, add a dash of lemon juice, vinegar, or white wine to fish and meat dishes. Try mustard, sugar, Worcestershire or soy sauce, red wine, bouillon cubes, drippings from a roast, or a tiny bit of ground cloves to improve broths. Try croutons, chives, garlic, thyme, bay, rosemary, and any of the garnishes suggested below. The garnish may be what is missing.

And a final admonition: Make sure the spoonful you are tasting is relatively cool. If it's very hot you won't be aware of its real flavor. Sometimes just letting a soup sit for half an hour can improve it, so when you aren't happy with your dish, walk away from it, then come back and taste again.

GARNISHES

A few threads of chopped green chives nestled in the center of a creamy vichyssoise—minced parsley greening a vegetable chowder—Boston bean soup flecked with dark red bacon bits—croutons—tiny sauce-filled *profiteroles*—dumplings—the garnishes for soups are meant to be bright and beautiful, but they have a flavoring job to do as well.

The accompaniment to a soup has almost as much importance as the garnish. Crackly-crusted, warm French bread, hot butter biscuits, crisp dinner rolls, even plain old saltines, taste really good with vegetable and meat soups. Corn bread is great with bean or ham- and sausage-flavored soups. Popovers are a delight with delicate cream soups. Cheese straws, cheese puffs, bread sticks, all crunchy nibbles, add texture that a bowlful of smooth soup may need to make it unforgettable.

Here are some of our family favorites.

SAUTÉED ALMONDS   Serves 4 to 6

    2 heaping tablespoons
      slivered almonds
    1 tablespoon butter

Melt butter in a small saucepan over medium heat, then sauté the almonds, stirring constantly until the almonds begin to turn golden brown. Drain on paper towel.

To serve: Place a heaping teaspoonful in each bowl of soup.

BREAD STICKS   Makes 60

    ¾ cup boiling water   2 egg whites, beaten to soft
    2 tablespoons shortening   peaks
    1 teaspoon salt   2 tablespoons milk
    ¼ cup tepid water   Coarse sea or kosher salt, or
    2 teaspoons sugar   sesame seeds
    1 package dry yeast
    3½ cups sifted all-purpose
       flour

1. In a large mixing bowl, combine boiling water, shortening, and salt; allow to cool. Stir the sugar and yeast into the tepid water; allow to rest until it begins to bubble, about 5 minutes in a warm room. Combine yeast mixture with 1½ cups of flour.

Stir in egg whites, and when these are absorbed, mix in the remaining flour. Knead 10 minutes on a floured board, then grease the mixing bowl, return the dough to it, cover and allow to rise in a warm place, about 1 hour or until doubled in bulk.

2. Punch the dough down, knead 2 minutes, then divide in half. Roll out one portion, making a large rectangle of dough $\frac{1}{3}$ inch thick. Cut into strips 6 to 8 inches long by $\frac{1}{2}$ inch wide. Roll these between your palms to round them. Place $\frac{1}{2}$ inch apart on a greased cookie sheet. Repeat with the other half. Allow to rise about $\frac{1}{2}$ hour or until doubled in bulk.

3. Preheat the oven to 400 degrees. Brush the sticks with milk and sprinkle lightly with coarse salt or sesame seeds. Place a bread pan half-filled with water in the bottom of the oven and bake the sticks until brown, 12 to 15 minutes. Cool and store in airtight containers.

GARLIC BREAD   Serves 6

This is a good way to use up a baguette at the point of going stale.

　1　stick soft butter
　1 to 2 large cloves garlic
　1　thin French or Italian loaf,
　　　18 to 20 inches long

1. Preheat the oven to 375 degrees.
2. In a small bowl mash the butter and crush the garlic into it. Mix well. Cut the bread into slices about 1 inch thick. Do not cut all the way through. Spread the garlic butter on the bread, buttering each side of each piece, then press the pieces back together. Wrap in foil and bake 20 to 25 minutes. Open the top and bake 5 minutes more.

To serve: Place the bread, still in its foil wrapper, in a long bread basket lined with a cloth napkin.

BUTTER BISCUITS   Makes 12

Oven-warmed, crisp French or Italian bread is wonderful with soup, and so are English muffins. When you haven't either, these fast biscuits are a good accompaniment.

        2 cups all-purpose flour   ½ teaspoon salt
        2 teaspoons baking powder   6 tablespoons butter
        2 teaspoons sugar   ½ to 1 cup milk

1. Preheat the oven to 450 degrees.
2. Sift flour, baking powder, sugar, and salt into a mixing bowl. Cut in the butter as for pie dough. Add milk, omitting the last bit if the dough is becoming too soft to hold its shape. Or place the dry ingredients and the butter in the bowl of a food processor fitted with the knife blade, and process until the butter is cut in evenly—about 15 seconds. With the processor running, add ½ cup of milk all at once down the food chute. Process about 10 seconds. With the processor running, continue adding milk until the dough begins to look soft.
3. Butter and flour a cookie sheet. Drop the dough onto it by the tablespoonful and shape into small mounds. Bake until golden brown, 12 to 15 minutes.

To serve: Heap in a basket lined with a cloth napkin and serve warm.

CARROT FLOWERS   Serves 6

        1 large carrot, peeled
        2 cups water or broth
        Sprigs of fresh parsley

Cut four lengthwise grooves in the carrot on opposite sides. Slice into very thin rounds. Boil rapidly for 3 minutes in water or broth. Drain.

To serve: Arrange on the soup with tiny sprigs of fresh parsley between slices.

CHEESE CRACKERS   Serves 4

12 soda crackers
2 tablespoons soft butter
2 tablespoons grated cheese
Paprika

1. Preheat the oven to 500 degrees.
2. Spread the crackers with the butter, sprinkle with cheese, and dust with paprika. Set in the oven to bake until lightly browned, about 5 minutes.

To serve: Serve hot as accompaniment to soup.

CHEESE PUFFS   Makes 30

These are tasty tidbits to use as garnishes for vegetable soups, particularly those with cabbage or broccoli, and for clear consommé.

½ pound sharp cheddar
  cheese, grated
¼ cup butter
½ cup all-purpose flour

½ teaspoon salt
½ teaspoon paprika
1 small bottle small stuffed
  olives, about 30, wiped dry

1. In a small bowl, with an electric beater on low, beat the cheese into the butter. Add the flour, salt, and paprika. Mix at low speed. Gather the dough into a ball, wrap in wax paper, and refrigerate 3 hours.
2. Pinch off one teaspoon of the dough, flatten it with your fingers, and wrap it around a stuffed olive. Leave the ends of the dough open. Roll gently between the palms of your hands until the sides of the dough adhere. Freeze, sealed in plastic, until soup time.
3. Bake as many as needed in the oven (preheated to 400 degrees) for 15 minutes or until golden brown. Do not defrost before baking.

To serve: Drop 2 or 3 into each bowl of soup just before serving.

CHEESE STRAWS
Serves 8 to 10

Homemade cheese straws are a treat, and they're easy to make. For a gala touch, offer them set into rings made of baked cheese-straw dough. One caution—they're fragile.

1 cup all-purpose flour	5 ounces butter
½ teaspoon salt	4 ounces firm cheddar
⅛ teaspoon pepper	cheese, finely grated
⅛ teaspoon dried mustard	2 egg yolks, beaten
⅛ teaspoon celery salt	1 egg white, lightly beaten

1. Preheat the oven to 425 degrees.
2. Sift together flour, salt, pepper, mustard, and celery salt. Cut the butter in bits and crumble the butter into the flour mixture with your fingers until it resembles fine bread crumbs. Toss the cheese lightly with this mixture.
3. Work the egg yolks into the flour mixture. Roll out firmly but gently on a well-floured board until about ¼ inch thick. Cut into fingers ¼ inch wide and 3 to 4 inches long. Gather up any pastry left, roll out again, and cut into rings with a doughnut cutter. Lay fingers and rings on lightly greased cookie sheets. Brush with egg white.
4. Bake 12 to 15 minutes or until golden brown.
5. Cool completely before removing from sheets. Gently lift straws with a spatula, as they are fragile and break easily when fresh.

CHEESE TOPPING
Serves 6

1 egg yolk, lightly beaten	Parmesan cheese
3 tablespoons grated	1 cup whipped cream

In a small bowl combine the egg yolk and the cheese. Fold into the whipped cream.

To serve: Spoon onto soup in ovenproof bowls and brown lightly under a broiler on high.

CHIVES AND PARSLEY
Serves 4 to 6

3 tablespoons finely minced parsley

1 tablespoon finely minced scallions or chives

Combine ingredients, and divide among 4 to 6 soup bowls.

CORN BREAD
Serves 6 to 8

Corn bread is very good from a mix. The flaw is the cost of the mix. From-scratch corn bread is first-rate and more economical.

1 cup yellow corn meal
1 cup all-purpose flour
¼ cup sugar
4 teaspoons baking powder
½ teaspoon salt

1 cup milk
1 medium egg
¼ cup butter
1 tablespoon bacon drippings

1. Preheat the oven to 425 degrees.
2. In a large bowl combine the corn meal, flour, sugar, baking powder, and salt. Mix the milk with the egg and beat into the dry ingredients. In the oven, melt the butter in the baking pan, then stir into the batter. Spread the bacon drippings over the warm baking pan, then pour the batter into the pan.
3. Bake 25 minutes or until it begins to brown lightly.

To serve: Allow to cool a few minutes. Serve in the baking pan or turn out onto a plate, whole.

CRÈME FRAÎCHE

Dollops of this are wonderful in cream soups, Mock Turtle Soup, and especially in chilled fruit soups.

½ cup sour cream
½ cup heavy cream

Stir the creams together, cover, and let rest at room temperature 3 to 4 hours. Chill.

To serve: Place a tablespoonful in each bowl of soup.

CROUTONS

When sliced French bread is going to go stale, everyday bread is headed that way, or you have leftover toast, remove the crusts and cut into ¼- to ½-inch squares. Allow to dry thoroughly, then store in airtight containers.

To serve: Place a tablespoonful in each bowl of soup.

LARGE CROUTONS

Cut sliced French or American bread into rounds or cookie-cutter shapes, allow to dry 24 hours in an unlighted oven, then store.

To serve: Butter well and place one or two in each soup bowl, then ladle the soup over the croutons.

CROUTONS, SAUTÉED OR FRIED IN OIL

To deep fry, heat shortening to 350 degrees. Place ½ cup of croutons at a time in the fryer basket and fry 10 to 15 seconds or until just golden brown. Drain on paper towel.

To pan fry, combine butter half-and-half with oil to a depth of 1 inch in a large, heavy skillet over moderately high heat. Heat until a crouton sizzles when dropped into the butter and oil. Sauté half a cup of croutons at a time until golden brown. Drain on paper towel.

To serve: Place a heaping tablespoonful of croutons in each bowl of soup.

CROUTONS, GARLIC-FLAVORED

Prepare Croutons, Sautéed, and shake them in a paper bag with 1 teaspoon of garlic salt.

To serve: Place a heaping teaspoonful in each bowl of soup.

CROUTONS, HERBED

Prepare Croutons, Sautéed, and shake them in a paper bag with 1 teaspoon of mixed herbs.

CROUTONS, BACON-FLAVORED

Prepare Croutons, Sautéed, but sauté them in bacon drippings.

CROUTONS, CHEESE-FLAVORED

1 cup croutons
1 tablespoon grated
   Parmesan cheese

1. Preheat the oven to 400 degrees.
2. Set croutons in a small baking dish and sprinkle with cheese. Bake until golden brown, about 10 minutes.

FRESH CROUTONS, SAUTÉED IN BUTTER

8 slices fresh white bread
1 stick butter

1. Preheat the oven to 250 degrees.
2. Remove crusts from the bread slices and cut slices into ¼- to ½-inch cubes. Dry in the oven 20 minutes.
3. Over medium heat, melt the butter in a large saucepan. When the butter stops foaming, drop in the cubes and sauté until golden on all sides. Don't let the butter burn. Drain on paper towel.

To serve: Place a heaping tablespoonful in each bowl of soup.

CUCUMBER GARNISH

Choose cucumbers whose skins are unwaxed.

½ cucumber
Sprigs of fresh parsley

With a fork score the cucumber skin heavily, along its length. Slice through the cucumber to make very thin rounds. Place a sprig of parsley in the center of each round and float 2 or 3 in each bowl of clear broth, particularly fish or veal broth, and on cream soup; or serve on the side of a mound of jellied consommé.

LIVER DUMPLINGS
Serves 8 to 10

Add these to broths and bouillons to make the soup heartier and more filling. Season the chopped liver to suit yourself.

½ cup bread crumbs
5 tablespoons milk
2 tablespoons oil
1 small onion, minced
¼ pound chicken livers, cut into halves
¼ cup all-purpose flour

1 teaspoon minced fresh parsley
¼ teaspoon salt
1/16 teaspoon marjoram
⅛ teaspoon pepper
1 medium egg, beaten
3 quarts broth

1. In a small bowl combine the crumbs and the milk, and allow to soak 1 hour.
2. In a large skillet over medium heat, warm the oil and sauté the onion until translucent, about 5 minutes. Add the livers and sauté 5 minutes, stirring so all pieces are lightly browned. Scrape the onions and liver onto a chopping board or into a processor, and mince. Add the flour, parsley, salt, marjoram, and pepper. Combine the egg with the bread crumbs soaked in milk, and beat into the liver mixture.
3. Bring the broth to boiling, scoop small mounds of liver mixture onto the tip of a demitasse spoon, and drop into the boiling broth. Cover and simmer 3 to 5 minutes or until done through. Remove with a slotted spoon, and keep warm until all the mixture is cooked.

To serve: Spoon 2 or 3 dumplings into each bowl of hot broth.

POTATO DUMPLINGS   Serves 10 to 12

Use old potatoes to make these. Start the night before so the riced potatoes have lots of time to dry—the dumplings will be lighter as a result.

4 medium potatoes, about 1 pound	$\frac{1}{16}$ teaspoon pepper
3 quarts water	1 medium egg, beaten
2 tablespoons salt	1 cup all-purpose flour
$\frac{1}{2}$ stick soft butter	$\frac{1}{2}$ cup bread crumbs
$\frac{3}{4}$ teaspoon salt	3 quarts broth

1. Boil the potatoes, unpeeled, in salted water until they can be easily pierced with a knife point. Drain, return to the heat, and shake to dry. When cool, peel, and force through a ricer onto a cookie sheet. Do not mash. Allow to dry several hours or overnight.
2. Scrape the potatoes into a large bowl, and beat in the butter, salt, and pepper. Blend in the egg. Beat in half the flour and half the bread crumbs. If the dough is getting dry, omit some of the flour when you beat in the remaining flour and crumbs. Scoop up by teaspoonfuls, and roll into 1-inch balls between your palms. Roll each ball in flour, and cook in boiling broth 5 to 7 minutes. Remove with a slotted spoon and keep warm until all are cooked.

To serve: Spoon 2 or 3 dumplings into each bowl of soup.

POTATO DUMPLINGS WITH CROUTONS

Prepare Potato Dumplings following the recipe above, but omit the half-cup of bread crumbs. Instead, press a sautéed crouton into the center of each dumpling before forming the ball. Proceed with the recipe, adding more flour if the balls are too soft to hold their shape.

FARINA DUMPLINGS   Serves 6 to 8

Add these to clear broths and bouillons.

1 medium egg	½ to ¾ cup cooked farina
½ teaspoon salt	1 tablespoon soft butter
¼ teaspoon pepper	2 to 3 quarts broth

1. Separate the egg. Put the white into a small bowl with the salt and pepper, and beat until frothy. Blend in the yolk. Slowly beat in the cooked farina and the butter; add as much farina as the mixture will hold. Let the dough stand 10 minutes to harden.
2. Just before serving, bring the broth to a slow boil, and drop dough by the half-teaspoonful into the soup. Simmer 4 to 5 minutes, and remove with a slotted spoon. Keep warm in a buttered bowl while you cook the remaining dough.

To serve: Place a few dumplings in each bowl of hot broth.

KREPLACH   Serves 8 to 10

These are noodle pastries filled with chopped liver and are a favorite of those who love Jewish cuisine.

Dough:

1 cup all-purpose flour	1 medium egg, lightly beaten
½ teaspoon salt	⅛ cup cold water

Filling:

½ cup chicken livers, halved	1 teaspoon grated onion
1 tablespoon chicken fat	¼ teaspoon salt
3 to 4 quarts chicken broth—	⅛ teaspoon pepper
Bella Kaplan's Recipe	
(page 47)	

1. In a small bowl combine the flour and salt, and stir in the egg. Add only as much cold water as necessary to hold the dough together and make it kneadable. Knead in the bowl or on a floured board until smooth, about 5 minutes. Let rest 30 minutes. Flatten the ball and roll it out on a floured board ¼ to ⅛ inch thick. Cut into 18 2½-inch squares.

2. In a saucepan over medium heat, sauté the livers in the chicken fat until tender, about 5 minutes. Turn the livers onto a cutting board and chop fine. Degrease the saucepan with a tablespoonful of chicken broth, and scrape onto chopped livers. Combine livers with the onion, salt, and pepper. Taste and add more salt if needed.
3. Drop ½ teaspoonful of filling into the center of each dough square. Moisten the dough edges with cold water, fold over to make a triangle, and with the tip of a fork moistened in cold water, press the edges of the dough firmly together. Rest the triangles on a floured board 20 minutes, then turn them over and let stand another 20 minutes.
4. Cook in boiling broth 10 to 15 minutes.

To serve: Spoon 2 or 3 into each bowl of broth.

LEMON FLOWERS

  1 thick-skinned lemon
  Sprigs of fresh parsley

Roll the lemon on the counter, pressing hard, to make it juicier. With a sharp knife, remove 4 to 6 lengths of peel. Slice across the lemon to make very thin rounds.

To serve: Place a sprig of parsley in the center of each round and float in hot broth or on jellied consommé.

MUSHROOM FLOWERS   Serves 6

  6 large mushrooms, caps
    about 2 inches in diameter
  6 small sprigs parsley

Wipe the mushrooms clean and cut away the rounded tops, making flat surfaces. Cut 3 very thin rounds from each cap, and with a sharp knife serate the edges.

To serve: Float on hot broths and garnish each slice with a tiny sprig of parsley.

POPOVERS   Makes 10

These are wonderful with light cold soups and with delicate cream soups. The key to making them rise properly is to beat the eggs a lot, and to heat the baking dish well before adding the batter. Make just before serving.

2 medium eggs	½ teaspoon salt
¾ cup milk	¼ cup oil, butter, or bacon
¼ cup cold water	drippings
1 cup sifted all-purpose flour	

1. Heat the oven to 450 degrees, and place an ungreased muffin tin in the oven.
2. Beat the eggs until thick and lemon-colored. Stir in the milk combined with the water and then the flour combined with the salt.
3. Remove the muffin tin and grease each cup. Return to the oven for 1 minute. Spoon the batter into the cups, filling each ⅔ full. Bake at 400 degrees for 12 minutes. Lower heat to 325 degrees and bake 20 minutes more. Do not open the oven door during the baking.

To serve: Remove from the tin, pile into a napkin-lined bread basket, and cover loosely.

MINIATURE *PROFITEROLES*   Makes 5 to 6 dozen

These are elegant, tiny pastries the shape of a cream puff, filled or unfilled, to float on the soup at a dinner party. You must have a pastry tube to make them, but it can be an inexpensive tube with plastic fittings.

½ cup water	1 medium egg, lightly
¼ cup butter	beaten, minus 1
¼ teaspoon salt	teaspoonful
½ cup all-purpose flour	1 teaspoon water
1 medium egg	

1. Preheat the oven to 350 degrees.
2. In a small saucepan over medium heat, bring the water to a boil, reduce heat to very low, and at once stir in the butter, cut into small pieces, and the salt. As soon as the butter has melted pour in all the flour, beating with a wooden spoon until the mixture peels away from the sides of the pan and is very smooth. Remove the saucepan from heat. Make a well in the center of the mixture; let cool 5 minutes. Beat the eggs one at a time into the well. Beat the dough until smooth and glossy after each addition. The dough will be firm enough to retain a shape, but very soft.
3. Make two sizes of puffs: Fit a pastry bag with a ¼-inch tip, fill with dough, and press a ¼-inch round the size of a pea onto an ungreased cookie sheet. Holding the tip close to the top of the pea-sized piece of dough, press another little bit of dough out. Make 4 dozen of these. Then make larger puffs by pressing out a 1-inch round the size of half a small walnut, and holding the tip close to the top of the walnut-sized round, press out another little mound. Wet a finger and gently press down the points of puffs that end in a sharp peak: the tops should be gently rounded. Brush the tops of the larger puffs with the reserved teaspoon of egg mixed with the teaspoon of water. Bake at 350 degrees for 20 minutes. Do not open the oven door. Turn off the heat, and allow to dry 10 minutes.
4. Allow the puffs to cool in a dry, warm kitchen until ready to use. They should be crisp when you add them to the soup. If you eat one and it is less than crunchy, crisp for 2 or 3 minutes in the oven at 250 degrees.
5. Cut larger puffs in half with a sharp knife and fill with whipped cream for fruit soups, or with any hors d'oeuvres stuffing, like chopped liver, or ham or chicken, or grated cheese mixed with mayonnaise.

To serve: Drop 6 to 8 of the small size—2 or 3 of the larger size—into each bowl of soup just before it is served.

Dividends: Allow extras to cool, then store in an airtight container or in the refrigerator or the freezer. Place frozen puffs in an oven at 250 degrees for 5 to 10 minutes to thaw and crisp before serving.

ROYALES Makes 2 dozen

These are custard cut-ups in plain or fancy shapes. They should be made several hours before they will be needed so the custard has time to set. This is a basic, simple *royale:* Escoffier has many complex recipes for other types, including fish and chicken and creams.

1 teaspoon soft butter	1 tablespoon mashed
1 egg plus 2 yolks	vegetable, meat, or fish for
¾ cup hot chicken broth	flavoring, optional

1. Preheat the oven to 325 degrees. Half fill a cake tin with water, and set it in the oven.
2. Butter a small, flat baking dish.
3. Beat the egg and yolks together in a small bowl, then beat in the hot broth and the optional flavoring. Pour through a strainer into the baking dish. The depth should be about ¼ inch. Remove the surface bubbles. Place the dish in the cake tin in the hot oven, and bake 20 minutes. Insert a small, sharp knife in the center of the custard. When the knife comes out clean, the custard is ready. Remove dish, and allow to cool several hours. Unmold onto a clean board or plate, and cut into diamonds or other attractive shapes.

To serve: Place a few in each bowl of soup or consommé.

SPAETZLE Serves 8 to 10

These tiny German noodles flavored with spices are served as a potato substitute and as a garnish for soups. Make your own or buy dried by the box in the supermarket. They're also called "pinched noodles."

1 cup all-purpose flour	Tiny pinch paprika
½ teaspoon salt	⅛ cup cold water
1 medium egg	3 quarts broth
Tiny pinch grated nutmeg	1 tablespoon butter

1. In a small bowl combine the flour and the salt, and stir in egg and spices, to make a stiff dough. Add only as much cold water as necessary to hold the dough together and make it

kneadable. Knead in the bowl or on a floured board until it is smooth, about 4 minutes. Let it rest 30 minutes. Flatten the ball, or roll it out ¼ inch thick on a floured board. With your thumb and forefinger pinch off ½-inch pieces: pinch these noodle bits to flatten them. Drop them into rapidly boiling broth and cook 7 to 8 minutes. Lift out with a strainer, and keep warm in a buttered bowl while you cook remaining dough.

2. Allow extras to dry, and store in an airtight container until needed. Add dried spaetzle to cooked broths and boil until tender.

To serve: Place a few in each bowl of soup or broth.

WHIPPED CREAM, SALTED   Serves 4

½ cup heavy cream
Salt
Paprika

Whip cream until it will hold its shape, then stir in salt to taste. Dust with paprika.

To serve: Drop one tablespoonful in the center of each bowl of soup.

ZUCCHINI FLOWERS   Serves 6

¼ small, very green zucchini
6 squash blooms, optional

Lengthwise, remove wedges from the zucchini in four equally spaced places. Slice into very thin rounds—almost paper thin.

To serve: Float several on each bowl of hot or cold soup with a small squash bloom, if available, on top of one of the slices.

BROTHS, STOCKS, CONSOMMÉS

Broth—stock—is a bouillon made with meat, fowl, fish, or vegetables. In recent years it has become something of a sacred cow among food buffs. Much as I squirm when faced by *other* food buffs' pretentions, this is one I indulge, too. The difference between a soup (or a stew) made with broth and one made with water is considerable—clear, distinct, meaningful, everything you've ever heard it was.

Broth is the word I prefer for "stock" but as far as I can make out, both mean the same thing. "Broth" sounds warmer. Consommé is a clear soup, or a jellied clear soup, that is made starting with broth as a base. *Consommé double* is a French term applied to rich clear soups made from broth. Escoffier refers to the procedures that make consommé as *clarification:* don't confuse Escoffier's term *clarification* with instructions for "clarifying" stocks and consommés given in American cookbooks.

To "clarify," American style, the cooked broth is cooled, skimmed of surface fat, placed in a large kettle and to it are added two egg whites beaten to soft peaks, and the shells, crushed fine. The broth is brought to a boil as you stir. As soon as it foams, it is removed from the heat, stirred once or twice, and left five minutes. The broth is then dripped through a colander lined with a linen or cotton napkin. Or the broth is clarified toward the end of the cooking, unskimmed.

This instruction for clarifying, American style, turns up usually when a broth is to be used to make a jellied consommé or an aspic. It does not turn up in all broth recipes. There's a simpler clarifying process intended to clear broths of murkiness. A description of it appears below among the basic rules for making broths.

Instructions for *clarification* in Escoffier's manner involve adding fresh ingredients to the broth and making a whole new version of it, as one does to make a *consommé double.*

Jellied consommé is usually what you get when you chill a good broth or a consommé: the animal and fowl or fish bones that give the broth its flavor produce the substance that jellies the dish. You may add unflavored gelatin at the rate of one envelope (one tablespoon) for every two cups of broth to get a firmer jellied consommé, or a consommé firm enough for use as an aspic.

HANDLING BROTHS

Broth is very easy to make. You'll get pretty good broth simply by combining and boiling beef, chicken, veal, or fish with herbs and water and a little salt (see Chicken Broth à la Supermarket). However, to produce a superior broth you need a few special but easily located ingredients, a little more patience, and knowledge of a few simple rules:

Don't peel vegetables for broths. Peels improve color and flavor.

Do buy older meats and fowl for making broths. Older animals have more flavor. Escoffier was very firm on the subject.

Do choose meat attached to bones: the flavor is better, and there's gelatin in those bones. Shin, neck, brisket, short ribs (you'll have too much fat, but the flavor will be good), flanken (ribs), chuck, veal knuckles, and big old fowl are all good for making broths.

Don't add more salt to broths than recipes specify: the broths go into soups which usually have their own salt quotas.

Do consider budgeting for a big stock pot (see Chapter 1), a good, heavy-gauge kettle that can hold six quarts or more.

To skim or not to skim the broth as it cooks is a question. For eye appeal, broths should be skimmed. The initial boiling sends bubbling to the surface coagulated blood and liqueurs (Escoffier said albumins) from meat, fish, herbs, and vegetables that later settle in the broth, making it a bit murky. Those particles are flavorful and also nutritious, and should be kept when the stock will make soups. Skim, however, when you are making broth for consommé that will become jellied consommé or an aspic, because clarity will affect the look of the dish.

You'll find handsome broth skimmers in kitchen equipment shops—long-handled, flat strainers that do the job very well. But a small, ordinary, fine strainer works well, too. Bring the broth to a moderate boil over medium heat, uncovered. A scummy froth will form in a few minutes; keep skimming this off until it stops forming. Remove scum adhering to the sides of the kettle. When scumming ends reduce the heat, cover, and start the broth on its long round of simmering.

To further clarify a broth, there are many steps possible. I suggest that after the cooking you strain the broth through a double thickness of cheesecloth.

STORING BROTHS

We store broth in the refrigerator for up to two weeks. Broth will keep longer, but eventually it starts to lose its firmness and develops a sour odor. Broth to be kept more than two weeks, I freeze in 8-ounce plastic cups covered with a double thickness of plastic wrap held in place by a rubber band; before using, I boil a stored broth two to three minutes.

In summer, freeze broth in ice cube trays, then bag loose cubes. The cubes can be popped into cold tomato and vegetable drinks, or melted down for use in soups: two standard cubes measure a quarter-cup of broth (or water).

I do not skim fat from just-cooked broth intended for future use: the fat rises as the broth cools and acts as a seal. I do remove fat before using the broth in a recipe. To degrease broth you have just made, refrigerate, and when the fat has risen to the surface, skim off and discard.

WHICH BROTH TO CHOOSE?

The recipes in this book based on broth call for plain chicken broth or beef broth, for the most part. Every cook has a special recipe for the basic broth used in cooking, and you will develop one that suits you. Meanwhile, here are some classic recipes to experiment with. Any of the light broths (All-Purpose White Stock, for instance) will be excellent in place of chicken broth in my recipes, and any of the dark broths (from Pot-au-Feu in Chapter 3 to Save-It-Up-Broth, below) will be excellent where recipes call for beef broth.

THE LIGHT BROTHS AND STOCKS

Light, dry, delicate broths made with chicken, veal, and combinations of these and other meats, are the basis for delicious fruit soups, Edwardian creams, and veloutés. All-Purpose White Stock, below, is the classic recipe for this purpose, long and slow to cook, wonderful to have in the larder. Other recipes in this group are less costly to make, and faster. But it is true that the finer the broth, the finer the soup or consommé you will make with it.

ALL-PURPOSE WHITE STOCK— *FOND BLANC ORDINAIRE*

Makes 3 to 4 quarts

This is the basic stock or broth in the French cooking arsenal. Escoffier made it with 3 pounds of shin beef, 3 pounds of any lean beef (*older* animals), the bones of an old fowl (tastier than young), turnips, carrots, leeks, parsnips, and boiled it for 12 hours and up. It is delicate and perfect for use in making cream soups, veloutés, and anywhere chicken broth is called for. Ask the butcher to crack the bones.

3 pounds veal bones, cracked
2 pounds veal shank or shoulder or trimmings
2 pounds chicken giblets, backs, necks, wing tips
1½ tablespoons salt
6 quarts cold water
2 medium carrots, cut into chunks
2 medium onions, cut into chunks

2 medium leeks, halved
2 large stalks celery
4 sprigs parsley
1 medium bay leaf
1 teaspoon dried thyme
4 whole cloves
8 peppercorns
Coarse sea or kosher salt

1. In a large kettle or stock pot over high heat, combine bones, meat, chicken parts, salt, and water. Skim until scum stops forming; wipe the scum from the sides of the pot. Add the vegetables and skim as before. Add parsley, bay leaf, thyme, cloves, and peppercorns, tied into a small cheesecloth square. Cover partially, reduce heat, and simmer 4 hours. As the water falls below the level of the ingredients, replenish the supply.
2. Line a colander with 2 thicknesses of cheesecloth and strain the broth through it. Discard bones, bony chicken parts, and herbs. Scoop vegetables and meat into an ovenproof bowl. Pour 4 to 6 cups of broth over this meat. Allow the remaining broth to cool, then refrigerate or freeze for future use in soups and consommés.

Dividends: Serve the meat with vegetables and a little degreased hot broth in large soup plates. Pass coarse sea or kosher salt, and offer French bread as an accompaniment.

VEAL BROTH
Makes 1 quart

2 pounds veal bones from back, shin, knuckle, or shoulder
1 calf's foot or knuckle
1 carrot, cut into chunks
2 leeks, green removed, quartered
2 large stalks celery, minced

2 teaspoons salt
5 peppercorns
3 whole cloves
2 quarts water
1 teaspoon lemon juice
Coarse sea or kosher salt

1. In a large kettle over medium heat, combine all the ingredients except the lemon juice and coarse salt. Bring to a boil, then simmer, covered, 1½ hours. Add lemon juice and cook 1 minute.
2. Line a colander with 2 thicknesses of cheesecloth and strain the broth through it. Discard the bones and herbs. Allow the broth to cool, then refrigerate or freeze for future use in soups or consommés.

Dividends: Serve meat scraps and vegetables with a little broth in large soup plates. Pass sea or kosher salt, and offer French bread as an accompaniment.

SAVE-IT-UP BROTH
Makes 2 to 3 quarts

1 pound meaty beef bones
1 pound meaty chicken bones
6 chicken giblets
1 pound meaty veal neck bones
1 large carrot, scraped
1 parsnip, scraped
1 stalk celery and leaves
1 large onion
4 whole cloves

1 bay leaf
½ teaspoon dried chervil
½ teaspoon dried thyme
½ teaspoon marjoram
6 peppercorns
2 sprigs parsley
1 tablespoon salt
3 beef bouillon cubes
4 quarts cold water
Coarse sea or kosher salt

1. In a large kettle over medium heat, combine all the ingredients except the coarse sea or kosher salt. Cover, bring to a boil; reduce heat at once and simmer 4 hours.
2. Line a colander with 2 thicknesses of cheesecloth and strain the broth through it. Strip the meat from the bones and discard bones, cloves, bay leaf, and peppercorns. Allow the broth

to cool, then refrigerate or freeze for future use in soups or consommés.

Dividends: Serve the meat scraps and giblets with vegetables and a little degreased hot broth in large soup plates. Pass coarse sea or kosher salt, and offer French bread as an accompaniment.

CHICKEN BROTH—BELLA KAPLAN'S RECIPE   Serves 6 to 8

Bella Kaplan was the grandmother of my friend, writer Marian Asne. She served this light, clear broth Friday night with fine noodles for supper, and on Saturday she served the chicken and vegetables cold. This recalls the French recipe for *poule-au-pot,* in which the broth is served with the chicken and vegetables when just made, and the chicken meat may be served later with a *béchamel* sauce.

2 1½ pound chickens, cut up, including gizzards, heart, and neck, trimmed of fat
Garlic salt
⅛ teaspoon pepper
3 large sprigs dark, coarse parsley
3 large branches fresh dill
3½ quarts water
1 large clove garlic
1 medium onion, cut in sixths to halfway down

2 fat carrots, quartered
2 large stalks celery, trimmed of leaves, cut in thirds
1 large fresh parsnip, trimmed, halved
Salt
6 ounces egg noodles, cooked

1. Sprinkle chicken parts all over with garlic salt and pepper. Tie parsley and dill together with string. In a large kettle over high heat, bring the water to a rapid boil and add chicken, herbs, garlic, and vegetables. Bring back to a boil, skimming until scum stops forming. Wipe scum from sides of kettle. Cover, lower heat, and simmer 2½ hours.
2. Lift the chicken into a casserole; cover and keep warm. Salt the broth to taste, then drain into a soup tureen. Add the vegetables to the chicken; discard garlic and herbs.

To serve: Divide cooked noodles among 6 or 8 large soup bowls, and ladle soup over them. About 9 cups of broth should remain after cooking. When soup is finished, serve chicken and vegetables into same bowls, and offer bread with it. Refrigerate or freeze leftover broth.

CHICKEN BROTH À LA SUPERMARKET   Makes about 1 quart

Here is the simplest, least expensive chicken broth I know for use as a base for soup recipes. Just gather up the fresh or frozen packaged necks, gizzards, and livers from supermarket chickens, toss into the kettle, and cook 4 hours. The broth is golden-brown, rich, dry—tasty enough to be made into soup by adding half a cup of rice or noodles and cooking until they are tender. I often do this one in the slow-cooker.

3 quarts water
2 teaspoons salt
1/8 teaspoon pepper
1/4 small bay leaf
1/4 teaspoon dried thyme
6 each : chicken necks, gizzards, livers, hearts, wing tips
1 small onion, stuck with 4 whole cloves

1 large sprig parsley
1/8 teaspoon dried dill
1 medium carrot, peeled, cut up
1 stalk celery and leaves, cut up
Salt

1. In a large kettle over high heat, combine all the ingredients, cover, and bring to a boil. Reduce heat and simmer for 4 hours.
2. Line a colander with 2 thicknesses of cheesecloth and strain the broth through it. Reserve only the broth. Allow to cool, salt to taste, then refrigerate or freeze for use in soups and consommés.

CHICKEN BROTH—FAST   Makes 4 cups

4 level teaspoons chicken bouillon granules or 4 chicken bouillon cubes
4 1/4 cups water
1 thin slice onion

2 sprigs parsley
1/4 small bay leaf
1/8 teaspoon dried thyme
1/3 cup dry white vermouth, optional

In a small saucepan over medium heat, combine all the ingredients except the vermouth. Bring to a boil, cover, and simmer 5 minutes. Add vermouth and cook 2 minutes. Strain through cheesecloth. Discard herbs. Use broth as directed in recipe.

CHICKEN BROTH FOR CHINESE SOUPS Makes about 3 quarts

This is my from-scratch recipe for chicken broth to make Chinese and other Oriental soups.

5 pounds chicken
4 quarts water
2½-inch slices fresh ginger root or 1 teaspoon ground ginger

1 large scallion, cut into 1-inch pieces
1 teaspoon soy sauce
Salt

1. In a large kettle over high heat, combine the chicken, water, ginger root, and scallion. Cover and bring to a boil. Skim the surface until scum stops forming. Cover, reduce heat, and simmer 2 hours.
2. Remove the chicken, add the soy sauce, and salt to taste. Allow the broth to cool, then refrigerate or freeze for future use in Oriental recipes.

Dividends: Save the chicken meat and put aside 2 cups of the broth to make a Chicken à la King with ginger overtones.

CONSOMMÉ DOUBLE OF CHICKEN

See *Petite Marmite* on page 94. Though it is intended primarily as a boiled dinner, the extra broth created has more flavor than the chicken broths above or the All-Purpose White Stock, and is a delicious base for the consommé recipes that follow.

FISH BROTHS

A classic recipe for a broth whose flavor recalls bouillabaisse and the Mediterranean follows, along with a recipe for a quick fish stock that can serve as a *court bouillon* for cooking fish.

FISH BROTH   Makes 2½ quarts

This makes a very good soup all by itself. By adding milk or cream, and clams, oysters, leftover bits of lobster or crab, you can turn it into a heavenly main course. If you wish, you may make this broth from 2 pounds of fish instead of fish trimmings. In that case, serve the fish with a little broth for dinner; reserve the balance.

1 cup chopped onion	½ teaspoon dried thyme
1 large leek, white only, chopped	¼ teaspoon fennel seed
1 cup olive oil	¼ teaspoon saffron threads
6 large ripe tomatoes or 1 16-ounce can of tomatoes and liquid, chopped	½ teaspoon grated orange peel
4 large cloves garlic, crushed	2 pounds trimmings from white fish, such as sea bass, cod, haddock, hake, halibut, flounder, whiting
6 sprigs parsley	2½ quarts water
	2 teaspoons salt

1. In a large saucepan over medium heat, sauté the onion and the leek in the oil 5 minutes. Do not allow to brown. Stir in the tomatoes and garlic, and sauté 5 minutes. Add the remaining ingredients, bring to a boil; cover, reduce heat, and simmer 40 minutes.
2. Line a colander with 2 thicknesses of cheesecloth. Strain the broth, allow it to cool, then refrigerate or freeze for future use in soups and consommés.

FISH BROTH—FAST   Makes 2 cups

Here is a substitute for fish broth. If the recipe you are working with already includes thyme, omit the thyme here.

1 8-ounce bottle clam juice	⅛ teaspoon dried thyme
½ teaspoon strained lemon juice	Salt and pepper

Combine all the ingredients in a small saucepan over medium heat. Bring to a boil, cover, and simmer 5 minutes. Turn off heat and allow the broth to rest 5 minutes. Add salt and pepper to taste. Use as directed in the recipe.

VEGETABLE BROTH
Makes 1 to 2 quarts

Here's a simple yet delicate and delicious vegetable broth to use as a base for soups in place of meat broths. It is suitable in most recipes calling for chicken, veal, or beef broth.

For a very special vegetable broth, see the recipe for *Petite Marmite* in Chapter 3.

4 medium carrots, chopped	1 medium bay leaf
4 scallions, chopped	4 large sprigs parsley
2 medium onions, chopped	½ teaspoon dried thyme
2 large celery ribs and leaves, chopped	Tiny pinch tarragon
	2 teaspoons salt
4 leeks, chopped	¼ teaspoon pepper
3 tablespoons butter	Salt and pepper
3 quarts water	

1. In a large saucepan over medium heat, sauté the vegetables in the butter, stirring constantly, 15 minutes. Do not let them brown. Stir in the water and add the herbs and seasonings. Cover, bring to a boil, reduce heat, and simmer 2 hours.
2. Line a colander with 2 thicknesses of cheesecloth and strain the broth through it. Add salt and pepper to taste. Allow the broth to cool, then store in refrigerator or freezer for future use.

Dividends: Serve the vegetables with a little broth as a side dish, or purée them with 1 cup of broth and serve as a cream of vegetable soup.

HEARTY BROTHS AND STOCKS

Beef broth—*le fond brun*—that follows, is typical of the hearty broths used to base consommés and strongly-flavored soups. Less costly versions of strong broths, and quick recipes, are included in the group below. But when you want to splurge on a soup or a consommé for a gala event, plan to make Pot-au-Feu (see Chapter 3) and hoard the broth for your special purpose.

BEEF BROTH—*LE FOND BRUN*   Makes 2 to 3 quarts

Use this where beef broth is called for. It makes a wonderful base for hearty gravies as well. Pour a little, or dissolve 2 or 3 frozen cubes of it into the hot skillet steak has fried in to make a wonderful gravy. Have the butcher crack the bones for you.

2 pounds beef : shin, neck, brisket, flanken, chuck
2 pounds beef shin bones or other beef soup bones, cracked
1 knuckle of veal and a little meat
4½ quarts cold water
1½ tablespoons salt
2 teaspoons drippings from a beef roast, or bacon drippings

2 carrots, cut into chunks
2 parsnips, cut into chunks
2 large leeks, halved
2 large stalks celery and leaves
4 sprigs parsley
1 medium bay leaf
1 teaspoon dried thyme
4 whole cloves
3 large cloves garlic
8 peppercorns
Coarse sea or kosher salt

1. Preheat the oven to 450 degrees.
2. Remove the meat from the bones, tie it together, and place it in a large kettle or stock pot with the water and salt, over high heat. Cover.
3. Spread the bones in a large saucepan, sprinkle them with a little melted fat or drippings. Roast in the oven 30 to 40 minutes, until well colored.
4. When the stock comes to a boil, lower heat and skim scum as it rises. When it stops forming, wipe the scum from the sides of the pot. Add the vegetables, and remove the scum as before. Tie the herbs, cloves, and peppercorns into a small cheesecloth square, and add to pot.
5. When the bones are browned, turn them into the kettle. Use a little broth to loosen the drippings in the saucepan and turn that into the broth. Cover, reduce heat, and simmer 4 hours.
6. Line a colander with 2 thicknesses of cheesecloth and strain the broth through it. Discard bones and herbs, scoop the vegetables and the meat into an ovenproof bowl; untie the meat. Pour 4 to 6 cups of broth over the meat. Allow the remaining broth to cool, then refrigerate or freeze for future use in soups and consommés.

Dividends: Serve the meat with the vegetables and a little degreased hot broth in large soup plates. Pass coarse sea or kosher salt, and offer French bread as an accompaniment.

BEEF BROTH—LIGHT AND EASY

Follow the recipe for Basic Beef Broth, but omit the browning of the bones. The result is a lighter flavored broth.

BEEF BROTH—SIMPLE   Makes 2 to 3 quarts

3 pounds beef shank meat and bones, cracked
2 medium carrots, cut into chunks
1 large onion, unpeeled, cut into chunks
4½ quarts water
2 large stalks celery and leaves, cut into chunks

1 large parsnip, cut into chunks
1½ tablespoons salt
¼ teaspoon dried thyme
1 small bay leaf
Coarse sea or kosher salt

Follow the procedures for roasting bones and cooking broth given under Basic Beef Broth (see page 52).

BEEF BROTH—FAST   Makes 4 cups

4 level teaspoons beef bouillon granules
4¼ cups water
1 thin slice onion
1 small clove garlic

2 sprigs parsley
1 whole clove
4 peppercorns
1 teaspoon dried thyme
⅓ cup dry sherry, optional

Combine everything but the sherry in a small saucepan over medium heat. Bring to a boil, cover, and simmer 5 minutes. Add sherry and cook 2 minutes. Strain through cheesecloth. Discard herbs. Use broth as directed in recipe.

CONSOMMÉ DOUBLE OF BEEF

See Pot-au-Feu in Chapter 3. A *consommé double* is a broth whose flavor is sharpened by the addition of more meat. The broth remaining from pot-au-feu is perfect for use as a base for any of the consommé variations noted below. Or serve the pot-au-feu consommé hot with minced parsley, or chilled and jellied with a lemon wedge.

BEEF TEA   Serves 3

This is easy to make in a slow-cook pot. Set at 200 degrees—slow —and cook overnight, using only 3 cups of water. Beef Tea is said to be a strengthening drink and is usually made for people recovering from illness.

1 pound lean beef	2 sprigs parsley
3½ cups water	½ teaspoon salt
1 small carrot, chopped	¼ teaspoon pepper
1 large slice onion	Lemon Flowers (page 37)

1. Preheat the oven to 300 degrees.
2. Chop the beef in a food processor, or put it through a meat grinder. In a *cocotte* (or a dutch oven) combine the meat with the water and add the vegetables, parsley, salt, and pepper. Place in the oven and cook 3 hours. Line a colander with 2 thicknesses of cheesecloth and strain the broth through it. Chill broth in the refrigerator. When the fat has risen to the surface skim it off and discard. Reheat the broth.

To serve: Ladle into consommé cups and garnish with Lemon Flowers.

GAME CONSOMMÉ

Makes 1½ to 2 quarts

This is made from the remains of roasted game birds.

Skin and bones of 2 grouse or
    pheasants
1 large onion, sliced
1 large carrot, sliced
2 whole cloves
8 peppercorns
2 large sprigs parsley
½ teaspoon dried thyme
⅛ teaspoon ground mace
1 small bay leaf
1 teaspoon sugar

6 juniper berries
2½ quarts Veal Broth
    (page 46), fat removed
½ cup dry sherry
2 quarts water
2 egg whites
2 egg shells
Salt and pepper
1 ounce lean ham, chopped
Lemon Flowers (page 37)

1. In a large kettle over medium heat, combine the skin, bones, vegetables, herbs, and spices with the broth and sherry. Cover and bring to a boil. Reduce heat and simmer 3 hours, adding water to maintain original level.
2. Line a colander with a double thickness of cheesecloth, and strain the consommé through it. Reserve only the broth. Place the consommé in the refrigerator to chill. When the fat has risen to the surface, skim it off and discard. Follow the steps for clarifying the broth described on page 42 of the introduction to this chapter.

To serve: Ladle into consommé cups and garnish with chopped ham and Lemon Flowers.

CONSOMMÉS—TO SERVE HOT OR COLD

Here is a handful of classic consommés to be made from the broths and stocks above. Any of the clear consommés here can be served chilled in a cup set in a bowl of cracked ice, or hot. If a consommé fails to gel after chilling for twelve to twenty-four hours, you may heat it and add one envelope (one tablespoon) of gelatin for every two cups. But it's rare that a good broth fails to gel.

CONSOMMÉ WITH CROUTONS
Serves 4 to 6

4 to 6 cups Pot-au-Feu broth
  (page 70), or beef broth
1 recipe Croutons, Sautéed
  (page 32), or other
  crouton recipe

Remove the fat from the chilled broth, and reheat to boiling. Ladle into consommé cups and garnish with croutons.

JELLIED CONSOMMÉ
Serves 4 to 6

4 to 6 cups jellied Pot-au-Feu
  broth (page 70), or other
  beef broth
¼ cup cold water, if needed

1 envelope (1 tablespoon)
  unflavored gelatin, if
  needed
4 to 6 Lemon Flowers (page 37)

Remove the fat from chilled jellied broth. If the consommé is less than firm, add the gelatin dissolved in the water. Chill until firmly set. Break the jelly apart with a fork and serve in chilled bowls set, if you wish, in bowls of cracked ice. Garnish with Lemon Flowers.

CONSOMMÉ *CHIFFONNADE*
Serves 8

¼ medium head of Boston or
  a small head of iceberg
  lettuce, shredded fine
½ cup sorrel leaves

2 tablespoons butter
8 cups hot All-Purpose
  White Stock (page 45) or
  chicken broth, fat removed

In a saucepan over medium heat, sauté the lettuce and sorrel leaves in the butter, stirring constantly, 2 minutes or until just wilted. (This is a *chiffonnade*.)

To serve: Divide the *chiffonnade* among the consommé cups and ladle the hot broth over it.

CONSOMMÉ CRÉCY Serves 4

4 cups All-Purpose White
  Stock (page 45) or chicken
  broth, fat removed
5 tablespoons quick-cooking
  tapioca

Royales, flavored with 1
  tablespoon carrot purée
  and cut into lozenge shapes
  (page 40)
Carrot Flowers (page 28)

In a kettle over medium heat, bring the broth to a rapid boil and sprinkle the tapioca into it. Reduce heat and cook until tapioca becomes transparent, about 10 minutes.

To serve: Ladle soup into consommé cups and garnish with *Royales* and Carrot Flowers.

CONSOMMÉ FORESTIÈRE Serves 6

½ pound fresh mushrooms,
  quartered
2 tablespoons butter
⅛ teaspoon salt
6 cups beef broth, fat
  removed

½ cup heavy cream
1 tablespoon dry sherry
3 mushrooms caps, sliced
  thin
½ teaspoon chopped fresh
  chervil or tarragon

1. In a kettle over medium heat, sauté the mushrooms in the butter, stirring, 5 minutes. Add the salt and stir in the broth. Reduce heat, cover, and simmer 8 minutes.
2. Purée in a blender or a food processor, 2 cups at a time, then return purée to the kettle. Raise heat to medium, stir in the cream and sherry, and heat to just below boiling.

To serve: Ladle into consommé cups and garnish with sliced mushroom caps and a pinch of chopped herb.

CONSOMMÉ WITH FRESH HERBS
Serves 6

This recipe would be equally good with other herbs—basil and tarragon, for instance, or chervil—whatever you grow and love.

6 cups Pot-au-Feu broth
  (page 70), or beef broth,
  fat removed
1 sprig each of parsley and
  thyme

2 or 3 chive stems
6 chive blossoms, or sprigs of
  parsley or thyme

Pour 1 cup of Pot-au-Feu broth, or Beef Broth into a blender or food processor, add the sprigs of fresh herbs, and blend for half a minute. Pour the remaining consommé or broth into a kettle over medium high heat, bring to a boil, add the puréed herbs, and remove from heat at once. Stir, then let rest 5 minutes.

To serve: Ladle into bowls and garnish with chive blossoms or herb sprigs.

CONSOMMÉ GARNI
Serves 4

This turns up on French menus: it means consommé that has a garnish. Here's one version, but there can be many others.

4 cups beef broth, fat
  removed
4 Lemon Flowers (page 37)

12 pimiento-stuffed green
  olives, chopped

In a kettle over medium heat, bring the broth to a boil and add the chopped olives. As soon as the broth boils again, remove from heat.

To serve: Ladle into consommé cups and garnish with Lemon Flowers.

CONSOMMÉ JULIENNE
Serves 4 to 6

This is a classic consommé. It will be pretty only if the pieces of vegetable are of equal sizes—about 2 inches long and ¼ inch thick, and remain unbroken in the cooking.

1 medium carrot, cut into
matchstick lengths
1 small parsnip, cut into
matchstick lengths
1 small leek, cut into
matchstick lengths
¼ cup shredded green
cabbage

2 tablespoons tiny green
peas
1 teaspoon brown sugar
2 tablespoons butter
5 cups beef broth, fat
removed
1 teaspoon minced fresh
chervil

In a saucepan over medium heat, sauté the vegetables with the sugar in the butter, stirring gently, 5 minutes. Add 1 cup of broth. Cover, reduce heat, and cook until tender, about 5 to 10 minutes.

To serve: When ready to serve, pour the remaining 4 cups of broth over the vegetables, heat to boiling, and ladle into consommé cups. Garnish with minced chervil.

CONSOMMÉ MADRILÈNE   Serves 6

6 cups beef broth, fat
removed
2 large ripe tomatoes, peeled
¼ cup Madeira, optional

½ teaspoon minced fresh
chervil
1 tablespoon minced red
pimiento

In a kettle over medium heat, bring the broth to a boil. Reduce heat and rub the tomatoes through a sieve into the boiling broth. Add the wine, if you wish, and simmer 1 minute. Strain the broth and reheat.

To serve: Ladle into consommé cups and garnish with chervil and diced pimiento.

JELLIED *CONSOMMÉ MADRILÈNE*   Serves 6

1 recipe *Consommé
Madrilène*
1 envelope unflavored
gelatin (1 tablespoon)

¼ cup cold water
Lemon Flowers (page 37)

To the hot *Consommé Madrilène* add the gelatin dissolved in the water. Chill until set. Break the jellied consommé apart with a fork and serve in chilled bowls set, if you wish, in bowls of cracked ice. Garnish with Lemon Flowers.

CONSOMMÉ MAISON   Serves 6

A rule of thumb when making consommés that will be served jellied is to prepare broth or stock allowing one pound of meat for every *pint* of water, which makes a very strong broth. The usual proportion is one *quart* of water for each pound of meat, but if there is plenty of bone included in the soup ingredients list, the broth will gel, too. In my experience, however, almost any long-cooking, meaty broth made with bones will gel and is very good. Cold jellied consommé is refreshing on hot days, and makes an elegant first course when nicely garnished.

6 cups jellied beef or chicken broth, fat removed
1 tablespoon strained lemon juice
6 Lemon Flowers (page 37)
6 sprigs parsley
Coarse sea or kosher salt

To serve: Spoon jellied consommé into consommé cups, and divide lemon juice among them. Garnish with Lemon Flowers and sprigs of parsley, and season with a grating of salt, or a small pinch of coarse sea or kosher salt.

To make ahead: May be prepared in advance, but keep chilled until ready to serve.

CONSOMMÉ MIMOSA   Serves 4

Mimosa is a beautiful flowering tree or shrub, with fluffy, yellow blooms as tiny as a pinhead. *Consommé Mimosa* is a broth garnished with yellow, green, and a dab of red.

4 cups hot chicken broth, fat removed
½ recipe *Royales,* cut into small circles (page 40)
2 tablespoons minced chives
2 tablespoons chopped ripe tomato pulp

To serve: Ladle the broth into consommé cups and garnish with *Royales,* chives, and tomato.

CONSOMMÉ MOUSSELINE
Serves 4 to 5

4 cups All-Purpose White
Stock (page 45), or
chicken broth, fat removed
3 tablespoons quick-cooking
tapioca

2 tablespoons dry sherry
2 medium egg yolks
½ cup heavy cream
Miniature *Profiteroles,* small,
optional (page 38)

1. In a kettle over medium heat, bring the broth to a boil, sprinkle tapioca into it, reduce heat, and cook until tapioca becomes transparent, about 10 minutes. Add the sherry and cook 2 minutes.
2. In a small bowl beat the yolks lightly. Stir 1 cup hot broth into the eggs, then add mixture to kettle, stirring. Reheat, but do not let it boil. Stir in the cream.

To serve: Ladle into consommé cups. Drop a few Miniature *Profiteroles* into each cup just before it is served, if you wish.

CONSOMMÉ PRINTANIER
Serves 4

This is a spring consommé made with the first vegetables from the garden—tiny peas, sugar peas, baby carrots, young snap green beans, young turnips. You can toss in thinnings from the lettuce row, too, just before serving.

2 tablespoons each of 3 or
4 garden vegetables—
chopped or grated
1 teaspoon brown sugar
4¼ cups chicken or beef
broth, fat removed

½ recipe Chives and
Parsley, optional
(page 31)

In a kettle over medium low heat, simmer the vegetables with the sugar in ¼ cup of broth, stirring, until tender, about 8 to 10 minutes. Don't let them brown. Stir in the remaining 4 cups of broth, bring to a boil, and turn off heat.

To serve: Ladle into consommé cups and garnish with Chives and Parsley if you wish.

HOLIDAY CONSOMMÉ

Serves 4 to 6

You could make this with leftover clam broth, too.

2 cups bottled clam juice
1 cup chicken broth
⅛ cup dry white wine
3 egg yolks, lightly beaten

¼ cup heavy cream
⅛ teaspoon pepper
1 tablespoon minced parsley

In a kettle over medium heat, bring clam juice and chicken broth to a simmer, cover, and cook 5 minutes. Beat the wine into the egg yolks, then beat a little hot broth into the wine-egg mixture. Beat mixture into the broth. Remove the soup from heat, and stir in the cream and pepper.

To serve: Ladle into consommé cups and garnish with parsley.

Dividends: Nice chilled.

WINE CONSOMMÉ

Serves 4

4 cups beef broth, fat
    removed
½ cup dry red wine
½ teaspoon sugar
½ teaspoon strained lemon
    juice

Salt and pepper
Croutons, Garlic-Flavored
    (page 32)

In a kettle over medium heat, bring the broth to a boil and add the wine and sugar. Reduce heat and simmer 3 minutes; add the lemon juice. Turn off heat, cover, and let rest 5 to 10 minutes. Add salt and pepper to taste.

To serve: Ladle into consommé cups and garnish with Croutons, Garlic-Flavored.

Three
THE HOSPITALITY POT

The soups in this chapter are as hearty as stews, too filling to serve as a first course but just right for the feeding of hungry multitudes. I think of them as main-course soups for one-dish dinners, true hospitality pots.

The first time I ever saw a hospitality pot in action in the ancient Swedish style—that is, taking in all sorts of leftovers— was in the kitchen of Sally Larkin Erath's little Cape Cod cottage overlooking a salty bay in Chatham, Massachusetts. The stove had one deeply recessed burner that accommodated a big stock pot. Here Sally made soups and glorious chowders. One night when she was heating broth intended as a first course to a sedate little dinner of leftover cold turkey, the whole of Chatham, it seemed, arrived intent on being fed. To accommodate the first arrival (a neighbor who was without electricity), she added a cupful of baked ham scraps to the soup pot, along with another cupful of broth. The second drop-in (a large, hungry high school football player) inspired her to mix up a batch of biscuits and to add the turkey, chopped, to the soup, along with leftover corn kernels and broad noodles. She also added more broth. While the soup simmered and the biscuits baked, Sally kept tasting and adding—dried thyme, a scrap of bay leaf, salt, pepper, a small clove of minced garlic, a half-cup of dry white wine. When she ladled the thick, fragrant broth into big soup plates, she sprinkled each liberally with finely minced parsley.

Yumm!

"Squeamish!" Sally would say, poking a leftover down into the thick soup. "This is all perfectly good food!"

Spur-of-the-moment hospitality pots, like Sally's, surely are the ancestors of the written recipes in this chapter, recipes for hearty meat and vegetable dishes that fall somewhere between stews and soups. They are creations of the heart, intent on feeding multitudes from whatever falls to hand.

Sally often began hers by dicing a creamy white slab of salt pork and rendering it for ten to fifteen minutes in a big heavy kettle over a slow fire. But modern recipes more often begin with the sautéeing of an onion in butter or oil. Rendered goose fat is almost as fine as butter for this purpose, and so is really good chicken grease, the congealed fat in the pan in which a chicken has been roasted.

BROWNING MEATS FOR SOUPS

The recipes here usually give you oil or butter in which to brown meats, but you can often substitute a little fat taken from the meat to be browned. Render it in the saucepan or kettle so that a couple of tablespoons of liquid fat are sloshing around, then discard the crisped bits and put the meat into the fat.

More robust soups, especially the main course soups here and in Chapter 6, call for browning of the meat as a first step. Don't skimp on the browning. Today's meats are mass-produced, often frozen and sometimes refrozen, and generally, they are tasteless. The browning of the meat may be the only flavor (almost) brought to the soup by the meat.

Where to brown meats? A big stock pot or a dutch oven may offer enough surface to brown a couple of pounds of meat at a time. The average 4-quart kettle will do only a quarter or a third of three 1-pound lamb breasts, or three pounds of cut-up chicken at a time. I often brown meats in a big cast-iron saucepan, then transfer to the kettle or stock pot. If you make such a transfer it is vitally important that you add a little liquid to the bottom of the browning pan and scrape up all the drippings browned there. That's sheer flavor, and the soup needs it!

ACCOMPANIMENTS FOR MAIN-COURSE SOUPS

Most main-course soups need something crunchy and baked to go with them—oven-warmed French or Italian bread, for instance, well done English muffins, butter biscuits, crackle-fresh dinner rolls—all are just right with the meat soups that follow. I prefer warm, fresh corn bread with the ham and bean dishes (and nutritionally, that is a sound mix). Croutons, on the other hand, may be enough for you—just a bit of crunch under tooth. Bread sticks can satisfy, and so can cheese straws.

GARNISHES

Few of the main-course soups have garnishes other than a dab of color that comes from minced parsley, dill, or some other green herb. Most are so thick that they don't really need anything more floating in them! A group of soups, below, includes dumplings, and egg and dairy products such as custard and scrambled eggs. And these ingredients serve as their own rich garnishes.

TIMING AND SLOW-COOK POTS, AND PRESSURE COOKERS

The main-course soups take half an hour or so to pull together, even with a food processor to help. Most of these cook in two to four hours. And a few take longer. In a slow-cook pot on low (200 to 240 degrees) they would benefit from cooking ten to twelve hours. The meat recipes in this chapter are ideal for slow-pot cooking. But some may turn out a little watery because they have been planned for more rapid cooking in which there is greater water loss in evaporation. To strengthen the flavor, strain and boil the broth on high until the flavor pleases you.

You can make some of these soups in a pressure cooker (see Chapter 12).

DIVIDENDS

Virtually all the hearty, main-course soups are at least as good the second day and can be made ahead. Generally, they are thicker the second time around and benefit from being thinned and stretched by at least one or two cups of broth, or wine and broth. Add liquid stretchers such as broth and water by the cupful, not the quart, and taste as you add. You may need additional seasonings. Add wine by the half-cup; you may find it will taste better if a matching quantity of water is added. If wine is used, cook the soup over low heat for five or ten minutes before serving to eliminate the flavor of raw wine. Milk is a good additive to thick vegetable stews.

MEATS FOR MAIN-COURSE SOUPS

Main-course soups are where all those delicious meat cuts too tough for roasting come into their own. Easy on the pocketbook as well, they are first-rate in flavor and nourishment, but they need plenty of slow simmering for their flavor to develop in just the right way.

BEEF: Beef, with pork, is the meat most often used in soups, and there are any number of beef cuts suitable for main-course soups. When choosing a cut naturally marbled, choose one whose marbling is plentiful but not broad. Avoid cuts whose fat is yellowish or grayish. Compare colors and select pieces whose meat is bright rather than deep red, and choose pieces whose bones are soft-looking and have a reddish color.

The cuts listed here are all suitable for soups. Some are not inexpensive; look for sales on these, and buy and freeze with future soups in mind.

Any pot roast (buy when on sale and freeze)

Beef plate (this includes ribs and spareribs, Yankee pot roast, and is the section behind the brisket)

Top or bottom round (buy when on sale and freeze)

Chuck

Brisket of beef (boneless breast, unless you buy the whole, which includes ribs)

Brisket, cured (corned beef—boneless)

Short ribs (flanken or flunken)

Spareribs

Riblets

Neck roast

Neck (bone in)

Neck pieces (these are bones without meat, the equivalent of soup bones, but not a suitable substitute when soups call for neck, bone in, or meaty neck bones)

Shank (fore or aft, also shin: see the caution above regarding neck bones)

Shin (also called shank and marrow bones)

Oxtails

Soup bones (meatless, usually sawed shin or knuckle)

Also suitable are beef cuts for stewing, and lean ground chuck or round. Don't make soup with fatty hamburger.

VEAL: Veal is young beef. It is very expensive, and there's little meat on its bonier parts, the parts which in beef are used for soup making. Veal and veal bones are included in some recipes for broth (see Chapter 2) and in some of the recipes here. But it has a flavor all its own and is not a substitute for beef.

Neck (usually boned)

Breast (chest and plate including rib ends)

Shank (fore shank usually cross cut with slices of bone; hind shank includes veal for *osso buco*, containing lots of marrow)

Bones (meatless, usually sawed shin or knuckle)

Knuckle (soup bones)

LAMB: Lamb is young mutton (or mutton is old lamb). It makes very good soup! This is one meat not finer in flavor for soups when older; choose fine-textured cuts with firm meat and bones that are red, moist, and porous. Avoid meat that is dark red, fat that is yellowish, and bones that are dry-looking and white. That is, avoid them if you can; we don't often have a wide variety of lamb cuts to choose from in our supermarkets. Those often used for soups are:

Neck (bone in)

Breast of lamb (chest ribs, riblets, and spareribs in a single block)

Shank (fore shank and hind shank, which is the tip end of a leg of lamb roast)

Bones (meatless, usually sawed shin or knuckle)

POT-AU-FEU

Pot-au-feu resembles *Grande Marmite* and *Petite Marmite*, slow-cooking meat-and-vegetable broths that are French classics. Some cookbooks treat them as one recipe with variations. The basic ingredients are similar: lean beef, brisket or plate of beef, knuckles, shin or marrow bones, carrots, turnips, onion, celery, and the French *bouquet garni* of herbs, bay, thyme, parsley, and cloves. Pot-au-feu and *Petite Marmite*, below, include veal. Some French recipes add cabbage cooked apart in a little broth from a pot-au-feu, and often the marrow from the bones is spread on slightly stale French bread or toast and served on the side rather than placed in the tureen, as suggested here.

A major difference between recipes, in my mind, is that *Grande Marmite* (much like Beef Broth—*Le Fond Brun* in Chapter 2) is essentially a method for making broth for use in cooking, and the meat and vegetables are cooked in the water four or five hours from the beginning—so that by the time you eat them, they are overcooked. Whereas in a pot-au-feu, the boiled dinner aspect is more important than the broth. The bones are cooked with the herbs in water to make a broth to which the meat is added later and cooked only until tender. The vegetables go in the last hour so as to retain their freshness and flavor. For *Petite Marmite* the object of the best recipes, in my view, isn't to make good broth, but to make a good boiled dinner *in broth* with lots of vegetables. *Joy of Cooking* refers to this as *poule-au-pot*, but *poule-au-pot* in France is a chicken boiled in broth, which then is served in its broth, or in a *sauce béchamel* made from the cooking broth.

Here is a classic recipe for a pot-au-feu I found in a French cookbook from the last century. The author dislikes veal but recommends chicken parts along with beef and marrow bones:

> *Mettez dans la marmite la viande de boeuf ficelée, cassez les os, quelques jarrets de boeuf et os à moelle; ne mettez pas de veau, le bouillon blanchirait; faites partir à feu modéré en écumant à mesure; lorsque votre bouillon n'écume plus, ajoutez-y les légumes; carottes, navets, poireaux, un oignon piqué d'un clou de girofle, une branche de céleri, faites partir et retirez du feu, laissez bouillir pendant six ou sept heures aux moins, dégraissez et passez le bouillon après l'avoir gouté.*
>
> *Si vous avez quelques os, cous, pattes, gésiers de volailles, mettez-les dans votre bouillon; il n'en aura que plus de saveur.*

Which translates this way (rather literally):

Put in a kettle the tied beef, break the bones, some beef knuckles and marrow bones; do not add veal, the broth could lighten; cook over a moderate flame, skimming as needed; when the broth stops foaming, add the vegetables; carrots, turnips, leeks, and onion stuck with a clove, a stalk of celery, set to cook and reduce the fire, allowing it to boil for six or seven hours at least, degrease and strain the broth after having tasted it.

If you have a few bones, necks, feet, gizzards of fowl, put them into your broth; it will be more flavorful as a result.

Here is the recipe my family uses.

POT-AU-FEU   Serves 10 to 12

3 pounds beef marrow
   bones, cut up
1 medium onion, sliced
1 large carrot, sliced
1 large leek, halved
1 large stalk celery, sliced
2 teaspoons drippings from
   a beef roast, baked
   chicken, bacon, or oil
4½ quarts water
1½ tablespoons salt
1 medium bay leaf
2 sprigs parsley
1 teaspoon dried thyme
8 peppercorns
4 whole cloves

2 pounds lean bottom or
   top round of beef
2 pounds brisket of beef,
   beef plate or chuck,
   boned, rolled
10 to 12 small carrots,
   scrubbed
10 to 12 small white turnips,
   peeled
10 small leeks, whites only
10 stalks heart of celery
Salt and pepper
1 tablespoon chopped
   parsley, optional
Coarse sea or kosher salt

1. Preheat the oven to 450 degrees.
2. Spread the bones in a large saucepan. Place around them the onion, carrot, leek, and celery, and sprinkle drippings or oil over the bones. Roast in the oven 30 to 40 minutes, until bones are well colored.
3. In a large kettle or stock pot over high heat, bring to a boil the water and salt with the bay, parsley, thyme, peppercorns, and cloves tied into a small cheesecloth square. When the bones are browned add them and the roasted vegetables to the kettle. Use a little of the hot water to loosen the drippings in the saucepan, and turn that into the kettle. Lower heat and skim scum as it rises. When it stops forming wipe the scum from the sides of the pot. Cover and cook 2 hours. Add enough water to bring broth back to its original level.
4. Add all the beef. Skim away scum as before. Cover and simmer 3 to 4 hours, until tender.
5. In the last hour of cooking lay the carrots, turnips, leeks, and celery on top of the meat. Cover and simmer 1 hour.
6. Line a colander with 2 thicknesses of cheesecloth and strain the broth through it. Taste, and add salt and pepper if needed. Remove as much fat from the top of the broth as you can.

To serve: Discard the herb bag, and roasted vegetables. Place the meat in a large tureen. Gently press the marrow from the bones and set on the meat. Discard the bones. Set the simmered carrots and turnips around the meat, and the leeks across the top. Reheat the broth and ladle over the meat and vegetables.

Garnish with a sprinkling of chopped parsley. Serve the boiled beef and broth in big soup plates and pass coarse sea or kosher salt. (In some restaurants the broth is served first, and the meat and vegetables as a second course.)

Dividends: The meat is excellent the next day served with a vinaigrette dressing accompanied by boiled potatoes. Leftover broth is a magnificent *consommé double* to serve hot or cold, or to use as a base for the consommé recipes in Chapter 2, or wherever a good beef broth is called for.

To make ahead: Complete through Step 3, then finish later. Boiled dinners can rest in their bouillon for several hours before being served.

OXTAIL SOUP
Serves 6 to 8

Oxtail is the skinned tail of a mature beef animal. The meat is dark and flavorful but needs lots of cooking. It's very good!

2 pounds oxtail
1 pound veal knuckle
6 medium carrots, chopped
3 small white turnips, chopped
1 large onion, stuck with 3 whole cloves
1 tablespoon salt

5 quarts water
1 pound ground beef chuck
2 tablespoons butter
1 tablespoon potato starch or cornstarch
Salt and pepper
3 tablespoons minced parsley

1. In a large kettle over high heat, combine oxtail, veal knuckle, carrots, turnips, onion, salt, and 4 quarts of water. Cover, bring to a boil, reduce heat, and simmer 3 hours, adding water to maintain original level.
2. In a saucepan over medium heat, brown the beef chuck in the butter, stirring. Sprinkle potato starch or cornstarch over the meat and sauté 1 minute. Scrape into the broth. Pour a little broth into the saucepan and scrape drippings back into broth. Cover and simmer 1 hour.
3. With a slotted spoon lift the bones from the soup. Discard the bones and the onion. Degrease the broth; add salt and pepper to taste. Return the meat to the broth and reheat.

To serve: Ladle into large soup plates and garnish with parsley.

To make ahead: Tastes even better made the day before.

OLD-FASHIONED OXTAIL AND BARLEY SOUP

Serves 6 to 8

Barley is a cereal grain used in the making of beer and whiskeys. Boiled in soups for about 45 minutes, it adds a mellow richness generations of soup buffs have associated with the long-simmering hearty soups Mama made.

2½ pounds oxtail	1 large carrot, chopped
1 tablespoon beef drippings or oil	2 large stalks celery, chopped
1 medium onion, chopped	1 6-ounce can tomato paste
3 quarts water	½ teaspoon marjoram
1½ teaspoons salt	½ teaspoon dried basil
¼ teaspoon pepper	¼ cup pearl barley
¼ cup chopped parsley	

1. In a large kettle or stock pot over medium heat, sauté the oxtail pieces in the drippings or oil until well colored on all sides. Stir in the onion and sauté 10 minutes. Add all the remaining ingredients except the barley, lower heat, cover, and simmer 3 hours. Add the barley and simmer 1 hour.
2. With a slotted spoon lift the oxtails from the soup. Discard the bones. Degrease the broth. Add salt and pepper to taste. Return the meat to the soup and reheat.

To serve: Ladle into large soup plates.

To make ahead: Tastes even better made the day before.

BEEF AND BARLEY SOUP WITH DRIED LEGUMES

Serves 6 to 8

This recipe goes easy on the meat, but is rich and thick with dried legumes, and easy to make. Nice with garlic bread.

1 pound beef shank
1 tablespoon beef drippings or oil
1 large onion, sliced
2 pounds beef soup bones, cracked
4½ quarts water
1½ tablespoons salt
½ teaspoon marjoram
1 medium bay leaf
2 sprigs parsley
½ teaspoon dried thyme

8 peppercorns
4 whole cloves
1 cup green split peas
½ cup dried lentils
¼ cup white beans
2 tablespoons pearl barley
2 large carrots, chopped
2 large stalks celery, chopped
Salt and pepper
Carrot Flowers (page 28)

1. In a large kettle or a stock pot over medium high heat, sauté the beef shank in the drippings or oil until meat is colored on all sides. Add the onion and sauté 5 minutes. Add the soup bones, ½ the water, and salt. Add the marjoram, bay, parsley, thyme, peppercorns, and cloves tied into a small cheesecloth square. Bring to a boil, reduce heat, cover, and simmer 1 hour.
2. Meanwhile, in a kettle over high heat, combine the remaining water, the peas, lentils, beans, barley, carrots and celery. Bring to a boil, boil 2 minutes, turn off heat, cover, and leave until first stage of meat cooking is complete.
3. Turn legumes and their water into the beef broth. Cover and simmer 2½ to 3 hours or until legumes have completely disintegrated. Taste, and add salt and pepper if needed.

To serve: Discard the soup bones and herb bag. Cut the meat from the shank bone into 2-inch chunks and place in a large tureen. Gently press marrow from the shank bone and spread over the meat. Discard the shank bone. Reheat the broth and ladle over the meat. Garnish with Carrot Flowers.

To make ahead: May be made several hours ahead. Very good reheated the next day.

CORNED BEEF SOUP
Serves 6

This is my variation on corned beef and cabbage. Don't omit the potatoes, or the broth will be too salty. This really does serve only 6, by the way, because most people ask for seconds! I serve Corned Beef Soup with crusty bake shop breads—challah and crisp sesame-topped Italian—a green salad, and shortcake or cheesecake.

3 pounds corned beef brisket	2 big cloves garlic, sliced
3 quarts water	1 large sprig fresh dill
12 peppercorns	1 large carrot, shredded
1 medium onion, stuck with 5 whole cloves	1 large white turnip, shredded
1/8 teaspoon allspice	6 small potatoes, peeled, or 3 large, peeled and halved
1 large bay leaf	
Leaves from tops of 4 stalks celery	1/2 head green cabbage, sliced thin
1 quart water	Sour cream

1. Wash the brisket thoroughly in cold running water. In a large kettle or a stock pot over high heat, combine the brisket, 3 quarts water, peppercorns, onion, allspice, bay, and celery leaves. Cover, bring to a boil, reduce heat, and simmer 2½ hours.
2. Slice the meat into 3 flat pieces, each with some fat. Add 1 quart water, garlic, dill, carrot, turnip, and cook 1 hour.
3. Add the potatoes and cook 15 minutes. Add the cabbage and cook 15 minutes.

To serve: Discard the onion and bay. Divide the meat and potatoes among large soup plates, and ladle broth and cabbage over them. Serve sour cream on the side.

To make ahead: Good made a few hours earlier. Or complete through Step 2, then finish just before serving.

MEATBALL SOUP
Serves 6 to 8

I omit the mint leaves, but this is a variation on a Mexican recipe, and the original includes the mint, so try it. A piece cut from a pork roast or center cut pork chops (less expensive than loin) are suitable for making the meatballs.

1 medium onion, chopped	¾ pound beef round
1 large clove garlic, chopped	¾ pound lean pork
2 tablespoons oil	1½ teaspoons salt
1 8-ounce can tomato sauce	¼ teaspoon pepper
3 quarts beef broth	1 medium egg, lightly beaten
1 large carrot, sliced into thin rounds	⅓ cup raw rice
½ cup peas or chopped green beans	1 tablespoon chopped fresh mint leaves, optional, or parsley

1. In a large saucepan over medium heat, sauté the onion and the garlic in the oil 5 minutes. Stir in the tomato sauce, broth, carrots, and peas or beans. Reduce heat, cover, and simmer while making the meatballs.
2. In a food processor or a meat grinder, chop the meats. Stir in the salt, pepper, egg, and rice. To make the meatballs quickly, hold the ground meat mixture in your left hand, pinch off a teaspoonful or a bite-size piece with your right hand, roll it into a ball in your right hand or against your left wrist or on the countertop, then drop into the simmering soup. Cover and simmer 30 minutes.

To serve: Ladle into soup plates and garnish with mint leaves, if you wish, or parsley.

To make ahead: Complete through Step 1, ready the meatballs, and complete before serving.

STEAK SOUP   Serves 4

A steak-flavored soup that stretches that costly meat cut so a little serves many. Takes about 20 minutes to make.

1 pound thin chuck steak, bone in	4 cups beef broth
3 medium onions, sliced	½ cup water
1 small clove garlic, sliced	⅛ teaspoon dried thyme
¼ teaspoon salt	½ small bay leaf, crumbled
⅛ teaspoon pepper	Cheese Puffs (page 29) or grated Parmesan cheese

1. Cut the fat from the chuck steak and cut the meat into ¼-inch strips.
2. In a large saucepan over medium high heat, render the fat, discard it, and brown the meat strips and bones. Add the onions and sauté about 10 minutes, until lightly browned. Add the garlic, salt, and pepper. Stir in the broth and water, and scrape up the meat drippings on the bottom of the saucepan. Add the thyme and bay. Lower heat, cover, and simmer 10 minutes.

To serve: Discard the bones. Ladle into soup plates and garnish with Cheese Puffs or stir in Parmesan cheese.

To make ahead: May be made several hours earlier.

SHORT RIBS AND BARLEY SOUP   Serves 6 to 8

Choose short ribs with as little fat as possible.

3 pounds short ribs of beef	3 large ripe tomatoes, quartered, or 24 ounces canned, stewed tomatoes
1 medium onion, chopped	
1 small clove garlic, minced	
½ teaspoon salt	3 large carrots
¼ teaspoon pepper	4 ounces dried mushrooms
2 quarts beef broth	3 large stalks celery
1 quart water	2 large sprigs parsley
1 cup barley	1 sweet red pepper
Salt and pepper	

1. Cut bits of fat from the ribs of beef and render them in a large saucepan over medium high heat. Add the ribs and brown on all sides. Add the onion and sauté 10 minutes. Add the garlic, salt, and pepper. Stir in the broth and water, and scrape up the meat drippings from the bottom of the saucepan. Add the barley and tomatoes, reduce heat, cover, and simmer 1 hour. Add the carrots and mushrooms, and cook 1 hour. Add the celery, parsley, and pepper, and simmer ½ hour. Add water if broth is too thick. Add salt and pepper to taste.

To serve: Ladle into big soup plates.

To make ahead: May be made many hours in advance.

LAMB AND SPLIT PEA SOUP, BAKED   Serves 6

Other lamb soups we like are in Chapters 6 and 8. Here's an interesting variation.

2 quarts water	6 peppercorns
1 cup dried split peas	1 tablespoon raw rice
1 pound lamb neck or shank	1 small carrot, chopped
½ teaspoon dried thyme	1 medium onion, chopped
1 large clove garlic, sliced	Salt and pepper
1 teaspoon salt	

1. Preheat the oven to 300 degrees.
2. In a large baking dish with a cover, combine the water, peas, meat, herbs, seasonings, rice, and vegetables. Cover and place in the oven. Bake 3 to 4 hours or until the meat is very tender and the peas have disintegrated. Add water if too thick. Add salt and pepper to taste. With a slotted spoon lift the lamb from the soup. Discard the bone and the peppercorns.

To serve: Cut the meat into small pieces and divide among soup plates. Ladle the soup over the meat.

To make ahead: May be made several hours ahead.

LAMB BONE AND BEAN SOUP   Serves 8 to 10

Here's another soup recipe that turns the shank end of a leg of lamb—the part of a leg of lamb roast that becomes almost inedible when roasted—into a super supper soup! You need about 2 pounds of lamb shanks, including meat with the bone in. The average shank weighs about 1 pound.

2 pounds lamb shank	2 16-ounce cans tomatoes and liquid
1 tablespoon lamb drippings or oil	5 large cloves garlic
2 medium onions, sliced	2 medium bay leaves
4 quarts water	1 teaspoon celery seed
3 large leeks, whites only	1 tablespoon dried summer savory
3 small white turnips, chopped	8 peppercorns
1 small red pepper, chopped	1½ tablespoons salt
1 small green bell pepper, chopped	½ cup dried large white northern beans
6 large mushrooms, chopped	½ cup dried baby lima beans
	½ cup dried red beans
	Salt and pepper

1. In a large kettle or a stock pot over medium high heat, sauté the lamb shanks in the drippings or the oil until the meat is colored on all sides. Add the onions and sauté 5 minutes. Add half the water, and vegetables, and the canned tomatoes and liquid. Crush the garlic into the kettle and add the herbs, tied into a small cheesecloth square, and the salt. Cover, bring to a boil, reduce heat, and simmer 1 hour.
2. Meanwhile, in a kettle over high heat, combine the remaining water with all the beans. Bring to a boil, boil 2 minutes, turn off heat, and leave until the first stage of meat cooking is complete.
3. Turn the beans and their water into the lamb and vegetable broth. Cover and cook 2½ hours or until the beans are completely tender. Add a little water if the soup becomes too thick. Taste and add salt and pepper if needed.

To serve: Discard the herb bag. Cut the meat from the shank bone into 2-inch chunks and place in a large tureen. Gently press the marrow from the shank bone and spread it over the meat. Reheat the broth and ladle over the meat with the vegetables. Discard the bones.

To make ahead: May be made several hours ahead. Very good the next day, but rather thick; stretch with tomato juice or with a little red wine, and simmer 3 or 4 minutes.

LAMB AND EGGPLANT SOUP   Serves 6

I also make this with breast of lamb, cut into individual ribs, and lamb shank, bone in, saved from a leg of lamb roast. If you have drippings or gravy left from a lamb roast—add them. Very, very good!

1 large eggplant	1 teaspoon cinnamon
¼ teaspoon salt	½ cup barley
½ cup olive oil	8 cups water
2 large onions, chopped	1 tablespoon salt
2 pounds boneless stewing lamb, cut into 2-inch pieces	⅛ teaspoon pepper
	½ teaspoon ground coriander
	¼ teaspoon ground cumin
3 large ripe tomatoes, chopped, or 1 28-ounce can chopped tomatoes	¼ teaspoon dried thyme
	1 small clove garlic
	1 cup sour cream
2 tablespoons lemon juice	

1. Cut the eggplant into 2-inch cubes, skin on; salt and set in a colander to drain for 30 minutes.
2. In a large saucepan over medium heat, sauté the eggplant in half the oil until golden, about 10 minutes. Remove with a slotted spoon and add remaining oil and the onions. Sauté the onions 5 minutes, then add the lamb pieces and sauté until brown on all sides, about 10 to 15 minutes. Stir in the tomatoes, scraping up the pan juices. Reduce heat, cover, and simmer 20 minutes. Add the lemon juice, cinnamon, barley, eggplant, and water. Cover and simmer 1 hour or until meat is tender. Add salt, pepper, coriander, cumin, thyme, and crush the garlic into the broth. Stir well, cover, and cook 20 minutes.

To serve: Ladle into bowls and garnish with dollops of sour cream.

To make ahead: May be made hours or a day ahead.

SURF AND TURF SOUP   Serves 8

This is a combination of beef broth and seafood we love. It is exquisite made with fresh tiny shrimp and fresh clams, and almost as good made with the ingredients proposed here, which come from a can. I chop everything, including meats, in the food processor.

1 medium onion, chopped	1 6½-ounce can minced
3 tablespoons olive oil	clams and liquid
¼ pound ham, minced	1 cup raw rice
¼ cup shelled almonds, chopped fine	½ cup frozen peas
	2 6-ounce cans tiny shrimp
2 tablespoons tomato paste	and liquid
¼ cup water	2 hard-boiled eggs, chopped
6 cups beef broth	

1. In a large saucepan over medium heat, sauté the onion in the oil until translucent, about 5 minutes. Push the onion to the edge of the pan and sauté the ham and almonds until the pan bottom is browning. Stir in the tomato paste mixed with the water and scrape up the brown morsels stuck to the saucepan bottom. Add the broth and clams, and bring to a boil, uncovered. Reduce heat and add rice. Simmer, partially covered, 20 minutes or until rice is almost done. Add the peas and the liquid from the shrimp. Cover and turn off heat.
2. Just before serving add the shrimp, stir well, and reheat.

To serve: Ladle into big soup plates and garnish with chopped egg.

To make ahead: May be completed through Step 2 and finished just before serving.

PORK AND BACON SOUPS

Pork, and that includes fresh and smoked (or cured) hams, is as popular with soup makers as beef. Almost every part of the pig is used. The good soup cuts aren't always available at my supermarket, so when they turn up I buy and freeze. Ham hocks, usually cured, and trotters (pigs' feet) have special qualities: cured hocks add a flavor like smoked ham to soups, and the trotters bring a rich, creamy texture.

Center cut ham (smoked or cured; buy when on sale and freeze to use any time baked)

Daisy ham (brand name for smoked butt)

Ham hocks (pigs' leg bones with skin and a little meat; usually smoked or cured)

Pigs' feet (fresh, these dainty pure white "trotters" give a wonderful, rich quality to soups)

Neck bones (new on the market—use where fresh ham hocks are called for)

Back bones (new on the market; see above)

Pork ribs (new on the market; use where spareribs are called for)

Salt pork (It is salted, not smoked, and is cubed and sautéed to render fat for soups and bean dishes. Look for creamy white pieces, with a good-sized strip of meat in the center. Don't confuse this with fatback, which has no lean. Another name for salt pork is "white bacon"—but don't try to use it as bacon!)

Sausage (Chorizo is a hot Spanish sausage great in soups and bean pots. Hot Italian sausage is similar. Polish sausage and Italian sweet sausage, sweeter and milder, are used where "sweet" sausage is called for. Avoid buying sausage that looks as though it is sweating grease.)

Smoked butt (all-meat oval to use wherever baked or boiled ham is called for)

Spareribs (fresh, not cured; buy when on sale and freeze)

Pigs' ears and tails also are used in soups. The famous Belgian *Hochepot*, in Chapter 6, shows how. But these aren't available in most markets. Still, if you have some handy, they're worth a try in the hearty multimeat broths.

BEANS, BONES, AND HAM SOUP — Serves 8

Center cut ham is a large oval slice from a smoked ham roast. It has a small round bone in the center and is great for use in soups when you have no leftovers from a baked ham roast.

4½ quarts water
1 tablespoon salt
1 veal knuckle
1 veal shank
2 pounds beef shank
1 pound baked ham or center cut ham slice
6 medium carrots, quartered
1 medium onion, chopped
2 large leeks, white only, halved
4 medium cloves garlic, sliced
1 small bay leaf
½ teaspoon dried thyme
2 large sprigs parsley
6 peppercorns
5 whole cloves
1 pound dry white beans
1 medium cabbage (green or white) cut into 8 wedges
2 pounds garlic sausage or sweet Italian sausage
Salt and pepper
16 slices French bread

1. In a large kettle or a stock pot over medium heat, bring half the water to a boil with the salt, meat and bones, ham, carrots, onion, leeks, and garlic. Add the bay, thyme, parsley, peppercorns, and whole cloves tied into a small cheesecloth square. Cover and simmer 1 hour.
2. Meanwhile, in a kettle over high heat, bring the beans and the remaining water to a boil. Boil 2 minutes, turn off heat, cover, and leave until the meat has simmered 1 hour. Then add beans and water to the large kettle, cover, and simmer 1½ hours. Add the cabbage and sausage to the soup and simmer 1 hour, uncovered. Taste, add salt and pepper if needed, and a little water if the broth has become too thick.

To serve: Discard the soup bones and herb bag. With a slotted spoon lift the shanks, knuckle, ham, and sausage from the soup, and cut the meat into 2-inch pieces. Arrange the meat on a large platter with the cabbage around it. Gently press the marrow from the shank bones and spread over the meats. Discard the bones. Reheat the broth and ladle a little over the meat. Bring the platter to the table with the reheated broth in a tureen beside it. Pass French bread heaped in a bread basket.

To make ahead: May be made several hours in advance.

BEAN, BASIL, AND SAUSAGE SOUP　　　　Serves 6 to 8

This is an adaptation of a classic Mediterranean soup enriched with a *pesto* sauce. It is ready in about 45 minutes and is delicious! There's a lot of garlic, but you'll not notice it in the finished soup.

1 large onion, minced	4 cups beef broth
4 large cloves garlic, minced	¼ cup raw broken spaghetti
½ bunch parsley and stems, chopped	pieces
⅔ cups olive oil	1 cup thinly-sliced chorizo or Polish sausage, or minced ham
1 16-ounce can stewed tomatoes or 3 very ripe large tomatoes, chopped	1 cup tightly packed basil, fresh or frozen
2 tablespoons tomato paste	½ cup grated Parmesan cheese
½ teaspoon dried oregano	
5 cups pinto, pink, red, or white beans, cooked or canned, and liquid	

1. In a large saucepan over medium heat, sauté the onion, 2 cloves of garlic, and parsley in ⅓ cup oil for 2 minutes. Stir in the tomatoes, tomato paste, and oregano. Reduce heat and cook, uncovered, until thick, 10 to 15 minutes. Add 2 cups of the beans and 1 cup of broth. Cover and simmer 10 minutes. Purée in a blender or a food processor, 2 cups at a time, or press through a sieve. Return to the kettle with remaining beans and broth. Add spaghetti bits and cook until tender, 10 to 12 minutes. Add the sausage, cover, and cook 10 minutes.
2. In a blender combine the remaining garlic and oil, the basil and Parmesan, and purée until smooth, about 2 to 3 minutes.

To serve: Stir the basil purée (*pesto*) into the soup, heat through, and ladle into big bowls.

Dividends: Use leftovers as a sauce for spaghetti. To stretch, add tomato sauce and/or beef broth.

To make ahead: Complete through Step 1, then finish just before serving.

RED BEANS AND HAM HOCK SOUP   Serves 10 to 12

2 pounds ham hocks
3 quarts water
1 pound red or pinto beans
4 large onions, sliced
4 large cloves garlic, sliced
½ green bell pepper, sliced
2 medium bay leaves
½ teaspoon saffron threads

2 Polish sausages, sliced
2 pigs' feet, halved
4 medium potatoes,
   quartered
1 small head cabbage, cut
   into 10 to 12 small wedges
Salt and pepper

In a large kettle or a stock pot over high heat, combine the ham hocks, water, and beans, bring to a boil. Cover, reduce heat, and simmer 20 minutes. Add the onions, garlic, pepper, bay leaves and saffron, and cook 20 minutes. Add the sausages and the pigs' feet, and cook 2 hours. Add the potatoes and cook 45 minutes. Add water if the soup is becoming too thick. When the potatoes are tender, lay the cabbage wedges on top of the soup, cover, and cook 15 minutes. Add salt and pepper to taste.

To serve: With a slotted spoon remove the hocks, and pigs' feet if anything remains of them, from the broth, and cut the meat into 2-inch pieces. Discard the bones and the bay leaves. Arrange the meat in a large shallow tureen with the potatoes and cabbage around it. Taste the broth and add salt and pepper if needed. Reheat and ladle over the meat and vegetables.

To make ahead: Gets better every day, but will need thinning. Use chicken broth as a stretcher.

HAM AND POTATO CHOWDER   Serves 4

This is a rather coarse soup with a smoky flavor. It is so thick you can almost stand a spoon in it. Ready in half an hour if you have a food processor.

1 medium onion, minced
¾ cup minced ham
½ cup minced celery
1½ cups minced potatoes
¼ cup butter

1½ teaspoons salt
¼ teaspoon pepper
3 tablespoons all-purpose
   flour
3 cups milk

1. In a saucepan over medium low heat, sauté the onion, ham, celery, and potatoes in the butter, stirring, about 20 minutes.
2. Remove from heat and stir in the salt, pepper, and flour. Stirring constantly, add the milk. Return to heat and continue to cook, stirring, until thick. Add more milk if needed.

To serve: Ladle into bowls.

To make ahead: Complete through Step 1, then finish just before serving.

BLACK BEAN, RED BEAN, AND SAUSAGE SOUP

Serves 10 to 12

¼ pound salt pork, diced
3 large cloves garlic, minced
3 quarts hot water
½ cup black beans
1 cup kidney or red beans
2 large carrots, chopped
3 large stalks celery, chopped
1 small bunch scallions, chopped
1 cup shredded cabbage

6 beef bouillon cubes
1 teaspoon fresh or frozen basil, or ½ teaspoon dried
1 28-ounce can tomatoes
¾ cup raw broken spaghetti pieces
¾ pound Polish sausage, sliced, or 1½ cups diced ham
Salt and pepper

In a large saucepan over medium heat, sauté the salt pork and the garlic until brown and crisp. Add the water and the beans; cover, reduce heat, and simmer 2 hours. Add the carrots, celery, scallions, cabbage, beef bouillon cubes, and basil. Cook 1 hour. Add the tomatoes, spaghetti pieces, and sausage or ham, and cook 30 minutes. Add salt and pepper to taste. Add a little water if broth is too thick.

To serve: Ladle into large soup plates.

To make ahead: Excellent the next day but will need thinning with more broth.

KALE AND SAUSAGE SOUP   Serves 4 to 5

Kale is a spinach-flavored, vitamin-loaded relative of cabbage. Where spinach won't grow well, kale is raised and used in its place in salads and as a boiling green. Plantlets removed to thin a row of kale in the garden make good soup. Use only the tender green part of kale to make soup: discard the stalks.

6 cups beef broth	½ pound kale, shredded fine
3 medium potatoes, peeled, diced or chopped	3 tablespoons olive oil
	Salt and pepper
½ pound linguica, chorizo, or other spicy, garlic sausage	

1. In a large kettle over medium heat, bring the broth and potatoes to a boil. Reduce heat, cover, and simmer until potatoes are tender, about 15 to 20 minutes. Purée soup in a blender or a food processor, 2 cups at a time, or press through a sieve. Return purée to the kettle.
2. Prick sausage lightly and place in a small skillet with just enough water to cover. Bring to a boil, lower heat, and simmer, uncovered, 15 minutes. Drain sausage well and slice into ¼-inch-thick pieces.
3. Bring soup to a boil, add kale and olive oil. Reduce heat and simmer until kale is tender, 5 to 10 minutes. Add sausage and simmer a minute more. Add salt and pepper to taste.

To serve: Ladle into piping hot soup plates.

CORN SOUP WITH SPARERIBS   Serves 6

A mild, pale but hearty soup flavored by the cumin in it. It's different—the ribs come out almost sweet. The liquid may evaporate drastically; be sure to add more before it finishes cooking, so you'll have enough broth for everyone.

2 pounds spareribs, cut into serving pieces	1 small clove garlic, minced
1 teaspoon salt	1 small onion, chopped
1 teaspoon ground cumin	1½ tablespoons cider vinegar
¼ teaspoon black pepper	12 cups cold water
½ teaspoon dried oregano	2 cups corn kernels or 1
1 small bay leaf, crumbled	16-ounce can corn and liquid

| 2 cups shredded raw | 1 cup milk |
| potatoes | Salt and pepper |

1. Place the spareribs in a large bowl and sprinkle with salt, cumin, pepper, oregano, bay, garlic, onion, and vinegar. Add 1 cup water and marinate overnight, or at least a few hours.
2. In a large kettle over high heat, combine the ribs and their marinade with the remaining water. Cover, bring to a boil, reduce heat, and simmer 2 hours.
3. Add the corn (and liquid if canned) to the broth, along with the potatoes and milk. Simmer until potatoes are tender, about 15 to 20 minutes. Add salt and pepper to taste.

To serve: Ladle into soup plates.

To make ahead: Complete through Step 1, then finish just before serving.

TAKE AN OLD COCK

Escoffier invited us to choose an "old cock" to make stocks and broths, because, he said, the meat of older animals is rich and flavorful. In America I've never found a cock for sale where I shop. I have seen fowl, a term for a hen aged ten months or more, and these make good broth (poor chewing unless they are in broth), but they are more expensive than broilers. Try fowl instead of broiler chickens for soups, and decide for yourself if the difference is worth the price.

The chickens that reach the supermarket these days are not generally very good. Mass produced, they don't compare in flavor with birds that have roamed a barnyard. To improve soups these chickens leave insipid in flavor, add degreased pan drippings from roast chickens, or add bouillon cubes. I also save up bones and well-browned skin from baked chickens to add to soups. Chicken feet and chicken carcasses added to broths and soups help the consommé gel more firmly. Necks, backs, and wings are sometimes sold at good prices, and these can strengthen the flavor of chicken soups, too.

Don't buy cut-up chicken: it's the worst chicken buy there is. You pay more per pound, and meanwhile, the butcher subtracts parts you could use for soup and which are free when you cut the bird up yourself.

Do select chicken with care. Fresh-killed chickens are best because chicken meat is more perishable than red meat (and fish and shellfish are more perishable yet). Unpackage, wash, and rewrap loosely before storing chicken in the refrigerator. Use within two or three days of purchase. If you buy frozen chicken, avoid birds showing brownish patches on the skin: this usually indicates poor freezing practices. Choose birds with stiff breastbones: they are older, and should have more flavor.

And when you've made a chicken soup, if the flavor is insipid, let me repeat the suggestion above: Add bouillon cubes, powders, or other chicken-flavored bits and pieces to solve the problem.

OLD-FASHIONED CREAM OF CHICKEN SOUP   Serves 8

Chicken soup was simmered hours in the old days—this way— and the results are especially good. It will be best if you can locate the kind of chickens that peck on the ground and consort with roosters, but even supermarket chicken does good things in this recipe. There are little pockets of pure chicken fat just inside the cavities of most chickens, and that's what is called for in this recipe. Butter or fat rendered from salt pork may be used instead, about 2 tablespoons.

Fat from chicken, cut up
- 4 pounds chicken, cut up
- 1 veal knuckle, cut up
- 1 large onion, chopped
- 2 large carrots, cut into big slices
- 3½ quarts cold water
- 4 big sprigs parsley
- ½ teaspoon thyme
- 1 small bay leaf
- 1 small onion, stuck with 4 whole cloves
- 2 large stalks celery and leaves, cut into large pieces
- 1 tablespoon salt
- 8 peppercorns
- 1 cup heavy cream
- 3 tablespoons all-purpose flour
- 2 egg yolks

Salt and pepper

1. In a large kettle over medium high heat, sauté the chicken fat until rendered, about 10 minutes. Remove fried bits and discard. Sauté chicken pieces, veal knuckle, onion, and carrots until meat is very well browned. Add water and bring to a slow boil. Skim scum forming on top of broth for 5 minutes or until it clears, then add herbs, celery, salt, and peppercorns. Cover, lower heat, and simmer 2 hours. Remove chicken breasts to a shallow plate and cover with broth. Continue to cook broth, covered, another 2 hours. Strain into a large bowl.

Discard bones and skin. Reserve meat. Cool broth until grease thickens on top, and skim it off. Dice breast meat (only) and return to broth. Return broth to kettle and heat.

2. Combine cream and flour in a small bowl, and stir in egg yolks. Stir in 1 cup hot broth, then return to kettle. Cook, stirring, until broth is just below boiling, about 3 minutes. Add salt and pepper to taste.

To serve: Ladle into soup bowls.

Dividends: Reserved boiled chicken and vegetables not used in broth make a nice light meal. If flavor is bland, season with salad dressing. The broth makes a great base for almost any other soup.

To make ahead: Complete and store in refrigerator, covered, or in freezer. Store in 1- or 2-cup lots to make measuring broth easy when you are using it as a base for another soup.

POULE-AU-POT

Some claim this is *Petite Marmite* (see page 94), but when we make *Poule-au-Pot* in the Hériteau clan, we substitute a 4-pound stewing fowl, or ordinary chicken, for the 4 pounds of beef in step 4 of the recipe for Pot-au-Feu. If we have handy a half dozen chicken necks, wings and backs, we add these in step 3 of the Pot-au-Feu recipe, and discard these bony parts along with the chicken carcass before serving the soup. In Madeleine Hériteau's house sometimes the chicken was served cut up with a little plain chicken broth and vegetable, and other times it was served with a *béchamel* sauce made by pouring a little broth into a *roux,* and enriching it with cream, beaten with a raw egg yolk and a little hot broth.

CREAM OF CHICKEN NOODLE SOUP   Serves 8

1 recipe Old-Fashioned Cream of Chicken Soup (page 88)	½ to ⅓ cup uncooked broad egg noodles per cup of broth

Bring broth to a boil, add noodles, and cook 7 minutes.

CREAM OF CHICKEN SOUP WITH RICE   Serves 8

1 recipe Old-Fashioned
  Cream of Chicken Soup
  (page 88)

2 tablespoons cooked white
  rice per cup of broth

Bring broth to a boil, add rice, and simmer 3 minutes.

CHICKEN SOUP WITH CUSTARD   Serves 6

A rich, creamy chicken soup with delicious custard squares added.

⅓ cup butter
⅓ cup all-purpose flour
1½ quarts hot chicken broth
1 cooked chicken breast,
  chopped
1 tablespoon minced
  parsley

⅛ teaspoon dried thyme
¼ small bay leaf
1 cup heavy cream
Salt and pepper
1 recipe *Royales* (page 40)

In a large saucepan over low heat, heat the butter until very lightly browning; stir in the flour. Add the broth, beating constantly, and cook until bubbly. Add the chicken, parsley, thyme, and bay. Add the cream and heat to just below boiling. Add salt and pepper to taste.

To serve: Ladle into soup plates and divide the *royales* among the plates.

CHICKEN CORN SOUP   Serves 8 to 10

3 pounds cut-up chicken and
  giblets
3 quarts water
1 tablespoon salt
⅛ teaspoon pepper
¼ teaspoon saffron threads
2 cups narrow noodles

2 cups corn kernels or 1
  16-ounce can corn and
  liquid
Salt and pepper
1 teaspoon chopped parsley
2 hard-boiled eggs, chopped

1. In a large kettle over high heat combine the chicken, water, salt, pepper, and saffron. Cover, bring to a boil, reduce heat,

and simmer until tender, about 45 minutes. With a slotted spoon remove the chicken pieces from the broth, cut the meat into 2-inch pieces, and return to the broth. Discard skin and bones.

2. Bring broth to a boil, add the noodles, the corn (and liquid if canned) and simmer, uncovered, 15 minutes. Add salt and pepper to taste.

To serve: Ladle into bowls and garnish with parsley and chopped egg.

To make ahead: Complete through Step 1, then finish just before serving.

CHICKEN AND RICE SOUP   Serves 8 to 10

Yes, the spinach in this recipe does cook as long as the chicken, which certainly is a departure for me. But that's the way it is! This is reminiscent of an old Scottish recipe, Cockaleekie, in Chapter 6.

Fat from the chicken	2 medium leeks, shredded
1 large onion, chopped	½ cup chopped parsley
1 3-pound chicken	1 tablespoon salt
3 quarts water	¼ teaspoon pepper
1 cup raw rice	1 tablespoon turmeric
½ cup yellow split peas	12 pitted prunes
1 10-ounce bag washed spinach, chopped	Salt and pepper
	8 sprigs mint

1. In a large kettle over medium heat, sauté the lumps of chicken fat you will find near the cavity until about 2 tablespoons have been rendered. Discard the crisped bits. Sauté the onion in the fat until golden brown. Add the chicken, water, rice, peas, spinach, leeks, parsley, salt, pepper, and turmeric. Bring to a boil, reduce heat, and simmer 45 minutes.

2. Add the prunes and simmer 15 minutes. With a slotted spoon lift out the chicken; cut up the meat, discard bones and skin, return meat to the broth, and reheat. Add salt and pepper to taste.

To serve: Ladle into bowls. Garnish each with a sprig of mint.

To make ahead: Complete through Step 1, then finish just before serving.

CHICKEN SOUP WITH SCRAMBLED EGGS   Serves 6

Cook the scrambled eggs very slowly: the flavor will be better.

1½ quarts chicken broth
1 small clove garlic
2 large scallions, chopped
1 small cucumber, peeled, sliced thin
4 tablespoons dry sherry
1 1-inch piece ginger root, minced fine

1 tablespoon butter
3 eggs
¼ cup heavy cream
¼ teaspoon salt
¼ teaspoon Hungarian paprika, optional
2 tablespoons minced parsley

1. In a kettle over medium heat, bring the broth to a boil. Crush the garlic into the broth, then add the scallions, cucumber, sherry, and ginger. Cover, reduce heat, and simmer 20 minutes. Strain the soup and return to the kettle.
2. In a small saucepan over medium low heat, melt the butter, and cook the eggs beaten with the cream, salt, and paprika, stirring constantly.
3. Reduce heat under the broth and scrape the eggs into the kettle; heat gently 3 minutes.

To serve: Ladle into soup bowls and garnish with parsley.

To make ahead: Complete through Step 1, then finish just before serving.

VEGETABLE SOUP MEALS

Soup meals don't have to include meat. The recipes below are among the most filling in the book. In addition, there are many soups in Chapters 5 and 7 thick enough to make completely satisfying dinners. Even the lighter vegetable soups can be turned into satisfying meals by the addition of cheese-topped toast like the toast in Potato Soup with Dill and Cheese Toast, below, croutons, and some of the heartier garnishes in Chapter 2.

When you are making vegetable soups, watch out for those with potatoes. When potatoes are old, they are starchier and take up more water, so you can—depending on the state of your potatoes—find your soup thicker than you want it. The solution is simple: Add more water and cook a bit longer—another ten minutes.

Potatoes also absorb a great deal of salt, so you may find soups with potatoes in them in need of quite a bit more seasoning.

Here's a clue to how to solve the problem of oversalted soup: Peel a potato and add to the soup in thick slices; simmer 5 minutes, taste, add more potato, then simmer again about 10 minutes. That should do it.

Cabbage, on the other hand, can make soups too sweet. The solution can be a teaspoon or two of vinegar. Try a little vinegar added to a bit of the soup in a small bowl; if you like the result, add some vinegar to the broth.

Celery tends to add a salty taste, so go lightly with salt in celery soups.

Carrots, especially old, dark red carrots, can be a sweetener, so don't add more of these than the recipe calls for.

RICH CABBAGE AND POTATO SOUP   Serves 8 to 10

Good first course for a hearty meal with pork or another broiled meat.

12 slices bacon, cut into ½-inch pieces
1 large onion, chopped
6 scallions, chopped (with greens)
½ small white cabbage, chopped
4 large potatoes, peeled, diced

8 cups chicken broth
2 cups shredded Jarlsberg or Swiss cheese (½ pound)
1 cup light cream
Salt and pepper
1 cup Croutons, Sautéed in Butter (page 33)

1. In a large kettle over medium heat, sauté bacon until translucent. Add onion, scallions, and cabbage, and cook, stirring continuously, 5 minutes.
2. Add potatoes and broth. Bring to a boil, lower heat, and simmer, covered, 40 minutes.
3. Stir in cheese, and continue to stir until it is all melted. Stir in cream, and add salt and pepper to taste.

To serve: Ladle into soup bowls and garnish with croutons.

Dividends: Purée in a blender or a food processor, and stretch with broth.

To make ahead: Complete through Step 2, then finish just before serving.

PETITE MARMITE Serves 8

The word *marmite* is French for a large clay pot which was the cookware of an earlier century, and when this soup is made in an earthen *marmite* it is better! When I went to live with the Bertrand family in their farmhouse in southern France, the corners of the barn had piles of these wonderful pieces—some for washing dishes, others for cooking over an open fire—disgarded, alas, by Mme. Bertrand, who found it easier to wash modern metal pots. You might prefer to cook the cabbage and even the vegetables apart in a little broth.

2 pounds beef shin or marrow bones, cut up
2 pounds soup bones
1 medium onion, sliced
1 large carrot, sliced
1 large leek, halved
1 large stalk celery, sliced
2 teaspoons drippings from baked chicken
4½ quarts water
1½ tablespoons salt
1 medium bay leaf
2 sprigs parsley
1 teaspoon dried thyme
8 peppercorns
4 whole cloves
Necks, wings, backs of 4 chickens

1 3-pound chicken with giblets
1 pound beef brisket, plate, or shin meat
3 medium carrots, quartered
3 large leeks, quartered
6 small white turnips, halved
1 small head green cabbage, shredded
Salt and pepper
8 to 12 slices French bread, toasted
½ cup grated Gruyère cheese
Coarse sea or kosher salt

1. Preheat oven to 450 degrees.
2. Spread the bones in a large saucepan. Place around them the onion, carrot, leek, and celery, and sprinkle drippings over the bones. Roast in the oven 30 to 40 minutes, until bones are well colored.
3. In a large kettle or stock pot over high heat, bring to a boil the water and salt with the bay, parsley, thyme, peppercorns, and cloves tied into a small cheesecloth square. When the bones are browned add them and the roasted vegetables to the kettle. Use a little of the hot water to loosen the drippings in the saucepan, and turn that into the kettle. Lower heat and skim scum as it rises. When it stops forming wipe the scum from the sides of the pot. Cover and cook 3 hours.
4. Add the chicken, giblets, and beef. Add enough water to cover the ingredients. Bring to a boil. Skim scum as before. Cover

and add carrots, leeks, turnips, and simmer 1 hour or until the meat is tender. If the chicken is tender before the beef, remove the chicken and vegetables and keep warm while the beef finishes. Another half hour should be enough. Add the cabbage for the last 15 minutes of cooking.

5. Line a colander with 2 thicknesses of cheesecloth and strain the broth through it. Taste, and add salt and pepper if needed. Remove as much fat from the broth as you can.

To serve: Discard the chicken parts, giblets, soup bones, herb bag, and roasted vegetables. Remove the meat from the chicken carcass and cut it and the beef into large chunks. Place in a tureen. Gently press the marrow from the shin or marrow bones and spread on the toasted bread. Keep warm. Discard the bones. Set the cabbage, carrots, turnips, and leeks around the meat. Reheat the broth and ladle it over the meat and vegetables. Serve *Petite Marmite* in large soup plates. Pass grated Gruyère and toast, coarse sea or kosher salt.

Dividends: The cold vegetables are excellent served the next day as a first course. Leftover broth is very good *consommé double.*

To make ahead: Complete through Step 3, then finish later.

WINTER VEGETABLE SOUP WITH BARLEY   Serves 6 to 8

5 cups water	¾ cup chopped onion
1 16-ounce can whole tomatoes and liquid	⅔ cup chopped green bell pepper
3 beef bouillon cubes	1 small bay leaf
⅔ cup pearl barley	2 tablespoons firmly packed brown sugar
1 cup chopped carrots	
1 cup chopped white turnip	1 sprig basil leaves, frozen or fresh
1 cup cut-up green beans, frozen or fresh	Salt and pepper

In a large kettle over medium high heat, combine water, tomatoes, and bouillon cubes; cover and bring to a boil. Reduce heat, break up tomatoes, and stir in barley. Cover and simmer 30 minutes. Add vegetables, bay, sugar, and basil; cover and simmer 1 hour. Add salt and pepper to taste.

To serve: Ladle into bowls.

To make ahead: Tastes better made several hours or a day before.

WINTER CABBAGE SOUP WITH
POTATO-HAM DUMPLINGS

Serves 8

4 cups shredded winter
  cabbage
4 tablespoons butter
2 tablespoons dark brown
  sugar, firmly packed
2 quarts chicken broth

Potato-Ham Dumplings
2 small onions, chopped

4 tablespoons butter
¾ pound cooked ham, diced
6 medium potatoes, boiled,
  peeled
2 egg yolks, beaten
1½ teaspoons salt
¾ cup sifted all-purpose.
  flour

1. In a kettle over medium heat, sauté the cabbage in the butter
   until it begins to brown. Add sugar and continue to cook,
   stirring constantly, until blended. Add the broth, cover, and
   simmer 45 minutes.
2. In a skillet over medium heat, sauté the onions in the butter
   until translucent. Stir in the ham and sauté 5 minutes. Set
   aside.
3. Put the potatoes through a ricer into a bowl. Beat in the egg
   yolks, salt, and flour. Knead lightly into a dough, and shape
   into 2 8-inch rolls. Pinch off pieces of dough from each roll;
   flatten gently and cover each with 1 tablespoon of the ham
   mixture. Gather up edges of dough around the ham and shape
   into a dumpling, sealing edges carefully.
4. Add the Potato-Ham Dumplings to the broth, cover, and simmer 15 minutes. Do not remove the cover until you are ready
   to serve or the dumplings will be heavy.

To serve: Ladle into soup bowls; divide dumplings among the
bowls.

To make ahead: Complete through Step 3, then refrigerate the
dumplings. Bring them back to room temperature and cook just
before serving.

POTATO SOUP WITH DILL AND
CHEESE TOAST

Serves 6

Choose a good Brie that is almost runny to make this soup. It's
a delicious recipe, by the way, in which to use up an end piece of
cheese.

1 large onion, minced	½ cup half-and-half
3 tablespoons butter	3 cups milk
1 pound potatoes, chopped	Salt and pepper
3 cups water	6 slices French bread,
1 tablespoon salt	toasted and buttered
4 large sprigs fresh dill	Brie

1. In a saucepan over medium heat, sauté the onion in the butter 10 minutes. Add the potatoes and cook, stirring, until they begin to look soft, about 15 minutes. Add the water and salt, and scrape up the crust browning on the bottom of the sauce-pan. Reduce heat, cover, and cook 15 minutes or until potatoes are well done. Snip the dill into the broth. Purée in a blender or a food processor, 2 cups at a time, or press through a sieve. Return to the saucepan, and stir in the half-and-half and milk. Add salt and pepper to taste, and turn heat to very low.
2. Turn broiler to medium. Spread the Brie over the toast and broil until the cheese melts.

To serve: Ladle the soup into plates and float 1 slice of toast in each.

To make ahead: Complete through Step 1, then finish just before serving.

POTATO SOUP WITH HAM AND CHEESE   Serves 6

Follow the recipe for Potato Soup with Dill and Cheese Toast, but add 1½ cups chopped baked ham, 1½ cups grated mild cheddar cheese, and garnish with ½ cup of croutons instead of the cheese toast.

RICH MUSHROOM SOUP WITH VERMOUTH   Serves 6

With a salad, this makes a nice meal—no meat needed!

2 tablespoons olive oil
2 tablespoons butter
2 cloves garlic, minced
1 medium onion, chopped
1 pound mushrooms, sliced thin
3 tablespoons tomato paste
2 tablespoons sweet red vermouth
4 cups chicken broth

2 tablespoons minced fresh parsley
1 teaspoon chopped fresh basil
4 egg yolks
2 tablespoons grated Parmesan cheese
Salt and pepper
6 slices Italian bread, toasted, and buttered

1. In a heavy saucepan over medium heat, heat oil and butter, and sauté garlic and onion until onion is translucent, about 5 minutes. Add mushrooms and sauté, stirring, about 5 minutes, then stir in tomato paste, vermouth, broth, and herbs. Cover and simmer 10 minutes.
2. Beat egg yolks and cheese until eggs are thick; beat 1 cup of hot soup into the eggs, then turn egg mixture into saucepan, stirring. Reheat, but do not boil. Add salt and pepper to taste.

To serve: Place a piece of toast in the bottom of each bowl and ladle soup over slice.

To make ahead: Complete through Step 1, then finish just before serving.

TOMATO SOUP WITH CHEESE   Serves 6

3 medium leeks, whites only, sliced
2 large stalks celery, sliced thin
2 tablespoons butter
1/2 pound mushrooms, sliced thin
1/4 teaspoon salt
1/8 teaspoon pepper

3 cups half-and-half
1 16-ounce can tomato sauce
1/4 teaspoon dried thyme
Salt and pepper
6 small very ripe tomatoes
1/4 pound Swiss or Jarlsberg cheese, grated
Milk
1 tablespoon minced parsley

1. In a saucepan over medium heat, sauté the leeks and the celery in the butter until the leeks become translucent, about 7 minutes. Add the mushrooms, and sauté, stirring, 5 minutes.

Season mushrooms with salt and pepper. Stir the half-and-half into the mixture, then stir in the tomato sauce. Add the thyme, and salt and pepper to taste. Reduce heat.

2. Dip the tomatoes in boiling water for half a minute, then skin them and cut out enough of the center of each to make room for ⅙ of the cheese. Stuff each tomato with the grated cheese.

3. Float the tomatoes in the soup, open end up, and simmer until they are soft, about 15 minutes. Add a little milk if too much liquid is evaporating from the soup.

To serve: Set 1 tomato in each soup plate, then pour hot soup over the tomatoes. Garnish with parsley.

To make ahead: Complete through Step 2, then finish just before serving.

TOMATO AND CRAB SOUP   Serves 6 to 8

Crab is one of the many flavors that go beautifully with tomato. Flaked crab meat is out of sight in price, but sometimes there are leftovers—?

1 small onion, minced	4 large ripe tomatoes
1 medium celery stalk, chopped	(about 2 pounds), chopped
5 tablespoons butter	1½ cups flaked crab meat
5 tablespoons all-purpose flour	2 cups light cream
4 cups hot milk	Salt and pepper
¼ teaspoon dried thyme	¼ to ½ cup medium dry sherry
⅛ teaspoon baking soda	

1. In a large saucepan over medium heat, sauté the onion and celery in the butter until the onion becomes translucent, 5 to 7 minutes. Stir in the flour. Beating constantly, add the milk, and cook, stirring, until bubbly, 1 to 2 minutes. Turn off heat.

2. In a smaller saucepan over medium high heat, place the thyme and tomatoes, and cook, stirring, about 10 minutes. Turn off heat, stir in the soda, and purée in a blender or a food processor, 2 cups at a time, or press through a sieve.

3. Stir the tomatoes into the cream sauce, and add the crab meat and the cream. Add salt and pepper to taste, and as much sherry as you like. Reheat to just below boiling.

To serve: Ladle into soup bowls.

SUMMER VEGETABLE SOUP
Serves 8 to 10

If you have a nice beef broth, you really can put any vegetables into it, simmer away, add a thickener, like rice, and your favorite herbs and come up with a great meal. Use this combination as a guide, but don't think you have to stick to just these vegetables. "Shell" beans are the kind grown for drying: you'll find them on the market late summer, looking like big, lumpy pea pods. They shell just as peas do.

3 quarts beef broth
1/4 pound salt pork, diced
1 cup fresh shell beans, about 1/2–1 pound
4 cups spinach or other leafy greens
1 cup peas or chopped green beans
2 stalks celery, chopped
1 small green cabbage, shredded
4 small carrots, chopped
5 medium potatoes, chopped
1 small onion, chopped
1/2 cup raw rice
1 teaspoon minced fresh sage
1 tablespoon chopped parsley
2 cloves garlic, minced
Grated Parmesan cheese or sour cream

In a large kettle over medium high heat, combine broth and salt pork, bring to a boil, cover, reduce heat, and simmer 30 minutes. Add all other ingredients except cheese or sour cream, and simmer, covered, 1 hour.

To serve: Ladle into soup bowls and garnish with cheese or sour cream.

Dividends: Great as a leftover. Stretch with broth or milk.

To make ahead: You can make it days ahead, but add cabbage only at the final heating, and cook 30 minutes or until tender.

RICH CREAM OF VEGETABLE SOUP   Serves 6 to 8

This purée is enriched with eggs and cream. A very filling soup that needs little else to make a complete meal. Pod peas are also called snow peas—peas in tender, edible pods.

1 large leek, chopped	¼ teaspoon dried thyme
3 parsnips, chopped	½ small bay leaf
3 carrots, chopped	2 teaspoons salt
4 large stalks celery and leaves, chopped	¼ teaspoon pepper
	4 tablespoons butter
2 cups pod peas, broken in half	4 tablespoons all-purpose flour
1½ quarts water	1 quart hot milk
1 cup firmly packed shredded spinach leaves	2 egg yolks
	½ cup heavy cream
6 stalks parsley, minced	Salt and pepper to taste

1. In a large kettle over medium heat, place leek, parsnips, carrots, celery, pod peas, and water. Cover and cook 30 minutes. Purée in a blender or a food processor, 2 cups at a time, or press through a sieve. Return to kettle, turn heat to medium high, add spinach, parsley, thyme, bay, salt and pepper. Cover and simmer 10 minutes more.
2. In a small saucepan over low heat, melt the butter and stir in the flour. Beating constantly, add milk, and cook, stirring, until bubbly, 1 to 2 minutes. Stir into vegetable purée and heat to just below boiling.

To serve: Beat egg yolks until thick and lemon-colored. Stir in cream. Whip into purée, and ladle into soup bowls.

ZUCCHINI SOUP ITALIAN STYLE   Serves 8 to 10

Serve this as party fare when served with lots of garlic bread, salad, and a filling dessert, like pie à la mode, or cheesecake.

1 pound Italian sausage, hot or sweet, casing removed
2 cups chopped celery
8 small zucchini, sliced ½-inch thick
1 cup chopped onion
8 to 10 large ripe tomatoes (about 4 pounds), chopped
2 large cloves garlic, minced
2 teaspoons salt
½ teaspoon dried basil
¼ teaspoon dried thyme
¼ teaspoon dried rosemary
1 teaspoon dried oregano
1 teaspoon sugar
2 green peppers, seeded, chopped
4 to 5 tablespoons grated Parmesan cheese

1. In a large kettle over medium heat, brown the sausage, breaking it into chunks with two forks as it cooks. Pour off fat, add celery, and cook, stirring, 10 minutes. Add everything but the peppers and cheese, scraping the kettle bottom to dissolve caramalized sausage bits. Cover, lower heat, and simmer 20 minutes. Add peppers and cook 10 minutes.

To serve: Ladle into soup bowls and sprinkle a heaping teaspoon of cheese into each.

Dividends: Very good cold with a tablespoon of sour cream.

To make ahead: Can be made hours or the day before, but in that case undercook the green peppers a little so they stay a bright green. They'll finish cooking in the heat of the soup and will soften when you reheat the soup later.

Four

WHEN THE BOATS
COME IN

Most of the recipes in this chapter make a main course. With gourmet ingredients like lobster and shrimp, mussels and clams, these are among the most exotic soups around. Though costs are threatening to put fish and seafood onto the endangered list, when fish is used in a soup, a little goes a long way. If you live near water, or vacation by the sea, very often you can find your own ingredients at the shore, or at the local fish co-op, or from fishing boats at reasonable prices.

My father, Marcel Hériteau, was born in Les Sables D'Olonne, a fishing village on the Atlantic coast of France between Biarritz and Nantes. Today there are more yachts than fishing boats in Les Sables, but as a boy he learned to stalk mussels and to locate fishy delicacies on the salty shores of his hometown, and he taught me how and where, and later on, he taught my children.

Anytime we've gone to the sea together, *Papa chéri* is out of the car before it has come to a stop, and off down the beach or over the rocks to see what the sea has provided for the evening meal. Most often there are mussels, sometimes tiny snails you steam and pick out from their shells with a bent pin to dip in a garlic-rich sauce. Sometimes there are crayfish. From my father the boys have learned to be good fishermen and how to buy a big fish for a few dollars when the boats come in at the local fishermen's wharf. A whole fish so fresh its eyes still sparkle makes a super supper, and leftovers are the base for broths and chowders. With such a fish and a few shore delicacies—mussels, clams, a small lobster or two—you can make a magnificent bouillabaisse, and shore people have from the beginning of time.

In New England in the early days, chowders and fish soups and stews were staple foods. It was easy to cook one-pot meals over the fire in the hearth, and spoons were easier to come by than forks. The word "chowder," by the way, comes from the French word *chaudière*, which means "hot pot"—the big iron pot in which a soup of some sort bubbled all day long as it hung over the fire.

The late Sally Erath, a wonderful New England lady who wrote *Cooking for Two,* and pepped up Cape Cod in her later days, used to say she loved chowders "as much for the sense of thrift I enjoy when I dig my own clams as for the fun of being on the beach with the tide far out, and the wind fair and the sun warm on my back."

BY ANY OTHER NAME

The differences between the various shore soups are distinct, but rather subtle:

Stew describes a recipe in which the fish is stewed briefly in butter, seasoned with salt, pepper, sometimes paprika or nutmeg, and served swimming in a rich milk or cream broth.

Bisque is very similar to stew, but the broth is thickened with a *roux*—a cream sauce made of butter and flour—or thickened some other way. I often use a tablespoonful of instant mashed potato powder.

Chowder is more complex. The broth is usually based on onions sautéed in butter and thickened by simmering with diced (chopped if you use a food processor) potatoes, preferably old potatoes because they thicken a sauce more readily than do new potatoes. When the broth is ready, you add the fish or shellfish and then milk or cream. In early recipes mashed potatoes were sometimes used as the thickener for a chowder. Daniel Webster's Chowder in this chapter is one example of this use of potatoes.

Fish soup, like fish chowder, often begins with onions sautéed in butter, but usually the broth is without milk and includes many other vegetables and condiments. Fish soups like bouillabaisse and *cioppino* have grown out of the ingredients available. Bouillabaisse is from southern France, the Mediterranean area, and fish and shellfish native to that region—the day's catch—go into it. *Cioppino* is native to the Italian colony in San Francisco, so it is flavored with and based on foods available there.

BUYING FISH AND SHELLFISH

One reason inland Americans are not keen on fish is that the fish they ate in childhood often was not absolutely fresh. Fish deteriorates the minute it dies—that's why lobsters are stored, alive, in tanks of water, and oysters in barrels with moist dirt. It is wise to buy fishy things from a good fish shop, to insist on smelling it to make sure it is briny—*not* fishy—and to demand lobsters that are lively. The fish's eye tells how fresh it is, too: if it is bright and clear, the fish is fresh. Scales should be shiny. A dull, blue-hazed, slightly sunken eye means an old fish. When you are buying a piece of fish without the head, the gleam of the scales, the odor, and the shop owner's ethics are what you must rely on.

When you get the fish home, use it as soon as possible. Store live lobsters in the refrigerator (clams, oysters, mussels, too). Wash fish and store in the coldest part of the refrigerator and use the same day: it will never be fresher, and therefore, never better. Fresh fish can be held frozen and will be very good. Freeze it by setting it on the floor of the freezer, or in a flash freeze unit. Be sure it is heavily wrapped in freezer paper.

Fish soups freeze well, though the texture of the fish may not be quite as it is when it has not been frozen.

Just how good commercially frozen fish and shellfish, such as oysters and clams are, depends a lot on the brand. Generally, I find clams, and shucked oysters in pints, quite good, but often the frozen fish is not as fine. Do without fish rather than serve dubious fish!

CLEANING FISH AND SHELLFISH

Cleaning shore catches and buys from fishing boats requires care. Wash a fish and clean it by slitting the lower abdomen and removing what is inside. Wash again. Use the head and other trimmings to make broths and bases for soups, as suggested below.

Wash shellfish such as lobsters, crabs and shrimp, and those called mollusks, the oysters and clams, in cold running water, *but do not soak them.* Lobsters drown in fresh water! Scrub clams under cold running water with a stiff brush. To clean grit inside soft-shell clams—and you *must*—place them in a large enamel pan with brine (one tablespoon salt to each quart of water), toss in a handful of corn meal, and let stand for twenty-four hours. The clams will stretch their necks clear of the water and spit water and grit until they are clean. To clear hardshell clams and the big quahogs, scrub away all sand with a stiff-bristled brush under cold, running water.

To clean mussels: Under cold running water, with a small, sharp knife in hand, remove the clinging seaweed and scrape away the little barnacles usually attached to the shells. If you don't they'll steam loose in the cooking and drop into the opening shells of their neighbors, to end up under your teeth! Snap each mussel hard between thumb and forefinger, trying to separate the shells: sometimes they are sand-filled rather than fish-filled. The snapping usually locates that kind of dud.

To open shellfish to make a soup, use a clam or an oyster knife. (See page 128.) But if you get stuck, set them in a baking dish at 325 degrees—oven or broiler—and check in two to three minutes. Usually, they'll pop open enough for you to complete the job with an ordinary knife. Use them at once.

FISH BROTHS

Gourmet recipes for fish soups often begin by calling for liberal quantities of *fumet,* fish stock or broth. Most recipes here do not because they include such liberal quantities of fish that all that is needed is water. However, fish broth is worth making and storing if you have freezer space because it is a wonderful base on which to improvise soups. Frozen in 1-cup batches, as described in Chapter 2, these keep well for six months or more in the freezer. To a good fish broth you can add leftover cooked fish, lobster, or shellfish. Liven the broth with a bit of dry white wine, or sweeten it with cream and butter, thicken it with potato powder or mashed potatoes, or rice, and you have a from-scratch main course, a real delight served with warm, crusty French bread. Add salad and fruit, and you have a whole meal.

Fish broth generally is made from the parts trimmed from a whole fresh fish. To make a hearty *fumet*, expect to use three to four heads of two- to five-pound fish, with the backbones, tails, and gills; that equals about two pounds of fish. A basic measurement would be for each quart of water, use one pound of fish.

The great chef, Escoffier, my idol, was very particular about all stocks, including fish. He recommended for *fumet* only sole or whiting, a name used to refer to a slender Atlantic shore fish, and to hake and species of European cod. Here is an adaptation of Escoffier's *fumet* recipe:

FISH BROTH—ALL-PURPOSE   Makes about 7 cups

Any type of white fish may be used to make fish broth—flounder, bass, cod, and their variations, sole, scrod, whiting, snapper, etc.

2 quarts cold water	1 small bay leaf
2 pounds (4 to 6 cups) trimmings: heads, bones, tails	1/4 teaspoon dried thyme 3 large sprigs parsley, chopped
1 medium onion, sliced	1 cup white wine, optional
1 small carrot, sliced thin	Salt and pepper

1. In a large kettle over high heat, place all the ingredients except salt and pepper; cover and bring to a rapid boil. Reduce heat, skim scum until rapid formation stops, then simmer, uncovered, 20 minutes.
2. Strain through a colander lined with 2 thicknesses of cheesecloth. Return to broth any good chunks of fish in the trimmings, and add salt and pepper to taste. Use the broth as directed, or store in the refrigerator, or freeze, covered, in 1-cup lots for future use. (If you freeze, omit returning fish meat to broth.)

FISH BROTH—CLASSIC RECIPE   Makes about 4 quarts

I make this in what I call a "chicken casserole"—a big cast-iron saucepan, enameled and lidded. Peel the onions under running water to avoid weeping.

2 tablespoons salt	4 pounds sole or whiting:
½ pound (about 8) small white onions, peeled	heads, trimmings, bones
	Juice of 1 lemon, strained
2 quarts boiling water	2 cups dry white wine
2 tablespoons butter	4 quarts cold water
1 medium bunch parsley stalks	

1. In a large saucepan that has a lid, over high heat, add salt and onions to boiling water. Boil 3 minutes, drain, and chill onions quickly under cold running water. Discard blanching water.
2. Return the saucepan to medium low heat, melt the butter, and layer in the saucepan the blanched onions, parsley stalks, and fish trimmings. Sprinkle with lemon juice, cover and cook, shaking the pan gently now and then. When trimmings begin to exude a white substance, moisten with the white wine, cover, shake gently once or twice, remove lid, and cook over medium high heat until liquid has reduced by about half. Add cold water, raise heat, bring liquid to a boil, skim until scum stops rapid formation, reduce heat and simmer, uncovered, 20 minutes.
3. Strain through a colander lined with 2 thicknesses of cheesecloth, and use the broth as directed, or store in the refrigerator, or freeze, covered, in 1-cup lots for future use.

FISH BROTH—MEDITERRANEAN STYLE   Makes about 7 cups

    1 recipe Fish Broth,
        All-Purpose (page 107)
    ½ teaspoon saffron threads
        or turmeric

Complete recipe for Fish Broth, All-Purpose, then stir in saffron or turmeric. Bring to a boil, remove from heat, and proceed with recipe.

FISH BROTH FROM THE STEAMER　　　Makes 2 quarts

Broth left over from steaming lobster, clams, mussels, or other shellfish or fish makes an elegant basic broth for use in soup recipes including seafood. If the original broth was cooked without herbs, for each 2 quarts of plain broth add:

1 small bay leaf	1 small carrot, sliced
½ teaspoon dried thyme	Salt and pepper
1 small onion, sliced	

In a kettle over high heat, combine broth and all ingredients. Bring to a boil, turn off heat, and let rest 5 minutes. Strain before using, or storing in refrigerator, or freezing, covered, in 1-cup lots for future use.

POTAGE MME. BERTRAND　　　Serves 4

Here is a great clear fish soup to make with a good base of fish broth. Its flavor depends on a really good olive oil. (Always store olive oil in the refrigerator or it will go rancid.)

1 small onion, chopped	¼ teaspoon anise seed
1 medium carrot, chopped	½ teaspoon grated orange
1 large stalk celery, chopped	rind
1 medium clove garlic,	1 small bay leaf
chopped	¼ teaspoon dried thyme
2 tablespoons olive oil	2 sprigs parsley
1 tablespoon tomato paste	½ recipe *Rouille* (page 198)
5 cups fish broth	4 slices French bread,
¼ teaspoon saffron	toasted

1. In a medium kettle over medium heat, sauté the onion, carrot, celery, and garlic in the oil until the onion becomes translucent, and vegetables are lightly browned, about 10 minutes.
2. Stir in the tomato paste, broth, and herbs. Bring to a boil, and simmer, uncovered, 20 minutes. Strain, reserving only the broth. Add salt and pepper to taste.

To serve: Spread *rouille* on the bread slices, and place in the bottom of broad soup bowls. Ladle broth over the bread.

To make ahead: Soup may be made a day ahead; prepare *rouille* toast just before serving.

POTAGE MME. BERTRAND
WITH FISH FLAKES   Serves 4

A wonderful soup made from leftover cooked fish, hearty enough to be a main course, with a tossed salad, crusty bread, and a filling dessert, such as pie or rice pudding.

1 recipe *Potage Mme.*
    Bertrand (page 109), made
    with 4 cups fish broth and
    1 cup dry white wine
	1 to 2 cups flaked, cooked
	    white fish or shellfish, such
	    as lobster, crab, mussels,
	    soft-shell clams

Complete *Potage Mme. Bertrand* through Step 2. Reheat strained broth, and add cooked fish or shellfish. Heat to boiling.

To serve: Ladle soup over *rouille*-spread toast.

FISH BROTH FROM COOKED SCRAPS   Makes 6 to 8 cups

This is a way of salvaging those meaty bits of lobster or crab you can't quite get at. The resulting essence is a wonderful base for bisques, soups, chowders, or soups of your own creation.

4 cups cooked shellfish shells
    and scraps
2 cups cold water
	4-6 cups cooking liquid from
	    seafood
	Salt and pepper

Combine all ingredients except salt and pepper in a large kettle over high heat, cover, and cook 20 minutes. Cool. Strain through a colander lined with 2 thicknesses of cheesecloth. Add salt and pepper to taste. Use as fish broth, following recipe directions, or store in refrigerator, or freeze, covered, in 1-cup lots for future use.

SHRIMP

Shrimp costs relate to size: the "colossal" size, about ten to a pound, are the most expensive, and the miniatures, dozens to a pound, are less so, but what a chore it is to shell them! Medium-size shrimp, which are medium in price, too, are just as good, if not quite as glamorous, for use in soups as the giants.

Green or raw shrimp—in the shell—are my choice for every use. Bagged, frozen, shelled, and deveined, partially or fully cooked shrimp are the easiest to use. The green shrimp must be shelled and deveined. But the frozen deveined type are usually tasteless. I think the producers cook them in dishwater. Oregon Freeze Dry Foods' freeze-dried shrimp, large or small, are very flavorful. These are deveined, shelled, semicooked, and take just a few minutes to plump up in lukewarm water.

Raw shrimp are gray-green-pink, and it takes only minutes in boiling water for them to be cooked. They are cooked just as soon as they turn deep pink all over. When used whole in soups, raw shrimp generally are cooked in the soup, then taken out and shelled and deveined. When intended for a bisque, for instance, in which the shrimp is ground up as a thickener for the soup, already-shelled shrimp may be used. Miniatures are shelled before use in the soups: Drop them into boiling, salted water with a bay leaf, an onion, 1/8 teaspoon dried thyme, parsley, and take them out in one minute, then shell them. This size does not require deveining. Use the cooking water from the miniatures to make the soup.

To devein shrimp, unwind the shell, starting on the underside. Grasp a bit of the shell between thumb and forefinger, pull the shell up over the back and you will sense the next move. To devein the shrimp, make an incision 1/8 inch deep down the center back with a sharp knife, then scrape or rinse out the dark vein that runs down the back.

SHRIMP SOUP   Serves 4

Great party fare! You may use raw shrimp to make this, but cook them first in the 8 cups of boiling water this recipe calls for, with the herbs listed below the water, then shell and devein the shrimp as described above.

1 cup dry white wine
1 pound shrimp, shelled and deveined
1 small leek, sliced thin
2 medium onions, chopped
1 small carrot, chopped
3 tablespoons olive oil
2 tablespoons all-purpose flour
8 cups boiling water

⅛ teaspoon dried thyme
⅛ teaspoon dried rosemary
4 sprigs parsley, minced
1 inch zest of lemon
1 tablespoon salt
⅛ teaspoon pepper
1 egg yolk
2 tablespoons minced parsley

1. In a kettle over medium high heat, bring wine to a boil, add shrimp and simmer 10 minutes, covered. Remove from heat, and drain; reserve wine and shrimp.
2. In a saucepan over medium heat, sauté the leek, onions, and carrot in the oil until the onion is translucent, about 5 minutes. Stir in the flour. Beating constantly, add the wine and boiling water. Cook, stirring, until bubbly, 1 to 2 minutes. Add thyme, rosemary, parsley, lemon, salt, and pepper, reduce heat, and simmer 40 minutes.
3. Purée the shrimp with a little cooking liquid in a blender or a food processor, 2 cups at a time, and turn into the broth. Cover and simmer 15 minutes. In a small bowl beat the egg yolk and stir in ½ cup of broth. Scrape the mixture back into the soup, and stir.

To serve: Ladle into bowls and garnish with parsley.

To make ahead: Complete through cooking. Just before serving, reheat and add egg yolk.

SHRIMP BISQUE   Serves 4 to 6

You can use shelled, deveined shrimp to make this, or a quality freeze-dried product: just omit Step 2.

2 cups water	6 tablespoons butter
½ medium onion, chopped	2 tablespoons all-purpose
1 small bay leaf	flour
¼ teaspoon dried thyme	4 cups milk
1 teaspoon salt	1 cup heavy cream
⅛ teaspoon pepper	¼ teaspoon paprika
1½ pounds raw shrimp in the shell	3 tablespoons dry cooking sherry
2 tablespoons minced onion	Salt and pepper
	1 tablespoon minced chives

1. In a large kettle over high heat, bring the water to a rapid boil with the onion, bay, thyme, salt, and pepper. Drop in the shrimp, bring back to a boil, reduce heat, cover, and simmer barely 3 minutes or until shrimp are pink all over. Drain, and discard bay leaf; reserve broth.
2. Shell and devein shrimp. Return shells and broth to kettle, and over high heat, boil shells, uncovered, 5 minutes. Drain, and discard shells. Reserve broth.
3. Purée shrimp and broth in a blender or a food processor, 2 cups at a time.
4. In a saucepan over medium heat, sauté the minced onion in the butter until translucent, 3 to 5 minutes. Stir in the flour. Beating constantly, add shrimp purée and milk, and cook, stirring, until bubbly, 3 to 4 minutes. Stir in cream, paprika, and dry sherry, and heat to just below boiling.

To serve: Ladle into bowls and garnish with chives.

Dividends: Freezes very well. Good mixed with other soups, like vegetable creams, or stretched with clam juice or chicken broth, milk or light cream.

To make ahead: Complete hours or a day before using, but add garnish just before serving.

CRABS

Fresh crabmeat is sold by the pint, cooked, at the shore, and sometimes inland you find buys on the big Alaskan king crab legs. If you catch your own, try a gumbo, or cook the crabs, draw the meat, and make the bisque described below. I cook crabs by dropping them live into lots of rapidly boiling water with 1 to 3 tablespoons of salt, a small bay leaf, ½ teaspoon dried thyme, 8 peppercorns, 4 sprigs parsley. Cook for 5 minutes after the water returns to a boil.

Cool the crabs before drawing the meat. Pry off the backs (called the "apron"), and break off the large claws and legs. Crack the legs and draw out the meat. Crack the claws. If the claws are going into a bouillabaisse, return them to the broth with the drawn meat. Break the body in half along its length, and with a knife point or a lobster pick, draw the meaty nuggets from the knuckles. The morsels of yellow liver and orange roe are considered delicacies, but neither the gray feathery gills nor the cartilage is edible.

CRAB BISQUE   Serves 6 to 8

Lobster left over in legs and knuckles from a lobster feast can be used instead of crab in this recipe. So could almost any tasty cooked fish.

½ cup finely minced celery
3 tablespoons butter
3 tablespoons all-purpose flour
1 pound (2 cups) cooked crab meat, cartilage removed
1 quart milk, scalded

Salt and pepper to taste
2 tablespoons sherry, optional
6 very thin slices lemon with rind
2 hard-boiled eggs, sliced
1 pint half-and-half

In a saucepan over medium heat, sauté the celery in the butter until golden, about 5 minutes. Stir in the flour. Beating constantly, add the milk and cook, stirring, until bubbly. Add the half-and-half, the crab, salt and pepper to taste, sherry, if you wish, and bring to just below boiling.

To serve: Place 1 slice of lemon and slices of egg in big soup bowls and ladle the bisque over them.

Dividends: Nice cold. Stretch with clam juice.

To make ahead: Complete through addition of crab, salt, and pepper, then finish just before serving.

CRAB AND SHRIMP GUMBO   Serves 6

A very satisfying meal, this gumbo is made with the small blue crabs that weigh about 8 ounces, and which are found in the South and often in shallow waters farther north.

5 quarts cold water	2 large cloves garlic, minced
5 small dried hot chilies	½ pound okra, sliced, or ½
1 large bay leaf	10-ounce package frozen
1 teaspoon dried thyme	okra
1 small lemon, sliced thin	¾ cup chopped green pepper
1 tablespoon salt	1 teaspoon cayenne
1 pound medium shrimp	½ teaspoon Tabasco sauce
10 blue crabs	1 small bay leaf
4 tablespoons butter	½ teaspoon dried thyme
4 tablespoons all-purpose flour	Salt and pepper
½ cup chopped onion	6 cups cooked rice

1. In a large kettle over high heat, place the water, chilies, bay, thyme, lemon, and salt; bring to a rapid boil. Drop in the shrimp, tied into a square of cheesecloth, and cook until they are pink all over, 3 to 5 minutes; then remove. Drop in crabs, cook 5 minutes, and remove with tongs. Boil the broth rapidly while you shell and devein the shrimp (reserve shells), and draw meat from the crabs. Return shrimp shells to the broth in the cheesecloth bag. Boil broth to reduce it. It is ready when it is reduced to 3 quarts.
2. In a large saucepan over low heat, melt the butter and stir in the flour. Beating constantly, add the onions and garlic, and cook 5 minutes, stirring. Add the okra and green pepper, and continue to cook, still stirring. Pour in the broth, add the cayenne, Tabasco, bay, thyme, crabmeat, and claws. Reduce heat, and simmer 1 hour, partially covered. Remove shrimp shells, add shrimp, and simmer 2 minutes. Add salt and pepper to taste, and add more Tabasco if you like it hot.

To serve: Divide the rice among the soup bowls and ladle the gumbo over it. Provide lobster crackers to finish breaking open claws.

To make ahead: Excellent made the day before and reheated, but add shrimp at the last minute.

LOBSTER

Lobster meat in cans, or cooked and sold by the pint, is very expensive, though that may change. So popular is this shellfish—and so profitable—that lobster "farms" are springing up all over the place. Meanwhile, you can usually salvage enough lobster meat from boiled lobster dinners to make a bit of chowder or soup. Most diners abandon the meat in the legs and knuckles, and many disdain the delicious tomalley (liver—gray-green) and coral (undeveloped roe—coral-colored).

If you buy lobsters to make soups, expect to draw one pound of lobster meat from tail, claws, legs, and knuckles of a 1¼-pound lobster. One-clawed lobsters and soft-shelled lobsters that have just cast their former shell are less expensive and have less meat. Cook lobster as recommended for crab (page 114), allowing twenty minutes' cooking time after water has returned to a rapid boil after the addition of the lobster.

To remove the meat from a cooked lobster, set it on its back and cut down the middle all the way to the end of the tail. Crack the claws and knuckles and twist off the legs. A lobster pick or a small fork will help remove meat from tail and claws, and can pull out a lot of the meat in the legs and knuckles along the edges of the body.

PRAWNS AND CRAYFISH

Prawns are 3- to 4-inch long shrimplike shellfish that look like baby lobsters or crayfish. Crayfish usually have large tails and very sweet meat, and are larger. Lobster recipes taste very good with crayfish or prawns as a substitute. Cook five minutes in boiling water to which you have added the herbs used in cooking crab or lobster. Shell before using the meat.

LOBSTER STEW BOSTON STYLE   Serves 4 to 6

This is a very simple way to turn cooked lobster meat into a delicious and delicate stew.

1 pound cooked lobster meat (1 1¼ pound uncooked lobster), chopped	1 teaspoon paprika
½ cup butter	4 cups milk
	1 cup heavy cream
	Salt and pepper

116

In a saucepan over medium heat, sauté the lobster meat in the butter with the paprika until lightly colored, but not brown. Pour in milk and cream and heat to just below boiling. Add salt and pepper to taste.

To serve: Ladle into soup bowls.

Dividends: Stretch leftovers with clam juice and this becomes Lobster Stew Casco Bay Style.

To make ahead: May be made a day ahead.

LOBSTER BISQUE   Serves 6

A bisque of lobster is very similar to a stew, but it is thickened with flour. This will be a richer bisque if you have cooked the lobster yourself, and can substitute 2 cups of the water the lobster cooked in for the cold water called for here.

2 pounds cooked lobster meat (2½ pounds uncooked), chopped	6 tablespoons butter
	4 tablespoons all-purpose flour
2 cups cold water	1 teaspoon salt
3 cups milk	Paprika
1 cup heavy cream	

1. In a saucepan over medium low heat, combine lobster and water. Cover, bring to a simmer, and cook 30 minutes. Purée in a blender or a food processor, 2 cups at a time. Return to kettle, stir in milk and cream, and scald.
2. In a saucepan over low heat, melt the butter and stir in the flour. Beating constantly, add the broth and cook, stirring, until bubbly. Add salt and paprika to taste.

To serve: Ladle into soup bowls.

Dividends: Leftovers are very good stretched with clam juice. Or mix in leftover cooked steamers, mussels, or haddock flakes, and make a whole elegant new soup.

To make ahead: Better made hours or a day ahead, but do not boil when reheating.

LOBSTER CHOWDER   Serves 6 to 8

A richly flavored chowder that includes the gray-green tomalley and white substance found in the shells of lobsters and crabs that are not quite full.

3 quarts water	1 medium onion, chopped
½ tablespoon salt	4 tablespoons butter
1 small onion, peeled	2 tablespoons all-purpose
1 small bay leaf	flour
¼ teaspoon dried thyme	4 cups scalded milk
8 peppercorns	Salt and pepper
4 sprigs parsley	1 tablespoon minced
1 small carrot, split	parsley
2½ pounds uncooked lobster	Chowder crackers
1½ cups potatoes, chopped	

1. In a kettle over high heat, bring water, salt, onion, bay, thyme, peppercorns, parsley, and carrot, to a rapid boil. Drop lobsters in head first, cover tightly, and when water returns to a rapid boil, reduce heat and simmer 20 minutes. Remove lobsters from broth, reserving 4 cups broth and herbs. Remove lobster meat as described on page 116. Reserve tomalley and white substance, and chop lobster. Return lobster shells to the kettle with the reserved broth, and simmer 15 minutes. Strain, discard shells, and return broth to kettle and add potatoes. Cover, and cook rapidly until potatoes are tender, about 15 minutes.

2. In a saucepan over medium heat, sauté the onion in the butter until lightly browned, about 10 minutes. Blend in the tomalley and white substance, and stir in the flour. Beating constantly, add the scalded milk, and cook, stirring, until bubbly, 1 to 2 minutes. Stir in the lobster meat, potatoes, and broth. Simmer 5 minutes. Add salt and pepper to taste.

To serve: Ladle into bowls, garnish with parsley, and serve crackers on the side.

Dividends: Stretch with clam juice: it's first-rate!

To make ahead: Delicious made hours or a day ahead, but do not boil when reheating.

LOBSTER SOUP PORTUGUESE STYLE   Serves 6 to 8

Chicken broth and a dab of sherry make this perfectly delicious
—different from the all-fish recipes that precede it. But to be at
its best, the chicken broth should be homemade.

3 quarts water	3 cups chicken broth
1 tablespoon salt	4 slices white bread, crusts
1 small onion, studded with	trimmed
4 whole cloves	2 tablespoons butter,
¼ teaspoon tarragon	melted
8 peppercorns	1 cup heavy cream
4 sprigs parsley	2 tablespoons sweet sherry
1 small carrot, split	or Madeira
1 small bay leaf	Salt and pepper
2½-pounds uncooked lobster	

1. In a kettle over high heat, bring water with salt, onion, tarragon, peppercorns, parsley, carrot, and bay to a rapid boil.
   Drop lobster in head first, cover tightly, and when water returns to a rapid boil, reduce heat and simmer 20 minutes.
   Strain broth, reserving lobster and 3 cups broth. Remove
   lobster meat and cut claws and tail into big chunks. Save
   tomalley and white substance in shell.
2. In the kettle over high heat, combine the lobster and chicken
   broths, and add the bread. Stir until the bread disintegrates.
   Stir the melted butter into the tomalley and white substance,
   and add to the soup, along with lobster meat and chunks, and
   add cream. Heat to just below boiling. Flavor with sherry or
   Madeira if you wish. Add salt and pepper to taste.

To serve: Ladle into soup bowls.

Dividends: Leftovers are excellent stretched with more milk,
cream, or a little more chicken broth.

To make ahead: Complete through addition of bread to broths.
Finish just before serving.

LOBSTER STEW DOWN EAST STYLE   Serves 4 to 6

Down East refers to the Maine coast, where lobster is plentiful, and this recipe is more generous with the lobster than recipes that have developed in places where lobster is less easy to get.

2 pounds cooked lobster meat (2½ pounds uncooked), chopped, plus tomalley and coral from the lobsters and white substance found in lobster shells	½ cup butter 4 cups milk, scalded Salt and pepper

In a saucepan over low heat, sauté tomalley, coral, and white substance from lobsters in the butter for 5 minutes. Add the lobster meat and cook another 4 minutes, stirring. Remove from the heat and allow to cool slightly, then slowly stir in scalded milk. Allow stew to stand several hours.

To serve: Over low heat reheat to just below boiling, stirring, then add salt and pepper to taste, and ladle into soup bowls.

Dividends: Excellent the next day: delicious cold.

To make ahead: Must be made ahead.

LOBSTER À LA NAGE   Serves 4

Two lobsters done this way make a very satisfying meal for four. A cool white wine—Blanc de Blancs type—and crusty French bread and butter complete the meal nicely. An easy party dish.

1 large onion, minced	6 sprigs parsley
1 large stalk celery, minced	6 peppercorns
2 medium carrots, minced	2 1½-pound uncooked
1 medium leek, sliced thin	lobsters
4 cups water	4 tablespoons butter
2 cups dry white wine	Salt
½ teaspoon dried thyme	Cayenne
1 medium bay leaf	

1. In a large kettle over high heat, combine onion, celery, carrots, and leek with water, wine, thyme, bay, parsley, and peppercorns. Bring to a rapid boil, cover, reduce heat, and simmer 15 minutes.

2. Put the lobsters into the broth. Raise the heat to bring the kettle back to a boil, then cover, reduce heat, and simmer 20 minutes. Lift out the lobsters, and turn off the heat. Set the lobsters on their backs, and cut them down the middle. Crack the claws and the knuckles. Pour juices from lobsters back into kettle, raise heat, stir in butter, and add salt and cayenne to taste.

To serve: Place halved lobsters in large soup bowls and pour broth over them.

CLAMS FOR SOUPS

Clams for soups and chowders may be purchased in the shell by the dozen or by the pound. They also are sold shucked by the pint. I generally don't buy canned clams for soups: too expensive, not very good. The large hard-shell clams, called quahogs by the Indians, are the best for chowders. Cherrystone clams, which are about 3 inches, and littlenecks, which are about 1½ inches, are just right for use in combination fish soups, like bouillabaisse. If you have lots of soft-shell clams for the digging, free, and want to use them to make chowder or soup, go ahead, but realize you will need many more of these—how many depends on their highly variable size—than of the quahog type. And be sure you get all the sand out, following the instructions on page 106.

About quantities: As a rule of thumb, one pint of clams makes soup for six to eight if combined with several other ingredients. Allow six of the small hard-shell types per serving for soups in which clams are the only ingredient. Two dozen average-size cherrystone clams, shucked, measure about one pint, including the liquid. I find a pint of shucked clams includes about 24 clams and 1 cup of liquid. (The liquid from cherrystone clams and oysters often is referred to as "liquor.")

CLAM STEW
Serves 4 to 6

A takeoff on oyster stew, this was very popular in Victorian families. Each portion here makes a satisfying main course, especially if served with lots of crisp crackers or hard rolls.

1 small onion, chopped
4 tablespoons butter
2 dozen clams, shucked, and liquor
1 teaspoon Worcestershire sauce, optional
1/4 small bay leaf
1/8 teaspoon dried thyme
3 cups half-and-half
Salt and pepper
Chowder crackers, optional
Paprika

In a saucepan over low heat, sauté the onion in the butter until soft, 5 to 7 minutes. Add the clams, their liquor, and the Worcestershire, if you wish, along with the bay leaf and thyme. Cover and simmer gently 10 minutes. Add half-and-half, season to taste with salt and pepper, and heat through without boiling.

To serve: Remove bay leaf. Break crackers, if you wish, into each bowl, and ladle stew over them. Garnish with paprika.

CLAM BISQUE
Serves 4

This bisque is thickened with rice rather than with a *roux*. Make it with soft-shell clams. It's a good recipe to use with leftover cooked steamers, as long as they aren't overcooked.

2 cups soft-shell clams (3 to 4 dozen), and liquor
1 cup water
4 cups combined cooking water and liquor from clams, fish broth (any type), or bottled clam juice
1/2 cup uncooked rice
1 medium celery stalk, chopped
1/4 small bay leaf
1/8 teaspoon dried thyme
1 cup half-and-half
Salt and pepper
1 tablespoon finely minced parsley

In a large saucepan over medium heat, place clams and water, cover, and steam until all are open. Shuck the clams, reserve the liquor, and discard the shells. Chop clams and return to saucepan with liquor, fish broth or clam juice, rice, celery, bay, thyme.

Raise heat and bring to a slow boil; cover, reduce heat, and simmer 15 to 20 minutes or until rice is tender. Remove bay. Purée in a blender or a food processor, 2 cups at a time, or press through a sieve. Return to the saucepan, add the half-and-half, salt and pepper to taste, and heat to just below boiling.

To serve: Ladle into soup bowls and garnish with parsley.

Dividends: Very good the next day stretched with more half-and-half and chowder crackers.

To make ahead: Keeps well for hours or a day or two.

MANHATTAN CLAM CHOWDER   Serves 8

This is the other way to make clam chowder, sometimes called Rhode Island style. It is colored by tomatoes and contains various vegetables, depending on the season. You can add peas for color, corn for New England flavor.

1 large onion, chopped	1 pint shucked clams,
2 tablespoons bacon or	minced, and liquor
pork roast drippings	1 pint bottled clam juice
1½ cups chopped carrots	Salt and pepper
½ cup chopped celery	1 tablespoon minced
2 cups chopped potatoes	parsley
2 cups Fish Broth (All-	3 cups chopped tomatoes,
Purpose or Classic, see	fresh or cannned
pages 107 and 108)	
or water	

In a saucepan over medium heat, sauté the onion in the drippings until translucent, about 5 minutes. Stir in carrots, celery, potatoes, tomatoes, and fish broth, or water. Bring to a boil, cover, lower heat, and simmer 15 minutes. Add clams and their liquor, clam juice, turn off heat, and let stand at least half an hour. Just before serving, reheat to just boiling but do not boil.

To serve: Ladle into soup bowls and garnish with parsley.

Dividends: Excellent reheated and stretched with milk.

To make ahead: Better made hours or a day ahead.

NEW ENGLAND CLAM CHOWDER   Serves 6

This is Sally Erath's chowder recipe, made with the big hard-shell clams you pick from the sea floor off Cape Cod. As a substitute, use about 2 quarts small hard-shells, or 1 pint shucked clams. Use old potatoes; they thicken a chowder best. Sally served this chowder with hard New England biscuits soaked in cold milk, split, and placed in the bottom of the soup bowl before the chowder was ladled in.

12 large quahogs and liquor	1 teaspoon salt
1 cup water	⅛ teaspoon pepper
¼ pound salt pork, diced	¼ small bay leaf
1 large onion, chopped	⅛ teaspoon dried thyme
4 medium potatoes, chopped	4 cups half-and-half or milk
2½ cups boiling water	Chowder crackers

1. In a large saucepan over medium heat, place clams, cover, and steam until all are open. Shuck the clams, reserve the liquor, and discard the shells. Chop clams. If chopped in a processor, leave them there.
2. Place the saucepan over medium heat, and sauté salt pork until golden brown, 5 to 7 minutes. Add onion and sauté 5 to 7 minutes, until translucent. Add potatoes and sauté 2 minutes more. Add clams, their liquor, 2½ cups boiling water, salt, pepper, bay, and thyme. Cover and cook 15 minutes. Add milk and simmer 15 minutes. Remove bay.

To serve: Ladle chowder into bowls and offer crackers on the side.

Dividends: Great the next day. Stretch with milk or cream, dot with butter.

To make ahead: Better when made several hours before serving.

MUSSELS

My family prefers these to soft-shell clams (steamers). Shiny black with blue markings, they're still free for the picking where rocks and pebble beaches meet salt water. In recent years they've appeared in the fish shops of Manhattan, especially in those owned by Orientals, who seem to know better than we do how very special mussels are!

Mussels are sold by the pound in the shell, unless they are quite large. Then they are sold by the dozen. About 6 or 7 dozen medium mussels make about five pounds.

If you have the opportunity at the shore, pick your own. They're well worth the effort. Picking is easy: Just pull large mussels free from the rocks or gravel they are clinging to. Choose mussels growing as close to the lowest point of low tide as you can reach. Those that never are out of the water are my choice. But before you go mussel picking, check with local authorities: all shellfish are poisonous when the "red tide" is running. This is a condition that occurs in warmer months.

For general information on cleaning mussels, turn to page 106 of this chapter.

MUSSEL SOUP CLEMENCE
Serves 6

A creamy version of Mussels à la Marinière, inspired by the way my French grandmother handled leftover mussels.

⅓ cup minced shallots	1 small bay leaf, crumpled
½ cup butter	1 cup dry white vermouth
5 pounds medium mussels	2 cups half-and-half
1 tablespoon minced parsley	4 teaspoons butter
½ teaspoon dried thyme	¼ cup minced parsley

1. In a large kettle over medium heat, sauté shallots in the butter until translucent, about 5 minutes. Add mussels, parsley, thyme, bay, and vermouth. Raise heat and bring to a boil, cover, lower heat, and simmer about 8 minutes, shaking the pan often. When all the mussels are open, they are done. Lift mussels into big soup bowls with a slotted spoon.
2. Add milk or half-and-half and butter to the kettle, bring to a boil, then add parsley, stir 30 seconds, and ladle at once over mussels.

To serve: Serve as soon as ready.

Dividends: Shuck any remaining mussels into any leftover broth. Reheated with some additional milk or cream, salt and pepper, this makes a nice chowder.

MUSSEL SOUP ITALIAN STYLE   Serves 6

As richly flavored as your favorite Italian dishes, this makes a one-dish dinner. Serve with Italian bread and follow with a little salad and fruit.

1 medium onion, minced
2 large stalks fennel and tops, minced
4 large cloves garlic, minced
4 sprigs fresh basil, minced, or 1 tablespoon dried
½ cup olive oil
⅛ teaspoon black pepper
1 cup dry white wine

2 pounds ripe plum tomatoes, chopped, or 2 16-ounce cans tomatoes
1 tablespoon grated orange rind
⅛ teaspoon dried rosemary
1 cup tomato juice
5 pounds medium mussels
6 sprigs basil

1. In a large kettle over medium heat sauté onion, fennel, garlic, and basil in the oil until onions are golden brown, about 10 minutes. Stir in pepper and wine, scrape up pan juices, and simmer 3 to 4 minutes. Add tomatoes, orange peel, rosemary, and tomato juice. Cover, lower heat, and simmer, stirring occasionally, 12 to 15 minutes.
2. Add mussels, raise heat, bring to a boil, then cover, lower heat, and simmer about 8 minutes, shaking the pan often. When all the mussels are open, they are done.

To serve: Ladle into big bowls and garnish with a sprig of basil.

Dividends: Shuck any remaining mussels into remaining broth. Reheated with a little additional clam juice or milk, this makes a nice soup.

To make ahead: Follow through Step 1 several hours ahead. Complete just before serving.

SOLE AND MUSSEL SOUP   Serves 4 to 6

This is a soupy version of what is called a *matelote* in good French restaurants. Be sure the cider you use is dry. Substitute dry white wine if dry cider is unavailable.

4 tablespoons butter
2 tablespoons oil
1 pound sole or flounder fillets, cut into 2-inch pieces

1 medium onion, chopped
¼ pound fresh mushrooms, chopped
½ teaspoon salt
¼ teaspoon pepper

1½ cups dry cider
2 cups fish broth (All-Purpose or Classic, see pages 107 and 108)
2 tablespoons brandy, optional
2 dozen mussels
¼ cup cold water

3 tablespoons butter
3 tablespoons all-purpose flour
1 cup light cream
4 to 6 slices French bread
1 tablespoon butter
1 tablespoon oil

1. In a large saucepan over medium heat, melt the butter in the oil. Sauté the fish until lightly browned. Stir often. Remove the fish and keep warm. Place the onion in the saucepan and sauté 1 minute, then add the mushrooms and stir-fry 5 minutes more. Lay the fish on top of the mushrooms, add salt and pepper, cider, broth, and brandy if you wish. Bring to simmer, reduce heat, cover, and cook 8 minutes more. Remove the saucepan and keep it warm.

2. Place the mussels and the water in a kettle over medium high heat, cover, and cook, shaking often, until mussels open, 4 to 6 minutes. Remove the kettle from heat. Reserve six mussels in their shells. Shell the others and place with the sole. Return kettle and mussel liquid to heat, and boil until reduced by half. Pour over the fish. Lower heat to medium low, and in the same kettle, melt the butter and stir in the flour. Add the cream and cook, stirring, until bubbly, 1 to 2 minutes. Gently pour in sole or flounder, mussels, and their liquid. Raise heat a little and cook until hot through.

3. Return the saucepan to medium high heat. Melt the butter in the oil, and sauté the bread until browned on both sides.

To serve: Ladle fish soup into large bowls and garnish with reserved mussels and fried bread.

OYSTERS

When we lived in Westport, Connecticut, there was a beach where you could pick up a dozen or two small, salty oysters of the size called "bluepoint," 2 to 4 inches long, as you gathered mussels by the bucket. All free. Beaches where oysters are free are rare, but oysters in the shell, even free, are not my choice for stews and soups. Those shucked and by the pint are just as good cooked as the in-shell oysters, and they're easier on the cook. To open oysters, you must have an oyster knife, and a sharp one. These are fat-handled, with a round, thin tip. You must pry this tip into the oyster between the shells at the narrow end of the oyster, and this the oyster does not like and therefore strongly resists. Then you must pry off the top shell. I usually cut my fingers, either on the knife or on the knife-sharp oyster shell. Better are the shucked oysters sold by the pint, either fresh or frozen and thawed, than cut fingers and bent tempers. In a soup or stew, one pint serves four.

The real trick in making very good oyster stew or soup is to avoid overcooking the oysters. Oysters are done when the edges are curled, and that begins to happen almost the minute they hit the boiling liquid. Overdone, they are tough and tasteless.

OYSTER STEW GRAND CENTRAL STYLE   Serves 8

Old seafood hands in New York still beat a path to Grand Central Station's Oyster Bar restaurant. It seems much as it must have been when it opened in 1912. Here's a chef's-eye view of the Bar's famous oyster stew.

2 cups milk	½ teaspoon salt
2 cups light cream	½ teaspoon celery salt
2 pints shucked oysters and	⅛ teaspoon pepper
liquor	⅛ teaspoon paprika
2 tablespoons butter	Oyster crackers

1. In a kettle over medium heat, bring the milk and the cream to scalding, and turn off heat.
2. In a small saucepan over high heat, bring the drained oyster liquor to boiling. Pour a quarter cup of the liquor into another small saucepan, and add the butter. Turn the heat off under the first. Turn the oysters into the second small saucepan, turn the heat to medium, and cook, uncovered, shaking the pan constantly, until all the oysters are curled at the edges, about 4 minutes. Turn the heat up under the milk and cream. Pour the oysters into the milk and cream, add oyster liquor and all the remaining ingredients except the crackers. Stir one minute more.

To serve: Pour into very hot soup bowls and pass the crackers.

DANIEL WEBSTER'S CHOWDER Serves 10 to 12

The recipe here was modernized by Boston's Garland School of Homemaking years ago and became a favorite of its board of directors. I've cut in half the amount of fish called for, so this is a lighter version yet of the very heavy, rich fish chowders popular in the last century.

"Hard biscuit" is also called "sea biscuit" and hard-tack. It is an unleavened biscuit, about three inches across, really hard. You put the point of a knife into the side seam and push and pry, and it will pop apart into two halves. Because it is hard to start with, it doesn't go stale, and was common fare on fishing boats that would stay at sea for days and weeks at a time. I find it at supermarkets in shore communities where it is popular for use in and with chowders and fish soups and stews.

4 tablespoons minced onion	4 whole cloves
½ pound salt pork, chopped	8 black peppercorns
1 quart mashed potatoes	⅛ teaspoon allspice
½ pound hard biscuit, broken	4 pounds fish fillets, cut into
¼ pound fresh mushrooms,	2-inch pieces
chopped	25 shucked oysters and
3 slices lemon with rind	liquor
½ teaspoon dried thyme	8 to 10 cups boiling water
¼ teaspoon grated nutmeg	1 quart dry red wine
⅛ teaspoon ground mace	Chowder crackers

1. In a large kettle over medium heat, sauté onion and salt pork until crisp, 10 to 15 minutes. Stir in mashed potatoes, biscuit, mushrooms, lemon, and spices.
2. Set fish and oysters on top, pour in boiling water to cover. Bring to a boil, stirring very gently. Reduce heat and simmer until fish begins to look opaque, then add wine, and simmer 10 minutes. Remove peppercorns, whole cloves, and lemon.

To serve: Ladle into bowls and pass the crackers.

To make ahead: Complete through Step 1, then finish just before serving.

OYSTER CHOWDER   Serves 8

We used to start Thanksgiving Dinner with a big platter of icy cold oysters and lemon wedges, but with soaring prices, we've switched to oyster chowder, which takes fewer oysters to feed family and guests. This is a delicious and very rich soup.

2 medium onions, chopped
2 medium potatoes, chopped
3 tablespoons butter
6 cups milk
1 pint heavy cream
2 cups bottled clam juice
1 sprig celery leaves, minced
½ small bay leaf, crumpled

1 teaspoon salt
¼ teaspoon pepper
⅛ teaspoon dried thyme
⅛ teaspoon grated nutmeg
2 pints shucked oysters and liquor
1 tablespoon cream sherry, optional

1. In a large saucepan over medium heat, sauté the onions and potatoes in the butter 10 minutes. Add milk, cream, clam juice, herbs, and spices. Bring to scalding, lower heat, and simmer 20 minutes. Purée in a blender or a food processor, 2 cups at a time, or press through a sieve.
2. Turn oysters and their liquor into a small saucepan. Cook, uncovered, over medium heat, shaking the pan constantly, until all the oysters are curled at the edges, about 4 minutes. Pour the oysters into the purée and turn off heat. Stir in the sherry if you wish.

To serve: Ladle into big bowls.

To make ahead: Complete through Step 1, then finish just before serving.

OYSTER BISQUE YANKEE STYLE   Serves 4

This is similar to an oyster stew, but it is much thicker and richer—flavored with bread crumbs and butter.

1 dozen bluepoint oysters, shucked, or 1 pint shucked oysters and liquor
2 cups chicken broth
¾ cup fresh bread crumbs
1 medium slice onion
2 small stalks celery, chopped
1 teaspoon minced parsley

1 small bay leaf, crumpled
1 tablespoon butter
1 tablespoon all-purpose flour
2 cups milk
Salt and pepper
½ cup heavy cream, whipped with ¼ teaspoon salt
Crackers

1. Cut firm part of oysters from soft belly. Reserve soft part and liquor.
2. In a large saucepan over medium heat, combine firm part of oysters, broth, bread crumbs, onion, celery, parsley, and bay. Simmer, uncovered, 3 minutes. Remove bay. Purée broth in blender or food processor, 2 cups at a time.
3. Melt the butter in the saucepan over low heat, and stir in the flour. Beating constantly, add the purée and the oyster liquor. Raise heat to medium and stir in the milk and soft part of oysters. Cook 2 minutes. Lift oysters from broth with a slotted spoon and purée with 1 cup of broth. Combine both purées and reheat. Add salt and pepper to taste.

To serve: Ladle into bowls and garnish with salted whipped cream. Serve crackers on the side.

To make ahead: Complete through Step 2, then finish just before serving.

GREENFIELD CORN AND OYSTER STEW — Serves 8

Corn, oysters, and clams were part of the diet of the shore Indians who helped our forebears learn to live on the American continent—and all three blend well together in this historical stewy soup.

3 tablespoons butter
2 cups celery (6 to 8 stalks and leaves), minced fine
3 tablespoons all-purpose flour
1 teaspoon salt
⅛ teaspoon paprika
1 small bay leaf
1 cup bottled clam juice
3 cups milk
2 cups corn kernels, fresh or canned with juice
1 pink shucked oysters and liquor
1 cup heavy cream

In a large saucepan over medium heat, melt the butter and sauté the celery 5 minutes or until golden. Stir in the flour, add salt, paprika, and bay, and beating constantly, add the clam juice, milk, and corn. Cook, uncovered, 20 minutes. Stir in oysters and liquor, and cook until all oysters are curled at the edges, about 4 minutes. Remove from heat. Stir in the cream.

To serve: Ladle at once into hot soup bowls.

To make ahead: Complete through cooking of the corn, and just before serving, add the oysters and then the cream.

OYSTER, SHRIMP, AND OKRA GUMBO   Serves 12

Full of the special flavors of the South. This is a meal in itself.
Serve with hard rolls and butter. Wear gloves to seed and cut
up the hot pepper: they're dynamite!

1 whole 3 to 4 pound
  broiler, split
2 teaspoons salt
4 sprigs parsley
2 stalks celery, chopped
1 medium carrot, sliced in
  rounds
1 small onion, studded with
  4 whole cloves
2 large cloves garlic
8 peppercorns
5 quarts cold water
2 medium onions, chopped
1 small hot red pepper,
  seeded, chopped

2 cups cooked ham,
  chopped
1 teaspoon salt
½ teaspoon cayenne
⅛ teaspoon chili powder
1 pound okra, sliced, or 1
  10-ounce package frozen
  okra
1 pink shucked oysters
½ pound small shrimp,
  cooked, shelled
2 tablespoons filé power
2½ cups cooked rice
3 tablespoons minced
  parsley

1. In a large kettle over medium high heat, combine chicken with
   salt, parsley, celery, carrot. Add the onion stuck with cloves,
   the garlic, and peppercorns, knotted into a cheesecloth square.
   Add water and cook, uncovered, over medium heat 1 hour.
   Skim away scum that forms during first few minutes of cooking. Remove chicken and drain broth into a cool bowl and set
   in refrigerator. Skin and bone chicken and cut into 2-inch
   pieces. When fat has risen to top of broth, remove and reserve.
2. Spoon 2 tablespoons of chicken fat from the broth into the
   kettle and sauté the chopped onions and pepper over medium
   heat until onion is translucent, about 5 minutes. Add ham and
   sauté 5 minutes. Add chicken pieces, broth, salt, cayenne, and
   chili powder. Cover, reduce heat, and simmer 1 hour.
3. Add okra and cook 15 minutes. Add oysters and their liquid,
   and cook until edges of all the oysters are curled, about 4
   minutes. Add shrimp and cook 1 minute. Remove from heat.
   Mix ½ cup of broth with filé powder and stir into broth. Bring
   to scalding but do not boil. Taste and add salt and pepper if
   needed.

To serve: Divide cooked rice among bowls and ladle gumbo over
it. Garnish with parsley.

Dividends: Very good reheated.

To make ahead: Complete through Step 2, then finish shortly before serving.

CONCH, SCALLOPS, AND ABALONE

Scallops are shellfish, mollusks, as are oysters and clams. The edible part is a flat, round muscle that holds together two beautifully scalloped shells, like the Shell Oil signs. Tiny "bay" scallops half an inch or so in diameter, are very expensive and exquisitely tasty. The larger scallops are less expensive and perfect for soups and stews. They are sometimes referred to as "sea" scallops. Both types are found on the Atlantic and the Pacific coasts and in bays.

Abalone is found only on the West Coast. It is a sea snail and lives in a beautiful pearl-lined shell shaped like an ear. Chances are you will be buying it already prepared for cooking.

NANTUCKET SCALLOP CHOWDER   Serves 6

This may be made with the exquisite little bay scallops that are so costly, but it's just as good made with the big sea scallops that abound along the New England coast.

2 medium onions, chopped	¼ teaspoon dried thyme
4 tablespoons butter	4 cups scalded milk
1 pint scallops, chopped	Salt and pepper
1 cup diced potatoes	1 tablespoon minced dill
2 cups boiling water	

In a saucepan over medium heat, sauté the onions in the butter until translucent, about 5 minutes. Sauté scallops in the butter 3 minutes, then remove with a slotted spoon. Add potatoes, toss with butter and onion, then pour in boiling water, thyme, and simmer, covered, 12 to 15 minutes or until potatoes are tender. Add scallops and milk, and simmer 15 minutes. Add salt and pepper to taste.

To serve: Ladle into soup bowls and garnish with dill.

Dividends: Delicious reheated. Stretch with milk or clam juice.

To make ahead: Complete through cooking of potatoes, and finish shortly before serving.

SCALLOP CHOWDER NOVA SCOTIA STYLE   Serves 4

This is an easy-to-make fisherman's recipe from that great Canadian bay where the tides sometimes are seventy feet high, the Bay of Fundy. And the cod fishing is just great.

4 cups cold water	1 cup chopped carrot
1 teaspoon salt	1 cup chopped celery
⅛ teaspoon pepper	2 tablespoons butter
½ pound scallops, cut into ½-inch pieces	1 cup milk
	1 cup chicken broth
½ pound cod, cut into 1-inch pieces	Salt and pepper
	1 tablespoon chopped chives
1 cup chopped potato	

1. In a large kettle over high heat, bring the water with the salt and pepper to boiling. Add scallops and cod, reduce heat and simmer, uncovered, until the fish becomes opaque, about 5 minutes. Strain. Reserve fish and return broth to kettle. Raise heat to high.
2. Stir the potato, carrot, and celery into the broth, and simmer, uncovered, until vegetables are tender, about 15 minutes. Add the butter, milk, and chicken broth to the kettle. Turn half the fish and scallops into the kettle. Purée the chowder in a blender or a food processor, 2 cups at a time, or press through a sieve. Return purée to the kettle.
3. Add remaining fish and scallops, heat to just below boiling. Add salt and pepper to taste.

To serve: Ladle into soup bowls and garnish with chives.

Dividends: Very good reheated.

To make ahead: Complete through Step 3, reheat, and add chives just before serving.

SCALLOPS À LA NAGE   Serves 4

Coquilles St. Jacques is a famous French shellfish dish—scallops in a creamy mushroom sauce with bits of shrimp, and served on a scallop shell. This recipe is a delicious variation: a party soup.

1 small onion, minced	1 small carrot, minced
2 medium stalks celery, minced	4 sprigs parsley minced
	1 large leek, sliced thin

1 small bay leaf
1 teaspoon salt
¼ teaspoon pepper
2 tablespoons butter
1 pint scallops, small, or large, halved

2 tablespoons butter
1 cup milk
1 cup heavy cream
Cayenne
1 cup dry white wine

In a large saucepan over medium heat, sauté the onion, celery, carrot, parsley, and leek with the bay leaf, salt, and pepper in the butter, stirring, 10 minutes. Add the wine and scrape up the pan juices. Simmer until reduced by half, 8 to 10 minutes. Stir in the scallops and butter and stir 2 minutes. Add the milk and cream, scrape up the pan juices, and cook 1 minute. Add cayenne to taste.

To serve: Ladle into bowls.

ABALONE STEW   Serves 4

Abalone is one good reason to go to the West Coast, but it's tough to prepare unless it has been tenderized. Frozen, tenderized steaks reach the Atlantic Coast on occasion. If you have fresh abalone, slice it across the grain to ¼ inch thickness, and with a wooden mallet pound—and pound—and pound, until it is absolutely limp.

1 large onion, chopped
1 large clove garlic, minced
⅓ cup minced green bell pepper
2 large potatoes, chopped
4 tablespoons butter
1 small bay leaf
½ teaspoon dried thyme

½ teaspoon dried oregano
¼ teaspoon dried basil
1 8-ounce can tomato juice
3 cups water
2 tenderized abalone steaks, chopped
Salt and pepper

In a saucepan over medium heat, sauté the onion, garlic, and pepper with potatoes in the butter until the onion is translucent, 5 to 8 minutes. Stir in remaining ingredients except abalone, and bring to a boil. Cover, reduce heat, and simmer until potatoes are tender, about 12 to 15 minutes. Add abalone and simmer 8 to 10 minutes. Add salt and pepper to taste.

To serve: Ladle into soup bowls.

To make ahead: Complete through cooking of the vegetables, then finish shortly before serving.

CONCH CHOWDER Serves 6 to 8

Conch (pronounced *konk*) is the mollusk found in the beautiful conch shell. It's strongly flavored and can be very tough unless tenderized before using, even in a soup. Fresh conch is sold from fishing boats and in shops in Florida and along the Gulf Coast, and fresh is considered better than canned or frozen. Cut off the tough black end and the curled-up tip, and pound until very thin, then wash thoroughly before using.

8 large or 14 medium conchs, tenderized	1 teaspoon salt
	2 quarts water
¼ pound salt pork, chopped	1 tablespoon dried thyme
2 medium onions, chopped	1 small bay leaf
3 large stalks celery, chopped	1 6-ounce can tomato paste
	1 teaspoon lime juice
1 medium green pepper, chopped	Salt and pepper
	¾ cup heavy cream or evaporated milk
1 large carrot, chopped	
3 small potatoes, chopped	

1. Cut the conchs into ½-inch squares.
2. In a large kettle over medium heat, sauté the salt pork until the fat is rendered, then discard crisped bits. Stir in the onions, celery, pepper, carrot, and potatoes. Sprinkle with salt, reduce heat to medium, and cook, stirring, 10 minutes. Add the conchs, water, thyme, bay, tomato paste, and lime juice. Cover, bring to a simmer, reduce heat, and cook about 1 hour or until the conch is very tender. Add salt and pepper to taste.

To serve: Add the cream or evaporated milk, and ladle into bowls.

To make ahead: May be made several hours ahead.

COMBINATION SEAFOOD SOUPS

Bouillabaisse is one of the most famous combination seafood soups, but wherever there is an ocean, at least one rich, wonderful soup combining local herbs and local seafood has been invented.

The recipe given for bouillabaisse (page 196) is my favorite, but *real* bouillabaisse is different. The Bertrands, my friends in southern France, made it over an open fire in the backyard of their shore house. Into a big caldron half filled with water they put garlic, onions, tomatoes, basil, thyme, bay, salt, and pepper.

After these had simmered while the men fished, the catch went into the pot—fish, big and small, clams, mussels, sea urchins, crayfish, all of it. The fish cooked another 20 to 30 minutes, then the broth was served with big chunks of fresh French bread, butter, cheese, wine, and the dessert was fruit.

The progress approach to using fish and shellfish, illustrated in Sailaway Chowder, is one of my favorites.

FISH SOUP ADRIATIC STYLE   Serves 6

Like bouillabaisse, this is a recipe invented to use a fisherman's catch. Squid, cinnamon, and vinegar give it a piquant flavor. Choose tiny squid: they are the most tender.

2 pounds fish, such as sea trout, snapper, flounder, bass	2 teaspoons salt
	⅛ teaspoon pepper
	7 cups water
1 pound squid, 8-ounce size	1 small onion, chopped
1 small leek, chopped	1 small bay leaf
1 large stalk celery, chopped	1 stick cinnamon
2 medium cloves garlic, minced	2 sprigs parsley
	Salt and pepper
¼ cup olive oil	12 slices stale French bread
2 tablespoons wine vinegar	

1. Remove and reserve fish heads. Discard squid bone and ink sac; scrape skin with a sharp knife, wash, and cut squid into ½-inch pieces.
2. In a saucepan over medium heat, sauté the leek, celery, and garlic in half the oil until leek is translucent, 5 to 6 minutes. Add fish heads and squid. Sprinkle with vinegar and simmer, scraping up pan juices, until vinegar is gone. Add salt, pepper, and water; bring to a boil. Cover, reduce heat, and simmer 40 minutes. Strain. Reserve squid and broth. Pick flesh from fish heads and return to broth. Discard fish bones. Mash vegetables back into the broth.
3. In a saucepan over medium heat, sauté onion in remaining oil until translucent, about 5 minutes. Add fish bodies, bay, cinnamon, and parsley. Stir 3 minutes, turning fish often. Pour in squid and broth, and simmer 15 minutes, scraping up pan juices. Remove cinnamon and bay. Add salt and pepper to taste.

To serve: Arrange bread in bowls and ladle soup over, dividing fish among bowls.

CIOPPINO
Serves 4

A fisherman's catch recipe from the Italian colony in San Francisco, this is a companion piece to the French bouillabaisse, but it is strongly flavored with tomatoes. It's simpler than the French recipe, since you omit the whole business of preparing a fish broth from the fish trimmings.

2 medium onions, chopped
4 scallions, chopped
2 large cloves garlic, minced
⅓ cup chopped parsley
1 large green bell pepper, chopped
¼ cup olive oil
1 16-ounce can tomato purée
1 8-ounce can tomato sauce
3 cups cold water
½ cup dry white wine
1 tablespoon sugar
2 teaspoons salt
¼ teaspoon marjoram

¼ teaspoon dried oregano
¼ teaspoon pepper
1 small bay leaf
⅛ teaspoon dried rosemary
⅛ teaspoon dried thyme
2 1-pound lobsters, or 4 large lobster tails, or 12 large shrimp in the shell
1 pound fillets of white fish, such as haddock, whiting, cod, cut into 2-inch pieces
1 dozen cherrystone or littleneck clams
1 tablespoon chopped parsley

1. In a large saucepan over medium high heat, sauté the onions, scallions, garlic, parsley, and pepper in the oil until the onions begin to brown lightly, about 10 minutes. Add the tomato purée and sauce, water, wine, sugar, salt, and herbs. Bring to a boil, cover, reduce heat, and simmer 20 minutes.
2. Bury the lobsters or shrimp in the broth and cook 10 minutes for lobster, 3 minutes for shrimp. If using shrimp, remove and keep warm. Add the fish and cook 2 minutes. Set the shellfish on top, cover, and cook 8 minutes. Turn off heat. Take lobsters from broth, place on their backs, and slice down the middle. Crack the claws and knuckles. If using shrimp, shell, leaving tail shell on, and devein. Return lobster or shrimp to the broth, and reheat briefly.

To serve: Divide fish and shellfish among large soup plates, ladle broth over them, and garnish with parsley.

To make ahead: Complete through Step 1, then finish just before serving.

FISH SOUP ITALIAN STYLE   Serves 8

Variations on this theme are served all around the Mediterranean. Frozen rock lobster tails might be used instead of shrimp, and croutons instead of fried bread.

24 shellfish, such as mussels, soft-shell clams or cherrystones, and large shrimp
¼ cup olive oil
1 small onion, chopped
2 medium cloves of garlic, chopped
4 sprigs parsley, chopped
4 large ripe tomatoes, chopped
½ cup chopped fresh fennel tops

1 teaspoon saffron threads
1 teaspoon salt
¼ teaspoon pepper
2 pounds assorted fish fillets, such as flounder, haddock, cod
8 cups cold water
1 tablespoon butter
2 tablespoons olive oil
8 slices French bread
8 sprigs fresh parsley

1. Place the shellfish and 2 tablespoons of the oil in a large saucepan over medium heat. Cover and cook, shaking often, until mussels and clams open and shrimp are pink all over, 4 to 6 minutes. Turn off heat. Lift out the shellfish. Pour juices into a small bowl. Shell mussels and clams. Shell and devein shrimp. Place shellfish in the bowl with the pan juices.
2. Return the saucepan to medium heat with 2 tablespoons of oil, and add onion, garlic and parsley. Sauté until onion becomes translucent, about 5 minutes, then add tomatoes, fennel, saffron, salt, and pepper. Simmer, stirring, until sauce thickens. Add fish and water to cover. Scrape up pan juices, cover, and simmer 8 minutes. Stir in shellfish and their juices. Turn off heat. Pour into a large tureen
3. Return the saucepan to medium high heat. Melt the butter in the oil and sauté the bread until browned on both sides.

To serve: Place one slice of bread in each soup bowl and ladle soup over it, dividing fish and shellfish evenly among bowls. Garnish each bowl with a sprig of parsley.

Dividends: Leftover broth makes an elegant base for other fish soups. Freeze it if you can't use it within a day or two.

SAILAWAY CHOWDER

Makes 2 meals for 4 people

Here's a two-meal shore dinner designed for easy entertaining and big families, and named for dancer Sylvia Dick's Long Island home. The first day's dinner is a chowder rich in scallops, followed by chicken lobsters served with drawn butter. (Chicken lobsters are those under 1½ pounds each.) The second day's dinner, tangy with the broth the scallops and lobster were cooked in, is a fish soup with big portions of any fresh fish, including bluefish.

½ stick butter
2 large Bermuda onions, chopped
3 large potatoes, chopped
2 large carrots, chopped
3 quarts cold water
1 to 2 pounds whole fresh fish
2 medium bay leaves
8 peppercorns
½ teaspoon dried thyme
2 tablespoons salt

4 sprigs fresh parsley, minced
¼ pound bay scallops
4 chicken lobsters
½ pint heavy cream
4 tablespoons butter
½ stick butter
2 tablespoons strained lemon juice
4 pats butter
4 sprigs fresh parsley

1. In a large kettle over medium heat, melt the butter and sauté the onion until translucent, about 5 minutes. Add the potatoes and carrots, stir well, and sauté 5 minutes. Add the water. With a large, flat, sharp knife, fillet the fish, removing the flesh from the bones. Reserve for second meal. Tie the bones, with fish heads and trimmings, bay leaves and peppercorns, into a large square of cheesecloth, and add to the kettle with thyme, salt, and parsley. Raise heat, and when the kettle is boiling, reduce heat and simmer 1½ hours.

FIRST MEAL:

2. Wrap the scallops in cheesecloth and simmer in the broth until opaque, 5 to 10 minutes. Remove scallops from broth, and set aside 4 cups of broth. Keep warm.
3. Place lobsters in remaining simmering broth, cover, and cook 20 minutes more after broth returns to a boil. Meanwhile—

To serve scallops: Divide the reserved broth among 4 bowls; untie scallop bag, and divide scallops among bowls. Divide cream and butter among bowls. This constitutes your first course.

To serve lobster: Place butter in a small saucepan over medium heat, add lemon juice, and simmer together until butter froths. Remove lobsters from broth, set on backs, cut down the middle, and crack claws and knuckles. Place one lobster on each plate with a small bowl of drawn butter and lemon, and serve at once. This is the second course.

SECOND MEAL:

4. Return to the broth leftover bits of lobster and shells, tied into a cheesecloth square. Bring to a boil over medium high heat when ready to prepare second meal. Thin with a little water if broth seems too thick. Place fish fillets in boiling broth, cover, reduce heat and simmer 8 minutes.

To serve: Discard cheesecloth with lobster shells, and ladle broth and fish into 4 bowls. Place a pat of butter and a sprig of parsley in each.

SOLE, FLOUNDER, AND OTHER WHITE FISH

Most of the white fish on either coast are interchangeable in recipes. As a matter of fact, I can't think of a white fish that can't be used in place of any other white fish. Cooking times for most are the same, especially when fish is cut into 2-inch chunks. A fat, thick, dense fish obviously will take a little more time than a delicate tail piece of flounder, but fish flakes and is completely opaque when cooked, so it isn't hard to tell when the fish is finished.

Sole and flounder are interchangeable. Flounder is less expensive and makes first-rate soups and chowders. Cod and its relatives, like whiting, and haddock and its relatives, like snapper and scrod (small haddock), are interchangeable, too. Cod and haddock are interchangeable as well, though haddock has the finer flavor and is more expensive.

Sea bass, snapper, and sea trout can replace each other in most dishes, and go very well together in a medley recipe.

Don't hesitate to buy tail ends and side bits, chowder chunks, and other less desirable pieces of fish for making chowders and soups. You may have to remove some bones, but that is the only drawback. However, whatever you choose to make your fish soups and chowders with, be sure the fish is the freshest you can get. That's one rule worth repeating again and again. If it smells fishy, don't buy it!

Frozen fish is perfectly fine for soups, too, but be sure the brand is famous for the freshness of its product.

OLD-FASHIONED FISH CHOWDER
Serves 8

Every scrap of the fish went into our grandmother's "chowdy," and it was garnished with tough crackers that were soaked in milk before they were added to the broth.

1 4-pound cod or haddock	4 cups half-and-half or milk,
2 cups cold water	scalded
2-inch cube salt pork, diced	1 tablespoon salt
1 medium onion, sliced thin	⅛ teaspoon pepper
4 cups thinly sliced medium	3 tablespoons butter
potatoes	Chowder biscuits
2 cups boiling water	

1. Remove fish head, tail, gills and bits near the gills, and skin the body. With a large, sharp, flat knife fillet the fish, and cut into 2-inch pieces. Put fish trimmings into a large kettle. Reserve the fillets. Add cold water to kettle, bring to simmer over medium heat, cover, and cook 10 minutes. Drain and reserve the broth. Discard fish parts.
2. In a large saucepan over medium heat, sauté the salt pork 5 minutes. Add the onion and sauté until soft, about 5 minutes. With a slotted spoon, remove pork bits and reserve. Add potatoes and boiling water to the saucepan, scrape up pan juices, cover, and cook 5 minutes. Add fish and reserved broth, cover, and simmer 10 minutes. Add pork scraps, half-and-half or milk, salt, pepper, and butter, and heat to just below boiling.

To serve: Ladle into bowls and pass the crackers.

Dividends: Excellent stretched with a little milk.

To make ahead: Good made a day before.

FISH CHOWDER PORTUGUESE STYLE   Serves 8

Follow the recipe for Old-Fashioned Fish Chowder, but season in the last 15 minutes of cooking with ½ teaspoon saffron threads and 1 tablespoon of white vinegar.

FISH CHOWDER WITH TOMATO   Serves 8

Follow the recipe for Old-Fashioned Fish Chowder, but add a 14-ounce can of whole tomatoes in purée, or tomato purée when you add the potatoes. Season in the last 15 minutes of cooking with ½ teaspoon saffron threads and 1 tablespoon of white vinegar.

FISH CHOWDER BOSTON STYLE   Serves 8

Follow the recipe for Old-Fashioned Fish Chowder, but double the quantities of water, and include 1 small bay leaf, ½ teaspoon dried thyme, 1 stalk of celery, chopped, in the water the fish trimmings are cooked in. Use ½ pound of salt pork, and stir 4 tablespoons all-purpose flour into the fat before adding the potatoes and boiling water. Use 2 cups of milk instead of 4 cups of half-and-half, and do not use butter—the fat from the extra amount of salt pork will be enough.

NAUSET CHOWDER   Serves 8

Follow the recipe for Old-Fashioned Fish Chowder but stir 2 tablespoons all-purpose flour into the salt pork fat before adding the potatoes and boiling water. Reduce potatoes to 2 cups, and chop them instead of slicing. Garnish with parsley sprigs.

Nauset is a magnificent beach on Cape Cod, which juts, like a bent arm, into the Atlantic for fifty miles or so. It's south of Boston and one of the early areas of settlement by Europeans in America, as historic, in its way, as Plymouth Rock.

FLOUNDER CHOWDER   Serves 6 to 8

Flounder and sole, filleted, are boneless and therefore everyone's favorite fish. The expensive lemon sole and Dover sole are too exquisite to use in a chowder. Instead, select an inexpensive gray flounder or catch your own for use in fish soup recipes.

3 large onions, chopped	$\frac{1}{2}$ teaspoon dried thyme
4 tablespoons butter	1 medium bay leaf
2 quarts cold water	1 to 2 pounds flounder, cut
4 medium potatoes, chopped	in 2-inch pieces
1 tablespoon salt	2 tablespoons minced
10 peppercorns	parsley

1. In a saucepan over medium heat, sauté the onions in the butter until translucent, 6 to 7 minutes. Add remaining ingredients except the fish and parsley, bring to a boil, cover, reduce heat, and simmer 15 to 20 minutes or until potatoes are tender. Purée in a blender or a food processor, 2 cups at a time, or press through a sieve.
2. Add the fish pieces and simmer uncovered 30 minutes more.

To serve: Ladle into bowls and garnish with parsley.

Dividends: Stretch with milk. Reheat without boiling.

To make ahead: Complete through Step 1, then finish just before serving.

FISH CHOWDER WITH WINE, FRENCH STYLE   Serves 6

Here's a French chowder—*chaudrée*—in which the potatoes are used whole, rather than cut up as in American chowder recipes.

3 medium onions, chopped	1 clove garlic, minced
4 tablespoons butter	1 teaspoon salt
1 small bay leaf	3 cups dry white wine
3 whole cloves	3 cups water
1 sprig fresh dill	3 pounds cod, haddock,
2 sprigs parsley	whiting, or flounder, cut
6 peppercorns	into 2-inch pieces
6 to 12 very small new potatoes, peeled or scraped	

1. In a saucepan over medium heat, sauté the onions in the butter until translucent, about 5 minutes. Add the bay, cloves, dill,

parsley, and peppercorns tied into a small cheesecloth bag. Add potatoes, garlic, salt, wine, and water. Scrape up pan juices, cover, reduce heat, and simmer 15 minutes. Remove the potatoes, and keep warm in a tureen.

2. Add the fish, cover, and simmer 15 minutes. Strain broth and measure. Place fish in tureen and discard herb bag. If broth measures more than 4 cups, return to saucepan, raise heat, and boil to reduce to desired quantity. Pour over potatoes and fish.

To serve: Ladle into bowls, dividing potatoes and fish among them.

To make ahead: Complete through Step 2, then finish just before serving.

POOR MAN'S LOBSTER SOUP   Serves 6

Very fresh young haddock just off a fisherman's boat, poached 20 minutes and served with drawn butter, can taste like lobster. And it makes an elegant soup. But to catch the flavor of lobster, it must really be very fresh.

1 quart cold water	1 cup mashed potatoes or
1 tablespoon salt	cracker crumbs
1/8 teaspoon pepper	1 small slice onion, grated
2 large sprigs fresh dill, or	2 teaspoons strained lemon
1 teaspoon dried	juice
1/8 teaspoon dried thyme	4 tablespoons butter
1 pound haddock fillets	2 tablespoons minced
1 10¾-ounce can condensed	parsley
tomato bisque	

In a kettle over high heat, bring the water with the salt, pepper, dill, and thyme to a rapid boil. Add the fish, reduce heat, cover, and simmer 15 minutes. Discard dill sprigs. Stir in bisque, potatoes or cracker crumbs, onion, and lemon juice. Simmer 5 minutes.

To serve: Ladle into bowls. Dot with butter and garnish with parsley.

BASQUE FISH SOUP WITH GARLIC
Serves 6 to 8

This is the ultimate basic fish recipe. Use it with any white fish you encounter.

4 medium onions, chopped	1½ pounds cod, haddock,
¼ cup olive oil	hake, or other white fish,
2 quarts cold water	cut into 2-inch pieces
⅛ teaspoon dried thyme	¼ cup butter
⅛ teaspoon tarragon	2 medium cloves garlic,
1 small bay leaf	minced
2 large sprigs parsley	6 to 8 thick slices French
1 teaspoon salt	bread
⅛ teaspoon pepper	

1. In a saucepan over medium heat, sauté the onions in the oil until translucent, about 6 minutes. Add the water, herbs, and seasonings, bring to a rapid boil, and add the fish. Reduce heat and simmer, uncovered, for 1 hour.
2. About 20 minutes before the fish will be done, melt the butter in a saucepan over medium heat, sauté the garlic 1 minute, then sauté the bread slices on either side until well browned.

To serve: Place a slice of sautéed bread in each bowl and ladle the soup over it. Save the last of the soup to rinse out the bread sautéeing pan, then pour over bread slices.

Dividends: Reheat and stretch with milk or clam juice.

To make ahead: Complete through Step 1, then finish just before serving.

HADDOCK CREAM SWEDISH STYLE   Serves 8

This is a Swedish velouté, a creamy soup enriched with eggs. It's time-consuming, but very, very good.

2 quarts cold water	1 3-pound haddock
1 tablespoon salt	3 tablespoons butter
8 peppercorns	3 tablespoons all-purpose
3 whole cloves	flour
6 medium carrots, cut in	2 cups milk
strips	2 egg yolks
Tops and leaves of 1 bunch	½ cup heavy cream
celery	Salt and pepper
Half bunch parsley, chopped	

1. In a kettle over high heat, bring the water with the salt, peppercorns, and cloves to a rapid boil. Add the carrot strips and cook until just tender; remove gently and reserve. Put the celery and parsley into the broth, cover, reduce heat, and simmer 1 hour. Strain broth, and discard vegetables and herbs. Return broth to kettle and bring back to a boil.
2. Place the whole fish in the broth, cover, reduce heat, and simmer 20 minutes. Lift out the fish. Remove and discard skin, bones, head, tail, and gills. Break flesh into small flakes.
3. In a saucepan over low heat, melt the butter and stir in the flour. Beating constantly, add the broth and the milk, and cook, stirring, until bubbly. In a small bowl, beat the egg yolks until thick and lemon-colored. Stir in the cream. Stir 1 cup hot broth into the egg mixture, then return mixture to the soup. Stirring, heat to just below boiling. Gently fold in carrot strips and fish. Add salt and pepper to taste.

To serve: Ladle into bowls.

Dividends: Very good reheated. Stretch with cream.

To make ahead: Complete through Step 2, then finish before serving.

STRONGLY FLAVORED FISH

Salmon and mackerel are delicious but strongly flavored fish not much used for soups. However, tail pieces and other trim from either these or other flavorful seafoods, make good soup when handled as described below in the recipe for Salmon Soup with White Wine.

The perch recipe here is one to use with eels, or small carp, or tiny bluefish—almost anything, in fact, the day's catch brings.

SALMON BISQUE   Serves 4

This begins with cooked salmon. It's a recipe I use to employ fatty tail pieces and untidy chunks of salmon left over from a buffet dinner of cold salmon where guests helped themselves and demolished the fish in the process.

> 2 cups cooked salmon
> 1 cup salmon cooking liquid, fish broth, or bottled clam juice
> 4 tablespoons butter
> 4 tablespoons all-purpose flour
>
> 4 cups milk, scalded
> Salt and pepper
> 1/8 teaspoon grated nutmeg
> 1 tablespoon minced fresh dill

1. Flake salmon and discard bones. Pour over it cooking liquid, fish broth, or clam juice. Purée in a blender or a food processor, 2 cups at a time, or press through a sieve.
2. In a saucepan over low heat, melt the butter and stir in the flour. Stir in the fish purée. Beating constantly, add the scalded milk, and cook, stirring, until bubbly. Season with salt and pepper to taste, and nutmeg. Let stand, one hour, covered.

To serve: Reheat to just below boiling, then ladle into bowls and garnish with dill.

To make ahead: Excellent made hours or a day ahead. Do not boil when reheating.

MESS O' PERCH SOUP   Serves 4

You can make this with little eels, too (and call it Eel Soup), or small carp. Since it includes fish bones, children are not fond of it. Perch is sold frozen by the pound in bags. Be sure it is a brand you can trust to have done a good job of freezing and maintaining the fish frozen. The perch are sold, whether fresh or frozen, cleaned, but otherwise intact. If you catch your own, clean the fish, but remove only the heads.

1 large leek, chopped	⅛ teaspoon dried sage
2 small carrots, sliced thin	1 small bay leaf
8 tablespoons butter	2 teaspoons salt
1 pound (about 24) perch, frozen or fresh, cut into 2-inch lengths	⅛ teaspoon pepper
	1 tablespoon minced parsley
1¼ cups dry white wine	8 thick slices fresh French bread
3 cups cold water	
⅛ teaspoon dried thyme	Butter

In a large saucepan over medium heat, sauté the leek and carrots in half the butter until the leek becomes translucent, about 5 minutes. Add the remaining butter and the fish pieces. Toss fish in the vegetables 2 minutes, then pour in the wine and scrape up the pan juices. Add water, thyme, sage, bay, salt, and pepper. Cover, bring to a boil, reduce heat, and simmer 20 minutes. Discard bay.

To serve: Ladle into bowls, garnish with parsley, and pass the bread and butter.

SALMON SOUP WITH WHITE WINE   Serves 6 to 8

Served with hot biscuits and a hearty salad, this can be a complete meal. It is most elegant made with salmon, but would be good made with mackerel or bluefish, too.

5 cups cold water	1 small bay leaf
1 cup dry white wine	4 peppercorns
1 teaspoon salt	1 pound fresh salmon,
1 small onion	wrapped in cheesecloth
1/8 teaspoon ground cloves	3 tablespoons butter
4 very thin lemon slices with	1 teaspoon finely minced
rind, halved	parsley
1 medium carrot, chopped	
2 sprigs fresh parsley	
1/4 teaspoon dried thyme	

In a large kettle over medium high heat, combine all ingredients up to the fish. Bring to a boil, reduce heat, and simmer, covered, 15 minutes. Add the fish, cover, and simmer 30 minutes or until fish flakes easily. Remove cheesecloth-wrapped fish and strain broth, discarding herbs and carrot, but not lemon. Open cheesecloth bag, break fish into big flakes, and return flakes to broth. Reheat but do not boil.

To serve: Ladle into bowls, dividing fish and lemon slices among them. Garnish with dab of butter and sprinkling of minced parsley.

To make ahead: May be made hours or a day ahead.

Five

CLEVER, THOSE EDWARDIANS

These are the soups my mother served at the beginning of just about every meal. You'll find most of them on menus in good restaurants, and they are beginning to make a comeback in the home. With high meat costs making the curbing of appetites a very good idea and our current concern with vegetarian thinking and slim, elegant bodies, the Edwardian/Victorian first course is a very good idea.

These soups have another big attraction, too. Think of the same old hamburger for dinner. Then think of beginning the meal with a creamy Purée of Peas, or a wonderful crunchy Watercress Soup (made from stem ends, naturally, for economy's sake). Or consider the economy omelet dinner (what's lower in calories and cost?) preceded by Curried Cream of Lettuce. It works! Everything looks caring, and good, and you fill up but not out, and the savings are significant.

A number of the soups in this chapter make wonderful luncheon fare, by the way, with or without a sandwich. Cream of Chicken Soup, the old-fashioned way, makes a great dinner. Just add hot biscuits! (You'll find lots more main-course soup recipes in Chapter 3.) But don't overlook the soups here when planning a party meal. The costs are minimal, and the effect very special when you can say you made the soup yourself. Cream of Chicken Soup—Rich, Favorite Mushroom Soup with a few slices of raw mushroom floating on top, Curried Avocado Soup—these are real luxuries, but we can afford them!

RICH APPLE SOUP   Serves 4 to 6

A tangy variation on chicken soup.

2 tablespoons butter	1½ cups Chicken and Rice
1 small onion, chopped	Soup (page 91)
1 large tart apple, grated	1 cup half-and-half
1 teaspoon turmeric	1 cup heavy cream
¼ teaspoon ground cumin	Salt and pepper

In a kettle over medium heat, melt the butter and sauté the onion until translucent, about 5 minutes. Add the apple and sauté until tender, 4 to 5 minutes. Stir in the turmeric, cumin, and soup. Simmer 10 minutes. Purée in a blender or a food processor, or press through a sieve. Return to the kettle, and stir in the half-

and-half and the heavy cream. Add salt and pepper to taste. Heat through, but do not let boil.

To serve: Ladle into consommé cups.

Dividends: Delicious chilled.

To make ahead: May be made hours or a day ahead.

CONSOMMÉ AND CREAM WITH APPLE   Serves 6 to 8

Really tart apples are needed to make this soup as it should be. Granny Smith is a good choice for the green apple, and don't peel either apple. Tossing the grated red apple with lemon juice helps prevent discoloration.

1 large onion	Salt to taste
2 cups boiling water	⅛ teaspoon paprika
1 large tart green apple	⅛ teaspoon turmeric
3 10-ounce cans beef broth	½ ripe red apple, chopped
1½ cups heavy cream	1 tablespoon lemon juice

1. In a small kettle over high heat, boil the onion in the water 2 minutes. Discard the water.
2. In a food processor, or with a hand grater, grate the onion and the green apple. Combine with the broth in a kettle over medium heat, cover, bring to a boil, reduce heat, and simmer 10 minutes. Purée in a blender or a food processor, 2 cups at a time, or press through a sieve. Return to the kettle and over low heat, stir in the cream, salt, paprika, and turmeric.
3. Toss the chopped apple well with the lemon juice.

To serve: Ladle hot broth into bowls and garnish with chopped apple.

Dividends: Nice as a cold soup, too.

To make ahead: Complete through Step 2, then finish just before serving, but don't chop the red apple until ready to serve the soup.

ELEGANT CREAM OF ARTICHOKE SOUP   Serves 4 to 6

Rich and just right to begin a party dinner. When artichokes are unavailable fresh, a package of small, frozen choke hearts may be used instead—about 8 ounces.

5 cups chicken broth	1 tablespoon cornstarch
1 small onion, chopped	4 tablespoons cold water
1 small leek, chopped	Salt and pepper
1 stalk celery, chopped	¼ cup dry sherry
Hearts of 4 cooked large artichokes	½ cup light cream

1. In a large saucepan over medium heat, place the broth and the vegetables; simmer, uncovered, 30 minutes. Purée in a blender or a food processor, 2 cups at a time, or press through a sieve. Return to saucepan.
2. In a measuring cup, dissolve cornstarch in the cold water. Over medium heat, stir the cornstarch into the soup, and cook until soup thickens. Add salt and pepper to taste.

To serve: Stir in sherry and cream, and serve at once.

Dividends: Serve leftovers cold with a sprinkling of chopped chives.

To make ahead: Complete through Step 2, then reheat just before serving and stir in sherry and cream.

CREAM OF ASPARAGUS SOUP   Serves 4 to 6

Raymond Oliver in that magnificent French cookbook, *La Cuisine,* enriches his Cream of Asparagus soup with 4 egg yolks and uses broth rather than milk and cream as the liquid. This version is lighter and makes a more suitable first course for a modern household.

½ cup sour cream	2 tablespoons butter
1 cup heavy cream	2 tablespoons all-purpose flour
1 pound asparagus, green part only, cut into 1- to 2-inch lengths	1 cup milk
4 cups chicken broth	Salt and pepper
	⅛ teaspoon ground mace

1. In a small bowl, place the sour cream and stir in the heavy cream. Cover and let rest at room temperature.

2. In a kettle over medium high heat, place the chicken broth and the asparagus pieces. Bring to a boil, cover, lower heat, and simmer 15 to 20 minutes or until asparagus is tender. Purée in a blender or a food processor, 2 cups at a time, or press through a sieve.
3. In the kettle over medium low heat, melt the butter and stir in the flour. Beating constantly, add the asparagus purée, and cook, stirring, until bubbly, 1 to 2 minutes. Stir in milk. Stir combined creams into the soup, add salt and pepper to taste, and mace, and heat to just below boiling.

To serve: Ladle into soup bowls.

Dividends: Excellent reheated. Stretch with milk or broth.

To make ahead: The basic soup, without the cream, may be made hours or days ahead. It stores and freezes well.

CURRIED AVOCADO SOUP   Serves 4 to 6

Avocados can be tasteless unless fully ripe, so choose fruit that is definitely soft to the touch without being mushy. You'll find a recipe for a cold avocado soup in Chapter 10, but this one is nice hot.

1 medium onion, minced	2 large ripe avocados
2 tablespoons butter	1 tablespoon strained lemon
2 teaspoons curry powder	juice
1 teaspoon turmeric	¾ cup sour cream
3 cups chicken broth	Salt and pepper

1. In a saucepan over medium heat, sauté the onion in the butter until translucent, about 5 minutes. Stir in the curry, turmeric, and broth. Bring to a boil, cover, lower heat, and simmer 3 minutes.
2. Halve the avocados, discard pits, scoop the meat out with a round teaspoon, and purée with lemon juice and hot broth in a blender or a food processor, 2 cups at a time, or press through a sieve. Return to the saucepan and heat gently, stirring in half the sour cream. Do not allow to boil. Add salt and pepper to taste, and more lemon juice if flavor seems bland.

To serve: Ladle into soup bowls and garnish with remaining sour cream.

BEET SOUP   Serves 4 to 6

A brilliant red soup with a sharp tang, made from crops you
harvest at the summer's end. So pretty it's also ideal to start a
holiday meal . . . make it with canned beets and a 16-ounce can
of cooked whole tomatoes if the garden is under snow.

6 small beets	Juice of ½ lemon, strained
2 large ripe tomatoes,	Salt and pepper
skinned, seeded, diced	Sour cream
2 cups beef broth	Minced parsley or chives
1 cup dry red wine	
1 small onion, stuck with 3	
cloves	

1. In a large saucepan over medium heat, simmer beets in enough
   water to cover, covered, about 8 to 10 minutes. Drain, reserving ½ cup cooking liquid. Slip skins from beets, and dice beets.
   Return to saucepan with reserved liquid.
2. Add tomatoes, beef broth, wine, onion, and lemon juice. Bring
   to a boil, reduce heat, cover, and simmer 10 minutes. Discard
   onions. Add salt and pepper to taste.

To serve: Ladle into soup bowls and garnish with a big dab of
sour cream and a sprinkling of minced parsley or chives.

Dividends: Reheat with light cream to stretch.

To make ahead: Complete through Step 1, then finish just before
serving.

FANCY CREAM OF BROCCOLI SOUP   Serves 6 to 8

This is so rich it makes a meal if it is served with hot butter
biscuits, and a salad. Four cups of broccoli is about what I get
when I peel the stems and chop stems, leaves, and tops of a small
bunch of broccoli.

1 bunch broccoli, chopped	2 egg yolks
8 cups chicken broth	1 cup heavy cream
2 tablespoons butter	Salt and pepper
2 tablespoons all-purpose	Ground coriander
flour	

1. In a saucepan over medium high heat, combine broccoli and
   broth. Cover and cook until broccoli is tender, about 15 min-

utes. Purée in a blender or a food processor, 2 cups at a time, or press through a sieve.

2. In the saucepan over low heat, heat the butter and stir in the flour. Beating constantly, add the puréed broccoli, and cook, stirring, until bubbly.
3. In a small bowl beat the egg yolks until thick and lemon-colored; stir in the cream and 1 cup of the purée. Return the egg mixture to the saucepan, add salt, pepper, and coriander to taste, and heat to just below boiling.

To serve: Ladle into soup bowls.

HEARTY CABBAGE SOUP   Serves 6 to 8

White cabbage is also called winter cabbage—the kind you find in the garden at the end of the growing season.

6 cups beef broth	Salt and pepper
2 medium onions, chopped	1 tablespoon all-purpose
2 medium carrots, chopped	flour
2 large stalks celery, chopped	2 tablespoons cold water
1 small white cabbage, shredded fine	½ cup sour cream
	2 tablespoons minced dill

1. In a large kettle over high heat, bring broth to boiling. Add onions, carrots, and celery. Reduce heat, cover, and simmer 15 minutes. Add cabbage, cover, and cook until vegetables are tender, about 15 minutes. Add salt and pepper to taste.
2. In a small bowl with a wire whisk, blend the flour and water into a paste. Stir in the sour cream and blend well.
3. Beat sour cream a little at a time into soup. Continue stirring over heat until soup is almost boiling, but do not boil.

To serve: Ladle into soup bowls and sprinkle with dill.

Dividends: Stretch leftovers with more beef broth.

To make ahead: May be completed hours before serving.

CABBAGE CREAM   Serves 4

The green cabbage found on the market in spring is the best kind
to use here.

½ medium green cabbage,   1½ quarts boiling chicken
   chopped   broth
4 medium potatoes,   ½ cup heavy cream
   chopped   Salt and pepper
4 large leeks, chopped   3 tablespoons butter

In a large kettle over medium heat, combine the vegetables and
boiling broth, and cook 15 to 20 minutes or until the potatoes
begin to look rubbed on the edges. Reduce heat, and stir in the
cream, salt and pepper to taste, and the butter.

To serve: Ladle into bowls.

CABBAGE SOUP L'ÉNARDIÈRE   Serves 6 to 8

This is the family recipe for cabbage soup. It's a basic broth you
can dress up with any handy vegetable—cooked or uncooked—
from shredded turnips to broccoli stems (peeled). Add uncooked
vegetables early, and cooked vegetables toward the end of the
cooking.

1 small onion, minced   1 stalk celery, chopped
2 tablespoons butter   1 small green cabbage,
2 quarts cold water   shredded
2 large potatoes, peeled,   1 tablespoon salt
   chopped   Salt and pepper
1 carrot, chopped   1 tablespoon butter
1 large sprig parsley   2 tablespoons minced parsley

1. In a saucepan over medium heat, sauté the onion in the butter
   until translucent, about 5 minutes. Add the water, raise heat,
   and bring to a boil. Add potatoes, carrot, parsley, and celery.
   Return to a boil, cover, lower heat, and simmer until potatoes
   begin to disintegrate, about 30 minutes. Mash potatoes in the
   kettle with a potato masher.
2. Add cabbage and salt. Simmer, uncovered, until cabbage is
   just tender but still green, 10 to 12 minutes. Add salt and
   pepper to taste.

To serve: Just before serving add butter and parsley to saucepan,
stir, then ladle soup into bowls.

CARROT AND CELERY SOUP   Serves 6 to 8

This is quick, easy, and wonderfully inexpensive—just as good made with winter vegetables as with the garden's fresh summer produce.

1 medium onion, chopped	2 teaspoons salt
3 tablespoons butter	⅛ teaspoon pepper
3 large carrots, chopped	⅛ teaspoon dried thyme
1 small head celery and leaves, chopped	1 cup light cream
6 cups water	2 teaspoons butter
1 large clove garlic, minced	1 tablespoon minced parsley

In a saucepan over medium heat, sauté the onion in the butter until translucent, about 5 minutes. Add the carrot and celery, and sauté, stirring often, until somewhat soft, about 10 minutes. Add the water, cover, and simmer over reduced heat 25 minutes. Add garlic, salt, pepper, thyme, and cook 1 minute, then stir in cream.

To serve: Ladle into soup bowls and finish with a bit of butter and minced parsley.

Dividends: Excellent reheated. Stretch by adding milk.

To make ahead: May be made hours or a day ahead. Finish just before serving.

CREAM OF CHICKEN SOUP—RICH   Serves 4 to 6

Good cream of chicken soups begin with a broth made with the chicken giblets, like the stock I call Chicken Broth à la Supermarket. Nice with rice or noodles added.

4 tablespoons butter	2 egg yolks
4 tablespoons all-purpose flour	½ cup heavy cream
5 cups hot Chicken Broth à la Supermarket (page 48)	Salt and pepper

1. In a kettle over low heat, melt the butter and stir in the flour. Beating constantly, add the broth, and cook, stirring, until bubbly, 1 to 2 minutes. Cover and simmer very slowly 30 minutes.
2. In a small bowl beat the egg yolks until thick and lemon-colored, then stir in the cream. Stir in 1 cup of hot broth, then add mixture to the kettle. Add salt and pepper to taste, and heat to just below boiling.

To serve: Ladle into soup bowls.

Dividends: This soup is used as a base for many other soups.

To make ahead: Complete through Step 1, and store in the refrigerator or freeze. Add eggs, or just cream, when ready to use.

CREAM OF CELERY SOUP   Serves 4

Tops and leaves of a large stalk of celery make about half a cup of chopped celery, so use the tops and save the stalks for other dishes.

1 small onion, chopped	2 cups hot veal broth
1 cup chopped celery	2 cups hot milk
2 tablespoons butter	⅛ teaspoon grated nutmeg
2 tablespoons all-purpose flour	Salt and pepper
	Chopped celery leaves

In a saucepan over medium heat, sauté the onion and celery in the butter until onion begins to be translucent, 5 to 7 minutes. Lower heat, and stir in the flour. Beating constantly, add hot broth and milk, and cook, stirring, until bubbly, 1 to 2 minutes. Cook at just below boiling for a few minutes. Season with nutmeg, add salt and pepper to taste.

To serve: Ladle into soup bowls and garnish with celery leaves.

Dividends: Excellent reheated. Stretch with milk or broth.

To make ahead: May be made hours or a day ahead.

CELERY ROOT SOUP

Serves 6 to 8

Celery root, or celeriac, is the knobby, golden-brown root offered in Oriental and special groceries. It makes a celerier-than-celery soup, greened by cups of fresh (or frozen) peas.

2 tablespoons butter	2 cups large green peas
1 small onion, chopped	2 cups milk
1 large celery root, peeled, diced or chopped	Salt and pepper
	1 cup Croutons, Sautéed in Butter (page 33)
1 large white potato, peeled, diced or chopped	Pinch ground mace
3 cups boiling water	

1. In a large kettle over medium heat, melt butter and sauté onion, celeriac, and potato, stirring constantly, 5 to 8 minutes. Add boiling water, cover, raise heat, and boil hard 10 to 15 minutes or until celeriac is tender. Add green peas, and cook 10 minutes or until peas are slipping their skins. Purée in a blender or a food processor, 2 cups at a time, or press through a sieve.
2. Return to kettle, add milk, and heat to just below boiling. Add salt and pepper to taste.

To serve: Ladle into soup bowls, divide croutons among them, and garnish with a bit of ground mace.

To make ahead: Complete to the point where peas are to be added, then finish shortly before serving.

CREAM OF CORN SOUP   Serves 6

This is almost as good, and a lot faster to make, prepared using a 20-ounce can of cream style corn and its liquid instead of corn kernels and milk.

2¼ cups raw corn kernels	⅛ teaspoon pepper
3 cups milk	⅛ teaspoon grated nutmeg
¼ cup minced onion	2 cups milk
3 tablespoons butter	1 cup light cream
3 tablespoons all-purpose flour	1 tablespoon minced chives
	1 tablespoon butter
1½ teaspoons salt	

1. In a small saucepan over medium heat, simmer corn with milk, uncovered, until very tender, about 10 to 15 minutes.
2. In a saucepan over medium heat, sauté the onion in the butter until translucent, about 5 minutes. Lower heat and stir in the flour. Beating constantly, add the hot corn and milk, and cook, stirring, until bubbly, 1 to 2 minutes. Add remaining ingredients except chives and butter, and heat to boiling, then cook 3 minutes, stirring occasionally.

To serve: Ladle into soup bowls and garnish with chives and a dab of butter in each bowl.

Dividends: Nice reheated with milk.

To make ahead: Keeps well for several days.

SPICY CORN SOUP   Serves 6 to 8

Followed by a blue cheese salad and a dessert, this makes a nice lunch.

1 medium onion, minced	3 cups (about 6 ears) raw corn kernels
4 tablespoons butter	
1 teaspoon dry mustard	6 cups chicken broth
1 teaspoon sugar	1 cup light cream
1 teaspoon salt	Tabasco sauce
1 tablespoon lemon juice	Paprika

In a large, heavy saucepan over medium heat, sauté onion in butter until translucent, about 5 minutes. Blend in mustard, sugar, salt, and lemon juice, and simmer a minute or two, stirring. Add corn and broth. Bring to a boil, cover, reduce heat, and simmer until corn is tender, about 10 minutes.

To serve: Add cream and a dash of Tabasco, and reheat, but do not boil. Ladle into soup bowls and dust with paprika.

Dividends: Delicious chilled.

To make ahead: Make days or hours before serving, but add cream and complete just before serving.

CURRIED CREAM OF LETTUCE SOUP Serves 4 to 6

This calls for a head of Boston lettuce, but you can use the equivalent amount of lettuce gathered either as thinnings from a newly planted row of lettuce, or as side leaves from a looseleaf type. Ruby oakleaf lettuce is pretty in this soup and tastes good.

6 scallions, chopped
3 tablespoons bacon or fat
  from ham roast
1 teaspoon curry powder
1 teaspoon tarragon
½ teaspoon turmeric
1 large head Boston lettuce,
  shredded
⅓ cup water
3 cups milk
1 cup light cream
Salt and pepper
3 hard-boiled eggs, chopped

1. In a large kettle over medium heat, sauté scallions in bacon or ham fat until translucent, about 5 minutes. Stir in curry, tarragon, turmeric, and cook, stirring, 1 minute. Add lettuce and water, cover, and cook until lettuce is tender, about 5 minutes.
2. Purée in a blender or a food processor, 2 cups at a time, or press through a sieve. Return to the kettle, stir in milk and cream, add salt and pepper to taste, and reheat to just below boiling.

To serve: Ladle into soup bowls and garnish with chopped egg.

LETTUCE SOUP WITH PEAS
Serves 6

In early spring when lettuce rows are popping in the garden and need lots of thinning, and when peas are ripening on the vine, make this delicate and delicious green soup.

1 medium onion, chopped	6 cups chicken broth
1 whole leek, chopped fine	½ cup heavy cream
3 tablespoons butter	Salt and pepper
1 big head of lettuce, shredded	1 teaspoon minced fresh mint
1 cup peas	
3 tablespoons all-purpose flour	

1. In a large kettle over medium heat, sauté onion and leek in butter until onion is translucent, about 5 minutes. Add lettuce and peas. Cover and cook about 5 minutes. Sprinkle with flour, stirring, then add broth, stirring continually until soup thickens.
2. Purée in a blender or a food processor, 2 cups at a time, or press through a sieve. Return to kettle, add cream, and heat to just below boiling. Add salt and pepper to taste.

To serve: Ladle into soup bowls and garnish with a bit of mint.

VICHYSSOISE
Serves 6

This is the most famous of iced soups—a beautiful creamy leek-and-potato concoction garnished with a bit of chervil or, if you prefer, chives and a chive bloom. This recipe calls for beef broth as the liquid, but it also is made with veal broth and chicken broth, and it is almost as good. Serve it in elegantly frosted glass bowls.

5 to 6 medium leeks, whites only, sliced thinly	1 cup heavy cream
4 tablespoons butter	Salt and pepper
4 cups beef broth	2 tablespoons minced fresh chervil, or chives and chive blooms
4 medium potatoes, sliced	
1 cup sour cream	

1. In a large saucepan over medium low heat, sauté the leeks in the butter, covered, until limp, 10 to 15 minutes. Leeks must

not color or brown. Add the broth and potatoes, cover, and simmer 40 minutes, or until potatoes are very tender. Purée in a blender or a food processor, 2 cups at a time, or press through a sieve. Chill several hours or overnight.
2. Combine sour and heavy creams; chill.
3. Blend soup and cream, and season with salt and pepper to taste.

To serve: Ladle into iced soup bowls and garnish with herbs.

Dividends: Vichyssoise makes a wonderful base for any leftover vegetable. See, for instance, the recipe for Watercress Soup in this chapter.

To make ahead: Best if the base is made well ahead, but add creams just before serving.

CREAM OF MUSHROOM SOUP   Serves 6

If you'd like a lighter soup as your cream of mushroom staple, substitute milk for cream here.

1 pound mushrooms, wiped clean, chopped	4 cups hot chicken broth
4 tablespoons butter	1 cup heavy cream
1 clove garlic, minced	Salt and pepper
6 scallions, chopped	3 to 6 white mushroom caps, sliced
4 tablespoons all-purpose flour	Chopped chives

In a large saucepan over medium heat, sauté the mushrooms in the butter with the garlic and scallions for 7 to 8 minutes, stirring. Stir in the flour, lower heat, and remove the saucepan to let it cool down a bit. Return to heat, and stir in the hot broth, beating constantly. Cook, stirring, until bubbly, 1 to 2 minutes. Stir in the cream, and add salt and pepper to taste, then sliced mushrooms.

To serve: Ladle into soup bowls and garnish with chives.

Dividends: Leftovers make a great beginning for other soups and can be used as sauce to enhance pan gravies.

To make ahead: Keeps well for several days.

FAVORITE MUSHROOM SOUP   Serves 4

This takes about 15 minutes to make, and it is divine—that's why it is my favorite. I use 8-ounce bottles of clam juice to make this (you never taste the clam, by the way) and the cleanest mushrooms I can find so all I have to do to prepare them is wipe them quickly.

½ pound mushrooms, chopped	3 cups bottled clam juice
3 tablespoons butter	1 cup heavy cream
Salt and pepper	¼ cup heavy cream, whipped
3 tablespoons all-purpose flour	

In a saucepan over medium heat, sauté the mushrooms in the butter, stirring, about 4 minutes. Season with salt and pepper to taste. Lower heat and stir in the flour. It will make a gummy roll. Cook another 2 minutes. Then, beating constantly, add the clam juice, stirring until well blended, 1 to 2 minutes. Cover and simmer 10 minutes. Stir in the cream, and remove from heat.

To serve: Ladle into soup bowls and garnish with whipped cream.

Dividends: Wonderful reheated with a little milk.

To make ahead: Complete the cooking, but don't add the cream until just before serving.

OYSTERS AND CREAM   Serves 6

An elegant soup for oyster lovers with lots of money (or an oyster farm nearby). Make this with shucked oysters or oysters you shuck yourself. Include the oyster liquor when measuring quantities. Makes a wonderful lunch followed by a salad of watercress, avocado, and endive with Roquefort cheese dressing, hot rolls and butter.

4 cups shucked oysters and liquor	Worcestershire sauce
2 cups half-and-half	4 teaspoons butter
2 large scallions, including green parts, minced	½ cup heavy cream

Purée the oysters and liquor in a blender or a food processor, 2 cups at a time. Stir in half-and-half, scallions, and add Worcester-shire to taste (a few drops). Turn into a kettle over medium heat, add the butter, and cook 7 minutes, stirring.

To serve: Pour the soup into small, ovenproof, ceramic crocks, float a little heavy cream on the top of each, and place under a hot broiler just long enough to brown lightly.

SEAFOOD CREAM FOR A PARTY   Serves 14 to 16

A wonderful rich soup to serve at a gala buffet. Cooling the cream sauce after its first cooking thickens it and enhances the flavor. You can select juicy lemons: they are firm but squishy. To get more juice from a lemon, roll it around under pressure on a countertop before you juice it. By "white" mushrooms, I mean fresh, clean, pretty mushrooms.

1 pound white mushrooms	4 drops Tabasco sauce
4 cups shucked oysters and liquor	1/4 pound butter
	2 1/2 tablespoons all-purpose flour
4 cups shucked cherrystone clams and liquor	1 quart heavy cream
Juice of 1 lemon	Salt and pepper
1 tablespoon Worcestershire sauce	3 to 4 fresh violets or nasturtium blossoms

1. Wipe the mushrooms clean with paper towel, chop coarsely, and combine in a large bowl with the oysters and clams and their liquor. Purée in a blender or a food processor, 2 cups at a time, and return to the bowl. Stir in the lemon juice, Worcestershire, and Tabasco. Cover and refrigerate an hour or two.
2. In a large kettle over very low heat, melt the butter, and stir in the flour. Beat in the cream and heat, stirring, until thickened, but do not let boil. Let rest at room temperature an hour or two.

To serve: Stir seafood purée into the cream sauce, add salt and pepper to taste, and heat to just below boiling, stirring, then ladle into a tureen. Float fresh flowers on top as a garnish.

Dividends: Excellent cold. Thin, if necessary, with a little milk.

To make ahead: May be made many hours ahead. After the cream sauce has cooled, refrigerate until ready to use.

CREAM OF PARSNIP SOUP   Serves 4 to 6

Here's what to do with leftover parsnips. Or carrots, or turnips, or butternut squash.

½ medium onion, minced	1 cup cooked parsnips
3 tablespoons butter	1 teaspoon salt
3 tablespoons all-purpose flour	⅛ teaspoon pepper
	¼ teaspoon paprika
4½ cups hot milk	Minced celery leaves

1. In a saucepan over medium heat, sauté onion in butter until translucent. Stir in flour. Beating constantly, add the milk, and cook, stirring, until bubbly, 1 to 2 minutes.
2. Purée with parsnips in a blender or a food processor, 2 cups at a time, or press through a sieve. Return to saucepan and heat to just below boiling. Season with salt, pepper, and paprika.

To serve: Ladle into soup bowls and garnish with celery leaves.

CREAM OF PEA SOUP   Serves 6 to 8

4 cups chicken broth	2 egg yolks
4 cups shelled peas	1 cup light cream
1 small onion, chopped	Salt and pepper
3 tablespoons butter	1 cup whipped cream
3 tablespoons all-purpose flour	(unsweetened)
	Hungarian sweet paprika

1. In a large kettle over high heat, bring broth to boiling, and add peas by the handful. Add more only as broth returns to brisk boil. Add onion and simmer 5 to 7 minutes, until peas are just tender but not losing their bright color. Purée in a blender or a food processor, 2 cups at a time, or press through a sieve.
2. In the kettle over low heat, melt the butter and stir in the flour. Cook, stirring, about 1 minute, then gradually add the purée, beating constantly.
3. In a small bowl beat the egg yolks until thick and lemon-colored, then beat about a cup of purée into the eggs. Beat egg mixture into the kettle, and over medium heat bring to

just below boiling. Add cream and salt and pepper to taste. Reheat to just below boiling.

To serve: Ladle into soup plates, add a big dollop of whipped cream, and dust generously with Hungarian sweet paprika.

PEA SOUP WITH DUMPLINGS　　　　　　Serves 4 to 5

Nice without the dumplings if you want a lighter soup.

4 cups shelled peas	½ cup dry white wine
1 teaspoon brown sugar	Salt and pepper
4½ cups boiling water	Dumplings (see recipe below)
4 tablespoons butter	Grated nutmeg
4 tablespoons all-purpose flour	

1. In a large kettle over high heat, add peas and sugar to boiling water, and boil until peas are tender, about 5 to 7 minutes. Purée in a blender or a food processor, 2 cups at a time, or put through a sieve. Return to kettle.
2. In a skillet melt butter over low heat, and stir in flour, cooking until bubbly. Stir in a cup of hot purée, and cook until thickened. Add thickened purée and wine to kettle, and salt and pepper to taste, bring to simmer, add dumplings, and cook as directed below.

To serve: Ladle dumplings and soup into deep bowls and garnish with a grating of nutmeg.

DUMPLINGS

6 eggs	½ teaspoon salt
½ cup all-purpose flour	⅛ teaspoon grated nutmeg
6 tablespoons soft butter	

In a small bowl combine all the ingredients until thoroughly blended. Let rest 20 minutes. Then drop by half-teaspoonfuls into simmering soup. After dumplings rise to the top, cook 5 minutes more.

POTATO SOUP   Serves 6 to 8

Caraway seeds and dill give this variation on potato and leek soup a distinctly northern European flavor. Nice with black bread, salad, and pie for an after-party supper.

5 large potatoes, peeled, diced or chopped	2 tablespoons minced dill
3 to 4 large leeks, white only, chopped fine	1 teaspoon salt
4 cups water	Pepper
2 cups milk	¼ cup sour cream
½ teaspoon caraway seed	Sweet butter
	Minced fresh dill

1. In a large saucepan over medium heat, bring potatoes, leeks, and water to boiling. Reduce heat, cover, and simmer until potatoes are tender, about 20 to 30 minutes. Mash vegetables in saucepan.
2. Add milk, caraway seeds, dill, salt, and pepper to taste. Cover and simmer until potatoes are very soft and soup thickens. Whisk in sour cream.

To serve: Ladle into soup bowls and garnish with a dab of sweet butter and a sprinkling of dill.

Dividends: Chill, thicken with more sour cream, and serve for lunch with black bread.

To make ahead: Complete to point where sour cream is to be added, then finish just before serving.

POTATO SOUP WITH CHEESE   Serves 6

This variation on the potato soup theme makes a wonderful lunch. Serve the toast on the side if you prefer: that will keep it crisp.

4 large potatoes, peeled, diced or chopped	4 cups milk
1 large onion, chopped	Salt and pepper
3 tablespoons butter	6 large slices French bread, toasted
2 cups water	Butter
2 large sprigs dill	6 large slices Jarlsberg cheese
½ cup light cream	

1. In a large saucepan over medium heat, sauté potatoes and onion in the butter, stirring, until onions become translucent, about 5 minutes. Add water, cover, and simmer until potatoes are tender, about 15 to 20 minutes. Snip dill into the soup, stir once, then purée with cream in a blender or a food processor, 2 cups at a time, or press through a sieve. Add milk to soup and return to saucepan. Season to taste with salt and pepper, and reheat without boiling.
2. Butter toast, top with cheese, and melt under broiler until bubbly.

To serve: Ladle soup into bowls and top with toast still bubbling hot from the broiler.

To make ahead: Complete through Step 1, then finish just before serving.

HEARTY SQUASH SOUP   Serves 6 to 8

The broth in this recipe is beef, and the flavor is stronger than in the other squash recipes given. Nice with hot dogs for an outdoor supper. It is served cold, but is nice hot, too.

1 small onion, chopped	1 large potato, diced
1 celery stalk, chopped	6 cups beef broth
1 medium carrot, chopped	2 teaspoons caraway seed
4 tablespoons butter	1 cup light cream
4 to 6 small summer squash (about 1½ pounds), stemmed, sliced thin	Salt and pepper
	Sprigs fresh dill

1. In a large kettle over medium heat, sauté the onion with the celery and carrot until the onion becomes translucent, 5 to 7 minutes. Add the squash and the potato, and sauté, stirring constantly, another 5 minutes. Add the broth and caraway seeds: cover and simmer until potatoes begin to disintegrate, about 15 to 20 minutes. Turn off heat and mash vegetables thoroughly with a potato masher.
2. Add cream and salt and pepper to taste. Chill 4 hours or overnight.

To serve: Ladle into soup bowls and garnish with snips of dill.

Dividends: Nice hot.

To make ahead: Best made the day before.

CREAM OF SPINACH SOUP   Serves 4 to 6

This is a little like Spinach Lemon Soup, but has a drier, slightly finer taste.

5 tablespoons butter	1 cup heavy cream
1/4 cup all-purpose flour	Salt and pepper
5 cups hot chicken broth	1/8 teaspoon grated nutmeg
6 to 8 cups closely packed chopped spinach leaves	1/2 cup Croutons, Sautéed in Butter (page 33)

1. In a large saucepan over low heat, melt the butter and stir in the flour. Beating constantly, add the broth, and heat until bubbly, 1 to 2 minutes. Add the spinach, cover, and cook until spinach is tender but still bright green, 3 to 5 minutes.
2. Stir in the cream. Heat to just below boiling, but do not boil. Add salt and pepper to taste, and add nutmeg.

To serve: Ladle into soup bowls and garnish with croutons.

GAZPACHO FRENCH STYLE   Serves 6 to 8

This version of the Spanish soup, page 350, includes more vegetables and a touch of tarragon.

2 tablespoons red wine vinegar	1/2 cup chopped green bell pepper
3 tablespoons olive oil	1/2 cup cucumber, seeded, chopped
1 large clove garlic	1/2 cup chopped onion
1/2 teaspoon tarragon	1 tablespoon minced parsley
6 large ripe tomatoes, chopped fine	1/2 tablespoon minced chives
2 cups tomato juice or water	Salt and pepper to taste
1/2 cup chopped celery	

Place the vinegar, oil, garlic, and tarragon in a blender and purée. Turn into a large serving bowl and add remaining ingredients. Combine well, and chill for 4 hours or overnight.

To serve: Ladle into chilled bowls.

To make ahead: This is better prepared a day or two in advance so flavors can blend and soup can chill thoroughly.

ICED NO-COOK FRESH TOMATO CREAM SOUP   Serves 6

The flavor of this one depends on the tomatoes' ripeness—it's good only if they really are delicious, juicy, deep red, ready.

6 very ripe large tomatoes (about 2½ pounds)
1 small onion
1 small clove garlic, optional
1 tablespoon minced fresh basil
1 teaspoon salt
⅛ teaspoon pepper

1 tablespoon olive oil
2 celery ribs
⅛ teaspoon allspice
Worcestershire sauce
Salt and pepper
1 pint heavy cream
6 lemon slices
6 sprigs fresh basil

Purée in a blender or a food processor: 3 tomatoes, onion, garlic, basil, salt, pepper, oil, celery ribs, allspice. Turn into a big pitcher. Purée remaining tomatoes and stir into pitcher. Add Worcestershire sauce to taste, and add salt and pepper if needed. Chill 4 to 6 hours.

To serve: Divide among soup bowls and pour cream into each just before serving. Garnish with a slice of lemon and a sprig of basil.

NO-COOK TOMATO AND AVOCADO SOUP   Serves 6

Here's a variation on the Iced No-Cook Fresh Tomato Cream Soup. The avocado must be ripe—soft but not mushy to the touch.

6 large very ripe tomatoes (about 2½ pounds)
6 scallions
1 small clove garlic, peeled
¼ bay leaf
2 cups beef broth

1 small avocado, halved, pitted, scooped out in teaspoon rounds
Salt and pepper
6 lemon wedges
½ cup sour cream

Purée in a blender or a food processor: 3 tomatoes, scallions, garlic, bay leaf. Turn into a big pitcher. Purée remaining tomatoes and stir into pitcher. Add broth and avocado rounds, and salt and pepper to taste. Chill.

To serve: Divide among soup bowls and float a lemon wedge and a spoonful of sour cream in each.

To make ahead: Best made several hours or the day before.

CREAM OF TOMATO SOUP   Serves 6

Very similar to the Quick Cream of Tomato soup (page 262), this is flavored with brown sugar and topped with whipped cream.

4 tablespoons butter	4 tablespoons all-purpose
1 small onion, minced	flour
1 tablespoon brown sugar	4 cups hot milk
4 very ripe large tomatoes	Salt and pepper
(about 2 pounds), chopped	1/2 cup heavy cream, whipped
2 tablespoons butter	Chive blooms

1. In a large saucepan over medium heat, melt 4 tablespoons of butter and sauté the onion until translucent, about 5 minutes. Stir in the brown sugar, and the tomatoes, and simmer, covered, 15 minutes. Purée in a blender or a food processor, 2 cups at a time, or press through a sieve.
2. In the saucepan over low heat, melt the remaining butter, and stir in the flour. Stirring constantly, beat in the milk, and cook, stirring, until bubbly, 1 to 2 minutes. Add the tomato purée, and cook, uncovered, until just below boiling. Add salt and pepper to taste.

To serve: Ladle into soup bowls and garnish with whipped cream and chive blooms.

Dividends: Nice cold.

To make ahead: Complete through Step 1, then finish just before serving.

CREAM OF TOMATO SOUP WINTER STYLE   Serves 6

This is quick and easy, a way to make from-scratch cream of tomato soup when the garden is asleep in winter.

1 16-ounce can whole	1/2 teaspoon dried basil
tomatoes	1/2 teaspoon dried oregano
1/4 cup chopped onion	1 teaspoon salt
1/2 cup chopped celery and	2 tablespoons tomato paste
leaves	1 tablespoon brown sugar
2 tablespoons butter	2 tablespoons butter

3 tablespoons all-purpose
  flour
2 cups beef broth

1 cup milk
Salt and pepper

1. In a saucepan over medium heat, simmer tomatoes, onion, and celery in butter with basil, oregano, salt, tomato paste, and brown sugar, uncovered, until celery is tender, 7 to 10 minutes. Purée in a blender or a food processor, 2 cups at a time, or press through a sieve.
2. Over very low heat, melt butter in saucepan, stir in flour, and, beating briskly, stir in broth to make a smooth, thick sauce. Beat in the milk, and add the puréed tomato mixture. Add salt and pepper to taste, and serve at once.

To serve: Ladle into soup bowls.

CREAM OF TOMATO SOUP BOSTON STYLE   Serves 4 to 6

This is an old-fashioned recipe.

8 ripe medium
  tomatoes (about 2
  pounds), chopped
2 tablespoons butter
1 tablespoon minced onion
½ teaspoon celery seed
½ teaspoon salt
½ teaspoon sugar
1 small bay leaf
½ teaspoon dried basil
1 whole clove

⅛ teaspoon baking soda
3 tablespoons butter
3 tablespoons all-purpose
  flour
1½ teaspoons salt
⅛ teaspoon pepper
2 cups milk
Salt and pepper
½ cup heavy cream,
  whipped

1. In a large kettle over high heat, simmer tomatoes in butter with onion, celery seed, salt, sugar, bay leaf, basil, and clove for about 10 minutes. Purée in a blender or a food processor, 2 cups at a time, or press through a sieve. Stir in soda.
2. Melt the butter in the kettle over very low heat, then stir in the flour, salt, and pepper. Add the milk, stirring constantly. Simmer, stirring, until thickened. Add salt and pepper to taste.

To serve: Just before serving stir tomato mixture into the hot cream sauce, and heat, stirring constantly. Ladle into soup bowls and garnish with a big dollop of whipped cream.

TOMATO BISQUE WITH MUSHROOMS   Serves 6

I usually use sliced stem ends of mushrooms to make this—about 2½ cups.

½ pound mushrooms, cleaned, minced	1 stalk celery, chopped
4 tablespoons butter	1 tablespoon brown sugar
2 cups chicken broth	3 tablespoons butter
3 very ripe large tomatoes (about 1½ pounds), chopped	2 tablespoons all-purpose flour
1 small onion, chopped	1 cup heavy cream
1 clove garlic, sliced	Salt and pepper
	⅛ teaspoon baking soda
	1 tablespoon minced parsley

1. In a saucepan over medium heat, sauté mushrooms in butter 2 to 3 minutes. Add broth, cover, and simmer 12 minutes. Purée in a blender or a food processor, 2 cups at a time, or press through a sieve.
2. Combine tomatoes, onion, garlic, celery, and sugar in the saucepan; cover and cook over medium heat 15 minutes. Purée as described above, and combine with mushroom mixture.
3. Melt butter in the saucepan over low heat, stir in flour, then beat in the heavy cream to make a smooth sauce. Allow to bubble, stirring constantly, for a few minutes over low heat, then stir in mushroom and tomato mixture. Add salt and pepper to taste, and baking soda. Heat to just below boiling.

To serve: Ladle into soup bowls and garnish with parsley.

DUTCH VEGETABLE SOUP WITH CREAM   Serves 8

This cooks for hours and can be made in an electric slow-cooker set on Low without losing its wonderful vegetable flavor. About 12 to 15 hours should do it.

6 medium leeks, chopped	¼ small head of cabbage, shredded
2 large potatoes, chopped	2 large celery stalks and leaves, chopped
3 parsnips, peeled, chopped	1 cup peas
3 large carrots, chopped	1 cup fresh lima beans, or ½ cup dried
3 very ripe tomatoes (about 1½ pounds), chopped	2 cups green beans, cut up

    3 quarts water   3 tablespoons butter
2½ teaspoons salt   ½ cup heavy cream
    ¼ teaspoon pepper   Fresh sprigs dill

1. Place all the vegetables and the water, with salt and pepper, in a large kettle over medium heat. Cover and simmer for 2 hours.
2. Purée in a blender or a food processor, 2 cups at a time, or press through a sieve. Return to kettle. Stir in butter and cream, and reheat without boiling.

To serve: Ladle into soup bowls and garnish with snips of dill.

Dividends: Stretch leftovers with milk. Very good.

To make ahead: Excellent the next day, so make it as much ahead as you wish.

VEGETABLE CREAM   Serves 4

You can make this with vegetables other than those listed here— as long as you include onions, turnips, and carrots.

    4 tablespoons butter   ½ cup chopped potato
    1 small onion, chopped   1 quart veal broth
    ½ cup chopped carrot   1 cup water
    ½ cup chopped turnip   Salt and pepper
        (yellow or white)   1 tablespoon minced parsley
    ½ cup chopped celery

In a large kettle over medium heat, combine butter and all vegetables except potato, and sauté 2 minutes. Add the potato, cover, and cook 2 minutes. Add the broth and water, cover, reduce heat, and cook 1 hour. Purée in a blender or a food processor, 2 cups at a time, add salt and pepper to taste, and reheat.

To serve: Stir the parsley into the hot soup, then ladle into bowls.

Dividends: Excellent base to which cooked leftover vegetables may be added to make a "new" soup. You will probably need to thin with a little liquid; either milk or broth will be good.

To make ahead: Very good the next day.

CREAMY VEGETABLE SOUP WITH CHEESE   Serves 8 to 10

This is very rich, based as it is on broth and dressed with cream. Bread, a bit of salad, and a dessert is all you need with this to make a complete meal.

4 tablespoons butter	6 cups beef broth
3 medium leeks, chopped	2 large potatoes, chopped
4 medium celery roots, peeled, chopped	2 cups milk
	1 cup heavy cream
3 large carrots, chopped	Salt and pepper to taste
3 stalks celery and leaves, chopped	8 to 10 slices French bread
	½ cup grated Swiss cheese
3 Belgian endives, sliced	Sprigs fresh parsley

1. In a large kettle over medium heat, melt the butter and sauté the leeks, celery roots, carrots, celery, and endives, covered, stirring now and then, about 20 minutes. Add broth and potatoes; cover and cook about 30 minutes. Lower heat, add the milk and cream; cover and cook about 15 minutes—but watch the pot to make sure it doesn't boil over.
2. Meanwhile, divide the cheese over the bread slices, and broil until bubbly and golden brown.

To serve: Ladle soup into bowls, and top each with a slice of bread and a sprig of parsley.

Dividends: Soup without bread is very good reheated.

To make ahead: Complete through Step 1, then finish just before serving.

Six

THE GREAT INTERNATIONAL SOUPS

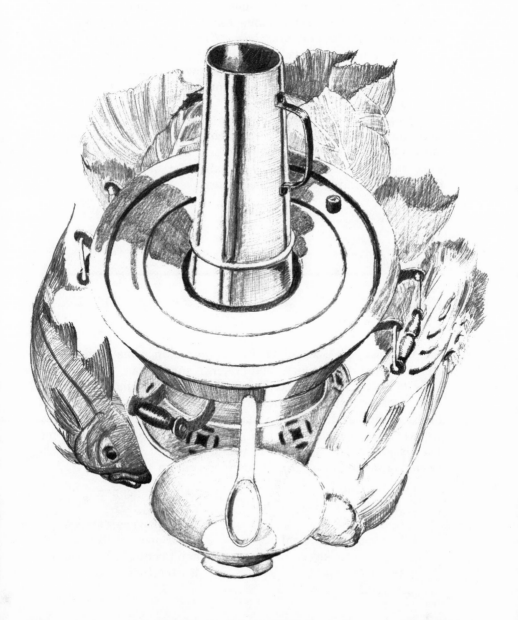

Nowhere is America's melting pot background more evident than in our cuisine. An informed cook taking a close look at many of the soups in our repertoire can discover lurking behind them a recipe from another land. In Chapter 9, Cream of Gruyère Soup is based on Western Europe's The King's Soup, and the recipe for Yogurt Soup with Spinach is Egypt's *Labaneya*. Most great soups from elsewhere have an American counterpart: *Tripe à la Mode de Caen,* which appears in this chapter, is made in Philadelphia under the title of Pepper Pot Soup.

So, if you remember a glorious soup from another continent and can't find the foreign name for it in the index, look it up according to its ingredients. *Crème Crécy* in this chapter is also known as Purée of Carrots, and Purée St. Germain many speak of as Purée of Peas. Borscht we all know as a Russian soup, but it is a plain or fancy form of beet soup and appears that way as often as it appears as borscht.

My apologies for the many very good national soup recipes that don't appear here. This world contains not five hundred but more like fifty thousand soup recipes, and we've had to leave some out. I've picked those I especially like, or that seem to me the most intriguing foreign specialties.

AFRICA

PEANUT SOUP   Serves 4 to 6

Soup made from roasted peanuts (*shorba* in some lands) is a North African specialty that turned up in our kitchens as Peanut Butter Soup. Sarah Tyson Rorer was a famous Philadelphia cooking school teacher at the turn of the century, and probably one of the first to make a peanut butter soup. Cecily Brownstone, a dear friend of many years' standing, gave me permission to use this version, which appeared some time ago in Cecily's famous Associated Press food column.

1 quart milk	¼ teaspoon pepper
1 cup creamy style peanut butter	1 small bay leaf
	1 tablespoon cornstarch
1 teaspoon minced onion	2 tablespoons water
¼ teaspoon celery seed	½ cup Croutons, Sautéed in
½ teaspoon salt	Butter (page 33)

1. In a saucepan over medium heat combine milk, peanut butter, onion, celery seed, salt, pepper, and bay leaf. Stirring constantly, cook until mixture smooths out.
2. In a small bowl combine the cornstarch and water, then stir into soup. Cook 1 minute. Remove bay leaf.

To serve: Ladle into soup bowls and garnish with croutons.

CHERBAH

This soup, made with lamb and vermicelli, is flavored with dried apricots, ingredients common to the cuisines of many North African lands. I omit the mint: go easy on it, unless you are a mint devotee.

1½ pounds meaty lamb shanks	2 tablespoons fresh mint, chopped
2 lamb bones, cracked or cut up	4 tablespoons oil
2 quarts water	4 large ripe tomatoes, chopped, or 1 16-ounce can whole tomatoes
1 tablespoon salt	¼ pound vermicelli
¼ teaspoon pepper	1 tablespoon lemon juice
¼ teaspoon cayenne	Salt
¼ pound dried pitted apricots	1 tablespoon chopped parsley and mint
4 medium onions, chopped	
3 medium green peppers, chopped	

1. In a large kettle over high heat, combine lamb, bones, water, salt, pepper, cayenne, and apricots. Cover, bring to a boil, reduce heat, and simmer 1½ hours.
2. In a saucepan over medium heat, sauté the onions, peppers, and mint leaves in the oil until the onions begin to be translucent, about 7 minutes. Stir mixture into the kettle, then add the tomatoes. Simmer 1 hour.
3. Lift out the bones, strip them of meat, and return the meat to the kettle. Discard the bones. Add the vermicelli and cook until tender, about 6 to 7 minutes. Stir in the lemon juice and add salt to taste.

To serve: Garnish with chopped parsley and mint.

To make ahead: May be made hours or a day ahead.

YAM SOUP   Serves 4

A little like pumpkin soup—Jack O'Lantern Soup, in Chapter 7, but hot, because of the chilies. Wear rubber gloves to handle the peppers. It's a Nigerian recipe.

1 small bunch scallions, chopped	1 pound yams, chopped
2 tablespoons peanut oil	3-4 cups beef broth
3 small chili peppers, minced, or 3 teaspoons of chili powder	Salt
	1 tablespoon minced parsley

1. In a saucepan over medium heat, sauté the scallions in the oil until translucent, about 5 minutes. Stir in the chilies, yams, and the broth. Cover, bring to a boil, reduce heat to very low, and simmer 30 minutes.
2. Purée in a blender or a food processor, 2 cups at a time, or press through a sieve. Return to the kettle. Add more broth if too thick. Add salt to taste and heat through before serving.

To serve: Ladle into bowls and sprinkle with parsley.

COCONUT SOUP   Serves 4

This exotic soup is an adaptation of a couple of West African recipes.

4 cups beef broth	1 tablespoon strained lemon juice
1 cup grated fresh coconut	1 teaspoon salt
½ to 1 cup coconut milk or cow's milk	1 thick slice fresh ginger, minced
1 small eggplant, peeled, cut into 2-inch chunks	1 tablespoon minced parsley

1. In a kettle over medium heat, combine the broth, coconut, and the milk; bring to a boil. Stir in the eggplant and the lemon juice, cover, and simmer 35 minutes.
2. Purée in a blender or a food processor, 2 cups at a time, or press through a sieve. Return purée to the kettle, stir in the salt and ginger, and cook 5 minutes.

To serve: Ladle into bowls and garnish with parsley.

To make ahead: May be made several hours ahead.

UNITED STATES

Chowders made from clams and oysters, and corn chowders, seem to be native to our shores, and you'll find recipes for them in this book. Greenfield Corn Chowder, Succotash Chowder, et al. recall our pioneer ancestors and the Indians who taught them what they knew about food collection in a very rich land. In this chapter we have made room for a few representative contemporary soups that seem to have originated here, and for samples from two great cooking traditions, the Pennsylvania Dutch and Creole.

BILLI-BI
Serves 6

I am guessing this is American, named for William B. Leeds (Billy B.), the American industrialist who loved it. It's yummy—mussels and cream. Remember to clean mussels thoroughly, as instructed in Chapter 4.

3 quarts mussels	½ cup heavy cream
1 cup dry white wine	Salt and pepper
4 cups fish broth	1 tablespoon minced parsley
2 large egg yolks	

1. In a large kettle over medium heat, combine mussels and wine. Cover and cook about 8 minutes, shaking the kettle often, until all the mussels are open.
2. Line a colander with 2 thicknesses of cheesecloth and strain the broth through it. Reserve 12 whole mussels. Remove the others from their shells, and combine them with the cooking liquid and the fish broth. Purée in a blender or a food processor, 2 cups at a time. Return purée to the kettle and bring to a boil over medium heat, then reduce heat to low.
3. In a small bowl beat the egg yolks well, then add the cream. Stir in a little hot broth, then return the egg mixture to the kettle. Heat to just below boiling. Add salt and pepper to taste.

To serve: Ladle soup into bowls and garnish with whole, reserved mussels and a bit of minced parsley.

CRANBERRY SOUP WITH BEETS   Serves 6

Shallots look and taste like a cross between onion and garlic. They're sold by the pound in specialty markets and are great for use with fish and in French cooking. If you don't have shallots, use the whites of 3 scallions and a small clove of garlic in this recipe. There's another version of this which includes a cup of chopped cabbage.

4 shallots, minced
1 tablespoon butter
1 16-ounce can whole small
  beets and liquid
3 cups chicken broth
1 pound cranberries, washed

½ cup sugar
¼ cup cream sherry
1 teaspoon grated orange
  rind
Salt and pepper
6 whole thin orange slices

1. In a saucepan over low heat, sauté the shallots in the butter 3 to 4 minutes.
2. Purée beets and their liquid in a blender or a food processor, and add shallots as you are finishing. Scrape beet mixture into a refrigerator dish that has a tight lid.
3. In the saucepan over medium high heat, combine broth, cranberries, and sugar, and simmer, uncovered, until the berries begin to pop, 5 to 7 minutes. Purée 2 cups at a time, and stir into beet mixture. Stir in sherry and orange rind; add salt and pepper to taste. Cover and chill 4 to 6 hours or overnight.

To serve: Ladle into soup bowls and garnish with orange slices.

CRANBERRY BORSCHT   Serves 4 to 6

I've never run into cranberries anywhere but in America, and to the best of my knowledge they are native to the salty bogs of the East Coast, notably Cape Cod. Another cranberry soup appears above.

⅔ cup cranberries
1½ quarts water
1 large onion, sliced
1 cup chopped cabbage
1 8- to 10-ounce can
  shredded beets
½ cup beet liquid from can

½ teaspoon salt
⅛ teaspoon pepper
1 tablespoon firmly packed
  light brown sugar
Salt and pepper
¾ cup sour cream
1 hard-boiled egg, chopped

In a kettle over medium heat, simmer the cranberries in the water until skins are popped. Mash through a strainer and discard seeds. Return to kettle with the onion and cabbage, and simmer 20 minutes. Add the beets, beet liquid, salt, pepper, and brown sugar, and heat through. Add salt and pepper to taste. Chill overnight.

To serve: Ladle into soup plates. Divide sour cream among them and garnish with chopped egg.

GOLDEN SOUP   Serves 4 to 6

Frozen food—and orange juice concentrate—may be America's main gift to the world of cooking!

1 medium onion, minced	1 tablespoon cold water
1 pound carrots, sliced thin	1 cup heavy cream
3 tablespoons butter	1 cup orange juice
2 cups chicken broth	¼ teaspoon grated nutmeg
1 cup water	Salt and pepper
1 tablespoon cornstarch	1 teaspoon minced chives

1. In a saucepan over medium heat, sauté the onion and the carrots in the butter until the onion begins to be translucent, 8 to 10 minutes. Add the broth and the water, cover, bring to a boil, reduce heat, and simmer until carrots are well cooked, about 15 minutes. Purée in a blender or a food processor, 2 cups at a time, or press through a sieve. Return purée to the kettle over low heat.
2. Combine cornstarch and cold water, stir into the purée, and continue to stir until it begins to thicken. Add the cream, orange juice, and nutmeg, and heat through. Season with salt and pepper to taste.

To serve: Ladle into consommé cups and garnish with chives.

Dividends: Nice chilled with a dab of sour cream.

To make ahead: May be made several hours ahead.

SHRIMP CREOLE SOUP   Serves 4 to 6

Gumbo filé, a khaki-colored powder made from crushed sassafras leaves, gives this Creole soup its special character. Okra is found fresh in season or frozen year round. Bottled filé is something to pick up when you are in a specialty food shop. For instructions on deveining shrimp, see Chapter 4.

1 small onion, chopped	3 cups beef broth
2 scallions, chopped	1 cup bottled clam juice
1 large clove garlic, chopped	½ cup raw rice
3 tablespoons butter	⅓ cup dry white wine
1 medium bay leaf	1 teaspoon lemon juice
1 cup halved very ripe	Pinch saffron threads
cherry tomatoes	1 pound raw shrimp
½ pound small okra,	Salt and pepper
stemmed, sliced in rounds	Filé powder
3 large sprigs parsley,	
chopped	

1. In a large saucepan over medium heat, sauté the onion, scallions, and garlic in the butter until onion is translucent, about 5 minutes. Add bay, tomatoes, okra, and parsley. Stir until moisture has evaporated. Add the beef and clam broths, the rice, wine, lemon juice, and saffron. Bring to a boil, reduce heat, cover, and simmer until the rice is tender, about 20 minutes.
2. Bury the shrimp in the rice, cover, and cook 3 to 5 minutes, just until the shrimp turn pink. Remove the shrimps, shell and devein, and return to the soup. Add salt and pepper to taste.

To serve: Add a dash of filé powder to each soup plate and ladle soup over the filé. Stir once and serve.

RIVVEL SOUP   Serves 6 to 8

The Pennsylvania Dutch like soup with lots of solids in it—floury noodles, dough balls, even popcorn. A few soups called Poor Man's Soup—brown, flour-thickened broths—were important to early settlers' diets in the months before the ground could be planted for vegetables. Rivvel means "lump," and this soup is full of lumps that look like rice. In its simpler versions, the rivvels are dropped into hot milk and seasoned.

1 cup all-purpose flour	2 quarts chicken or beef
1/2 teaspoon salt	broth
1 small egg, well beaten	2 tablespoons butter
2 cups corn kernels	

1. In a large mixing bowl combine the flour, salt, and beaten egg. Mix these together with your fingers until crumbly. These dough bits are the rivvels.
2. In a large kettle over medium heat, bring the broth to a brisk simmer, add the corn and the rivvels, stir, and simmer, uncovered, for 10 to 15 minutes.

To serve: Ladle into soup bowls and dot with butter.

BELGIUM

Some very fine dishes have come to us from Belgium. Here are two wonderful soups. *Hochepot* is antique, more fun to read than to try to accommodate, but *waterzooi* is one of the best of the thick chicken soups.

HOCHEPOT

Serves 20 or more

This is a wonderful old recipe attributed to Belgium by Countess Morphy in her *Recipes of All Nations* (1935), one of my favorite cookbooks for browsing. The amount of meat here is too much for moderns and impossible to find unless you live on a farm, but the broth must be spectacular. I've never found enough of the parts of the pig to make it.

1½ pounds fresh brisket of beef	1 small onion, stuck with 4 whole cloves
1½ pounds breast of lamb or mutton	1 small white cabbage, quartered
1½ pounds shoulder of veal	3 medium carrots, chopped
1½ pounds pigs' feet	4 medium leeks, chopped
¾ pound pigs' ears	½ small yellow turnip, peeled, chopped
½ pound pigs' tails	
4½ quarts water	4 stalks celery, chopped
1 large bay leaf	12 pearl onions, peeled
½ teaspoon dried thyme	12 chipolata sausages
2 large sprigs parsley	Salt and pepper

1. In a large kettle or a stock pot over high heat, combine the meat parts and the water, bring to a boil, and skim the scum until it stops forming. Add the herbs, cabbage, carrots, leeks, turnip, and celery. Cover, reduce heat, and simmer 3 hours. Add the pearl onions and the sausages; cover and simmer 1 hour.
2. Line a colander with 2 thicknesses of cheesecloth and strain the broth through it. Taste, and add salt and pepper if needed. Remove as much fat from the top of the broth as you can.

To serve: Discard the bay and the onion stuck with cloves. Remove the meat from the bones. I assume we also discard the parts of the pig. Set the meats and sausages in a large tureen. Place the coarsely chopped vegetables around the meats. Reheat the broth and ladle over the meats and vegetables.

WATERZOOI

Serves 8

This famous Belgian dish turns up in good cookbooks as a chicken soup. Belgians also know it as a fish soup made with wine, and that is how Escoffier recorded it. Here it's a chicken cream—a kind of *Blanquette de Poulet* soup. Made without wine it isn't *waterzooi* anymore, but it's delicious. A 4-pound fowl can be used instead of smaller birds.

¼ lemon, in a wedge	4 sprigs parsley
2 2-pound chickens, halved, and giblets from one	½ teaspoon dried thyme
4 large leeks, halved	8 peppercorns
4 large stalks celery and leaves, cut into large chunks	1 medium bay leaf
	2½ quarts chicken broth
	1 cup dry white wine, optional
2 large carrots, cut into large chunks	4 egg yolks, lightly beaten
9 small white onions, peeled	1 cup heavy cream
	¾ lemon, cut into 8 slices
4 whole cloves	Salt and pepper
¼ teaspoon ground mace	8 large sprigs parsley

1. Squeeze a few drops of lemon over the chicken halves, then rub them all over with the lemon wedge. In a large saucepan over medium heat, sauté the lumps of chicken fat you will find in the cavity until 2 to 3 tablespoons have been rendered. Discard the crisped bits. Sauté the chicken halves in the fat until golden brown all over, about 20 minutes. Add the giblets, leeks, celery and leaves, carrots, 8 onions, 1 onion stuck with 4 cloves, and the mace, parsley, thyme, peppercorns, and bay tied into a small cheesecloth square. Pour in the broth, and the wine if you wish. Cover, raise heat, bring to a boil, reduce heat, and simmer for 45 minutes. Lift the chicken halves from the broth, skin them, cut the meat into large chunks, and slice the giblets thinly. Discard the bones and skin, the herb bag, and the onion stuck with cloves.
2. Beat the yolks with the cream and pour a little hot broth into the mixture. Remove the broth from the heat and stir the mixture into the broth. Stir until the soup thickens slightly, 3 or 4 minutes. Return the meat and giblets to the kettle, add the lemon slices, and reheat over low heat, but do not boil. Add salt and pepper to taste.

To serve: Ladle into large soup plates, dividing the lemon slices among them. Place 1 large sprig of parsley on each lemon slice.

Dividends: Makes a nifty sauce for rice the next day.

To make ahead: May be made several hours or a day ahead.

GREAT BRITAIN

England, as the center of a colonial empire, was a melting pot for recipes. And some of the best from the British Isles are adaptations of the cuisine of exotic soils. Because Britain dealt in wool and so had abundant sheep herds, many good British soups include lamb or mutton.

COCKALEEKIE   Serves 12

An old Scottish recipe for a chicken soup flavored with leeks and enriched with prunes. In some Scottish households the prunes are omitted. (If you enjoy prunes in your soup try Chicken and Rice Soup in Chapter 3.)

1 4-to-5 pound fowl	¼ cup pearl barley
4½ quarts water	10 to 12 pitted prunes,
1 tablespoon salt	chopped
8 peppercorns	Salt and pepper
10 to 12 medium leeks,	2 tablespoons minced
whites only, cut into	parsley
lengths and halved	

1. In a large saucepan over medium heat, sauté the lumps of chicken fat you will find in the cavity until 2 to 3 tablespoons have been rendered. Discard the crisped bits. Sauté the bird in the fat until golden brown, about 20 minutes. Add the water, raise heat, and bring to a boil. Skim the scum until it stops forming. Add the salt, peppercorns, and leeks. Cover, reduce heat, and simmer 2½ hours. Add the barley and the prunes and simmer 1 hour.
2. Remove the chicken from the broth, cut up the meat, and discard the bones and skin. Remove as much fat from the broth as you can. Pull the meat into shreds (it will be very tender) and return to the soup. Add salt and pepper to taste. Heat through.

To serve: Ladle into large soup plates and garnish with parsley.

Dividends: Use extra broth as base for other soups.

To make ahead: Better made the day before.

MULLIGATAWNY SOUP I   Serves 8 to 10

This was called Curry Soup when first brought to Britain from its native land, India. *Mulegoo Thani* means "pepper-water," and depending on the heat in your curry powder, the soup may or may not justify its name. There are three main versions. One Mulligatawny is made like a mutton curry, but it simmers for 3 hours. The luxury version is made with a stewing hen or fowl, enriched with a *roux* and with cream. The Indian version is a curry made just with lentils. Mulligatawny is served with a bowl of rice on the side. Take a little rice on your soup spoon, dip up a little broth and chicken—that's the way my family handles it.

3 pounds breast of lamb or mutton	2 tablespoons chopped parsley
1 tablespoon butter	½ teaspoon dried thyme
2 medium onions, minced	1 small bay leaf
1 medium carrot, chopped	1 large clove garlic, minced
¼ small yellow turnip, chopped	2 teaspoons salt
2 tablespoons flour	2 tablespoons lemon juice
1 tablespoon curry powder	Salt and pepper
2½ quarts chicken broth or water	4 cups hot cooked rice

1. In a large kettle or stock pot over medium heat, sauté the meat in the butter until brown. Add the onions, carrot, and turnip, and sauté 8 minutes. Sprinkle with flour and curry powder, and stir in the broth or water. Scrape up the brown crust on the saucepan bottom. Add the parsley, thyme, bay, garlic, and salt. Bring to a boil, cover, reduce heat, and simmer 3 hours.
2. Lift out the bones, strip them of meat, and return the meat to the pot. Discard the bones and bay leaf. Add the lemon juice and cook 5 minutes. Add salt and pepper to taste.

To serve: Ladle into bowls and serve plain boiled rice in a small bowl on the side.

Dividends: Very good reheated.

To make ahead: May be made the day before. Degrease before reheating.

MULLIGATAWNY SOUP II   Serves 8 to 10

This starts out the way Mulligatawny is made in India, but with the addition of *roux* or *beurre manié* and cream, becomes a luxury British edition. *Roux* and *beurre manié* both describe a paste made by stirring flour into melted fat, but with *roux*, liquid is beaten into the paste, while with *beurre manié*, the paste is beaten into the broth.

1 3-pound chicken
2 tablespoons butter
3 small onions, chopped
1 large stalk celery, minced
½ red or green bell pepper, chopped
1 tablespoon curry powder
1 teaspoon ground coriander
½ teaspoon ground cardamom
½ teaspoon turmeric
½ teaspoon dried thyme
1 teaspoon ground cumin
1 tablespoon salt
2 quarts chicken broth

1 cup coconut milk, or ¾ cup milk blended with ¼ cup canned grated coconut, or combined with 1 tablespoon coconut cream
1 large bay leaf
3 tablespoons flour
1 cup heavy cream
1 teaspoon Maille white mustard
½ to 1 teaspoon garlic salt
Salt and pepper
4 cups hot cooked rice, optional

1. Cut up the chicken: separate breasts; cut off wings and divide at joints, separate drumsticks and thighs.
2. In a large saucepan over medium heat, render the fat from the chicken cavity and discard the crisped pieces. Add the butter, onions, celery, and pepper, and sauté 5 minutes. Stir in the curry, coriander, cardamom, turmeric, thyme, cumin, and salt. Add chicken pieces to the saucepan and sauté 20 minutes. Add the broth, coconut milk, and bay leaf, scraping up the browned bits stuck to the saucepan bottom. Add the chicken carcass. Cover, reduce heat, and simmer 1½ hours. Remove the chicken from the broth, skin the carcass, and strip meat from it. Skin the leg and wing pieces, discard carcass and skin, and return meat to the saucepan.
3. Skim 2 tablespoons of fat from the soup and put into a small saucepan. Place the saucepan over low heat and stir in the flour. Whip this *beurre manié* into the broth, beating rapidly, and cook, stirring, another 5 minutes. Stir in the cream, mustard, and garlic salt. Heat through, but do not boil. Add salt and pepper to taste.

To serve: Ladle into soup plates and serve plain boiled rice in a small bowl on the side if you wish.

Dividends: Excellent reheated.

To make ahead: May be made the day before.

SCOTCH BROTH—MARCEL HÉRITEAU'S
RECIPE   Serves 8 to 10

Scotch Broth is *the* way to use up a lamb bone and it is also a wonderful old dish. There are two recipes below: my father's— a hearty peasant dish—and a more authentic version, which is much like the famous Scotch Broth served at Lord & Taylor's Soup Bar in Manhattan. Substitute the bone of a leg of lamb roast, plus the shin portion and meat, uncooked, plus about 1 pound of lamb shoulder or breast for the meat in either of these recipes.

3 pounds lamb shoulder, bone in	2 teaspoons salt
	⅛ teaspoon pepper
4½ quarts water	1 cup pearl barley
1 medium bay leaf	3 tablespoons butter
2 medium carrots, chopped	2 tablespoons flour
4 medium stalks celery, chopped	Salt and pepper
	2 tablespoons chopped parsley
1 large leek, sliced	
2 large parsnips, chopped	

1. Cut the meat from the bones and discard as much fat as possible. Cut into small chunks. Separate the bones.
2. In a large kettle or stock pot over high heat, combine the bones, meat, and water, and bring to a boil. Reduce heat, skim until scum stops forming, and wipe scum from sides. Add the bay, cover, and cook 1½ hours. Add the vegetables, salt, pepper, and barley; cover and simmer 1 hour. Lift out the bones. Strip them of meat, and return the meat to the kettle. Discard bones and bay leaf.
3. In a small saucepan over low heat, melt the butter and stir in the flour. Whip this *beurre manié* into the broth, beating rapidly, and cook, stirring gently, 5 minutes. Add salt and pepper to taste.

To serve: Ladle into big soup plates and garnish with parsley.

To make ahead: Better made several hours earlier or a day ahead.

OLD-FASHIONED SCOTCH BARLEY BROTH Serves 10 to 12

Henry, the wonderful chef at Lord & Taylor's Soup Bar, gave out a recipe for his famous Scotch Broth, and included in it chicken bouillon and beef bouillon cubes. I don't know whether he realizes the earliest recipes for Scotch Broth included both chicken and beef. In any case, his recipe, like the Scottish recipe, calls for Scotch barley, which is barley husked and coarse-ground, and found here in health food stores. Pearl barley is husked and pale. Brown barley is unhusked and stays a little chewy, and I prefer it in my soups. Countess Morphy, in her wonderful book, *Recipes of All Nations,* says the Scottish custom is to serve the broth in one bowl and the meat in another with minced vegetables around it, topped by a little broth mixed with a teaspoon of prepared mustard and vinegar to taste, or nasturtium flowers warmed in butter, or chopped cucumbers.

2 pounds beef and lamb bones	2 medium leeks, sliced
4½ quarts water	2 large stalks celery, chopped
1 tablespoon salt	2 pounds lean, boneless shoulder lamb, cut into 2-inch pieces
8 peppercorns	
2 large sprigs parsley	Salt and pepper
1 teaspoon dried thyme	Chicken bouillon cubes or granules, optional
1 cup dried split peas	
1 cup Scotch or pearl barley	Beef bouillon cubes or granules, optional
3 medium carrots, chopped	3 tablespoons minced parsley
2 medium white turnips, chopped	
2 medium onions, chopped	

In a large kettle or a stock pot over high heat, combine the bones and water. Cover and bring to a boil. Reduce heat and simmer 2 or 3 hours. Add the salt, peppercorns, parsley, thyme, peas, and barley. Cover and simmer 1 hour. Add the vegetables, lamb pieces, and simmer 1 hour. Taste, and season with salt and pepper, or 1 or 2 bouillon cubes or 1 or 2 teaspoons granules, if you wish.

To serve: Remove the bones, ladle the broth into soup plates, and garnish with parsley.

To make ahead: Almost better made a day or two ahead.

CANADA

PEA SOUP

My mother was a Scotch-Canadian, and I grew up with her, so I am familiar with the Scotch heritage of our great neighbor to the north. However, the French Canadians have a more distinct cuisine. I will never forget a brown sugar and ice cream pie my best friend Rita Giroux's mother made for dessert on Sundays, and a glorious split pea soup like the one below. It resembles Poor Man's Split Pea Soup in Chapter 9. You can make this in a slow-cook electric pot; just combine everything but the croutons and cook on low for about 12 hours.

2 cups split dried green peas	6 peppercorns
3 quarts water	¼ teaspoon savory
½ pound salt pork, cubed	1 small bay leaf
3 medium carrots, chopped	2 large sprigs parsley
2 medium onions, chopped	Salt and pepper
1 small onion, stuck with 3 whole cloves	Croutons, Sautéed (page 32)

In a large kettle over high heat, combine the peas, water, salt pork, carrots, onions, the onion stuck with cloves, the peppercorns, savory, bay, and parsley. Cover, bring to a boil, then reduce heat and simmer 2½ to 3 hours or until the peas have disintegrated. Remove the bay, peppercorns, and the onion stuck with cloves. Season with salt and pepper to taste.

To serve: Ladle into bowls and garnish with croutons.

To make ahead: Wonderful made a day or two ahead.

FRANCE

The French love soup! They love it so much, the long list of favorites that follows doesn't even begin to give you an idea of the regional variety. A favorite French supper is a big bowl of thick soup served with crusty bread, then a salad, and cheese, which may be eaten with the salad or with fruit as dessert. For the big midday meal, an hors d'oeuvres course is traditionally followed by a light soup—probably a cream soup or a consommé —then comes the main course, salad, and dessert.

The group of recipes below includes some of our family favorites. A few others have become so closely identified with a type of soup that they appear in other chapters—vichyssoise is in Chapter 5 with the rich Edwardian soups, *Petite Marmite* and Pot-au-Feu are with the main-course soups in Chapter 3.

Soupe, potage (thick soup), *potée* (cooked in an earthenware container and usually including sausage), *bisque* (originally a soup thickened with rice), *velouté* (thickened with a *roux* or *beurre manié* of flour and butter), and *consommé* (clear or jellied broth) are some of the types of soups in France.

BOUILLABAISSE   Serves 4

One of the great dishes from southern France, this takes about one hour to make. Don't skimp on the saffron or the rind. *Rouille,* a strong garlic-flavored spread, is served with bouillabaisse in my favorite Manhattan restaurant, Le Marmiton, on East 49th Street. I place the bread with *rouille* in my bowl before I begin the bouillabaisse so that the flavor combines with the broth before I begin to eat.

1½ pounds unfilleted white fish, 2 or 3 types, such as haddock, flounder, cod	1 small bay leaf
	¼ teaspoon dried thyme
	4 sprigs fresh parsley
1 pound fish heads and trimmings, or chowder bits	¼ cup chopped scallions or yellow onion
	¼ cup olive oil
1 teaspoon dried fennel	1½ large cloves garlic, sliced
¼ teaspoon saffron threads	1 large ripe tomato or 1 cup canned, whole tomatoes, strained
1 teaspoon grated orange rind	

8 cups cold water	12 mussels
½ teaspoon salt	6 cherrystone clams or 12
¼ teaspoon pepper	soft-shell clams
1 medium lobster (1½	4 slices stale French bread
pounds) or 2 small	or thick toast
soft-shell crabs	1 recipe *Rouille* (below)

1. With a large, flat, sharp knife, fillet the fish, removing flesh from the bones. Reserve. Tie bones, with fish heads and trimmings or chowder bits, fennel, saffron, rind, bay, thyme, and parsley, into a large double thickness of cheesecloth. Set aside.
2. In a large, heavy saucepan over medium high heat, sauté the scallions or onion in the oil until it begins to brown lightly, 6 to 7 minutes. Add garlic and tomato, and sauté 5 minutes. Add water, scraping up the pan juices. Place the cheesecloth bag in the saucepan, add salt and pepper, bring to a rapid boil, and cook 15 minutes, uncovered.
3. Bury the lobster or crabs in the broth. Cover, reduce heat, and simmer 20 minutes. Remove lobster or crab and cheesecloth bag. Place fish fillets in the broth, set the mussels and clams on top, cover, and cook 8 minutes. Meanwhile, set the lobster or crabs on its (their) back(s), and slice down the middle. Crack claws and knuckles. If lobster, divide in half again, making two tail portions and two claw portions. Keep warm. Spread the *rouille* on the toast.
4. When the fish and shellfish are cooked, place lobster or crabs in a large soup tureen. Set the fish on top and arrange mussels and clams around the sides. Pour the broth through a colander, and mash the vegetables into the broth. Pour broth into tureen.

To serve: Divide fish and shellfish among four large bowls, and ladle soup over the top. Offer French bread spread with *rouille* on the side.

To make ahead: Complete through Step 2, and have everything else ready so you can finish the dish just before serving.

ROUILLE   Serves 4 to 6

This is a very strongly flavored spread that gives a big lift to fish stews. We place it, spread on toast or stale French bread, right in the soup bowl before we begin to eat, but some like to keep it on the side and nibble at it now and then.

½ cup French bread, cut into chunks
¼ cup cold water
4 to 6 cloves garlic, mashed

¼ to ½ teaspoon hot red pepper flakes
½ teaspoon salt
3 to 5 tablespoons olive oil

Soak the bread in the water for 5 minutes, squeeze dry with your hands. Mash the garlic with the salt and pepper in a bowl. Mash in the bread, and stir in the olive oil, a bit at a time. Wait for the preceding addition of oil to be absorbed before you add more. (It's like making a mayonnaise with eggs and oil.) If you overdo the oil, and the *rouille* begins to separate, break up another slice of bread and mash it in.

To serve: Spread on stale or toasted bread and serve with fish stews. Or pass as a sauce to ladle into fish soups.

CRÈME ARGENTEUIL   Serves 4 to 6

Good gardeners in France pride themselves on the delicate flavor of their blanched asparagus, asparagus mounded in soil so it matures before it is touched by air or sun, and therefore, silvery-gold in color. We call it "white" asparagus.

¼ cup sour cream
½ cup heavy cream
1½ pounds white asparagus
2 cups water

4 cups Old-Fashioned Cream of Chicken Soup (page 88)
Salt and pepper

1. In a small bowl place sour cream and stir in heavy cream. Cover and let rest at room temperature.
2. Snap bottoms from asparagus and remove asparagus tips. Discard bottoms. Peel stalks with potato peeler and cut into 1- to 2-inch lengths. Place stalks and tips in 2 cups boiling water over medium high heat and boil, uncovered, 5 minutes, or until tips are tender. Drain gently, and reserve vegetable and water.
3. Place the Cream of Chicken Soup in the kettle over high heat.

Add 1 cup of the reserved asparagus water and the stalks. Bring to a boil, cover, lower heat, and simmer until stalks are fork-tender, about 15 to 20 minutes. Purée in a blender or a food processor, 2 cups at a time, or press through a sieve. Return purée to the kettle, turn heat to medium, and stir in the cream mixture. Add salt and pepper to taste. Place asparagus tips in the soup and heat to just below boiling.

To serve: Ladle into soup bowls, dividing asparagus tips among them.

Dividends: Excellent reheated. Stretch with milk if necessary.

To make ahead: Complete the soup, but add cream and tips just before serving.

CRÈME CRÉCY   Serves 6

Made with tapioca as a thickener instead of rice, this is called *Purée Velours* in my hometown: it also is known as Purée of Carrots. Use richly colored red carrots and not young greenish ones for this.

1 small onion, minced	4 cups All-Purpose White
2 tablespoons butter	Stock (page 45) or
1 pound carrots, grated	chicken broth
¼ teaspoon dried thyme or	¼ cup raw rice
3 sprigs fresh	1½ cups heavy cream
1 cup water	½ cup Croutons, Sautéed in
½ teaspoon salt	Butter (page 33)
2 teaspoons brown sugar	

1. In a large saucepan over medium heat, sauté the onion in the butter until translucent, about 5 minutes. Stir in carrots, thyme, water, salt, and sugar. Bring to a boil, lower heat, and cook 10 minutes. Add broth and rice. Cover and cook until carrots and rice are very tender, 20 to 25 minutes.
2. Purée in a blender or a food processor, 2 cups at a time, or press through a sieve. Return purée to the saucepan, raise heat to medium, stir in cream, and heat to just below boiling.

To serve: Ladle into soup bowls and garnish with croutons.

Dividends: Nice cold or reheated. Stretch with milk.

To make ahead: Keeps well hours or a day or two.

CRÈME GERMINY   Serves 4

The other classic soup made with sorrel (sour dock) is called *Potage à l'Oseille*. The major difference between the two soups is that *Germiny* is made with broth instead of water, and the sorrel is boiled before it goes into the soup. *Germiny* is nice cold.

½ pound sorrel, shredded	3 egg yolks
2 cups water	¼ cup sour cream
1 teaspoon salt	¼ cup whipped cream
4 cups beef broth	Salt and pepper

1. In a large saucepan over medium heat, simmer the sorrel in boiling water with the salt for 10 minutes. Drain sorrel and discard cooking water. Press sorrel through the sieve; reserve.
2. Place the broth in the saucepan and bring to a boil over low heat. In a small bowl beat the egg yolks until thick, then stir in the sour and the whipped cream. Stir ½ cup of boiling broth into the egg mixture, then turn the mixture into the broth, stirring constantly. Heat to just below boiling, but do not boil. Stir in the sorrel, and season with salt and pepper to taste.

To serve: Ladle into soup bowls.

MOULES À LA MARINIÈRE   Serves 6

Another glorious mussel soup, fragrant with herbs and wine. When only a few mussels are allowed per person it becomes a first course; when a dozen or more mussels are provided per serving, it becomes a main course. Serve with crusty French rolls and butter. In another version of *Marinière*, 1½ cups of fine white bread crumbs are cooked with the mussels to make a more substantial sauce. I add a large clove of garlic, minced, to this dish.

½ cup minced shallots	1 tablespoon minced fresh
¾ cup butter	thyme or ½ teaspoon dried
5 pounds medium mussels	1 small bay leaf, crumpled
2 tablespoons minced	2 cups dry white wine
parsley	1 tablespoon minced parsley

1. In a large kettle over medium heat, sauté shallots in half the butter until translucent, about 5 minutes. Add mussels, parsley, thyme, bay, and wine. Cover, raise heat, and bring to a boil, then lower heat and simmer about 8 minutes, shaking the pan

often. When all the mussels are open, they are done. Lift mussels into big soup bowls with a slotted spoon. Discard bay.
2. Add remaining butter to the kettle, bring to a boil, then add parsley, stir 30 seconds, and ladle at once over mussels.

To serve: Serve as soon as ready.

Dividends: Shuck any remaining mussels into leftover broth. Reheated with milk or cream, salt and pepper, this makes a nice mussel chowder.

SOUPE À L'AILLE
Serves 6 to 8

Delicious. And only a gourmet will recognize the main ingredient. Note this calls for 2 heads—the whole thing—not cloves of garlic.

2 large heads garlic	2 sprigs parsley
2 cups boiling water	3 tablespoons olive oil
2 quarts cold water	3 large egg yolks
2 tablespoons salt	4 tablespoons melted butter
1/4 teaspoon pepper	6 to 8 pieces French bread,
2 large whole cloves	toasted and buttered
1/4 teaspoon sage	1/2 cup grated Swiss cheese
1/4 teaspoon dried thyme	

1. Separate the garlic cloves and scald 1 minute. Slip off and discard the skins and scalding water.
2. In a kettle over medium heat, combine the cold water, garlic, salt, pepper, cloves, sage, thyme, parsley, and oil. Bring to a boil, cover, reduce heat, and simmer 30 minutes. Remove from heat.
3. With a slotted spoon, lift out the cloves, parsley, and garlic. Discard parsley and cloves. Purée the garlic with 2 cups of broth, in a blender or a food processor, or press through a sieve.
4. In a medium bowl beat the egg yolks until thick. Whip in the butter, then the garlic purée, then one cup of broth. Whip this mixture into the kettle. Reheat to just below boiling, but do not boil.

To serve: Place a piece of French bread toasted and buttered, in the bottom of each soup bowl and sprinkle generously with cheese. Ladle the soup over the bread.

To make ahead: Complete through Step 3, then finish just before serving.

PISTOU

Serves 6

Pistou, a zucchini soup with garlic and basil for flavoring, is made in the south of France. If you don't overcook the zucchini, the soup will be a pretty green. Fresh limas and peas are best for the soup, of course, but frozen will do. The zucchini and basil must be fresh, however. Makes a very satisfying meal served with bread, cheeese, and a fruity dessert.

2 cups lima beans	2 large cloves garlic, crushed
6 cups boiling water	15 leaves fresh basil
1 teaspoon salt	3 tablespoons minced
1 cup peas	parsley
3 medium onions, chopped	2 egg yolks
3 tablespoons olive oil	¼ cup grated Parmesan
5 to 6 small zucchini, grated	cheese
1 tablespoon butter	⅓ cup olive oil

1. In a large saucepan over medium high heat, add limas to boiling, salted water and cook, uncovered, 15 minutes. Add peas and cook, uncovered, 10 minutes or until both vegetables are tender. Don't overcook: You are trying to preserve the green! Purée in a blender or a food processor, 2 cups at a time, or press through a sieve.
2. In the saucepan over medium heat, sauté the onions in the oil 3 minutes. Add the zucchini and sauté 2 minutes. Scrape lima and pea purée into the onion and zucchini, stir, and cook another 2 to 3 minutes.
3. In a mortar or a small bowl place the butter and mash the garlic into it with the back of a wooden spoon. Mash basil and parsley into the mixture until you have a green paste in the bowl. Mix in the egg yolks, cheese, and, drop by drop, the olive oil, working to develop a mayonnaiselike sauce.

To serve: Heat soup to just below boiling, but don't overcook or you will lose the color. Add a generous portion of the sauce to each bowlful of soup.

To make ahead: May be made hours or a day ahead. Keep sauce covered and refrigerate. Don't boil soup when you reheat it.

POTAGE BONNE FEMME   Serves 8

Leeks and potatoes made into soup are just about top favorites
with all manner of people in France. Leeks look like big—I mean
really big—scallions, white at the bottom and green on top,
and combined with potatoes, they make up the soup called *Potage
Bonne Femme* or *Potage Parmentier*. When you see *Soupe du
Jour* in a restaurant in France, chances are it is *Potage Bonne
Femme*—leek and potato soup—with leftover vegetables added.
The best watercress soup is made by adding watercress to vichyssoise, and vichyssoise is leek and potato soup with lots of cream
—the most elegant of all chilled soups.

It is really important when preparing leeks to make soups that
you get the leeks clean. Slice the leeks in half lengthwise, then
take the leaves apart, one by one, and wash each thoroughly under
cold water. Leeks put themselves together in an intricate way
that lets lots of fine dirt get down inside, and a little grit between
the teeth can do a lot to ruin a magnificent soup!

4 tablespoons butter	¼ teaspoon pepper
5 to 6 medium leeks, including several inches of green, washed, sliced	4 medium potatoes, peeled, sliced
4 tablespoons all-purpose flour	2 cups milk
	½ cup heavy cream
6 cups hot water	3 tablespoons butter
1 tablespoon salt	Minced chives

1. In a large saucepan over medium heat, melt the butter and
   sauté the leeks 5 minutes. Remove from heat to let the pan
   cool, then stir in the flour and then the hot water. Return to
   heat and add salt, pepper, and potatoes. Bring to a boil, cover,
   lower heat, and cook 30 to 40 minutes, until potatoes are very
   tender. With a potato masher, break up the vegetables in the
   soup. Add the milk and cream, and heat to just below boiling.

To serve: Ladle into soup bowls, dividing stringy leeks among
them, and garnish with butter and chives.

Dividends: Wonderful reheated with milk. Add cooked, leftover
vegetables and create your own *soupe du jour.*

To make ahead: Keeps well for several days.

PURÉE ST. GERMAIN   Serves 6

This is the classic way with fresh peas in France.

6 cups small fresh peas	4 cups chicken broth
6 cups boiling water	Salt and pepper
2 teaspoons salt	Sprigs chervil or parsley

1. In a kettle over high heat, drop the peas by the handful into boiling, salted water. Add more peas only as water returns to a brisk boil. Simmer 5 to 7 minutes, until peas are just tender but not losing their bright color. Drain, and discard the water.
2. Purée peas, with broth, in a blender or a food processor, 2 cups at a time. Return purée to the kettle, heat to boiling, and add salt and pepper to taste.

To serve: Ladle into soup bowls, divide butter among them, and garnish with sprigs of chervil or parsley.

SOUPE AUX MARRONS   Serves 6

This is an exquisitely delicate soup, wonderful for party dinners. In fall chestnuts are pretty good, but at other times of the year, you'll find many moldy ones among them, so buy 2 full pounds though you only need one and a quarter pounds for this recipe.

1¼ pounds chestnuts	1½ quarts chicken broth
4½ cups water	1 cup heavy cream
¼ teaspoon dried thyme	1 teaspoon Maille white
2 large sprigs parsley	mustard
1 small bay leaf	Salt
¼ teaspoon tarragon	Dry sherry, optional
½ teaspoon salt	

1. With a small sharp knife, make a deep cut across the top (point) of the shell of each nut. Place the chestnuts in a kettle over high heat with 2 cups of water. Cover, bring to a boil, and boil 10 minutes. Put the kettle into the sink and run cold water into it. Lift 3 or 4 chestnuts out at a time, enlarge the cuts, and peel outer, then inner skin. Discard skins.
2. Place the shelled nuts and the remaining water in a kettle over high heat, and add the thyme, parsley, bay, tarragon, and salt. Cover, bring to a boil, reduce heat, and simmer 15 to 20 minutes, or until chestnuts are tender. Drain chestnuts and discard the cooking liquid.

3. Pour the broth into the kettle and simmer with the chestnuts 10 minutes. Purée in a blender or a food processor, 2 cups at a time, or press through a sieve. Reheat with the cream and mustard. Add salt to taste. Add a few drops of sherry to a bowlful of soup, and if you like it, add a tablespoon or more sherry to the kettle.

To serve: Ladle into bowls.

To make ahead: May be made several hours before serving.

SOUPE À L'OIGNON   Serves 6

This is one of the most popular French soups—onion soup as it used to be served in that wonderful open air market that once centered Paris, Les Halles.

6 medium onions, sliced thin	2 ounces Swiss cheese, shredded
3 tablespoons butter	
6 cups beef broth	6 small slices French bread
¼ cup dry white wine	6 teaspoons grated Swiss cheese
Salt and pepper	

1. Preheat the oven to 325 degrees.
2. In a large kettle over medium low heat, simmer onions in butter until lightly browned, 7 to 8 minutes. Stir in the broth and wine. Cover and simmer for about 30 minutes. Season with salt and pepper.
3. Place 6 individual ovenproof ceramic soup pots on a cookie sheet. Pour the broth into the pots, dividing the onions evenly. Stir in the shredded cheese.
4. Break the bread into 1-inch chunks and place 2 or 3 in each pot. When the bread floats to the surface, sprinkle with grated cheese.
5. Bake in the oven for about 20 minutes, then set briefly under the broiler to brown the top.

To serve: Set pots on service plates.

To make ahead: For a party, complete Step 2 a day ahead. Shortly before serving, preheat oven as in Step 1; bring soup to a boil and complete Steps 3 through 5.

SOUPE PROVENÇALE   Serves 6 to 8

This is a variation on *Soupe à l'Oignon* and comes from the south of France, from the region called Provence. To an herb-flavored tomato and onion soup you add slices of bread and cheese, then you bubble the cheese under the broiler. Great Sunday night supper. You'll need ovenproof crockery pots.

2 large onions, sliced	½ teaspoon dried thyme
1 tablespoon olive oil	⅛ teaspoon basil
2 cloves garlic, minced	¼ teaspoon pepper
4 large, very ripe tomatoes	6 cups water
(about 2 pounds)	2 tablespoons olive oil
1 large green pepper,	6 to 8 slices French bread
slivered	½ cup grated Swiss cheese
1 teaspoon salt	(4 ounces)

1. In a large saucepan over medium heat, sauté the onions in the oil until golden and beginning to brown, about 10 minutes. Add garlic, tomatoes, green pepper, salt, thyme, basil, pepper, and water. Cover, raise heat until soup boils, then lower heat, and simmer for 30 minutes.
2. Turn broiler to high, and place soup pots on a cookie sheet.
3. In a large skillet over medium heat, heat the oil and sauté the bread on each side until golden brown. Place 1 slice in the bottom of each pot, and top with a portion of cheese. Ladle in hot soup, and when bread floats, add more cheese. Broil until cheese bubbles.

To serve: Set pots on service plates and serve at once.

SOUPE SOUBISE   Serves 4 to 6

This onion soup is named for a famous French sauce made with onions and veal.

2 large onions, sliced thin	⅛ teaspoon pepper
2 tablespoons butter	⅛ teaspoon grated nutmeg
2 tablespoons all-purpose	⅛ teaspoon dried thyme
flour	4 egg yolks
4 cups hot milk	1¼ cups half-and-half
2 cups hot veal broth	1 cup Croutons, Sautéed
1 teaspoon salt	(page 32)

1. In a saucepan over medium heat, sauté the onions in the butter,

stirring often, until translucent, about 7 to 8 minutes. Don't let the onions brown. Lower heat, remove the saucepan from the fire, and stir in the flour. Beating constantly, add the hot milk and broth, salt, pepper, nutmeg, and thyme. Return to heat and simmer, uncovered, 30 minutes, stirring occasionally.
2. In a small bowl beat the egg yolks until thick. Stir in the cream. Stir in 1 cup hot soup, then return to the saucepan. Heat to just below boiling.

To serve: Ladle into soup bowls and garnish with croutons.

Dividends: Excellent reheated. Stretch with veal broth but don't boil.

To make ahead: Complete through Step 1, then finish just before serving.

CREAMY CHICKEN SOUP WITH CURRY (SENEGALESE SOUP)
Serves 4

When you are in a hurry, start with canned cream of chicken soup to save the time of making the cream sauce in Step 1. Major Grey's chutney is my favorite, but any homemade fruit chutney may be used. This soup is excellent served hot, too. A richer, simpler version of this appears in Chapter 10, page 356.

2 tablespoons butter	2 egg yolks
2 tablespoons all-purpose flour	½ cup heavy cream
	Salt and pepper
2 teaspoons curry powder	4 tablespoons minced chives
1 teaspoon turmeric	2 tablespoons chutney, optional
1 cup cooked white chicken meat, cut into strips	4 cups hot chicken broth

1. In a large saucepan over medium low heat, melt the butter and stir in the flour, curry, and turmeric. Cook 1 minute. stirring. Beating constantly, add the hot broth and cook, stirring, until bubbly, 1 to 2 minutes. Raise heat a little, add the chicken, cover, and heat 5 to 10 minutes.
2. In a small bowl, beat the egg yolks until thick and lemon-colored. Add the cream and stir in 1 cup of broth, then return to the saucepan, and heat to just below boiling. Add salt and pepper to taste. Chill, covered, 4 to 6 hours or overnight.

To serve: Ladle into soup bowls and garnish with chopped chives and a little chutney if you wish.

TRIPE À LA MODE DE CAEN   Serves 8

Honeycomb tripe, the kind to use for this, is the lining of the
second stomach of a cow. There are other types of tripe, but this
is preferred. There are many ways of preparing tripe soup, a
soupy stew that cooks forever. Philadelphia Pepper Pot is the
nearest equivalent in this country—it's a simpler version of this,
made heartier by the addition of dumplings and sometimes enriched by a cup of heavy cream. Make this a day ahead and serve
with plain boiled potatoes.

4 pounds honeycomb tripe	6 whole cloves
2 large onions, sliced	10 peppercorns
4 carrots, sliced thick	2 teaspoons salt
4 leeks, sliced thick	¼ teaspoon allspice
1 calf's foot	2 quarts beef broth or
4 large cloves garlic	water
4 sprigs parsley	½ cup Calvados
1 small bay leaf	1½ cups sifted flour
½ teaspoon dried thyme	½ cup water

1. Preheat the oven to 300 degrees.
2. Cut the tripe into 3-inch squares. In a large dutch oven or a
   kettle with a close-fitting lid, lay out the vegetables, the tripe,
   and the calf's foot, split. Add the herbs and spices tied into a
   small cheesecloth square, the salt, allspice, and broth or water
   to cover, and the Calvados. Place the lid on the dutch oven or
   kettle. Mix the flour and enough water to make a dry but
   sticky dough, and roll it into a piece long enough to go around
   the lid. Use the dough to seal the lid closed. Bake 7 hours.
   Discard the pastry.
3. Line a colander with 2 thicknesses of cheesecloth and strain
   the broth into a large kettle. Place the tripe in a tureen with
   the meat stripped from the calf's foot. Discard bones, vegetables, herb bag, and garlic. When the broth has cooled, skim
   away as much fat as possible. Bring to a boil over high heat.

To serve: Pour the broth over the tripe and ladle the soup into
bowls.

GERMANY

Germans love soups and make them from fascinating combinations of ingredients—eels and beef, for instance, and oat groats and apples. In America, German soups are perhaps best known as based on wines and beer or ale. *Weinsuppe mit Makronen oder Biscuits*—wine soup made with macaroons or other sweet biscuits is one, and there's another with "snow eggs" (meringues), and at least one based on sparkling wine. Most of these recipes call for wine to be simmered with water, sugar, cinnamon, and lemon. Sometimes they are thickened with flour. I am including a beer soup, more for reading than making.

BIERSUPPE MIT MILCH   Serves 6

This is made with imported German beer. Try it only if you know you like beer soup.

1 quart imported sweet German ale
Juice of ½ lemon, strained
½ teaspoon grated lemon rind
1 stick cinnamon
1 tablespoon potato starch or cornstarch

1 tablespoon cold water
2 cups hot milk
2 large egg yolks, well beaten
Salt and pepper
Croutons, Sautéed (page 32)

1. In a kettle over medium heat, combine ale, lemon juice, rind, cinnamon, and bring to a boil. Reduce heat and stir in potato starch or cornstarch mixed with water. Stir until ale thickens and clears.
2. Whip ½ cup hot milk into the egg yolks, and scrape back into the remaining hot milk, then stir both into the ale. Heat to just below boiling. Season with salt and pepper to taste.

To serve: Discard the cinnamon stick and ladle the soup into mugs. Garnish with a few croutons.

HAMBURGER *AALSUPPE*   Serves 8

This is a famous German soup made with eels and beef, richer in flavor than the Eel Soup in Chapter 4. I've never made this one, so proceed with caution. I am including it because it is interesting to read.

1½ pounds eel, skinned, boned, cut into 2-inch pieces
1 tablespoon salt
2½ pounds lean stew beef, cut into 2-inch cubes
3 quarts water
2 medium onions, cut into big chunks
1 medium carrot, cut into big chunks
2 small turnips, halved
½ pound sorrel, washed, chopped
1 tablespoon salt
¼ teaspoon pepper
½ teaspoon sage
¼ teaspoon tarragon
¼ teaspoon dried thyme
1 cup frozen green peas
½ head small cauliflower, cut into florets
2 cups water
2 tablespoons white vinegar
1 small onion, sliced
¼ teaspoon dried thyme
½ cup dry white wine
2 egg yolks, lightly beaten
Salt and pepper
1 can pears, drained, quartered
1 teaspoon grated lemon rind

1. In a large bowl combine the eel pieces with the salt; set aside.
2. In a large kettle, combine beef and water with onions, carrot, turnips, sorrel, salt, pepper, and herbs. Cover, bring to a boil, reduce heat, and simmer 2 hours. Add peas and cauliflower, and cook 15 minutes.
3. Meanwhile, rinse the eel and place in a kettle over high heat with the water, vinegar, onion, and thyme. Cover, bring to a boil, reduce heat, and simmer 15 minutes. Strain, reserving liquid. Remove the eel from the bones and discard bones. Stir eel meat into the beef broth, and add the eel's cooking liquid and wine. Simmer rapidly 15 minutes. Remove from heat.
4. Beat ½ cup of the broth into the egg yolks, and scrape the mixture into the broth. Heat to just below boiling, but do not boil. Add salt and pepper to taste.

To serve: Ladle soup into bowls and garnish each with a few quarters of pear and a bit of lemon rind.

To make ahead: May be completed through Step 3, then finished just before serving.

GREECE

AVGOLEMONO

Serves 6

Lemon soup is *the* great Greek soup, as far as Americans are concerned. It is one of many similar soups made in other lands and perhaps the best. In Greece it often is based on lamb or mutton broth rather than on chicken broth, as here. *Stracciatella* is an Italian egg soup that is much like this, but that recipe adds 2 tablespoons of all-purpose flour to the eggs and ¼ cup grated Parmesan or other cheese. The flour will save the eggs from curdling if you overheat.

6 cups chicken broth	Salt and pepper
6 tablespoons raw rice	2 tablespoons minced mint
4 large eggs	leaves
3 tablespoons strained lemon juice	

1. In a kettle over medium heat, bring the broth to a boil, add the rice, reduce heat, cover, and cook 20 minutes.
2. In a large bowl beat the eggs until very frothy, then stir in the lemon juice. Whisk a cupful of hot broth into the eggs. Remove the broth from heat and in a slow stream, beat the eggs into the broth. Return the broth to very low heat and stir for a few minutes until the soup thickens. Don't let it boil. Add salt and pepper to taste.

To serve: Ladle into consommé cups and top with a little mint.

To make ahead: Complete through Step 1, then finish just before serving.

HUNGARY

This is another Middle European land where soups are important. Many are flavored with sweet Hungarian paprika, which is a trademark of Hungarian dishes such as goulash and Chicken Paprikash. Imported Hungarian paprika is an investment worth making.

GOULASH SOUP   Serves 8

A whole chili may heat this soup more than you like—you could use instead a few grains of red pepper.

3½ pounds boneless beef chuck or stew meat, cut into ½-inch cubes
2 tablespoons oil
3 tablespoons butter
3 large onions, chopped
3 large cloves garlic, minced
1 tablespoon sweet Hungarian or domestic paprika
2 quarts water
2 large green peppers, cut into narrow strips
1 tablespoon salt
½ teaspoon pepper
1 teaspoon caraway seed
4 large ripe tomatoes, peeled, seeded, chopped, or 1 16-ounce can tomatoes and liquid
1 small dried red chili pepper, crushed
2 medium potatoes, peeled, cut into eighths
Sour cream (Optional; traditionalists do not include sour cream)

1. In a large saucepan over medium high heat, sauté the meat in the oil until well browned on all sides. Reduce heat to medium. Melt the butter in the saucepan, add the onions and the garlic and sauté 5 minutes.
2. Stir in the paprika, water, green peppers, salt, pepper, caraway seeds, tomatoes, and chili. Cover, bring to a boil, reduce heat, and simmer 2 hours.
3. Add potatoes and simmer 20 minutes or until potatoes are tender.

To serve: Ladle into bowls and, if you wish, garnish with sour cream.

To make ahead: Best made the day before. Complete through Step 2, refrigerate overnight, skim the fat, then finish shortly before serving.

CREAM OF LIVER SOUP   Serves 6

In peasant homes this was made with pork liver. It is most delicious when you can afford fine fresh calf's liver, but it's very
good made with chicken livers, as here. They must be fresh.

1 small onion, minced	2 tablespoons butter
2 tablespoons butter	2 tablespoons all-purpose
⅓ pound fresh chicken	flour
livers, quartered	1 egg, well beaten
½ teaspoon salt	1 cup heavy cream
⅛ teaspoon pepper	Salt and pepper
1 tablespoon brandy	1 tablespoon minced parsley
6 cups hot beef or chicken	
broth	

1. In a saucepan over medium heat, sauté the onion in the butter
   3 minutes. Stir in the livers, salt and pepper them, sprinkle
   with brandy, cover, reduce heat, and sauté for about 5 minutes,
   tossing the contents of the pan often. Pour 1 cup of broth into
   the pan, scrape up the butter browning on the bottom, and
   purée the contents of the saucepan in a blender or a food
   processor, or press through a sieve.
2. Over low heat, melt the butter in the saucepan and stir in the
   flour. Beat the remaining hot broth into this *roux*, and continue
   to beat it as it bubbles and begins to thicken. Stir the purée
   into the broth.
3. Beat a little hot soup into the egg combined with the cream.
   Remove the soup from the heat and whip the egg mixture into
   the broth. Add salt and pepper to taste.

To serve: Ladle into bowls and garnish with parsley.

INDIA

DHAL MULEGOO THANI   Serves 6

This is a curry soup made with lentils. Be sure to use the pretty orange-red lentils—the brown lentils make it unattractive. In *Mulego Thani* you will recognize the name that became Mulligatawny when the recipe was brought home to the British Isles. *Dhal* is the word for lentils; pita is an Indian bread.

1 cup red lentils
7 cups water
1 small bay leaf
1 small onion, chopped
2 tablespoon butter
1 large clove garlic, minced
⅛ teaspoon red pepper or cayenne (more if you want it hot)

2 teaspoons turmeric
1 teaspoon strained lime or lemon juice
2 teaspoons salt
6 pita or English muffins, toasted
1 teaspoon ground coriander
½ teaspoon ground cumin

1. In a kettle over medium high heat, combine the lentils with the water and bay leaf, and bring to a boil, covered. Reduce heat and simmer until lentils are very soft, about 1 hour. Stir often.
2. In a small saucepan over medium heat, sauté the onion in the butter with the garlic, coriander, cumin, pepper or cayenne, and turmeric 5 minutes. Stir into the kettle of lentils. Stir in lime or lemon juice and salt. Simmer, covered, 15 minutes.

To serve: Ladle into bowls and serve with hot Indian pita or toasted English muffins.

To make ahead: Made a day or so ahead, it is very good.

RASAM   Serves 4 to 6

In India this is called "pepper water." It is a thin, hot, *digestif* soup served at the end of the meal, usually over rice. Several of the ingredients are found only in Eastern specialty shops, but you can make the clarified butter, known as *ghee;* just melt butter and spoon off the oily portion—that's clarified butter. Fresh coriander stems and leaves are sold as Chinese parsley in many Chinese markets, or as *cilantro* in Latin American grocery stores.

1 tablespoon tamarind pulp or 1 teaspoon instant tamarind
1 cup hot water
1 large clove garlic, sliced
½ teaspoon pepper
1 teaspoon ground cumin
4 cups cold water

2 teaspoons salt
2 tablespoons chopped fresh coriander
2 teaspoons clarified butter
1 teaspoon black mustard seeds
3 tablespoons curry powder
3 cups hot cooked rice

1. Soak the tamarind pulp in the hot water 10 minutes, then massage it between your fingers, squeezing the pulp into the water. Discard the seeds and fibers. If you are using instant tamarind, dissolve it in the hot water. Pour the tamarind water into a kettle over medium heat, and add the garlic, pepper, cumin, cold water, salt, and coriander. Bring to a boil, then simmer 10 minutes.
2. In a small saucepan over medium heat, warm the clarified butter and sauté the mustard seeds and curry. Scrape into the simmering soup. Simmer 3 minutes.

To serve: Serve in a small bowl or ladle over small bowls of hot rice.

ISRAEL

PASSOVER SOUP   Serves 6 to 8

This is probably more representative of Eastern European ethnic Jewish cuisine than of Israeli cooking. The matzo balls are made with matzo meal—ground matzo crackers. If you don't have chicken fat, use butter. Chicken broth can be made stronger by adding bouillon cubes.

2 large eggs, separated
3 tablespoons hot melted chicken fat or butter
8 cups strong chicken broth
½ teaspoon salt

½ teaspoon cayenne
¾ cup matzo meal
1 tablespoon finely minced parsley

1. In an electric mixer, beat the egg whites until stiff but not dry, and set aside.
2. In another bowl beat the yolks until thickening; dribble in the hot fat, then add ¼ cup of boiling broth, a little at a time. Add the salt and cayenne, turn the beater to low and slowly add the matzo meal. Fold the whites gently into the dough. Place in the freezer half an hour to stiffen, or chill in the refrigerator an hour.
3. In a big kettle or saucepan over medium heat, bring the remaining broth to a boil, reduce heat, and let it simmer rapidly. Break off pieces of dough the size of a small walnut and roll into balls between your palms. Drop into the broth and simmer 15 minutes.

To serve: Ladle into bowls and garnish with parsley.

To make ahead: Make the balls and refrigerate until ready to cook.

ITALY

MINESTRONE WITH FRESH TOMATOES   Serves 6 to 8

I tend to think of minestrone—the wonderful vegetable soup found in Italy—as made with tomato paste or without tomatoes at all. But here's a version that includes ripe tomatoes and other fresh vegetables.

2 cups fresh white beans	2 large ripe tomatoes, chopped
4 cups water	8 cups beef broth
½ cup olive oil	¼ cup elbow macaroni
4 onions, chopped	¼ teaspoon dried sage
2 leeks, chopped	1 tablespoon minced fresh basil
1 clove garlic, minced	1 tablespoon minced fresh parsley
1 stalk celery, chopped	Salt and pepper
2 cups green snap beans, cut into 1-inch pieces	Grated Parmesan cheese
2 small zucchini, chopped	
2 large potatoes, peeled, chopped	

1. In a large kettle over high heat, cook the white beans in the water, covered, 30 minutes or until tender.
2. In a small saucepan, heat the oil and sauté the onions, leeks, and garlic until the onion is translucent, 5 to 7 minutes. Scrape into the kettle. Add the celery, green beans, zucchini, potatoes, tomatoes, and broth. Cover and simmer 40 minutes. Raise heat, add the macaroni and herbs, cover, and boil for 20 minutes. Add salt and pepper to taste.

To serve: Ladle into soup bowls and sprinkle with Parmesan cheese.

To make ahead: Make a day ahead—tastes better! Add Parmesan at the end.

MEXICO AND LATIN AMERICA

Rich, bean-based soups are plentiful south of our borders. In Mexican homes, soup is a tradition at midday. The best of Latin American cooking is like the best of French cooking with a big dash of Spanish thrown in. Soups start with first-rate broths like those in Chapter 2, and include at least one clove of garlic. The herbs found in Latin America change the flavor. *Epazote,* for instance, and lemon and lime juice, and chili powder or peppers add the exotic touches tourists find so fascinating. A number of the bean-based soups in this book are of Latin American origin. Below are a couple of Mexican dishes you might enjoy.

SOPA DE FLOR DE CALABAZA Serves 8

This is made with pumpkin blossoms. You may never have enough blooms to spare to try it, but it's fun to read. *Epazote,* sometimes called *pazote* here, is an herb found in Puerto Rican markets in Manhattan and some other regions of the country.

1 pound squash blooms	2 quarts chicken broth
½ stick butter	1 sprig *epazote*
1 small onion, minced	Salt and pepper

1. Reserve 8 small blooms. Stem the others and chop coarsely. In a large kettle over medium heat, sauté the blooms in the butter with the onion until limp, 5 to 7 minutes.
2. In a kettle, heat the broth with the *epazote* until it begins to boil. Stir in the blooms with the onions, and heat 2 minutes. Add salt and pepper to taste.

To serve: Ladle into bowls and garnish each with a reserved bloom.

SOPA DE TORTILLA Serves 8

Tortillas are closely associated with Mexican cooking. Here's a way to use leftovers.

6 4-inch tortillas, cut into ¼-inch strips	½ cup oil
	2 quarts chicken broth

<table>
<tr><td>1 tablespoon ground
coriander
Grated Parmesan cheese</td><td>1 medium onion
2 cups tomato purée</td></tr>
</table>

1. In a large saucepan over medium heat, sauté the tortilla strips in the oil until crisp and beginning to brown. Drain and keep warm.
2. In a kettle over medium high heat, combine the broth with the onion and tomato purée. Simmer, uncovered, 5 minutes. Stir in the coriander, allow to boil up once, then turn off heat.

To serve: Divide the tortilla strips among the soup bowls and ladle hot soup over them.

SOPA SECA   Serves 4 to 6

It was the Spanish who brought both rice and noodles to Mexico where, for reasons unknown, they became the main ingredient in a course called *sopa seca,* "dry soup." *Sopa seca* is like the pasta course in an Italian meal, or like a *risotto*—served between a "wet" soup and the meat or fish entrée. Here's one made with tortillas.

1 medium onion, chopped	1 teaspoon salt
1 medium clove garlic, minced	1/4 teaspoon pepper
1/2 cup oil	1/4 teaspoon sugar
3 medium ripe tomatoes, chopped	18 small day-old tortillas
1/2 teaspoon dried oregano	1/2 pint heavy cream
	1 cup grated Parmesan cheese

1. Preheat the oven to 350 degrees.
2. In a saucepan over medium heat, sauté the onion and garlic in 2 tablespoons of oil until the onion is translucent, about 5 minutes. Add the tomatoes, oregano, salt, pepper, and sugar. Reduce heat and simmer, stirring, 5 minutes.
3. In a large skillet over medium heat, warm the remaining oil and sauté the tortillas until crisp but not brown. Drain on paper towel. Layer the sauce and tortillas in an ovenproof casserole with the cream and grated cheese, ending with cheese. Bake 15 minutes.

To serve: Spoon onto deep plates.

NEAR EAST

DRIED FRUIT SOUP I   Serves 4 to 6

This is a faintly sweet, gloriously exotic curry soup from the Near East—Iran/Persia, and much to my liking. The Dried Fruit soup below, #II, is a regional dish, and more for reading than for eating. Like Beer Soup, #II is included to make the book more completely representative of the soups of many lands.

¾ pound meaty lamb neck, or lamp shoulder chops	¼ teaspoon ground coriander
½ cup yellow split peas	½ teaspoon cumin
1 onion, chopped	¼ cup chopped, pitted, dried prunes
3 cups water	¼ cup chopped, pitted, dried apricots
1 teaspoon salt	
¼ teaspoon pepper	1 tablespoon strained lemon juice
1 teaspoon turmeric	
¼ teaspoon saffron threads	Salt

In a kettle over medium high heat, combine the lamb, and all the remaining ingredients except the fruits and the lemon juice. Cover, bring to boiling, reduce heat, and simmer 1 hour. Add the chopped fruit, and simmer uncovered 30 minutes more. Lift out the lamb, strip the meat and return it to the soup. Discard the bones. Stir in lemon juice, reheat 1 minute more, and season with salt to taste.

To serve: Ladle into bowls.

Dividends: Very nice cold, stretched with yogurt.

To make ahead: Delicious made ahead.

DRIED FRUIT SOUP II   Serves 4 to 6

Browsing among the soups in cookbooks of other lands, one finds many that are tempting to try. In Iran dried fruits are a staple, and soups like this one evolved in many households. It is sweet and sour, flavored with cinnamon and pepper, a fairly common combination in that region. I go very easy with the dried mint. Try this yourself before you serve it to company—it's quite special.

½ pound ground lean lamb	1 cup pitted dried prunes
1 small onion, minced	1 cup pitted dried apricots
¼ teaspoon cinnamon	1 cup chopped parsley
¼ teaspoon pepper	½ cup canned chick peas
½ teaspoon salt	½ cup vinegar
1 small onion, minced	⅓ cup sugar
2 tablespoons butter	1 tablespoon dried mint
6 cups water	¼ teaspoon cinnamon
3 teaspoons salt	¼ teaspoon pepper
½ cup raw rice	

1. In a large bowl combine meat, onion, cinnamon, pepper, and salt; mix well. Roll into balls the size of a small walnut.
2. In a small saucepan over medium heat, sauté the onion in the butter 5 minutes; set aside.
3. In a large kettle over high heat, bring the water to a rapid boil with the salt and rice. Cover, reduce heat, and simmer 15 minutes. Add prunes and cook 15 minutes. Add meatballs, apricots, parsley, chick peas, the sautéed onions and simmer, uncovered, 20 minutes. Add vinegar and sugar and cook 15 minutes.
4. Rub dried mint through a sieve into a small bowl, and combine it with the cinnamon and pepper. Add to the kettle 1 minute before removing the soup from heat.

To serve: Ladle into soup bowls.

To make ahead: May be completed through Step 3 a day or two ahead.

COLD YOGURT SOUP   Serves 4 to 6

Yogurt, lamb, dried fruit—these are some of the ingredients used in soups in the Near East. This one is Iranian in origin. You'll find other yogurt soups in Chapter 9.

½ cup golden raisins
½ cup hot water
3 cups plain yogurt
½ cup half-and-half
1 hard-boiled egg, chopped
6 ice cubes
1 small cucumber, peeled, seeded, chopped
2 to 3 large scallions, chopped

2 teaspoons salt
¼ teaspoon pepper
1 cup cold water
1 tablespoon chopped parsley
1 tablespoon chopped fresh dill

1. Soak the raisins in the hot water 5 minutes or until plump.
2. In a large mixing bowl combine the yogurt, half-and-half, egg, ice, cucumber, scallions, salt, and pepper. Drain the raisins, discard the water, and add to the bowl. Stir in the cold water, cover, and chill 4 hours.

To serve: Ladle into bowls and garnish with parsley and dill.

THE FAR EAST

Chinese cooking is more subtle than French, as varied as the imagination of the cook, and a sure cure for tired palates. The soups from the Orient are wonderfully inventive. Here are some of the most popular in our country. They'll be as good as the broth they are based on. In Chapter 2 you'll find a special recipe for Chicken Broth for Chinese Soups (page 49). Special ingredients, like Won Ton wrappers, are found in Oriental food shops, and more and more frequently, are carried by supermarkets and small greengrocers run by Koreans and Vietnamese.

There are charming little bowls and china spoons sold for serving Oriental soups—they are quite inexpensive in Chinese gift shops, and sometimes sold in five-and-dime stores.

The Thai soup *Tom Kah Kai* is brought to the table in my favorite Thai restaurant in a Mongolian hot pot, which has an alcohol or sterno flame to keep soup heating. Great fun! A dramatic way to present any Oriental soup.

BIRD'S NEST SOUP   Serves 4 to 6

Yes, this is made from real birds' nests, gelatinous material produced by the swifts that live in the South Sea Islands. You'll find
the nests at Chinese specialty shops. Soak them 3 hours or overnight, in cold water before using. Use a tweezers to pluck out
any remaining feathers, then rinse in clean running water. Chinese parsley is another name for fresh coriander.

5 cups Chicken Broth for Chinese Soups (page 49)	4 tablespoons cooked chicken meat, cut into thin strips
4 to 6 birds' nests, soaked, cleaned	1 tablespoon soy sauce
1 teaspoon salt	1 tablespoon Chinese parsley, minced
1 teaspoon cooked ham, cut into thin strips	

In a kettle over medium heat, bring the broth to a boil, and add
the nests and salt. Simmer, uncovered, 20 minutes. Add the ham,
chicken, and soy sauce. Simmer 1 minute.

To serve: Ladle into bowls and garnish with parsley.

EGG DROP SOUP   Serves 4 to 6

Another popular Chinese soup. Eggs are dribbled into broth
where they cook into fine, exotic strands.

4 to 6 cups Chicken Broth for Chinese Soups (page 49)	2 medium eggs
1 tablespoon cornstarch	1 large scallion, minced
½ teaspoon soy sauce	1 teaspoon Chinese parsley, minced
½ teaspoon salt	

1. Set aside 3 tablespoons broth and chill. In a kettle over medium
   heat, bring the remaining broth to a simmer. In a small bowl
   mix the cornstarch and the soy sauce with the cold broth, add
   the salt, and stir mixture into the soup until it thickens and
   clears.
2. Break the eggs into a small pitcher and beat very lightly.

To serve: With the broth simmering, pour the eggs into the soup
in a very thin, slow stream. Turn off heat at once. Stir once.
Divide the scallion and the parsley among the bowls, and ladle
soup into them.

HOT AND SOUR SOUP   Serves 4 to 6

This soup is one of my favorites because it uses so many exotic ingredients. (Yes, they are real tiger lilies, dried.)

¼ cup dried tree fungus
¼ cup dried tiger lilies
¼ cup dried Chinese
   mushrooms
1 cup boiling water
1 cake bean curd
3 cups beef broth
2 tablespoons cornstarch

½ cup cold beef broth
1 tablespoon soy sauce
½ teaspoon pepper
1½ tablespoons white wine
   vinegar
1 medium egg
1 teaspoon cold water

1. In a bowl combine the fungus, lilies, and mushrooms, and pour boiling water over them. Let soak 20 minutes. Drain, discard water, and squeeze all ingredients dry. Sliver the mushrooms.
2. In a kettle over medium heat, bring the broth to a simmer, and add the fungus, lilies, mushrooms, and bean curd. Simmer, uncovered, 10 minutes. Mix the cornstarch and cold beef broth, and stir into the soup until it thickens and clears. Add the soy sauce, pepper, and vinegar.

To serve: In a small bowl beat the egg with the water and pour into the simmering broth in a thin, slow stream. Turn the heat off at once. Stir once. Ladle into bowls.

WON TON SOUP   Serves 8

Won ton wrappers are flat small squares of rolled-out dough.

½ pound cooked fresh
   spinach, chopped, or
   1 10-ounce package
   frozen chopped spinach
4 cups cooked lean pork,
   chopped
1½ tablespoons soy sauce
½ teaspoon fresh ginger,
   minced

1 teaspoon salt
5 dozen won ton wrappers
1 egg, lightly beaten
2 quarts boiling water
8 cups Chicken Broth for
   Chinese Soups (page 49)
12 fresh spinach leaves,
   stemmed

1. In a food processor combine spinach, pork, soy sauce, ginger, and salt, process 1 minute.
2. Place about 1 teaspoon of the filling in each won ton wrapper as illustrated, roll like a cigarette, and seal by running a bit of egg along the inner and outer edges of the wrapper with

your finger. In a large kettle over high heat, cook the won tons in the boiling water, uncovered, 5 minutes. Lift from the water with a slotted spoon and drain in a colander. Spread out on a large platter while the others finish cooking: don't heap together—they'll stick.

To serve: In a large kettle over high heat, bring the chicken broth to a boil, add the won tons and the spinach leaves, bring back to a boil, turn off heat, and serve at once. Place 2 leaves in each bowl and divide the won tons among them, allowing 4 to 10 per person, depending on how many more courses the dinner will include.

To make ahead: Won tons may be made and refrigerated or frozen before cooking. Once cooked, they should be used at once to be at their best.

DAK KOOK
Serves 6

This is a thick Korean soup combining clams and chicken, easy to make. Remember to clean the shellfish thoroughly as described in Chapter 4. Add a bowl of rice to this and you have a complete meal.

1½ teaspoons minced ginger	1 tablespoon oil
1 large clove garlic, minced	18 small hard-shell clams or
3 small scallions,	mussels
minced	¾ pound fresh spinach,
1 chicken breast, boned,	stemmed and shredded
cut into matchstick strips	1 teaspoon sesame seed oil
6 cups Chicken Broth for	or a small bowl of soy
Chinese Soups (page 49)	sauce, optional

1. Heat a large soup kettle or a wok over medium high heat, and sauté the ginger, garlic, scallions, and chicken in the oil 30 seconds. Stir in the broth, cover, and bring to a rapid boil. Reduce heat and simmer 5 minutes. Add the clams or mussels, cover, and cook, shaking the kettle or wok often, until all the shellfish are open, about 8 minutes.
2. Raise heat and add the spinach, stirring. Remove the kettle from heat. Allow to stand until the spinach is completely wilted.

To serve: Add the sesame seed oil, if you wish, and ladle the soup into bowls, or pass a small bowl of soy sauce with the soup.

TOM KAH KAI   Serves 4

This is the recipe for chicken and coconut soup given me by Chef Thomas K. (as he writes his name) at Maneeya, a charming little Thai restaurant at 926 Eighth Avenue, in Manhattan. I *think* the name is *Tom Kah Kai*, unless that is the chef's name. In any case, he is wonderful, the food is good, and this soup is a delight. It is served at Maneeya in a Mongolian hot pot. It is exquisitely flavored with *kah*, which looks like ginger and tastes like an extraordinarily perfumed ginger. Thai fish sauce is clear and lighter than Chinese fish sauce. Fried peppers come bottled from Thailand, black-brown peppers cooked with carrots in oil.

4 cups Chicken Broth for Chinese Soups (page 49)	1 tablespoon Thai fried peppers
4 chicken bouillon cubes	1 tablespoon sugar
6 sliced *kah*	4 teaspoons strained lemon juice
1 cup coconut milk	
¼ cup dried Chinese mushrooms, slivered	1 cup boned chicken breast, cut into 2-inch pieces
1 tablespoon Thai fish sauce	

In a kettle over medium heat, bring the broth to a boil, and add the bouillon cubes, *kah*, coconut milk, mushrooms, fish sauce, peppers, sugar, and lemon juice. Simmer, covered, 10 minutes. Add chicken pieces and simmer 3 minutes.

To serve: Light the Mongolian hot pot and ladle the soup into the container. Leave a ladle in the dish and allow guests to serve themselves.

SHRIMP TEMPURA SOUP   Serves 4

This is served in a little Japanese health restaurant, near my Manhattan apartment, called Eden. It comes in a deep glass bowl that props solid deep-fried, batter-dipped tempura pieces upright so they can't soak in the broth and get mushy.

2 ounces cellophane noodles	1 tablespoon dry sherry
4 cups vegetable oil	1½ tablespoons fast-acting baking powder
1½ cups all-purpose flour	4 ¼-inch slices red cabbage
1½ teaspoons salt	4 ¼-inch slices sweet potato
1½ cups water minus 3 tablespoons	4 2-by-4-inch strips sweet green pepper
1 tablespoon vegetable oil	4 2-inch squares bean curd
4 3-inch broccoli florets	

4 large, thick onion rings	4 leaves Chinese cabbage,
16 big raw shrimp, shelled	chopped
and deveined	4 scallions, chopped
4 tablespoons soy sauce	Salt and pepper
8 beef bouillon cubes	Soy sauce
8 cups cold water	

1. Soak the noodles in cold water to cover.
2. Pour oil into deep fryer and set temperature at 425 degrees.
3. In a large, shallow bowl combine flour, salt, water, oil, sherry, and baking powder. Dip vegetable chunks and shrimp into batter, coat thoroughly, then deep fry until golden brown. Drain on paper towel and keep warm.
4. Meanwhile, in a kettle over medium heat, combine soy sauce, bouillon cubes, water, bean curd, and cabbage; bring to a boil, and cook 1 minute. Add soaked noodles and simmer over reduced heat 10 minutes. Add scallions and turn off heat. Salt, pepper, and soy sauce may be added to broth to suit your taste.

To serve: Divide noodles among bowls and pour in 1 to 2 cups of broth. Divide fried vegetables and shrimp among the bowls and set upright keeping them as far out of the broth as possible.

VEGETABLE SOUP JAPANESE STYLE   Serves 6 to 8

Delicate and lovely.

¼ cup dried Chinese	2 teaspoons oil
mushrooms	1 medium stalk green celery,
1 cup boiling water	sliced into very thin
1 cup cooked lean pork,	rounds
chopped	1 tablespoon soy sauce
6 cups Chicken Broth for	1 packed cup fresh spinach
Chinese Soups (page 49)	leaves
1 medium carrot, sliced very	¼ teaspoon minced fresh
thin	ginger

1. In a bowl combine mushrooms and water; soak 20 minutes. Drain, discard water, and sliver mushrooms.
2. Heat a large soup kettle or a wok over medium high heat and add the oil. At once stir in the mushrooms and pork, and stir-fry 5 minutes. Add the broth and bring to a boil. Add the carrot, celery, and soy sauce, and simmer 5 minutes. Add the spinach and the ginger, and stir until the spinach wilts.

To serve: Ladle into bowls at once.

RUSSIA

BORSCHT   Serves 10

Sour cream, called *smetana,* and dill are flavorings I associate with Russian food along with pickled beets, cucumbers, rye and pumpernickle breads. Borscht is the best-known of Russian soups, and it comes in many forms. The ingredients in the simple Beet Soup—Fast, in Chapter 7 are classic: you can make that recipe into borscht as most people know it. Just simmer the shredded fresh beets in butter instead of in broth, as in that recipe, and add the broth little by little until the beets are tender. Then turn the beets into the broth, mash them, and cook another 30 minutes. Strain, stir in the sour cream just before serving, or pass sour cream on the side along with a small bowl of snipped, fresh dill.

There are three other borscht recipes in this book—yes, it's that good, and it's easy—the Beet Soup in Chapter 5, which includes wine; the Icy Beet Soup in Chapter 10, which is very rich; and Marcel's Borscht in Chapter 11, which is very quick.

All of these combine beef broth, fresh beets, and sour cream, and a sweet-and-sour taste. In Siberia, borscht is made with buttermilk instead of broth. In the Ukraine and Poland, and in parts of Russia, borscht also is made with beef, veal, fish, or chicken broth and includes a great many vegetables. Here is an example of that type of borscht—it makes a whole meal and freezes very well, by the way.

2 medium onions, minced	2 teaspoons salt
½ stick of butter	6 peppercorns
2 pounds beets, chopped	½ cup red wine vinegar
2 medium purple turnips, chopped	3 quarts beef broth
1 medium celery root, chopped	1 pound potatoes, shredded
2 large parsnips, chopped	1 small green cabbage, shredded
2 16-ounce cans tomatoes an(liquid, or 4 tablespoons tomato paste	1 Polish sausage, cut into ½-inch slices
1 small bay leaf	2 cups sour cream
1 tablespoon firmly packed brown sugar	1 small bunch dill, snipped

In a large kettle or a stock pot, over medium high heat, sauté the onions in the butter 8 minutes. Stir in the beets, turnips, celery root, parsnips, tomatoes or tomato paste, bay, sugar, salt, peppercorns, vinegar, and 2 cups of the broth. Stirring constantly, bring to a boil, then cover, reduce heat, and simmer 30 minutes. Check occasionally to make sure vegetables aren't out of liquid. Add remaining broth and the potatoes, and cook 15 minutes. Add the cabbage and cook 15 minutes. Add the sausage and cook 15 minutes.

To serve: Ladle into large soup plates and pass sour cream and dill.

To make ahead: Excellent made hours or days ahead. Freezes well.

SCANDINAVIA

These cold countries have evolved hearty, stewy soups, just as you would expect. There's a Swedish pea soup rather like Canada's pea soup, but made with 1 cup dried yellow split peas and 1 pound pickled pork. It's called *Ärter Ock Fläok*. A Danish pea soup—*Gule Ärter*—is made with 2½ pounds fresh pork, 1½ pounds split peas, 2 sticks celery, 3 carrots, 4 leeks, 1 parsnip, salt, pepper, thyme. The Danes also make *Grönkall*—3 to 4 pounds pork simmered with carrots, leeks, *bouquet garni,* with a sliced whole cabbage added at the end. It is thickened with flour.

However, there's a lighter side to Scandinavian cuisine, one whose attention is centered on lovely, cool fruit soups and on European cooking. Some of these recipes appear below.

CHEESE SOUP DANISH STYLE   Serves 6 to 8

Danish Samsoe is rather like a mild cheddar, which might be used as a substitute.

½ cup chopped celery	1 cup firmly packed
4 large carrots, chopped	shredded Danish Baby
3 small leeks, sliced thin	Samsoe, Tybo, or Havarti
6 cups water	cheese
1½ teaspoons salt	3 egg yolks, lightly beaten
¼ teaspoon pepper	Salt and pepper
1 cup half-and-half	Chopped chives, optional

1. In a large kettle over high heat, combine celery, carrots, leeks, water, salt, and pepper. Cover, bring to a boil, reduce heat, and simmer 25 minutes. Purée in a blender or a food processor, 2 cups at a time, or press through a sieve. Return purée to the kettle.
2. Over medium high heat, bring the kettle to a boil and stir in the cheese. Stir until it is well blended. Season with salt and pepper to taste.
3. Pour half a cup of soup into the egg yolks. Scrape the yolks back into the kettle and stir 1 minute.

To serve: Ladle into soup bowls and garnish with chopped chives if you wish.

To make ahead: Complete through Step 1, then finish just before serving.

EGG SOUP   Serves 4

This is Swedish. There's a Spanish soup very like it further along. You'll need individual ceramic pots for this.

4 rounds Italian or French	4 cups hot beef broth
bread, ½ inch thick	½ cup grated Parmesan
4 tablespoons butter	cheese
4 large eggs	½ teaspoon minced dill
4 teaspoons chili sauce	

1. Preheat oven to 400 degrees.
2. In a large saucepan over medium heat, sauté the bread rounds in the butter until golden brown. Place a round in the bottom of each pot, and gently break 1 egg over each slice. Place a

teaspoon of chili sauce on each egg yolk. Pour 1 cup of hot broth into each pot, and sprinkle cheese on top. Set pots on a cookie sheet and place in the oven. Bake until the eggs are set, about 10 minutes.

To serve: Garnish each bowl with dill.

SØDSUPPE   Serves 8

This is good enough to be a dessert. It's an American adaptation of a Danish recipe for fruit soup and may be served hot or cold. You'll find many other fruit soups in Chapter 10.

8 cups combined cherry and plum juice from canned fruits, with water if needed to make 8 cups	½ orange, chopped
	½ lemon, chopped
	3 apples, cored, chopped
	3 peaches, pitted, chopped
1 cup sugar	2 sticks cinnamon
½ teaspoon salt	Salt or sugar
½ teaspoon tapioca	½ cup Croutons, Sautéed
1 cup pitted prunes	(page 32)
½ cup golden raisins	Sour cream

In a kettle over medium heat, combine the fruit juices and water with the sugar and salt. Cover and bring to a boil. Add the tapioca, fruits, and cinnamon sticks. Reduce heat and simmer, covered, 1 hour or until tapioca is soft and transparent. Taste, and add salt or sugar if needed.

To serve: To serve hot, garnish with croutons; to serve cold, chill several hours or overnight, and garnish with sour cream before serving.

SPAIN

Spain, with its Moorish and Roman heritage, and its proximity to France, has a cuisine that is both similar to and more exotic than either its neighbor to the north or Italy. Lots of olive oil is used—too much for the taste of some. Wonderful bean and sausage soups have come from Spain, and many of the soups in Chapter 12 are adaptations of these. Below are an egg soup, a variation on many popular in Spain, and a shrimp soup that is a good representative of the glorious seafood soups that have evolved on the Iberian peninsula.

SOPA CASTELLANO   Serves 6

This is an adaptation of a very ancient Castillian soup recipe whose feature is an egg cooked in broth. You'll need individual ovenproof ceramic pots to make this. It is hearty enough to be a main course if served with lots of crusty Portuguese bread.

1 large clove garlic, crushed	1 teaspoon paprika
1 small onion, minced	6 cups chicken broth
1/4 cup olive oil	Salt and pepper
3 slices white bread	6 eggs
4 ounces cooked ham	Paprika

1. Preheat the oven to 400 degrees.
2. In a large kettle over medium heat, sauté the garlic and the onion in the oil until the onion begins to be translucent, about 5 minutes. In a food processor mince the bread and the ham together, and stir into the onion. Sprinkle on the paprika and stir 2 minutes, but don't let the onions brown. Reduce heat. Stir the broth into the mixture a little at a time. Bring to a slow simmer and cook, uncovered, 10 minutes. Season with salt and pepper.
3. Pour the soup into individual ceramic pots and gently break an egg into each. Set pots on a cookie sheet and place in the oven. Bake until the eggs are set, about 10 minutes.

To serve: Garnish each bowl with a dash of paprika and set on a service plate.

SHRIMP SOUP MALAGUEÑA   Serves 6 to 8

In Malaga there are tiny shrimp that make a great soup. I've found these on the East Coast of the United States and in France. It's hard to have the patience to shell the wee shrimp, but they are very tasty, and the price, generally, is good.

1 pound unfilleted white fish, such as haddock, hake, turbot, flounder
1 medium onion, sliced
1 small bay leaf
2 sprigs parsley
7 cups cold water
¼ teaspoon dried thyme
½ teaspoon salt
¼ teaspoon pepper

½ pound fresh raw tiny shrimp
2 tablespoons dry sherry
½ cup fresh or frozen peas
1 egg yolk
2 teaspoons strained lemon juice
½ cup heavy cream
⅛ teaspoon ground nutmeg
2 teaspoons minced parsley

1. With a large, flat, sharp knife, fillet the fish, removing the flesh from the bones. Reserve. Cut the fish into 1-inch pieces. Tie the bones with the onion, bay, and parsley into a double thickness of cheesecloth. Place the bag in a big kettle over medium high heat with the water, thyme, salt, and pepper. Cover, bring to a boil, reduce heat, and cook 10 minutes. Add the shrimp, cover, return to a boil, and cook 5 minutes. Strain. Return the broth to the kettle with the cheesecloth bag but no heat. Shell the shrimp, placing the shrimp in a small bowl with just enough broth to cover them, and return the shells to the broth in the kettle. Cover, turn the heat to high, bring the broth to a boil, reduce heat, and simmer 10 minutes. Strain. Discard shells and bag.
2. Place the broth over medium heat, stir in the sherry, then add peas, fish pieces, and cook, uncovered, 4 minutes.
3. In a small bowl beat the egg yolk with the lemon juice. Stir in 1 cup of hot broth, then return to the soup. Add cream, nutmeg, shrimp and their broth to the kettle; heat to just below boiling, but do not boil.

To serve: Ladle soup into bowls and garnish with parsley.

Dividends: Leftover Shrimp Soup Malagueña, stirred into a *roux* and with a little more cooked, shelled shrimp, makes good creamed shrimp to serve on toast for light Sunday suppers.

To make ahead: Complete through Step 1, then finish just before serving.

Seven

SOUPS MY GARDEN TAUGHT ME

The soups in this chapter have mates in Chapter 5, creamy broths that were the staple first courses in the Edwardian meal —Cream of Mushroom Soup, Cream of Pea Soup, Fancy Cream of Broccoli Soup. Those Victorian/Edwardian soups are classics and the recipes should be followed fairly carefully. The vegetable soups in this chapter are different, quite able to accommodate the garden's plan, productivity, and season. Most of the recipes can take quite a bit of creative adjustment.

THE CONSERVATIVE SOUPS

Creativity is at the heart of conservation. You'll find a recipe here for most popular garden vegetables, from exotic Kohlrabi Cream to the very practical Too-Many-Tomatoes Soup. Many of the recipes can be jumping-off points for recipes of your own garden's invention. Poor Man's Asparagus Soup suggests ways to use stems of broccoli and other otherwise discarded vegetable parts. Soup from Greens suggests what can be done with not only kale and spinach, but turnip tops, beet tops, carrot and radish tops. Green Tomato Cream suggests that whatever the garden produces, there's some way to make soup with it!

Zucchini that has grown too big and tough, tomatoes that are slightly too ripe, and oversize beans that aren't preferred for soups make very good soups nonetheless. You will have to peel the big, big zucchini and squash because older skins are too tough, and you should seed big cucumbers, but these small efforts can turn second-class garden products into first-class eating.

Garden oddments, as well as over-productivity, have a place in the world of soups. The handful of tiny beans and cherry tomatoes that are too few to serve as a vegetable, make tasty variations on whatever is the day's soup theme. And when rows are overproducing but must be picked to keep productivity high, cook extras in 2-cup batches to make soup the next day or to freeze to make soup later. About two cups of cooked vegetables and a recipe of *Potage Bonne Femme* (Potato and Leek Soup) combine in what is called *soupe du jour*, the daily "house" soup in small French restaurants. Just as good is a combination of two cups cooked vegetable and cream of chicken soup, or chicken broth, or veal broth, enriched with milk or light cream, butter, seasonings, and garnished with herbs.

PREPARING GARDEN VEGETABLES FOR SOUPS

Garden vegetables and vegetables from local garden centers and roadside stands need thorough washing. Carrots need not be peeled if they are to be grated or chopped, but they do need scrubbing to avoid grit in the soup. Beans must be stemmed, and cucumbers and squash, too. Today the use of blenders in making soups just about makes peeling tomatoes obsolete—generally—but some tomato varieties have tough skins and should be peeled. It's easy enough: Grip the tomato on a spaghetti holder, or impale it on a fork, dip into rapidly boiling water, hold 15 to 30 seconds, remove, break the skin with a sharp knife, and pull skins off.

USING HERBS IN GARDEN SOUPS

A garnish of minced green brings a brilliant bit of color to the cream soups in particular. Use fresh herbs lavishly for color, but wisely for flavor. As a rule of thumb, use twice as much fresh herb, minced, as dried herb when substituting, and remember that herb leaves generally must be minced or bruised to bring out flavor. Pick herb tips, which are more flavorful as well as prettier than big leaves. (Picking tips encourages bushiness in the plant—and that's good!) Pick herbs in the midmorning period after dew has dried and before the sun draws out and dissipates their volatile oils.

Herb garnishes are somewhat interchangeable, but not entirely. Dill, chives, and parsley are the most common garden herbs available, and are nice in almost any creamy soup and most vegetable mixes. Parsley, thyme, and bay go well together. Chives are nice in anything including onions—which is most everything! Basil is heaven with tomatoes and most Italian cuisine. Dill is good with most German and Scandinavian dishes, but not with all that many French dishes.

Some herbs bloom: Borage has pretty blue flowers, and chives have a pink-lavender flower. They are edible, as are nasturtium blooms, and make especially pretty garnishes for soups.

TO MAKE AHEAD: CANNING AND FREEZING

Canned vegetable soups fresh from the garden can be rather good if you have the time and the equipment. The time isn't too great a problem. When you've finished cooking a soup, it's ready to process in a canner. Just pour into canning jars that are sterilized, process, seal, and store in a cool place.

But when you are canning, don't complete the soup through the addition of eggs and milk or cream. Consider the basic cooked soup as that portion to can, and plan to complete the soup just before serving.

Soups containing garden vegetables freeze well. Vegetables tend to lose their texture in the freezing process. If you wish, freeze the basic cooked soup if the vegetables are puréed and no texture is desirable.

HOT APPLE SOUP   Serves 4 to 6

Delicate—light—a nice way to begin a formal meal.

4 cups hot veal broth	½ teaspoon curry powder
1 large apple, peeled, grated	Salt and pepper
1 small onion, chopped	Sweet butter
1 cup light cream	

1. In a saucepan over medium heat, place broth, apple, and onion. Simmer until tender, about 10 minutes.
2. Purée in a blender or food processor, 2 cups at a time, or press through a sieve. Return to saucepan, stir in the cream, curry powder, salt, and pepper. Reheat, but do not let boil.

To serve: Ladle into soup bowls and add a dab of sweet butter.

To make ahead: Complete through Step 2, but do not reheat until ready to serve.

POOR MAN'S ASPARAGUS SOUP   Serves 6 to 8

Make this with stem ends of asparagus, those big green chunks you remove because they may not be tender enough to serve. But don't use the white, really tough bottom: they tend to be tasteless.

2 tablespoons butter	6 cups hot milk
1 small onion, minced	Salt and pepper
3 cups green stem ends of asparagus, cut into 1-inch lengths	2 tablespoons butter

1. In a heavy saucepan over medium heat, melt the butter and sauté the onion and the asparagus 5 to 8 minutes, stirring constantly. Add the milk and bring to a simmer. Cook until asparagus is tender.
2. Purée in a blender or a food processor, 2 cups at a time, or press through a sieve. Return to saucepan, add salt and pepper to taste, and reheat.

To serve: Ladle into soup bowls and divide butter among them.

To make ahead: Tastes better the second day.

ASPARAGUS SOUP   Serves 6

A tangy way with asparagus. Remove spears from heat before they lose the bright green that makes this soup pretty.

1 pound asparagus, trimmed, cut into 3- or 4-inch lengths	Grated zest and juice of ½ lemon
4 cups chicken broth	2 tablespoons all-purpose flour
2 tablespoons butter	Salt and pepper
1 small onion, grated	¼ teaspoon grated nutmeg

1. In a large saucepan over medium heat, simmer asparagus, uncovered, in broth until tender, 8 to 10 minutes. Purée in a blender or a food processor, 2 cups at a time, or press through a sieve.
2. In the large saucepan over low heat, melt the butter and simmer the onion with the lemon zest and juice until onion is tender. Stir in the flour and continue to cook until bubbly, about a minute longer.
3. Beat the asparagus purée into the flour mixture and cook, stirring constantly, until soup is hot and thick, then remove from heat.

To serve: Ladle into soup bowls and sprinkle with a bit of nutmeg.

BUTTER BEAN SOUP   Serves 6 to 8

Butter beans are those waxy yellow beans that ripen in mid-summer.

4 cups butter beans, cut into 1-inch pieces	2 cups milk, or more
	Salt and pepper
4 cups water	1/8 teaspoon grated nutmeg
1 teaspoon salt	4 tablespoons butter
1 slice onion	

1. In a medium kettle over high heat, place the beans, water, salt, and onion slice. Bring to a rapid boil, cover, and cook until beans are tender, 15 to 20 minutes.
2. Purée in a blender or a food processor, 2 cups at a time, or press through a sieve. Measure and return to the kettle, adding enough milk to make 6 cups. Raise heat and simmer the soup for ten minutes; milk will take on a slightly curdled appearance. Add salt and pepper to taste, and nutmeg.

To serve: Divide butter among soup bowls and ladle in soup.

To make ahead: May be made the day before.

GREEN BEAN SOUP   Serves 6 to 8

Bean lovers will love this. Don't overcook the beans, and the soup will be a handsome green. This, by the way, is a wonderful way to use up a bean crop that is ripening unevenly, providing you with some so thick they can't be cooked with skinny new beans.

2 tablespoons butter	2 cups veal broth
3 to 4 cups chopped green beans	Salt and pepper
	1/2 cup light cream
1 small onion, chopped	1 tablespoon snipped fresh dill
4 cups boiling water	
1 teaspoon salt	

1. In a kettle over medium heat, melt butter and sauté beans, stirring constantly, 5 to 8 minutes. Beans should be tender and still retain their bright green color. Add boiling water, salt, and broth; raise heat and simmer a few minutes more. Beans should taste cooked, but still have their color.

2. Purée in a blender or a food processor, 2 cups at a time, or press through a sieve. Return to kettle, reheat, and add salt and pepper to taste. Add cream and bring to just below boiling.

To serve: Ladle into soup bowls and garnish with dill snips.

STRING BEAN SOUP
Serves 4 to 6

Choose young beans fresh from the garden, and don't overcook. That's the secret to a very fine String Bean Soup. However, when the beans in the garden are getting big and tougher, a soup is the best way to use them—just make sure any strings are removed before you chop them.

1 medium onion, chopped	2 cups hot water
2 tablespoons of butter	1 teaspoon salt
2 cups beans, stemmed, chopped	¼ teaspoon pepper
	2 cups milk
2 tablespoons all-purpose flour	2 tablespoons minced parsley

1. In a saucepan over medium heat, sauté the onion in the butter until translucent, about 5 minutes. Remove the saucepan from heat and stir in the beans. Sprinkle with flour, combine well, then stir in the hot water and return to heat. Add salt and pepper, and cook, uncovered, stirring occasionally for 20 to 30 minutes or until beans are tender.
2. Purée in a blender or a food processor, 2 cups at a time, or press through a sieve. Return purée to the saucepan and mix in the milk. Heat to just below boiling.

To serve: Ladle into soup bowls and garnish with parsley.

BEET SOUP—FAST   Serves 6 to 8

The classic beet soup is borscht, a long-cooking stewy kind of soup made with beets and beef stock and lots of other vegetables. This simple garden-fresh soup isn't a replacement for the old-fashioned classic, but it is very good. Peel the beets with a potato peeler. To make a glorious pink Borscht, fold the sour cream into the beet soup before serving.

8 to 10 small beets, peeled, grated	1 teaspoon sugar
8 to 9 cups beef broth	1 tablespoon vinegar
1 tablespoon butter	Salt and pepper
	Sour cream

In a large kettle over medium high heat, place the beets and 3 cups of broth, cover, and simmer 15 minutes. Add remaining broth, cover, and cook until beets are soft, 10 or 15 minutes. Add butter, sugar, and vinegar, and simmer 20 minutes. Add salt and pepper to taste.

To serve: Ladle into soup bowls and garnish generously with sour cream.

Dividends: Good cold. Purée it before serving.

To make ahead: Complete through Step 1, then finish just before serving.

PLAIN BROCCOLI SOUP   Serves 4

You can make this with cauliflower instead of broccoli. I use mostly broccoli stems to make this one, peeled down to the tender part, plus the leaves, and I save a few bunches of broccoli florets, small ones, which I cook on top of the soup during the last few minutes, to make a garnish.

2 scallions, or 1 small yellow onion, chopped	2 cups hot chicken broth
2 cups chopped broccoli	2 cups hot milk
3 tablespoons butter	1/8 teaspoon ground cardamom
3 tablespoons all-purpose flour	Salt and pepper
	Broccoli florets

1. In a saucepan over medium heat, sauté the scallion or onion and the broccoli in the butter until onion begins to be trans-

lucent, 5 to 7 minutes. Lower heat and stir in the flour. Beating constantly, add the broth and milk, and cook, stirring, until bubbly, 1 to 2 minutes.

2. Purée in a blender or a food processor, 2 cups at a time, or press through a sieve. Add cardamom, salt and pepper to taste, and return to the saucepan; reheat to just below boiling.

To serve: Ladle into soup bowls and garnish with broccoli florets.

CREAM OF BRUSSELS SPROUTS SOUP   Serves 6 to 8

Potatoes thicken this cream soup. This same recipe can be used to make soup with almost any other vegetable, and the results are very good.

2 cups brussels sprouts (1 pint), trimmed, quartered	6 cups milk
3 tablespoons butter	Salt and pepper
3 cups chicken boiling broth or veal broth	1 cup hot Croutons, Sautéed in Butter (page 33)
2 medium potatoes, peeled, chopped	

1. In a large saucepan over medium heat, sauté the sprouts in butter 3 to 4 minutes. Add boiling broth and turn up the heat. Add potatoes and boil gently, uncovered, 10 to 15 minutes; potatoes should be disintegrating and sprouts should still retain some color.
2. Purée in a blender or a food processor, 2 cups at a time, or mash with a potato masher. Return to the kettle, add milk, and simmer to just below boiling. Add salt and pepper to taste.

To serve: Ladle into soup bowls and garnish with croutons.

FRESH CABBAGE SOUP   Serves 6 to 8

A gentle soup with a fresh, green look.

1 medium onion, sliced thin	Salt and pepper
2 tablespoons olive oil	1 teaspoon minced fresh
6 cups chicken broth	thyme
½ small green cabbage, shredded very fine	3 medium potatoes, chopped

1. In a large saucepan over medium heat, sauté onion in olive oil until translucent, about 3 minutes. Add broth and potatoes. Bring to boiling, cover, reduce heat, and simmer until potatoes are tender, about 15 minutes.
2. Purée in a blender or a food processor, 2 cups at a time, or press through a sieve. Return purée to saucepan, bring to a boil, add cabbage, and cook 3 minutes, uncovered. Add salt and pepper to taste.

To serve: Ladle into soup bowls and garnish with thyme.

To make ahead: Complete through Step 2, then finish just before serving.

CABBAGE AND APPLE SOUP   Serves 6 to 8

Begin a Hungarian meal with this. You might follow with a chicken paprikash, and *crêpes* stuffed with apricot preserves and topped with sour cream.

4 tablespoons butter	1 small clove garlic, sliced
1 small green cabbage, shredded fine	½ teaspoon brown sugar
	1 cup cooked fine noodles
1 large apple, peeled, cored, grated	½ teaspoon caraway seed
	Salt and pepper
6 cups veal broth	Hungarian sweet paprika

In a large kettle over medium heat, melt butter. Add cabbage and apple and sauté, stirring constantly, until cabbage begins to wilt, about 10 minutes. Add broth, garlic, and sugar. Bring to a boil; add cooked noodles and caraway seeds. Simmer, uncovered, just long enough for cabbage to be tender. Add salt and pepper to taste.

To serve: Ladle into small bowls and dust liberally with Hungarian paprika.

To make ahead: May be made many hours ahead.

SAVOY CABBAGE SOUP   Serves 8 to 10

Savoy is the cabbage with the beautifully wrinkled leaves. The flavor is a bit stronger than ordinary cabbage.

8 cups beef broth	2 tablespoons all-purpose
1 small savoy cabbage,	flour
shredded fine	Salt and pepper
2 tablespoons butter	½ cup sour cream
1 small onion, minced	½ cup grated Swiss cheese

1. In a large kettle over high heat, bring broth to boiling; add cabbage, reduce heat, and simmer, uncovered, 10 minutes.
2. In a saucepan over medium heat, melt butter and sauté onion until translucent. Sprinkle with flour, stir, and cook 3 minutes. Gradually stir in 4 cups of broth, then return mixture to the kettle and blend well. Simmer soup 10 minutes. Add salt and pepper to taste. Purée in a blender or a food processor, 2 cups at a time, or press through a sieve.
3. In a small bowl combine sour cream with ½ cup of purée; stir in another ½ cup of purée, then slowly return mixture to the kettle, stirring constantly.

To serve: Simmer until hot, then stir in cheese, and ladle into soup bowls.

Dividends: Great stretcher for pork stews.

To make ahead: Complete through Step 2, then finish just before serving.

CARROT SOUP IN THE TURKISH WAY   Serves 6 to 8

This tastes best made with brightly colored carrots. The little fingerling carrots from the garden, which are such a delicacy in a stew, don't seem hearty enough for this soup.

5 tablespoons butter	3 tablespoons all-purpose
6 large carrots, diced or	flour
chopped	½ cup milk
7 cups chicken broth	3 egg yolks
1 teaspoon sugar	Salt and pepper

1. In a large, heavy saucepan over medium heat, melt 2 table-spoons of butter and sauté carrots until lightly colored, about 10 minutes, stirring constantly. Add broth and sugar. Bring to boiling, cover, and simmer until carrots are very tender, about 30 minutes. Purée in a blender or a food processor, 2 cups at a time, or press through a sieve. Return to saucepan and simmer another 10 minutes.

2. In another large saucepan over low heat, melt the remaining 3 tablespoons of butter, and whisk in flour, stirring constantly, about 1 minute. Stir in milk, and cook until mixture boils, about 1 minute. Remove from heat and let cool 10 minutes. Whisk in the egg yolks, one at a time, beating constantly. Pour the purée into this mixture, beating constantly. Add salt and pepper to taste.

To serve: Ladle into bowls.

To make ahead: May be prepared hours ahead, but do not boil when reheating or the eggs may curdle or separate.

SWISS AND CAULIFLOWER SOUP   Serves 4 to 6

If your garden, or the supermarket, offers less-than-perfect cauliflower heads, cut away the brown parts and make this wonderful soup. It's hearty enough to make a light meal.

1 medium cauliflower, cut	2 tablespoons all-purpose
into smallest florets	flour
6 cups chicken boiling broth	1 cup light cream
1 cup grated Swiss cheese	Paprika
(4 ounces)	

1. In a heavy saucepan over medium heat, place cauliflower in boiling broth and simmer, covered, until cauliflower is tender, about 10 minutes.
2. In a small bowl combine cheese and flour, mixing well. Gradually stir cheese mixture into broth, stirring constantly until well blended and thickened. Purée in a blender or a food processor, 2 cups at a time, or press through a sieve. Return to saucepan, add cream, and heat to just below boiling.

To serve: Ladle into soup bowls and dust generously with paprika.

Dividends: Combine leftovers with drippings in degreased chicken cooking pan to make a rich sauce, or mix with pork drippings to serve on reheated pork slices.

CELERY SOUP EASY

Serves 4 to 6

This is a common or garden-variety celery soup; you'll find a Cream of Celery Recipe in Chapter 5.

1 tablespoon butter
1 teaspoon minced shallots
  or onion
4 cups milk

2 cups chopped celery
Salt and pepper
Butter

1. In a heavy saucepan over medium heat, melt butter, add the shallots or onion, and sauté until translucent. Add the milk and celery; cover and simmer until celery is tender, about 30 minutes.
2. Purée in a blender or a food processor, two cups at a time, or press through a sieve. Return to the saucepan, add salt and pepper to taste. Heat, but do not let boil.

To serve: Ladle into soup bowls and dot each serving with a generous dab of butter

Dividends: Nice cold.

To make ahead: Keeps for days.

GREEN CELERIAC SOUP   Serves 4 to 6

1 celeriac root, peeled, diced	1 medium slice onion
1 large potato, peeled, diced	2 cups large green peas
1 teaspoon lemon juice	2 tablespoons butter
2 cups milk	Salt
2 cups water	Paprika

1. Soak celeriac and potato in cold water to cover with lemon juice for 5 minutes. Drain and discard liquid.
2. In a large saucepan, heat milk to a simmer; add the celeriac and potato. Simmer until vegetables are tender, 13 to 15 minutes, then mash.
3. In a medium saucepan, bring the 2 cups of water to a boil; drop in the onion and peas. Simmer, uncovered, until peas are quite tender, about 10 minutes.
4. Purée peas and their liquid, in a blender or a food processor, two cups at a time, or press through a sieve. Beat the purée into the celeriac-potato mixture; add butter and salt to taste and simmer until hot, but not boiling.

To serve: Ladle into soup bowls and sprinkle with a generous dash of paprika.

Dividends: Leftovers make great flavoring for meat gravies.

CORN CHOWDER   Serves 6

This is the best corn chowder I've ever tasted—and very simple to make. The subtle flavor comes from the salt pork. Bacon is not a good substitute here, but bits of fat from a good ham roast can be used instead of the salt pork.

⅛ pound salt pork, diced	2 cups cooked corn kernels
1 small onion, minced	or 1 12-ounce can whole
¼ green pepper, seeded, minced	kernels and liquid
	2 teaspoons salt
3 large potatoes, chopped (about 3 cups)	1 quart milk
	¼ teaspoon paprika
2 cups boiling water	1 tablespoon butter

In a saucepan over medium heat, sauté the salt pork until brown and crisp. Remove crisped bits and reserve. Add the onion and the green pepper and sauté until the onion becomes translucent, about 5 to 7 minutes. Add potatoes and water, cover, and simmer until potatoes are tender, about 20 minutes. Add remaining ingredients, and heat to just below boiling.

To serve: Ladle into soup bowls and garnish with crisped salt pork bits and a dab of butter.

Dividends: Excellent reheated. Stretch with more milk.

To make ahead: May be made hours or a day ahead. Complete through Step 1, then finish just before serving.

CUCUMBER SOUP   Serves 6 to 8

You may make this from pickling cucumbers, which are small, but use twice as many. Chicken stock is nice if you have no veal broth.

½ cup butter	2 egg yolks
1 small onion, minced	1 tablespoon dry sherry
4 medium-large cucumbers, peeled, sliced thin	1 cup heavy cream
	Salt and pepper
3 tablespoons all-purpose flour	3 tablespoons finely minced parsley
6 cups hot veal broth	

1. In a large saucepan over low heat, melt butter and sauté onion and cucumbers until just tender but not browned. Sprinkle with flour and stir well. Gradually add the broth. Raise heat to medium, bring soup to a simmer, cover, and cook 10 minutes. Purée in a blender or a food processor, 2 cups at a time, or press through a sieve.
2. Beat the egg yolks in a large bowl until thick and lemon-colored. Stir in sherry and cream, then puréed cucumber. Reheat gently, and add salt and pepper to taste.

To serve: Divide parsley among soup bowls and ladle soup on top.

Dividends: Very good chilled.

To make ahead: Complete through Step 1, then finish just before serving.

JERUSALEM ARTICHOKE SOUP   Serves 6

Jerusalem artichokes are the small knobby roots of a species of American sunflower that is perennial and grows all over the country. The sunflowers are very tall and small-flowered. The flavor of the root is rather like a green artichoke and has the added virtue of being almost starchless. If you don't grow your own, usually you will find these offered at Oriental and specialty groceries toward the end of summer.

1 pound Jerusalem artichokes, scrubbed, chopped
2 cups water
2 teaspoons salt

4 cups milk
2 tablespoons sweet butter
1 teaspoon lemon juice
Freshly ground black pepper

1. In a kettle over high heat, place artichokes, water, and salt. Cover, bring to a boil, lower heat, and simmer 10 to 15 minutes, or until roots are tender. Purée in a blender or a food processor, 2 cups at a time, or press through a sieve. Return to kettle.
2. Add milk and reheat to just below boiling.

To serve: Ladle into soup bowls, divide butter among bowls, and add a bit of lemon juice to each bowl. Stir, then dust with a grating of pepper.

To make ahead: Complete through Step 2, then finish just before serving.

KOHLRABI CREAM   Serves 6 to 8

Kohlrabi is the vegetable garden's version of a flying saucer. The flavor resembles turnips and cabbage, and the texture is remarkably crisp.

1½ pounds chicken parts
8 cups cold water
1¼ teaspoons salt
1 small bay leaf
1 medium garlic clove, sliced
1 large sprig dill, or ¼ teaspoon dried
½ cup heavy cream
Salt and pepper

4 small to medium kohlrabi, peeled, cut into matchstick strips
2 tablespoons minced parsley
4 tablespoons butter
4 tablespoons all-purpose flour
2 egg yolks

1. In a large kettle over high heat, place the chicken and water, with the salt, bay, garlic, and dill, and bring to a rapid boil. Cover, lower heat, and simmer 30 minutes. Add the kohlrabi and cook another 30 to 40 minutes, until chicken is falling off the bone and kohlrabi is tender. Scoop chicken pieces out and cut meat from bones. Return meat to kettle, heat off.
2. In a small saucepan over medium heat, sauté the parsley in the butter 1 minute. Remove pan from heat and stir in the flour. Beating constantly, add a cup of hot broth. When smoothly blended, cook over low heat until bubbly, 1 to 2 minutes.
3. In a small bowl beat the egg yolks until thick and lemon-colored. Add the cream. Beat in the cup of hot thickened broth, then stir the mixture into the kettle, and heat to just below boiling. Add salt and pepper to taste.

To serve: Ladle soup into the bowls, dividing chicken meat among them.

To make ahead: Complete through Step 3. This is better when it has been cooked a few hours ahead of serving.

LEEK AND CELERY SOUP   Serves 4 to 6

Use the tops and leaves of celery heads to make this one. It's very economical and absolutely delicious!

1 cup minced celery tops and leaves	3 cups water
1 cup minced leek tops	2 teaspoons salt
1 medium-large potato, chopped	$\frac{1}{4}$ teaspoon pepper
3 tablespoons butter	1 cup milk
	1 tablespoon butter

In a saucepan over medium heat, sauté the celery, leek, and potato in butter 10 minutes, stirring often. Add the water salt and pepper, cover, and simmer over reduced heat 30 minutes or until vegetables are very soft. Mash in the saucepan with a potato masher. Stir in milk and reheat to just boiling.

To serve: Ladle into soup bowls and finish with a bit of butter.

Dividends: Excellent reheated. Stretch by adding milk.

To make ahead: May be made hours or a day ahead.

SOUP FROM GREENS

Serves 6

Kale, mustard, spinach, beet tops, and turnip tops—all these delicious greens make excellent soup. And, when the seedlings are beginning to crowd each other in the rows you have planted, the thinnings, well washed, make good soup. Africans eat carrot tops done this way, too. Greens have differing weights, depending on how much stalk is involved and how dense it is, so the measurement here is given in weight. About 6 to 8 cups shredded, packed greens should come out to about the right amount.

1 medium onion, chopped	4 cups chicken broth
4 tablespoons peanut oil	1 cup light cream
1½ to 2 pounds greens,	Salt
shredded fine	Cayenne

1. In a large saucepan over medium heat, sauté onion in oil until translucent. Add greens, cover, and cook until just wilted, about 2 minutes. Add chicken broth, cover, and simmer until greens are tender, about 10 minutes. Purée in a blender or a food processor, 2 cups at a time.
2. Return to saucepan; stir in cream. Add salt and cayenne to taste. Reheat, but do not boil.

To serve: Ladle into soup bowls.

Dividends: Stretch with additional broth.

ROSY LETTUCE SOUP

Serves 4 to 6

Any leafy lettuce from the garden, or the store for that matter, can be used to make this soup. You may also use the seedlings you thin from crowded rows of young lettuce; just be sure to stem them carefully and get all the sand out.

4 cups tightly packed, coarsely shredded leaf lettuce	4 cups hot chicken broth
	Salt and pepper
	1 teaspoon minced chervil or basil
4 tablespoons butter	
1 cup very ripe tomatoes, peeled, chopped	

In a large kettle over medium heat, sauté the lettuce in the butter until wilted, 2 to 3 minutes. Add the tomatoes and cook, stirring, 5 minutes more. Pour in the broth, bring to a boil, reduce heat, cover, and simmer 10 minutes. Add salt and pepper if needed.

To serve: Ladle into soup bowls and garnish with herb.

CREAM OF ONION SOUP PEASANT STYLE   Serves 4

If you have nothing in the house to make soup with but a handful of onions, milk, and eggs, you can make a delicious soup! You can use broth instead of milk, and it still is delicious!

2 cups chopped onion	4 egg yolks
3 tablespoons butter	⅛ teaspoon grated nutmeg
2 tablespoons all-purpose flour	Salt and pepper
4 cups hot milk	Chopped chives, optional

1. In a saucepan over medium heat, sauté the onion in the butter until translucent, about 5 minutes. Lower heat and stir in the flour. Beating constantly, add the milk and cook, stirring, until bubbly, 1 to 2 minutes.
2. In a small bowl, beat the egg yolks until thick and lemon-colored, then stir in 1 cup of hot broth. Beat the egg mixture into the soup. Reheat to just below boiling. Add nutmeg and salt and pepper to taste.

To serve: Ladle into soup bowls and garnish with chives if you wish.

Dividends: Leftovers are nice dressed with chopped watercress stems, minced parsley, or other herbs.

To make ahead: Complete through Step 1, then finish just before serving.

OYSTER PLANT (SALSIFY) CHOWDER   Serves 4

Salsify—which has a flavor only faintly reminiscent of oysters —is a root vegetable that tastes best after it has wintered in the ground. If you are buying seed to plant, choose the kind with black skin: the flavor is best. Use it to replace carrots or parsnips in soup recipes—or this way:

4 to 6 salsifies	⅛ teaspoon grated nutmeg
1 teaspoon lemon juice	1 teaspoon salt
1 tablespoon butter	5 peppercorns
1 small leek or onion, minced	⅓ cup diced celery
	1 teaspoon butter
3 cups milk	¼ cup small oyster crackers

1. Wash, scrape, and quarter the salsifies, and soak in cold water with lemon juice while sautéeing onions in Step 2.
2. In a saucepan over medium heat, melt the butter and sauté the leek or onion until translucent, about 5 minutes. Discard soak water and add salsify, milk, nutmeg, salt, peppercorns, and celery; bring to a boil. Lower heat and simmer, partially covered, until salsify is tender, about 10 minutes. Don't let the milk boil over. Purée in a blender or in a food processor, 2 cups at a time, or press through a sieve. Strain back into the saucepan, discarding peppercorns. Reheat briefly.

To serve: Ladle into soup bowls and garnish with a dab of butter and with oyster crackers.

PARSNIP CHOWDER   Serves 6 to 8

Parsnips are one of the few vegetables that keep well in the ground through the winter. When the frost first goes is the time to dig them—that's when they are sweetest. They are great in any vegetable soup and, in beef and veal casseroles, the secret ingredient replacing carrots that makes gourmet recipes very special. Cracker crumbs are a mellow-flavored thickener popular in my Scotch-Canadian grandmother's household.

⅛ pound salt pork, diced	1 cup chopped potato
1 small onion, chopped	2 cups boiling water
3 cups parsnips, peeled, chopped	1 teaspoon salt
	⅛ teaspoon pepper

⅛ teaspoon grated nutmeg	½ cup rolled cracker crumbs,
1 quart milk	optional
4 tablespoons butter	Salt and pepper

In a large saucepan over medium heat, sauté salt pork until crisp, about 10 minutes. Add onion and sauté 3 minutes. Add parsnips and potato, and sauté 2 minutes, stirring. Add boiling water, cover, lower heat, and simmer about 30 minutes or until potato is very tender. Stir in salt, pepper, nutmeg, milk, and butter. Stir in cracker crumbs, if you wish, and add salt and pepper to taste.

To serve: Ladle into soup bowls.

Dividends: Very good reheated.

To make ahead: May be made hours or a day ahead. Add cracker crumbs just before serving.

FRESH PEA SOUP   Serves 6

The trick here is to keep peas a bright green without under-cooking them. You can use sweet edible-pod peas, whole, instead of shelled peas.

8 cups veal broth	4 tablespoons butter
4 cups shelled peas	1 teaspoon minced fresh
Salt and pepper	chervil or mint
1 scallion, minced	

1. In a large kettle over high heat, bring the broth to boiling, and add peas and scallion by the handful. Add more only as broth returns to brisk boil. Lower heat and simmer 5 to 7 minutes, until peas are just tender but not losing their bright color.
2. Using a slotted spoon, reserve 4 tablespoons peas for a garnish. Purée remaining peas and broth in a blender or a food processor, 2 cups at a time, or press through a sieve. Return to the kettle, add salt and pepper to taste, and heat to boiling.

To serve: Divide butter among soup bowls and ladle in soup. Garnish each bowl with a bit of fresh mint or chervil, and reserved whole peas.

PEAS AND CARROTS SOUP   Serves 6

Chances are your garden won't have big, sweet full-flavored carrots ready in spring just when the peas are at their height— so use winter carrots from the supermarket to brighten this soup.

1 pound young peas in the pod	6 medium carrots (about ½ pound), diced or chopped
1 teaspoon dried thyme	4 large potatoes, peeled, diced or chopped
1 small bay leaf	
¼ teaspoon dried savory	2 tablespoons butter
1 small onion, peeled, chopped	Salt and pepper
8 cups water	2 tablespoons minced fresh parsley

1. Shell peas and discard blemished pods. In a small kettle bring remaining pods (washed), herbs, onion, and 4 cups of water to a rapid boil. Cover and simmer until liquid is reduced by half, about 2 hours. Strain, reserving the broth.
2. Return broth to kettle; add remaining water, carrots, and potatoes. Cover, raise heat, and boil until vegetables are almost tender, about 20 minutes. Potatoes should have begun to thicken soup. Add peas and cook until they are tender, 5 to 7 minutes. Add butter, and salt and pepper to taste.

To serve: Ladle into soup bowls and garnish with parsley.

To make ahead: Complete to the point where peas are to be added, then finish just before serving.

JACK-O'-LANTERN SOUP   Serves 6 to 8

I make this from the scoopings of meat taken from the big fall pumpkins we empty to make jack-o'-lanterns for Halloween. You can make it from canned pumpkin as long as it isn't seasoned. I find 6 cups of fresh pumpkin scoopings simmered, covered, for about an hour, reduces to about 2 cups of pumpkin pulp.

2 cups pumpkin pulp	2 tablespoons butter
3 cups chicken broth	½ cup light rum
½ cup chopped onion	1 teaspoon salt
½ cup chopped celery	⅛ teaspoon pepper
1 cup apple, chopped, peeled	3 tablespoons honey

½ teaspoon grated nutmeg	1 cup heavy cream
⅛ teaspoon ground ginger	2 or 3 cups milk
⅛ teaspoon cinnamon	Salt and pepper

1. In a large saucepan over medium heat, bring pumpkin, broth, onion, celery, and apple to a boil. Cover, reduce heat, and simmer about 20 minutes.
2. Purée in a blender or a food processor, 2 cups at a time, or press through a sieve. Return to saucepan, and stir in butter and rum. Simmer, uncovered, 1 to 2 minutes, stirring constantly. Stir in seasonings. Add cream and enough milk to make 8 cups of soup. Add salt and pepper to taste. Heat, but do not let boil.

To serve: Ladle into soup bowls.

To make ahead: Complete through addition of seasonings. Add cream and milk just before serving.

ANYTHING-GOES POTATO SOUP   Serves 6

Potatoes, especially old potatoes, are wonderful thickeners. With them you can make a soup base that can be combined with almost any leftover vegetable to make a hearty and delicious soup.

2 large potatoes, peeled, diced or chopped	2 cups chopped cooked vegetables
1 medium onion, chopped	Salt and pepper
3 tablespoons butter	2 tablespoons finely minced parsley
7 cups water	

1. In a large saucepan sauté the potatoes and onion in the butter, stirring, until the onion becomes translucent, about 5 minutes. Add water, cover, and simmer until potatoes are tender, about 15 to 20 minutes ; mash in the saucepan.
2. Purée the chopped cooked vegetables in a blender or a food processor, 2 cups at a time. Use some of the soup to liquefy the purée. Turn purée into saucepan, stir, and heat to boiling. Add salt and pepper to taste.

To serve: Ladle into soup bowls and garnish with parsley.

Dividends: Stretch with milk.

POTATO SOUP WITH TOMATOES   Serves 6 to 8

Here's a variation on the leek-and-potato theme, sharpened and brightened by the addition of tomatoes. It's a rich, thick soup to serve with big chunks of French bread. A salad including green peppers and cheese of a Swiss type, and a desert like apple pie could complete this meal.

6 medium potatoes, peeled, diced or chopped
4 medium leeks, white plus a bit of green, chopped
2 medium onions, chopped
4 tablespoons butter
4 large tomatoes, chopped
¼ teaspoon dried thyme

4 cups water
2 teaspoons sugar
Salt and pepper
1 tablespoon minced parsley
1¼ cups light cream
1 cup milk

1. In a large kettle over medium heat, sauté the potatoes, leeks, and onions in the butter, stiring until onions are translucent, about 5 minutes. Add tomatoes and continue to cook, stirring, until tomatoes are soft, about 5 minutes. If vegetables begin to stick to bottom, add some of the water. Add thyme, water, and sugar. Cover, lower heat, and simmer until potatoes are very soft, about 20 minutes.

2. Purée in a blender or a food processor, 2 cups at a time, or press through a sieve. Return purée to the kettle; season with salt and pepper to taste. Add cream and milk, and reheat to just below boiling.

To serve: Ladle into soup bowls and garnish with parsley.

To make ahead: Complete through Step 2, but don't add cream or milk until ready to serve.

SPINACH LEMON SOUP   Serves 6 to 8

Make this with spinach seedlings thinned from the garden row in spring, or use a pound of very fresh spinach from the supermarket. It's delicious either way. Half a 10-ounce package of frozen leaf spinach makes good soup, too.

8 cups chicken broth
1 large carrot, peeled, cut into matchstick strips
1 large stalk celery and leaves, chopped

6 to 8 cups closely packed spinach leaves
3 tablespoons butter
3 tablespoons all-purpose flour

2 tablespoons finely chopped parsley	3 egg yolks
1 tablespoon finely chopped dill	Juice of 1 lemon, strained
	Salt and pepper

1. In a large kettle over medium high heat, simmer broth with carrot and celery 15 minutes, covered. Add spinach, cover, and simmer 5 minutes. Use knife and fork to cut up spinach coarsely.
2. In a small saucepan over low heat, melt butter and stir in the flour. Beating constantly, add a cup of the spinach broth. Blend the mixture back into the kettle, and simmer over low heat, covered, 5 minutes.
3. In a small bowl combine egg yolks and lemon juice; beat until lemon-colored. Stir a cup of the hot broth into the egg mixture, then beat the mixture back into the saucepan. Heat to just below boiling, but do not let boil. Add salt and pepper to taste.

To serve: Ladle into soup bowls and garnish with herbs.

SUMMER SQUASH SOUP—COLD   Serves 6 to 8

Choose small squash so tender the skin is easily broken by a thumbnail. Nice made with zucchini, too.

3 medium onions, minced	1/8 teaspoon grated nutmeg
3 tablespoons butter	1/8 teaspoon ground coriander
6 to 8 small summer squash (about 2 pounds), stemmed, sliced thin	2 cups heavy cream
	Salt and pepper
8 cups chicken broth	1 tablespoon minced chives
1/2 teaspoon sugar	6 to 8 chive blooms

1. In a large kettle, over medium heat, sauté the onion in the butter until translucent, about 5 minutes. Add the squash and sauté, stirring constantly, another 5 minutes. Add broth, cover, and simmer until squash is tender, about 7 to 10 minutes.
2. Purée in a blender or a food processor, 2 cups at a time, or press through a sieve. Stir in sugar, nutmeg, and coriander. Add cream, and salt and pepper to taste. Chill 4 hours or overnight.

To serve: Ladle into soup bowls and garnish with chives and chive blooms.

To make ahead: Tastes best made the day before.

SUMMER SQUASH CREAM   Serves 6

Richer by far than plain Summer Squash Soup, this is a good choice for a dinner party. It is served hot.

1 medium onion, minced	1 small celery stalk, chopped
White of 1 leek or 2 scallions, chopped	1 tablespoon minced parsley
3 tablespoons butter	3 egg yolks
3 to 4 small summer squash (about 1 pound), stemmed, sliced thin	1 cup light cream
	⅛ teaspoon grated nutmerg
	Salt and pepper to taste
6 cups chicken broth	6 small sprigs fresh parsley

1. In a large kettle over medium heat, sauté the onion and the leek or scallions in the butter until translucent, about 5 minutes. Add the squash and sauté, stirring constantly, 5 minutes. Add broth, celery, and parsley. Cover and simmer until squash is tender, about 7 to 10 minutes.
2. Purée in a blender or a food processor, 2 cups at a time, or press through a sieve. Return purée to kettle.
3. In a small bowl beat egg yolks until lemon-colored. Stir in the cream, and beat in about 1 cup of the purée. Return the egg mixture to the kettle, stirring, and heat to just below boiling. Add nutmeg, and salt and pepper to taste.

To serve: Ladle into soup bowls and garnish with parsley.

Dividends: Nice cold.

To make ahead: Can be made ahead through Step 2.

BUTTERNUT-APPLE SOUP   Serves 6

Some recipes make this without peeling—just pop squash and its skin into the broth, and eventually scoop out the squash pulp and discard the skins. I prefer the flavor when the squash has been peeled, so I do it this way. Nice soup, and most people would never guess the content.

1 medium butternut squash (1 pound), peeled, seeded, chopped	1 medium onion, chopped
	¼ teaspoon dried rosemary
2 tart green apples, peeled, cored, chopped	¼ teaspoon marjoram
	6 cups chicken broth
	2 slices stale white bread

1 teaspoon salt	¼ cup heavy cream
¼ teaspoon pepper	¼ cup chopped walnuts

1. In a large kettle over medium high heat, simmer all the ingredients except the cream and nuts, covered, 45 minutes.
2. Purée in a blender or a food processor, 2 cups at a time, or press through a sieve. Return purée to the kettle. Stir in cream and heat to just below boiling.

To serve: Ladle into soup bowls and garnish with chopped nuts.

A WORD OR TWO ABOUT TOMATOES

Tomatoes for making soups should be really ripe, a deep, rich red, and juicy. If the tomatoes you pick or buy turn out to be poor in juice, or not as ripe as you hoped, you can enhance the tomato flavor in the soup by adding a tablespoon or two of tomato paste, or by using tomato juice or tomato sauce in the place of water called for in the recipe.

Generally speaking, a medium-size tomato weighs a quarter pound or a bit over, and, chopped, produces about half a cup of tomato pulp and juice.

A 1-pound 12-ounce can of whole tomatoes comes to about 3½ cups.

If you are buying your tomatoes fresh, buy by color. Garden-ripened tomatoes have an almost acid red, bright and sharp, with lots of yellow in it. Hothouse tomatoes generally are crimson, a pinker or bluer red. Commercial tomatoes picked green for shipping are orangy, never a really deep red. Both hothouse tomatoes and the commercial kind are apt to be all pulp and no juice— and not very good as a rule for making soup.

There are a whole lot of tomato recipes for soup here, because tomatoes are the most popular vegetable (actually, the tomato is technically a fruit) grown in the home garden, and almost every gardener has too many at some point in the year.

QUICK CREAM OF TOMATO SOUP   Serves 6

This is fast and easy. The flavor depends on your taste in herbs—and on how really ripe the tomatoes are. Use this recipe with fleshy tomatoes, like the plum and pear tomatoes, which are small and not very juicy but very flavorful.

4 tablespoons butter
1 large clove garlic, minced
4 tablespoons all-purpose flour
4 cups hot milk
Salt and pepper

8 to 10 plum or pear tomatoes (about 1½ pounds), chopped
½ cup mixed fresh herbs (basil, chervil, chives, parsley), minced

1. In a large saucepan over low heat, melt the butter and sauté the garlic 1 minute. Stir in the flour. Beating constantly, add the milk, and cook, stirring, until bubbly, 1 to 2 minutes.
2. Stir in tomatoes and cook, uncovered, until just below boiling, but do not let boil. Add salt and pepper to taste. Purée in a blender or a food processor, 2 cups at a time.

To serve: Stir the herbs into the hot soup and wait 1 minute, then ladle soup into bowls.

GARDEN FRESH TOMATO SOUP   Serves 8 to 10

10 large very ripe tomatoes
6 cups water
¼ cup chopped fresh parsley
1 small onion
½ teaspoon Worcestershire sauce
2 teaspoons salt
2 lemon slices

1 bay leaf
1 teaspoon peppercorns
4 whole cloves
½ cup grated carrot
½ cup minced green pepper
½ cup chopped celery
Sour cream
Minced fresh basil, optional

1. Wash and quarter the tomatoes and put them into a large kettle with the water, parsley, onion, Worcestershire, and salt. Crush the tomatoes with a potato masher. Tie lemon slices, bay leaf, peppercorns, and cloves into a square of cheesecloth and add to kettle. Cover and simmer until tomatoes and onions are soft, about 20 minutes. Remove herb bag and discard. Purée soup mixture in a blender or a food processor, 2 cups at a time, or press through a sieve.

2. Return purée to kettle. Add carrot, green pepper, and celery; reheat.

To serve: Ladle into soup bowls and add a dollop of sour cream to each. Or chill and serve with sour cream and a sprinkling of basil.

Dividends: Pour leftovers over chicken halves and bake 1 hour at 400 degrees. Makes a great casserole.

SAVORY TOMATO JUICE AND SOUP BASE   Serves 8 to 10

Noodles, celery chips, rice, almost any leftover vegetables, chopped, added to this tangy tomato base become grounds for a fine soup, but it's also a great tomato juice.

15 large ripe tomatoes (5–6 pounds), chopped	½ teaspoon dried thyme
1 cup chopped celery	2 teaspoons salt
½ cup chopped onion	1 tablespoon sugar
¼ cup strained lemon juice	2 teaspoons Worcestershire sauce
1 small bay leaf	1 teaspoon soy sauce

1. In a large kettle over medium heat, place tomatoes, celery, and onion. Cover and cook, stirring often, until tomatoes are soft, about 15 minutes. Press gently through a sieve.
2. Measure 12 cups of juice and return to kettle. Simmer, uncovered, for about 30 minutes; add remaining ingredients and simmer 10 minutes. Taste, and add salt and pepper if needed. Discard bay leaf.

To serve: Serve as juice, chilled, in tall glasses, or serve hot in soup bowls.

To make ahead: May be made days ahead and stored in refrigerator or freezer.

JELLIED TOMATO BOUILLON   Serves 4

Cubed and heaped into chilled bouillon cups, this is an elegant dish to begin a summer dinner, but it can also be used as a molded aspic to grace a party buffet table.

2 envelopes plain gelatin
½ cup cold water
2 cups Savory Tomato Juice (page 263), or canned tomato juice
2 beef bouillon cubes
1 teaspoon minced onion
¼ cup minced celery leaves

2 fresh basil leaves
1 teaspoon Worcestershire sauce
12 large ice cubes, or 2 cups crushed ice
Sprigs of basil or lemon slices

1. In a small bowl soak gelatin in cold water for 5 minutes.
2. In a small saucepan over medium heat, bring tomato juice, beef cubes, onion, celery, basil, and Worcestershire to a simmer. Add gelatin and stir until it is completely dissolved, 1 or 2 minutes.
3. Purée with ice cubes in a blender or a food processor, then strain into a 1-quart mold or bowl. Chill until set.

To serve: Break into 1-inch chunks with a couple of forks and serve in bouillon cups. Garnish with basil sprigs or lemon slices.

Dividends: Freeze leftovers in a sealed plastic bag and use as ice cubes for Bloody Marys.

HOT TOMATO–SWEET PEPPER SOUP   Serves 4

Make this with thoroughly ripe tomatoes in season. It takes just a few minutes and is delicious!

1 tablespoon olive oil
1 large onion, chopped
1 cup finely chopped green pepper
2 cups water
½ cup zucchini, sliced thin
1 tablespoon chopped parsley

4 large ripe tomatoes, peeled, chopped
1 clove garlic, crushed
Salt and pepper
1 tablespoon cider vinegar
1 teaspoon brown sugar
Tabasco sauce

1. In a large kettle over medium heat, heat oil and sauté onion, and pepper, stirring, until onion is translucent and beginning to brown. Add water, bring to a simmer, then add zucchini. Cover and cook until tender, about 3 minutes.

2. Add parsley, tomatoes, and garlic to broth; heat until tomatoes become tender. Season with salt and pepper to taste, then add vinegar and brown sugar. Check seasonings and add more if desired, then add a bit of Tabasco.

To serve: Ladle into big bowls.

Dividends: Nice chilled with dollops of sour cream and sprigs of dill.

To make ahead: Complete through Step 1, then finish just before serving.

TOO-MANY-TOMATOES SOUP   Serves 8

This is a tangy tomato soup made with herbs and filled with *al dente* grated vegetables from the garden.

10 large, very ripe tomatoes (about 3–4 pounds), chopped	2 thin lemon slices
	½ teaspoon Worcestershire sauce
1 large onion, sliced thin	2 teaspoons salt
3 tablespoons butter	½ cup grated carrot
4 cups water	½ cup grated green pepper
1 bay leaf	½ cup grated celery
1 teaspoon peppercorns	Salt and pepper
4 whole cloves	Sour cream

1. In a large kettle over medium heat, sauté tomatoes and onion in butter 10 minutes, then add water, bay, peppercorns, cloves, and lemon slices tied into a small cheesecloth bag. Add Worcestershire and salt. Cover, reduce heat, and simmer for 20 minutes. Remove spice bag, and purée soup in a blender or a food processor, 2 cups at a time, or press through a sieve. Return to kettle.
2. Add grated vegetables, and simmer, stirring, over medium heat, until carrots are *al dente,* a bit soft but still a bit chewy. Add salt and pepper to taste.

To serve: Ladle into soup bowls and garnish with sour cream.

Dividends: Heat it up and stretch with beef broth. Or serve chilled with snips of fresh dill.

To make ahead: Can be made a day ahead, but don't overcook grated vegetables; undercook so they'll be just right when served.

GREEN TOMATO GAZPACHO   Serves 8

Here's a cool, tart soup to make with green tomatoes. Choose fruit that has a white cast: the green-green tomatoes are too unripe. If the tomatoes are quite juiceless, you may want to add more water or wine. Make this the day before.

2 slices white bread, crusts removed	½ teaspoon salt
1 large clove garlic	2 tablespoons red wine vinegar
¼ cup olive oil	¼ teaspoon ground cumin
8 medium green tomatoes	¾ cup ice water
1 sweet red pepper, seeded, chopped	½ cup dry white wine
1 medium cucumber, peeled, chopped	Salt and pepper
1 large slice onion	¾ cup croutons, sautéed in olive oil

1. Break the bread into small bits and place in a bowl. Crush the garlic over it, and pour oil on top. Leave several hours. Do not refrigerate.
2. Skin the tomatoes with a potato peeler and cut them up; there should be about 4 cups. Purée the tomatoes, pepper, cucumber, and onion slice in a blender or a food processor, 2 cups at a time. Sprinkle salt, vinegar, and cumin over the bread and toss well. Purée with the vegetables in the blender or processor. Chill 4 to 6 hours or overnight.

To serve: Stir in the water and wine, add salt and pepper to taste, ladle into chilled bowls, and garnish with croutons.

FIERY TOMATO SOUP   Serves 4

Those beautiful little hot peppers sold in Southern states and in Mexico are the basis of this hot pot. Buy fresh peppers, wash and split them, discard all seeds, and wash again.

10 fresh small red, yellow, and orange hot peppers, chopped fine	3 tablespoons oil
	1 tablespoon butter
8 big tomatoes, peeled, chopped	3 tablespoons all-purpose flour
1 large onion, chopped	1 teaspoon grated lemon peel
1½ cups water	Fresh dill
1 cup cooked rice	Salt and pepper

1 teaspoon minced fresh basil	Sour cream

1. Purée peppers, tomatoes, and onion with water in a blender or a food processor, 2 cups at a time. Place purée in a large kettle over medium heat and simmer, covered, about 15 minutes. Purée once more, as above, or press through a sieve; return to kettle.
2. In a small saucepan over low heat, combine oil and butter, and stir in the flour; cook until bubbly. Gradually add a cup of the purée, stirring constantly until sauce thickens, then return to the kettle and cook, stirring, for 10 minutes. Stir in lemon peel; add salt and pepper to taste. Stir in cooked rice and heat through.

To serve: Ladle into soup bowls and garnish with sour cream and dill.

Dividends: Freeze leftovers and use later to stretch chili dishes.

To make ahead: Complete to the point where rice is to be added hours or days ahead, then finish just before serving.

GREEN TOMATO CREAM   Serves 4

When you have run out of bright ideas for the last few green tomatoes of the season, try this one. Nice with cheese sandwiches for a fall luncheon.

6 medium green tomatoes, chopped	3 tablespoons all-purpose flour
3 tablespoons minced onion	4 cups milk
4 cups water	Salt and pepper
¼ teaspoon baking soda	¼ cup crumbled cooked bacon
3 tablespoons butter	

1. In a saucepan over high heat, simmer tomatoes with onion in water for 20 minutes, or until mushy. Add ¼ teaspoon soda. Purée in a blender or a food processor, or press through a sieve.
2. In the saucepan over very low heat, melt the butter and stir in the flour. Stirring constantly, add the milk and simmer until sauce thickens. Stir in the tomato mixture, and season with salt and pepper to taste.

To serve: Ladle into soup bowls and garnish with bits of crumbled bacon.

CREAM OF TURNIP SOUP   Serves 6

Made with the delicious little white turnips of early spring, this is an elegant soup.

4 to 6 small white turnips, peeled, sliced	½ teaspoon sugar
1 medium onion, chopped	2 egg yolks
3 tablespoons butter	½ cup heavy cream
6 cups beef broth	Salt and pepper
2 medium potatoes, chopped	½ cup Croutons, Sautéed in Butter (page 33)

1. In a large saucepan over medium heat, sauté the turnips and the onion in butter until the onion begins to be translucent, about 7 to 10 minutes. Don't let vegetables brown. Add broth and potatoes, cover, and lower heat. Simmer until vegetables are very tender. Add sugar. Purée in a blender or a food processor, 2 cups at a time, or press through a sieve. Return to saucepan.
2. In a small bowl beat the egg yolks until thick and lemon-colored, then stir in the cream. Beat 1 cup purée into the egg mixture, then return the mixture to the saucepan, stirring. Heat to just below boiling. Season with salt and pepper to taste.

To serve: Ladle into soup bowls and garnish with croutons.

VEGETABLE SOUP WITH WINE   Serves 6 to 8

Peasants in Europe—they're the landowners—like a dash of wine in their soup, which often is the meal eaten before going off to work in the fields at dawn. Here's a Catalonian version of vegetable soup that includes white wine. Any dry white wine will do. Serve with crusty bread and butter.

2 medium onions, chopped	3 large ripe tomatoes (about 1½ pounds), chopped
2 large leeks, whites only, chopped	2 large potatoes, chopped
1 tablespoon olive oil	⅓ cup dry white wine
1 tablespoon butter	6 cups beef broth
1 large stalk celery and leaves, minced	Salt and pepper

In a large kettle over medium heat, sauté the onions and leeks in the oil and butter until the onion begins to be translucent, 5 to 7 minutes. Add the celery and tomatoes, cover, lower heat, and simmer until tomato is very soft, about 15 minutes. Add potatoes, wine, and broth. Cover and cook 30 minutes. Mash with a potato masher right in the kettle, and season with salt and pepper to taste.

To serve: Ladle into big soup bowls.

Dividends: Excellent reheated; stretch with more broth.

To make ahead: Make hours or a day ahead.

VEGETABLE SOUP WITH PEAS AND BEANS   Serves 6 to 8

Frozen green peas are easier to come by than fresh, unless you grow your own—and they are okay here.

1 large onion, chopped	2 quarts water
4 tablespoons butter	1 teaspoon sugar
2 large stalks celery and leaves, chopped	2 teaspoons salt
	1/4 teaspoon pepper
3 medium carrots, chopped	1/2 cup peas
2 medium tomatoes (about 1/3–1/2 pound) chopped	1/2 pound string beans, cut up (about 2 cups)
1/2 teaspoon fresh dill	1 tablespoon minced parsley
1/4 medium head of cabbage, shredded	

In a large kettle over medium heat, sauté the onion in the butter until translucent, about 5 minutes. Add celery, carrots, tomatoes, and dill; sauté, stirring, 2 to 3 minutes. Add cabbage, water, sugar, salt, and pepper. Cover, lower heat a little, and simmer until carrots are almost tender, about 15 minutes. Add peas and beans, and cook until tender, about 10 minutes more.

To serve: Ladle into soup bowls and garnish with parsley.

To make ahead: Can be made several hours ahead, but don't cook peas and beans completely. Remove from heat while their color is still bright green; reheat just before serving.

SEPTEMBER SOUP   Serves 6

Fall is the season when celery root, carrots, the yellow turnip called rutabaga, and cabbage are plentiful—the main ingredients in this version of vegetable soup.

6 tablespoons butter	6½ cups chicken broth
½ cup chopped celery root or celery	¼ head white cabbage, shredded
½ cup chopped carrot	½ head lettuce, shredded
½ cup chopped rutabaga or turnip	Salt and pepper
2 leeks, chopped	¼ cup minced parsley

In a large saucepan over medium heat, melt the butter and sauté the celery root or celery, carrot, rutabaga or turnip, and the leeks, stirring often, for 12 to 15 minutes, or until considerably softened. Add chicken broth, cover, and bring to a boil. Add cabbage, cover, and boil 8 minutes. Add lettuce, cover, and boil 8 minutes. All vegetables should be tender. Add salt and pepper to taste.

To serve: Ladle into soup bowls and garnish with parsley.

Dividends: Very good reheated. Add milk or broth to stretch.

To make ahead: Can be made hours or the day before.

CREAMY ZUCCHINI SOUP   Serves 4

Makes fresh zucchini into a wonderful soup with minimum fuss and time. Takes about 15 minutes to make. Nice chilled, too.

3 to 4 medium zucchini, unpeeled, sliced ¼ inch thick	2 cups chicken broth
	2 tablespoons butter
1 large onion, sliced thin	1 cup light cream
1 teaspoon salt	¼ teaspoon ground coriander
⅛ teaspoon pepper	2 tablespoons parsley, minced

1. In a kettle over medium heat, place zucchini, onion, broth, salt, and pepper. Bring to a rapid boil, uncovered. Stirring now and then, cook 10 minutes. Purée in a blender or a food processor, 2 cups at a time, or press through a sieve. Return to kettle.
2. Reheat to boiling, then stir in butter, cream, and coriander.

To serve: Ladle into soup bowls and garnish with parsley.

Dividends: Nice cold.

To make ahead: Complete through Step 1, then finish just before serving.

Eight

CREATIVE COOKING: TAKE A WILTED LETTUCE LEAF

When my French aunts go shopping for food, they start with a list of the leftovers in the larder: Leftovers with a few fresh ingredients can create a culinary event. Leftovers can cut in half the effort and cost of the next meal. Cooked (or leftover cooked) chicken is the basis of Chicken à la King. Make the cream sauce, add a bit of pimiento, and *voilà!* Now combine Chicken à la King with leftover chicken broth and you have an elegantly rich cream of chicken soup to garnish with paprika, and serve to cheers. In about five minutes!

This is an introduction to my theory—which may alarm the fastidious home economist—that almost anything left in the refrigerator can either make or enhance a soup. The recipe below, Thursday Night Soup, makes the point. This recipe is my variation on recipes creative cooks all over the world have evolved: a soup recipe to clear out the refrigerator (or the larder) before you go shopping to fill it up again. It's a "let's-make-room" soup. It can absorb anything except cabbagy leftovers, and its only flaw is that you can't ever make it the same way twice: you never have exactly the same set of ingredients hanging around!

THURSDAY NIGHT SOUP   Serves 6 to 8

This makes 4 to 5 cups of broth to which you can add just about anything the refrigerator can offer, except rank cabbage items. (Ham doesn't do much for it either.) To get it just right, you have to know what your family enjoys and do lots of tasting as you add ingredients.

3 medium onions, chopped	¼ teaspoon dried thyme
3 tablespoons oil	½ teaspoon sugar
1 6-ounce can tomato paste	1 to 2 cups solid leftovers,
4 cups water	cooked or raw
4 beef bouillon cubes	1 to 2 cups liquid
1 teaspoon salt	Condiments to taste
¼ teaspoon pepper	Garnish
1 small bay leaf	

1. In a kettle over medium heat, sauté the onion in the oil until lightly browned, about 10 minutes. Stir in the tomato paste. Reduce heat and cook 1 minute, stirring. Add water, bouillon cubes, salt, pepper, bay, thyme, and sugar. Cook 5 minutes, uncovered.
2. Add up to 2 cups solid leftovers—stray carrots, celery stalks and leaves, potatoes, peas, snap beans, lettuce. These may

be raw or cooked. If raw, mince or slice very thin, and cook 5 to 10 minutes or until tender, before adding. If cooked, simmer about 5 minutes before serving. Cooked meats (except ham) may be added: beef, hamburger leftovers, chicken, turkey, and veal are good. Cube before adding, and cook 5 minutes before serving. Fish or fish flakes (dried) may be added. Frozen vegetables, meats, or fish may also be added. Cooked dishes may be added—for instance, rice dishes, stews, spaghetti oddments, creamed vegetables, mashed potatoes. Raw spaghetti, noodles, and rice may be added, but these will require simmering 12 to 15 minutes, covered.

3. Add up to 2 cups liquid: milk, cream, buttermilk; any leftover soup that isn't cabbagy or contains ham or pork; the cooking water of vegetables or beef bouillon; leftover tomato juice, tomato cocktail mix, Bloody Mary mix; gravies; white or red wine, sherry (but not more than ½ cup), orange and grape-fruit juice.

3. Taste and season: add more salt, pepper, sugar, or paprika, a bit of wine, Worcestershire sauce, or those herbs that go so well with tomato-flavored soups—oregano, basil, and rosemary —¼ teaspoon each (dried) is enough of these. Cook 5 minutes after the final seasonings have gone in, then serve.

To serve: You can do some very creative things with bits of left-overs: a dab of sour cream or yogurt enhances a plate of soup; or a sprinkling of minced parsley or dill, or chopped watercress stems or sauerkraut, minced scallion tails or chopped celery leaves, sprouted soy beans or alfalfa sprouts; or croutons or stale bread sautéed in butter or olive oil with minced garlic.

Dividends: Plan to use up all of a soup that has lots of leftovers in it.

To make ahead: This may be made several hours ahead.

TURNING LEFTOVER VEGETABLES INTO CREAM SOUPS

Another way to use up leftover cooked vegetables is to turn them into cream soups. It's my solution to using up cabbagy leftovers. Here's the recipe I use for things like broccoli, brussels sprouts, cabbage, kale, and spinach. (I know spinach is not a cabbage, but it tends to be biting, and the cream softens its sting.) And follow-ing that are many more cream soups to make with all sorts of leftover cooked vegetables.

CREAM SOUP WITH CABBAGE FAMILY LEFTOVERS

Serves 5 to 6

Cauliflower, broccoli, cabbage, brussels sprouts (don't purée these in Step 1—just chop coarsely with a knife), and even kale and spinach (I know it isn't a cabbage relative, but it's nice in this recipe) may be used. If you don't quite have 2 cups of leftover cooked vegetables, complete the measure with mashed potato, cooked rice, or finely minced celery (sauté it with the onion).

2 tablespoons minced onion	2 cups leftover cooked
3 tablespoons butter	vegetables
3 tablespoons all-purpose	Salt and pepper
flour	¼ cup grated Cheddar,
2 cups hot milk	Gruyère, or Swiss cheese
2 cups chicken broth	⅛ teaspoon grated nutmeg

1. In a kettle over medium heat, sauté the onion in the butter until translucent, about 5 minutes. Stir in the flour. Lower heat and stir in the milk; cook, stirring, until bubbly, 1 to 2 minutes. Add the broth. Combine the leftover vegetables with 2 cups of the cream sauce, and purée in a blender or a food processor, 2 cups at a time, or press through a sieve.
2. Return to the kettle over medium heat. Add salt and pepper to taste. Heat to just below boiling, and stir in the cheese until just melted.

To serve: Ladle into bowls and garnish with nutmeg.

To make ahead: Complete through Step 1, then finish just before serving.

CREAM OF ARTICHOKE SOUP

Serves 5 to 6

You can make this with leftover cooked Jerusalem artichokes, mashed, or with leftovers scraped from the big globe artichokes. If you are working with cooked globe artichokes, scrape the meat from the artichoke leaves before they have quite cooled, remove the choke, and mash the heart with the meat scraped from the leaves. Cover and refrigerate until ready to use.

1 tablespoon minced onion	2 cups hot milk
3 tablespoons butter	2 cups chicken broth
3 tablespoons all-purpose	2 cups leftover cooked
flour	artichoke

½ teaspoon grated lemon rind

2 tablespoons butter
Salt and pepper

1. In a kettle over medium heat, sauté the onion in the butter until translucent, about 5 minutes. Stir in the flour. Lower heat and stir in the milk; cook, stirring, until bubbly, 1 to 2 minutes. Add the broth. Combine the artichoke with 2 cups of cream sauce, and purée in a blender or a food processor, 2 cups at a time, or press through a sieve.
2. Return to the kettle over medium heat. Add salt and pepper to taste, and add the lemon rind. Heat to just below boiling.

To serve: Ladle into bowls and add a dab of butter to each.

To make ahead: Complete through Step 1, then finish just before serving.

CREAM OF CARROT SOUP   Serves 5 to 6

Make this with carrots only, or with carrots combined with other vegetables—celery, peas, parsnips, turnips, cabbage, or potatoes.

2 tablespoons minced onion
2 tablespoons butter
2 tablespoons all-purpose flour
2 cups hot milk
2 cups cooked carrot and other leftover vegetables

2 cups chicken broth
Salt and pepper
2 tablespoons minced dill, parsley, or tarragon
1 tablespoon butter
Croutons, optional

1. In a kettle over medium heat, sauté the onion in the butter until translucent, about 5 minutes. Stir in the flour. Lower heat and stir in the milk; cook, stirring, until bubbly, 1 to 2 minutes. Add the broth. Combine the leftover vegetables with 2 cups of cream sauce, and purée in a blender or a food processor, 2 cups at a time, or press through a sieve.
2. Return to the kettle over medium heat. Add salt and pepper to taste. Heat to just below boiling.

To serve: Ladle into bowls and garnish with herb, butter, and croutons if you wish.

To make ahead: Complete through Step 1, then finish just before serving.

CREAM OF GREEN PEA SOUP   Serves 5 to 6

Make this with leftover cooked peas only (fresh or canned), or
with peas and carrots, celery, potato, or green beans.

1 small onion, minced
2 tablespoons butter
2 tablespoons all-purpose
   flour
2 cups hot milk
2 cups chicken broth
2 cups cooked peas and other
   leftover vegetables

Salt and pepper
1 teaspoon minced garlic,
   optional
1 tablespoon butter
Croutons, optional

1. In a kettle over medium heat, sauté the onion in the butter
   until translucent, about 5 minutes. Stir in the flour. Lower the
   heat and stir in the milk; cook, stirring, until bubbly, 1 to 2
   minutes. Add the broth. Combine the leftover vegetables with
   2 cups of cream sauce, and purée in a blender or a food
   processor, 2 cups at a time, or press through a sieve.
2. Return to the kettle over medium heat. Add salt and pepper
   to taste. Add garlic if you wish. Heat to just below boiling.

To serve: Ladle into bowls and garnish with butter and croutons,
if you decide to use them.

To make ahead: Complete through Step 1, then finish just before
serving.

CREAM OF SPINACH SOUP   Serves 5 to 6

Make this with spinach, kale, cress, sorrel, or celery.

1 small onion, minced
3 tablespoons butter
3 tablespoons all-purpose
   flour
2 cups hot milk
2 cups chicken broth
2½ cups cooked spinach and
   other leftover greens

Salt and pepper
⅛ teaspoon grated nutmeg
½ cup thinly sliced
   mushrooms, optional
1 tablespoon butter

1. In a kettle over medium heat, sauté the onion in the butter
   until translucent, about 5 minutes. Stir in the flour. Lower
   heat and stir in the milk; cook, stirring, until bubbly, 1 to 2

minutes. Add the broth. Combine the leftover vegetables with 2 cups of cream sauce, and purée in a blender or a food processor, 2 cups at a time, or press through a sieve.
2. In a small saucepan, sauté the mushrooms, if you are using them, in the butter over medium heat until they have rendered their liquid and begun to dry out.
3. Return purée to the kettle over medium heat, and scrape mushrooms, if you are using them, into the kettle. Add salt and pepper to taste. Heat to just below boiling.

To serve: Ladle into bowls. If you did not use the butter to cook the mushrooms, garnish with dabs of butter.

To make ahead: May be made several hours ahead. Stir often to keep the cream sauce from developing a tough skin.

CREAM OF SQUASH SOUP
Serves 5 to 6

Make this with summer squash, zucchini, or celery and squash.

1 small onion, minced	3 cups leftover cooked
3 tablespoons butter	squash
3 tablespoons all-purpose	Salt and pepper
flour	1/4 teaspoon dried savory
3 cups hot milk	1/4 teaspoon dried oregano
1 cup beef broth	1/8 teaspoon ground mace

1. In a kettle over medium heat, sauté the onion in the butter until translucent, about 5 minutes. Stir in the flour. Lower the heat and stir in the milk; cook, stirring, until bubbly, 1 to 2 minutes. Add the broth. Combine the squash with 2 cups of cream sauce, and purée in a blender or a food processor, 2 cups at a time, or press through a sieve.
2. Return the purée to the kettle over medium heat. Add salt and pepper to taste. Add savory, oregano, and mace. Heat to just below boiling.

To serve: Ladle into bowls.

To make ahead: May be completed several hours ahead.

CREAM OF SWEET POTATO SOUP Serves 5 to 6

Make this with mashed leftover sweet potatoes, pumpkin, yams, or winter squash such as butternut. Or make it with any of these combined with cooked celery or carrot.

2 tablespoons minced onion	Salt and pepper
2 tablespoons butter	¼ cup orange juice, optional
1 tablespoon all-purpose	Honey, optional
flour	¼ teaspoon each, cinnamon,
2 cups hot milk	ginger, mace, optional
2 cups chicken or beef broth	
2 cups leftover cooked	
vegetables	

1. In a kettle over medium heat, sauté the onion in the butter until translucent, about 5 minutes. Stir in the flour. Lower the heat and stir in the milk; cook, stirring, until bubbly, 1 to 2 minutes. Add the broth. Combine the leftover vegetables with 2 cups of cream sauce, and purée in a blender or a food processor, 2 cups at a time, or press through a sieve.
2. Return the purée to the kettle over medium heat. Add salt and pepper to taste. Add orange juice. If you wish, and sweeten with as much honey as you like. Combine the spices, if you wish, and stir into the soup. Heat to just below boiling.

To serve: Ladle into bowls.

To make ahead: Complete through Step 1, then finish just before serving.

CREAM SOUP WITH POTATO BASE Serves 6

You can use potatoes to make a creamy soup that includes leftover vegetables. Old potatoes, the kind sprouting and withering in early spring, thicken soups beautifully. Use them up this way.

2 large potatoes, chopped	Salt and pepper
1 medium onion, chopped	1 tablespoon minced parsley,
3 tablespoons butter	dill, savory, or other herb
7 cups water	Milk
2 cups leftover cooked	
vegetables	

1. In a kettle over medium heat, sauté the potatoes and onion in the butter until the onion begins to be translucent, about 5 to 7

minutes. Add the water, cover, and simmer until the potatoes are tender, another 15 to 20 minutes. Purée with the leftover vegetables in a blender or a food processor, 2 cups at a time, or press through a sieve.

2. Return the purée to the kettle over medium heat. Add salt and pepper to taste. Heat to boiling.

To serve: Garnish with minced herb and thin with a little milk.

To make ahead: Complete through Step 1, then finish just before serving.

TWO-PENNY SOUPS

We've made the point that soups are perhaps the least costly foods per serving. This group, based on potatoes, cabbage, and onions, is the biggest soup bargain around. You could think of it as the night-before-payday soup. To the basic recipe given below, you can add almost anything the refrigerator holds.

TWO-PENNY SOUP   Serves 8

3 medium onions, chopped	½ small bay leaf
3 medium potatoes, grated or chopped	¼ teaspoon dried thyme
3 tablespoons bacon or chicken drippings	½ head winter cabbage, shredded
3 quarts water	2 tablespoons minced parsley
1½ tablespoons salt	2 tablespoons butter, optional
10 peppercorns	

In a big kettle over medium heat, sauté the onions and potatoes in the drippings until the onion is translucent, about 10 minutes. Add the water, salt, peppercorns, bay, and thyme. Simmer, covered, 1 hour. Add the cabbage, cover, and cook 2 hours over low heat.

To serve: Ladle into bowls and garnish with parsley. Add a dab of butter to each bowl, if you wish.

Dividends: Great base for making soup from leftovers. (See following recipes.)

To make ahead: Keeps in the refrigerator; however, if kept for a long time it develops a strong cabbagy odor you may not like.

TWO-PENNY SOUP WITH CARROTS   Serves 8

1 recipe Two-Penny Soup
2 large carrots, grated

1 teaspoon brown sugar
Salt and pepper

Ten minutes before you complete the Two-Penny Soup recipe, add carrots and brown sugar. Complete the cooking, then add salt and pepper to taste.

TWO-PENNY SOUP WITH CRUMBS   Serves 8

1 recipe Two-Penny Soup
8 heaping tablespoons dried
    breadcrumbs
3 tablespoons butter

2 small cloves garlic, minced
3 tablespoons finely minced
    parsley

Garnish each serving of soup with crumbs and parsley sautéed in butter with garlic 1 minute.

TWO-PENNY SOUP WITH GREENS   Serves 8

1 recipe Two-Penny Soup
2 cupfuls chopped spinach
    stems or watercress stems,
    or 1 cup parsley stems

Three minutes before you complete the Two-Penny Soup recipe, add finely chopped greens, and complete the cooking uncovered.

TWO-PENNY SOUP WITH HAM LEFTOVERS   Serves 8

1 recipe Two-Penny Soup
Ham leftovers

Include in Two-Penny Soup recipe any portion of a ham bone, or scraps of leftover ham, even leftovers that are only fat. Discard leftovers before serving.

TWO-PENNY SOUP WITH HOT DOGS   Serves 8

1 recipe Two-Penny Soup
Leftover hotdogs

Include in Two-Penny Soup recipe any leftover hot dogs, sliced thin. Add 10 minutes before serving.

TWO-PENNY SOUP WITH PARMESAN   Serves 8

1 recipe Two-Penny Soup,   ½ cup grated Parmesan
  parsley omitted   cheese
2 tablespoons butter

To serve: Divide Two-Penny Soup among 8 small ovenproof crocks, the kind used for onion soup. Sprinkle Parmesan over each, add a dab of butter, and brown under the broiler on high.

THE HOSPITABLE POT

Soups accommodate almost any leftover. They also accommodate an almost infinite number of guests. Add a little broth, milk, tomato juice, or another tag end of soup, some rice, barley, and broken bits of spaghetti—and any soup will grow and grow to take in whoever needs tender, loving care at a moment's notice.

The recipe that follows is the first soup I ever took an interest in. My Scotch-Canadian mother had taught it to her French cook (or vice versa), so it has a French flavor, but it's made from the root vegetables of northern countries—the only vegetables available all winter long in the days before frozen vegetables and air travel. It is infinitely adaptable. It's best made with old potatoes, wrinkly the way they are at winter's end, that thicken a soup well, and from yellow turnips or rutabagas, though you can use instead the little white turnips of spring. I prefer big, thick winter carrots to skinny young ones: they're sweeter.

You can make the soup richer by adding more butter, or leaner by adding less. Or you can make it with oil—flavorful olive oil or plain vegetable oil. If you use olive oil, add a bit of basil and oregano to add an Italian accent. Cook it with the top off at a quick simmer, and it will soon boil down to a thick vegetable stew. Cook it in a slow-cooker, and it will be much thinner.

Since this soup accommodates almost any leftover, use it to practice your soup-stretching talents, first with the stretchers suggested here, then with whatever comes to hand or to mind.

And you can stretch it with almost anything you have in the refrigerator or the pantry.

MOTHER'S VEGETABLE SOUP   Serves 8 to 10

This is the first soup I learned to make and my favorite soup.

2 large onions, chopped	6 sprigs parsley, minced
¼ pound butter	1 small bay leaf
4 large carrots, chopped	¼ teaspoon dried thyme
½ small yellow turnip, chopped	1 tablespoon salt
	⅛ teaspoon pepper
6 large stalks celery and leaves, chopped	3 quarts water
	Salt and pepper
4 large potatoes, chopped	

In a large kettle over medium heat, sauté the onions in the butter until translucent, about 5 to 7 minutes. Don't let them brown. Add remaining ingredients, bring to a boil, cover, lower heat, and simmer 1½ hours or until potatoes have almost disintegrated. Soup will be thick. Add salt and pepper to taste.

To serve: Ladle into big bowls.

Dividends: Add almost any leftover, solid or liquid, to stretch.

To make ahead: Tastes better the second day.

BEANS AS A STRETCHER   Serves 6

4 cups Mother's Vegetable Soup	1 to 2 cups any cooked dried beans
Salt and pepper	Beef broth or water

Bring the soup to a boil, add the beans, heat 3 minutes. Add enough beef broth or water to thin it to the consistency you enjoy. Add salt and pepper to taste, and serve.

BREAD AS A STRETCHER   Serves 6

Stale French or Italian bread is great in soups—cut into cubes and sautéed in butter to make tasty croutons—or just chopped into slabs, buttered, with soup ladled over it, as here.

6 slices stale bread
Pinch dried thyme
4 cups Mother's Vegetable
   Soup

6 teaspoons butter
1 tablespoon minced parsley
   or dill

To serve: Place bread, sprinkled with thyme, buttered, then sprinkled with parsley, in the bottom of large soup bowls. Ladle very hot soup over slices.

CABBAGE AS A STRETCHER   Serves 6

4 cups Mother's Vegetable
   Soup
Salt and pepper

2 cups finely shredded green
   cabbage
2 cups water

Bring the soup to a rapid boil. Add cabbage and water; cook until cabbage turns bright green, about 7 to 8 minutes. Turn off heat before it yellows. Add salt and pepper to taste, and serve.

FISH AS A STRETCHER   Serves 6 to 8

4 cups Mother's Vegetable
   Soup
1 to 2 cups leftover cooked
   fish, boned
2 cups milk

Salt and pepper
1½ tablespoons butter
1 tablespoon minced
   parsley

Bring the soup to a rapid boil. Add the fish, and bring back to a boil. Cook 1 minute. Add the milk; bring back to a boil. Add salt and pepper to taste.

To serve: Ladle into bowls and garnish with butter and parsley.

MEAT AS A STRETCHER

Serves 6 to 8

4 cups Mother's Vegetable
Soup
½ 6-ounce can tomato paste
1 cup water
¼ teaspoon dried oregano
1 large clove garlic, minced

1 to 2 cups cooked leftover
meat such as beef, veal,
hamburger, beef stew,
meat sauce, chili con
carne, chicken, turkey

Bring soup to a rapid boil and add tomato paste, water, oregano, garlic, and leftovers. Bring back to a boil and cook, uncovered, 3 minutes. If too thick, add more water.

MILK AS A STRETCHER

Serves 6 to 8

4 cups Mother's vegetable
Soup
2 cups milk
¼ teaspoon saffron threads
or paprika, optional

Salt and pepper
Butter
Oysterettes, crumbled saltines,
or croutons

Bring soup to a boil. Add milk, and when it returns to a boil, add saffron or paprika, if you wish, and turn off heat. Add salt and pepper to taste.

To serve: Ladle into bowls, dot with butter, and add as many Oysterettes, crumbled saltines, or croutons as needed to make the soup as hearty as you want it to be.

PASTA AS A STRETCHER

Serves 6 to 8

1 cup broken spaghetti, elbow
macaroni, egg noodles,
spaetzle, rice, or any other
pasta or grain
2 cups water

4 cups Mother's Vegetable
Soup
Salt and pepper
Butter

Cook pasta in water until just soft. Add soup, bring to a boil, and cook until pasta is completely tender. Add salt and pepper to taste.

To serve: Ladle into bowls and garnish with butter.

TOMATO JUICE AS A STRETCHER   Serves 6 to 8

4 cups Mother's Vegetable   2 cups tomato juice
   Soup   Salt and pepper
½ cup minced celery

Bring soup to a boil, add celery and juice, and cook, covered, until celery is partially tender, about 10 minutes. Add salt and pepper to taste, and serve.

WINE AS A STRETCHER   Serves 6

4 cups Mother's Vegetable   ½ cup water
   Soup   Salt and pepper
1 cup dry red wine

Bring soup to a boil with wine and water; simmer 10 minutes, uncovered. Add salt and pepper to taste, and serve.

TURNING BONES INTO SOUP

Today we pay hard cash for the soup bones we used to be given free at the market. So before you discard *anything* related to meat, consider its potential for soup. Ham bones and turkey carcasses make soups we are all familiar with—but the magical properties of duck carcasses and pan drippings from meat and fowl roasts are less well known. Even the skin from a good ham can be puréed into a thick pea soup with glorious results! You may not want to go that far, but do boil it with your soup for flavor and nutrition.

CHICKEN SOUP VICTORIAN STYLE   Serves 8

Here's a basic approach to turning leftover chicken into soup. Make a cream sauce, add broth and leftover cooked or easily cooked raw vegetables, and cut-up chicken. Herbs and spices can be your own choice. Dill would be nice here, or you could try Italian herbs like basil or oregano.

1 small onion, chopped	¼ bay leaf
1 cup sliced mushrooms	⅛ teaspoon dried thyme
½ cup minced, canned pimiento, well drained, or ripe sweet red pepper	2 whole cloves
	½ cup all-purpose flour
2 tablespoons butter	2 quarts hot chicken broth
1 teaspoon salt	1 cup diced cooked chicken
⅛ teaspoon pepper	Paprika

In a saucepan over medium heat, sauté the onion, mushrooms, and pimiento or pepper in the butter until the onion begins to be translucent, 7 to 10 minutes. Add salt, pepper, bay, thyme, and cloves. Stir in flour. Beating constantly, add the broth, and cook, stirring, until bubbly. Add the chicken, reduce heat, and simmer 15 minutes before serving.

To serve: Ladle into bowls and garnish with paprika.

To make ahead: May be made a day ahead.

DUCK SOUP   Serves 4

Here's another way to use bird remains to make soup: Simmer the carcass, drippings, gravy, and so on, with seasonings and vegetables, remove the bones, thicken, and serve! You can do this on the top of the stove, as here, or in a slow-cooker (on Low all day), or in a pressure cooker (20 to 30 minutes). Reduce water to 4 cups for slow or pressure cooking.

Carcass and all remains from a duck, including pan drippings, gravy, meat, skin, bones	2 large stalks celery and tops
	1 teaspoon salt
	8 peppercorns
1 medium onion, chopped	1 small bay leaf
1 large carrot, chopped	2 whole cloves

8 cups water
½ to 1 cup mashed potatoes
  or 2 to 4 tablespoons
  instant mashed potato
  powder

Salt and pepper
2 tablespoons minced celery
  leaves

1. In a kettle over high heat, place duck carcass and leftovers, including as little fat as possible. Add vegetables, salt, peppercorns, bay, cloves, and water. Cover and bring to rapid boil. Lower heat and simmer 1½ hours. Strain. Place broth in freezer to encourage fat to rise to top. Pick over solids, discarding peppercorns, bay, cloves, bones, and skin. Reserve meat and vegetables.
2. Skim fat from broth, return to medium heat, and stir in potatoes or potato powder until as thick as desired. Add vegetables and meat, and heat to boiling. Add salt and pepper to taste.

To serve: Ladle into bowls and garnish with minced celery leaves.

To make ahead: Complete through Step 1, then finish shortly before serving.

TURKEY SOUP WILLIAMSBURG STYLE   Serves 10 to 12

A wonderful way to serve a crowd with leftovers from Christmas dinner!

3 large onions, chopped
3 large stalks celery and
  leaves, chopped
2 large carrots, chopped
2 cups water
½ pound butter
1 cup all-purpose flour

2½ quarts hot Turkey Broth,
  strained (page 288)
1 pint half-and-half
1 cup diced cooked turkey
1 cup cooked rice
Salt and pepper

1. In a saucepan over medium high heat, cook the onions, celery and leaves, and carrots in water, covered 20 minutes.
2. In a large saucepan over low heat, melt the butter and stir in the flour. Beating constantly, add the broth, then the half-and-half, and cook, stirring, until bubbly, 4 to 5 minutes. Add vegetables and their cooking liquid, and cook, stirring, 10 minutes. Add turkey and rice; add salt and pepper to taste.

To serve: Ladle into bowls.

To make ahead: May be made a day ahead.

TURKEY BROTH
Makes 2 to 3 quarts

The easiest way to make this is in a slow-cook electric pot as suggested below, but you could simmer it on top of the stove, covered, for three hours and get about the same results.

Carcass, pan drippings, gravy, leftover meat, skin, bones from a turkey
5 to 6 chicken wings, necks, or backs
2 quarts water
½ teaspoon dried thyme
1 small onion
3 whole cloves
1 small bay leaf
2 teaspoons salt
8 peppercorns
1 large carrot, cut into thick rounds
1 large stalk celery and leaves, cut up
3 tablespoons barley
Salt and pepper
1 tablespoon minced parsley

1. Place all ingredients except the barley, the last bit of salt and pepper, and the parsley in a slow-cooker, and set at 250 degrees. Cook covered, 3 to 6 hours. Add the barley and cook 45 minutes. Strain. Place broth in the freezer to encourage fat to rise to top. Pick over solids, discarding bones, skin, peppercorns, cloves, and bay. Reserve meat, vegetables, and barley.
2. Skim fat from broth, return reserved ingredients, and reheat. Add salt and pepper to taste.

To serve: Ladle into bowls and garnish with minced parsley.

Dividends: Makes a great soup base. To use it as a stock, strain out vegetables and freeze in 1-cup lots. Also, will usually gel to make an aspic. To make a molded turkey aspic, place chunks of turkey meat in a mold and fill with broth; cover and chill until set.

MARROW BONE SOUP
Serves 6

Marrow bones produce a wonderful soup, delicious with hot, crusty French bread.

6 cups veal broth
½ cup water
½ clove garlic, optional
4 beef marrow bones
8 large romaine lettuce leaves, cut into thin strips
Salt and pepper
1 tablespoon butter

1. In a large kettle over high heat, bring the broth to a rapid boil with the water (and the garlic if you wish). Add the bones; cover and boil 10 minutes. Remove the bones and re-

frigerate 1 hour. Draw the marrow out with a long, thin knife, and slice it into rounds ½ inch thick. Try not to break them up.

2. Over high heat, bring the broth back to a boil, and stir in the lettuce strips. Simmer until the lettuce is wilted and its color brightens—about 2 minutes. Remove the garlic (if used); add salt and pepper to taste. Place marrow rounds on lettuce in kettle, and heat 1 minute more.

To serve: Ladle into bowls and add a dab of butter to each.

To make ahead: Complete through Step 1, then finish just before serving.

SCOTCH BROTH WITH A LEFTOVER LAMB BONE
Serves 6

Use a meaty bone from a leg of lamb, including the shank part which usually dries out. To get the bone into the pot, twist the leg apart. It divides rather easily at the joint except for a small ligament which can be cut. Divided into four—one flat piece and three long bones—it fits into a 3- or 4-quart kettle.

1 large onion, chopped	8 to 9 cups water
3 tablespoons fat from lamb roasting pan, or butter	1 small bay leaf
	1 tablespoon salt
Bone from leg of lamb, and scraps of meat, pan drippings, gravy, omitting fat where possible	⅛ teaspoon pepper
	2 sprigs parsley
	½ cup barley
	3 tablespoons minced parsley
2 medium carrots, chopped	Salt and pepper
2 large celery stalks and leaves, chopped	

In a large kettle over medium heat, sauté the onion in the lamb fat or butter until translucent, about 5 minutes. Add lamb, carrots, celery, water, bay, salt, pepper, and parsley, and bring to a rapid boil. Cover, lower heat, and simmer 2 hours. Add barley and simmer 45 minutes. Discard bay leaf and remove bone. Chop meat on bone and return to kettle with any marrow in the bone. Discard bone. Stir in parsley, and add salt and pepper to taste. Heat.

To serve: Ladle into bowls.

To make ahead: May be made the day before.

BEEF BONE BROTH WITH OKRA   Serves 10 to 12

You may make this with packaged "soup bones" from the market, or from bones, meaty scraps, gravy, and drippings from a standing rib or other beef roast. If you use leftovers from a rib roast, remove as much of the fat as possible. If a lot of fat is floating on the broth surface when it is done, chill the broth long enough to bring all the fat to the top, then skim it off. A little fat is nice, but fatty broth can be distasteful.

1 large beef bone with meaty scraps, or soup bones and bits of meat	2 twenty-nine-ounce cans tomatoes and liquid
3 quarts water	2 medium bay leaves
3 pounds okra, chopped	2 medium onions, chopped
1 thick slice ham, bacon, or salt pork, diced	2 teaspoons salt
1 large whole clove garlic, peeled	⅛ teaspoon pepper
	1 cup cooked rice
	2 tablespoons minced parsley

In a large kettle over high heat, bring bones with meat and water to a rapid boil. Cover, reduce heat to medium low, and simmer 2 hours. Add okra, ham, bacon or pork, whole garlic clove, tomatoes, bay, onions, salt, and pepper, and cover. Simmer another hour, stirring occasionally. Add water if broth is too far reduced. Remove and discard bones, reserving any meat; discard bay leaves and garlic. Skim excess fat from soup. Cut up meat and return to broth. Stir in cooked rice.

To serve: Ladle into bowls and garnish with parsley.

To make ahead: May be kept for several days.

SPLIT PEA SOUP WITH HAM BONE   Serves 10 to 12

Never throw away a ham bone! It can be frozen if you don't have a soup coming up on the menu, wrapped in heavy foil with whatever meat and fat scraps remain. Ham bones and/or meat bring wonderful flavor to dried peas, yellow or green, lentils, lima beans, and other dehydrated legumes. Here's one of my family's favorite winter soups, a thick, tasty soup with meat—just perfect for after-sports snacking.

1 large onion, chopped	1 ham bone and scraps of
2 tablespoons butter	meat, fat, and skin
3 quarts water	1 cup minced celery
2 cups split green peas	1 cup minced carrot
(1 pound)	⅛ teaspoon dried savory
4 whole cloves	¼ teaspoon marjoram
1 medium bay leaf	1 tablespoon salt
2 large sprigs parsley	8 peppercorns

In a large kettle over medium heat, sauté the onion in the butter until translucent, about 5 minutes. Add the remaining ingredients. Raise heat and bring to a boil, then cover, lower heat, and simmer 3 to 4 hours. Stir now and then toward the end of the cooking, and add more water if soup thickens too much. It should be as thick as heavy cream whipped several minutes, but not stiff. Remove the ham bone, bay, cloves, and peppercorns. Cut up meat and return to the soup.

To serve: Ladle into mugs or bowls.

Dividends: Great the next day and freezes beautifully. Thin or stretch with broth, milk, or cream. Make it heartier by adding croutons if you have stretched it too thin.

To make ahead: May be made several days ahead.

GIZZARDS, HEARTS, AND ALL THAT

I can remember marketing with my mother in Canada during the thirties, when the butchers sold delicate pink-gray liver from a calf for five cents a pound. In those days, the butcher thought liver, gizzards, chicken necks, and other exotic meats were suited best to feline palates. And mother didn't disabuse him.

Today chicken livers are packaged and sold for lots more than five cents a pound. But even hearts make good soup, tough as they are, so don't overlook this kind of bargain. Often, the bargain comes home with the weekend's barbecue materials; save up chicken gizzards, livers, and other meaty exotics to make some of the soups below.

HEART AND SOUP BONE SOUP   Serves 10 to 12

Heart is an economical meat few cooks know how to handle. Calf heart is best. All hearts go into dishes that take quite a lot of cooking. This recipe is made a day ahead, as described here, but you could complete the first step overnight by putting everything into a slow-cook electric pot, set on Low. If you decide on that method, reduce the water to 8 cups and cook 8 to 12 hours, then refrigerate.

2 pounds beef soup bones	⅔ cup brown barley
12 cups water	2 large carrots, chopped
2½ teaspoons salt	2 large stalks celery and
5 peppercorns	leaves, chopped
⅛ teaspoon dried thyme	½ large onion, chopped
1 small bay leaf	Salt and pepper
3 whole cloves	½ cup finely minced parsley
1½-pound calf heart	

1. In a large kettle over high heat, combine beef bones with water, salt, peppercorns, thyme, bay, and cloves. Bring to a boil, cover, reduce heat, and simmer 1 hour. Add heart, cover, and simmer 1 hour. Add barley, cover, and simmer 1 hour. Refrigerate overnight.
2. Skim away fat. In a small saucepan over high heat, bring carrots, celery, and onion to a rapid boil with 2 cups heart broth and simmer, covered, 15 minutes. Meanwhile, remove meat from soup bones and dice. Discard fat, skin, and tubes from heart; dice. Over high heat, bring heart broth to a boil and add diced meats. When vegetables are done, add to broth. Add salt and pepper to taste.

To serve: Ladle into bowls and garnish with parsley.

TRIPE SOUP MEXICAN STYLE   Serves 10 to 12

The most famous dish with tripe—the stomach lining of an animal—is *Tripe à la Mode de Caen.* However, the Mexicans favor this one, which is considered a hangover remedy. Use fresh calf's feet, not smoked. Wash the tripe well before using, and remove any fatty bits. Cut into 2-inch sections. If you don't have a slow cooker, you can simmer this very slowly on the stove, tightly covered for 10 to 12 hours.

2 calf's feet
3 quarts water
5 pounds fresh tripe
3 cups hominy
3 large onions, chopped
4 cloves medium garlic,
   minced
1 tablespoon dried oregano

2 teaspoons coriander seed
1 tablespoon salt
¼ teaspoon pepper
Salt and pepper
4 scallions, chopped
¼ cup chopped mint leaves
Red Mexican chili sauce

In a slow-cook electric pot set at 250 degrees, place the calf's feet and water, bring to a boil, cover, and simmer 1 hour. Add tripe pieces, hominy, onions, garlic, oregano, coriander, salt, and pepper. Cover and simmer 6 to 7 hours. If broth is thin, remove cover, raise heat, and boil rapidly until reduced—½ to 1 hour. Add salt and pepper to taste.

To serve: Ladle into bowls, and offer chopped scallions, mint, and chili sauce on the side.

To make ahead: May be made several days ahead.

CHICKEN LIVER SOUP FOR GOURMETS   Serves 4 to 5

Save chicken livers in the freezer to make this one.

1 medium onion, chopped
2 tablespoons butter
6 chicken livers, halved
3 hard-boiled eggs, chopped
3 tablespoons butter
3 tablespoons all-purpose
   flour
3 cups hot chicken broth

½ 10-ounce package frozen
   chopped spinach, cooked
2 cups half-and-half
½ teaspoon tarragon
Salt and pepper
2 tablespoons minced
   parsley

1. In a saucepan over medium heat, sauté the onion in the butter 5 minutes. Add the livers, and sauté 5 minutes. Chop the liver-onion mixture. In a small bowl combine mixture, pan drippings, and eggs.
2. Return the saucepan to low heat; melt the butter and stir in the flour. Beating constantly, add the broth and cook, stirring, until bubbly, 1 to 2 minutes. Stir the egg-liver mixture into the broth. Add the spinach, the cream, and tarragon. Heat to just below boiling. Add salt and pepper to taste.

To serve: Ladle into bowls and garnish with parsley.

VEAL KIDNEY SOUP FOR GOURMETS   Serves 4

Fresh veal kidneys are a delicacy. When they are fresh, the color is on the pale side and the skin glistens. If you are buying from a butcher, sniff the kidneys and avoid those with a strong odor. Before using, wash the kidneys, slice in half, remove the outer membrane and discard with the core of fat and as much of the white veining as you can remove.

1 pair veal kidneys, diced	2 tablespoons butter
4 cups veal or chicken broth	¼ teaspoon salt
1 small onion, minced	1 tablespoon strained lemon
4 tablespoons butter	juice
4 tablespoons all-purpose flour	3 tablespoons Madeira
	Salt and pepper
1 cup heavy cream	2 tablespoons finely minced
1 pound mushrooms, chopped	parsley

1. In a saucepan over high heat, bring the kidneys and broth to a rapid boil. Lower heat, cover, and simmer 15 minutes.
2. In a small saucepan over low heat, sauté the onion in the butter 5 minutes. Stir in the flour. Beating constantly, strain the broth into this *roux,* and cook over low heat, stirring, until bubbly, 1 to 2 minutes. Add kidneys and cream, and turn off heat.
3. In a saucepan over medium heat, sauté the mushrooms in the butter 5 minutes. Sprinkle with salt and lemon juice. Stir the broth into the mushroom pan, stirring up pan juices. Add the Madeira, salt and pepper to taste. Heat 1 minute.

To serve: Ladle into bowls and garnish with lots of parsley.

GIZZARDS SOUP   Serves 6

Save the gizzard bag from packaged chicken in the freezer, and you'll always have enough scraps on hand to make this dish. Sweetbreads look like brain—white and grainy—but are glands from young animals, preferably veal. Before you use them, wash them well in cold water, and soak in the refrigerator in icy water to which you have added 1 tablespoon of white vinegar or lemon juice. After 2 hours, skin away the white membrane, change the water, and repeat the process.

6 cups water	1 cup sweetbreads
1½ teaspoons salt	2 chicken livers
5 peppercorns	½ cup sliced mushrooms
⅛ teaspoon dried thyme	3 tablespoons butter
1 thick slice onion	¼ teaspoon salt
2 stalks celery, cut into 2-inch pieces	3 tablespoons all-purpose flour
2 large carrots, cut into 2-inch pieces	2 egg yolks
	1 cup heavy cream
2 chicken gizzards	Salt and pepper
2 chicken hearts	

1. In a kettle over high heat, bring the water to a boil with the salt, peppercorns, thyme, onion, celery, and carrots. Add the gizzards and hearts; cover, reduce heat, and cook 10 minutes. Add sweetbreads, cover, and cook 10 minutes. Add livers, cover, and cook 5 minutes. Add enough additional water to return it to its original level, bring back to a boil, and turn off heat. Discard carrot and celery pieces. Collect meat with a slotted spoon, chop very coarsely, and return to broth.
2. In a saucepan over medium low heat, sauté mushrooms in butter 5 minutes. Add salt, then stir in flour. Beating contantly, strain the broth into this *roux*, and cook, stirring, until bubbly, 1 to 2 minutes. Scrape back into the soup kettle. Heat to just below boiling, then turn off heat.
3. Beat egg yolks until lemon-colored. Combine yolks and heavy cream, and stir into hot soup. Add salt and pepper to taste.

To serve: Ladle into soup bowls.

DICTIONARY OF USES FOR LEFTOVERS

BEANS, SNAP: A few raw beans, chopped and added to the soup for the last 5 minutes of cooking, make a good garnish. Use cooked leftover green beans to make Cream of Green Bean Soup—Fast, page 378. Use leftover cooked dried beans to thicken soups, and in vegetable soups.

BEER: Add beer to pea soups, beef broths, and any soups with ham in them.

BREAD: Cube stale bread or toast to make croutons; store in airtight container or bag.

BROCCOLI: Snip raw leaves to garnish soups. A few tiny florets, chopped and added to the soup for the last 5 minutes of cooking, make a good garnish. Use cooked broccoli leftovers in Cream of Broccoli Soup—Fast, page 378.

BUTTERNUT SQUASH: Use mashed cooked leftovers to make a variation on Cream of Parsnip Soup, page 168.

CAKE CRUMBS: Store in freezer or use fresh or stale. White, pound, and sponge cake crumbs give body to any of the cool fruit soups in Chapter 10; see especially Tangy Fruit Medley with Wine, and Apricot and Orange Soup—Fast, pages 348 and 384.

CARROTS: Raw, chopped, or thinly sliced carrots make colorful garnishes suitable for most soups. Use leftover cooked carrots to make Cream of Carrot Soup—Fast, or in Cream of Parsnip Soup, pages 379 and 168.

CAULIFLOWER: See *Broccoli*. Use leftover cooked cauliflower to make Cauliflower and Cheese Soup—Fast, page 379.

CELERY: Use minced leaves as soup garnishes. Dice celery and add to soups for last 5 minutes of cooking to add crunch. See also Celery Soup—Lean, and Cream of Celery Soup, pages 305 and 160.

COOKING WATER: Almost any cooking liquid can be used in a soup. Ham cooking liquid can be used to base dried bean and lentil soups—the result is almost as good as having a ham bone to cook with the soup. Store it in the freezer if you don't have an immediate use for it. Water used to cook almost any vegetable—except artichokes—and cabbage!—can be used instead of bouillon for vegetable soups and to add flavor to meat and bean soups.

CORN: Cut kernels from cooked cobs and store in freezer for future use in vegetable medley soups; Corn 'n Cheese Soup—Fast, and Corn Chowder—Fast, page 368. Use stripped corncobs to add flavor to soups like Succotash Chowder with Fresh Limas, page 326; discard cobs when cooking is over.

DRIPPINGS: Pan and roaster drippings from any meat but ham can be refrigerated for later use in a broth or soup; skim off the fat before adding to the soup.

FAT: Refrigerate fat from chicken for use in sautéeing vegetables going into chicken soups. Fat from pork or a ham roast can be used to sauté vegetables for almost any but a fish soup. Bacon fat can be used the same way, and is especially good for bean soups.

FISH: Fish trimmings may be used, if very fresh, in cooking certain fish soups and to make fish stocks. See Chapter 4 for this information and for use of water used in cooking shellfish and seafood.

HERBS: Herbs freeze well. Save leaves for garnishing finished soups; save stems to cook with soups as flavoring agents. Dill is especially valuable, as are parsley and chervil.

MUSHROOMS: Slice fresh white caps thin, making T-shapes, and float on soups as a garnish. Save stems to make any of the mushroom soups, and to add to vegetable, fish, and meat soups for flavor and as a garnish.

POTATOES: Mashed potatoes make an admirable thickener for any soup. Whip the hot broth into the potatoes, then return the potatoes to the soup. More salt will be needed after the addition of potatoes to soups. See Daniel Webster's Chowder, and Poor Man's Lobster Soup, pages 129 and 145.

SAUCES: A cup of almost any good sauce—meat or tomato sauce for spaghetti, chili sauce, cheese sauce—stretched with milk or broth can pass for a pretty good soup. A little sauce can be added to most any soup to stretch or brighten it. Or garnish cabbagy soups with dollops of cheese sauce; add chili sauce to meat soups; use *pesto* with Mediterranean recipes instead of *pistou*.

SPAGHETTI: Raw broken spaghetti can replace noodles or macaroni in most soups. Cooked spaghetti, added in the last few minutes of cooking, is a hearty stretcher for soup.

TOMATOES: Add oddments of tomato juice to any soup, but especially to vegetable soups, bean soups, meat soups, and fish soups like Manhattan Clam Chowder. It's a good stretcher. Add whole fresh or cooked or canned tomatoes to vegetable soups; float slices of fresh tomato on soups as a garnish.

WINE: Add odds and ends of wine—red, *rosé*, or white—to almost any soup early in the cooking. Stretch thick vegetable broths with wine, especially red. Flavor cream soups with a bit of sherry or Madeira.

Nine
LEAN AND LIVELY SOUPS

The soups in this chapter are lean and lively—nutrition and calorie conscious.

If you suspect as you settle down to a cozy bowl of soup on a mean winter night that your dinner is too fattening to be smart, you're giving in to that prejudice which says all good things are too costly, one way or another. Soups based on herbs, like those in this chapter, have been trusted as health-giving for centuries. Health is never too costly.

It's a fact that there's more nutrition per calorie and per dollar in soup than anywhere else. Meat, costly in calories and dollars, goes further to serve more people in a soup. And vegetables remain the backbone of most soups, and they are nutritious, and low in calories and cost, too.

Furthermore, cooked in soups, all the nutritional content of an ingredient is used. It isn't carried off in steam or thrown away in the cooking water, not burned in frying pans or dried up in ovens. Most soups are simmered, covered, from beginning to end, so everything the ingredients have to give goes to you.

Actually, credibility in nutritional content is something people accord to soups. But most of us suspect anything so rich must be fattening, so let's think about that. The real calorie-carrying ingredient is meat. Fats used for sautéeing onions, which base most soups, are suspect, too. Then there is the cream we call for so often, and the thickeners used to give vegetable soups body. Actually, a minimum of meat and fish goes into a soup to serve a maximum number of people: meat and fish often is as much a flavoring agent as a substantial element in soup. You get more taste per calorie, and that's often most of what you get. The same thing is true of butter, cream, and eggs in veloutés: divided among the number of portions in the soup, the overall calorie content can be surprisingly low.

For instance, a tomato soup without cream or milk comes to about 75 calories per portion. If it's the whole of lunch, that's pretty nifty! Gazpacho, a chilled tomato-based soup with some oil and lots of vegetables, comes to about 130 calories—not bad. A one-vegetable soup like borscht with a bit of sour cream comes to about 140 calories. A meatless dried bean soup ranges between 150 and 250 calories. Add sausage to the dried bean soup and the calories go up to 370 per portion, but for a rich, hearty, complete meal, that's reasonable. Split pea soup with ham comes to about 300 per portion. A corn chowder made with milk is about 225. Minestrone, about 260. Chilled cherry soup sweetened and topped with cream—only 200. Even the main-course soups that have everything in them can be surprisingly lean. The famous curried chicken soup called mulligatawny counts about 285 calories per portion. Scotch broth is about 400. Cheddar cheese soup is 350 to 390 depending on cream content. A bit of salad with vinegar dressing and a piece of fruit complete meals based on these soups, so even when the soup itself is very rich, the total caloric intake can be quite moderate.

And that's one of the glories of soup—it's filling and satisfying. And if you've been fighting with calorie-counting for years, it's soothing to feel comfortably full without feeling you've sinned against the lord of the fat farm.

You can trim down the calorie content of any soup fairly easily:

1. Use light cream (30 calories per tablespoon) instead of heavy cream.

2. Use milk instead of light cream (or half-and-half).

3. Use 1 egg instead of 2 in veloutés.

4. Buy low-fat yogurt, cheeses, milk, etc.

5. Cut meat and fish quantities in half. Ditto cream.

6. Use cornstarch or instant mashed potato powder (at 30 calories per tablespoonful) for thickeners instead of whole potatoes (at 100 per medium potato).

7. Cut butter or oil used to sauté ingredients in half, or skip it altogether, and simmer ingredients in bouillon instead of sautéeing in butter.

8. Skim the fat from broths: chill them first, and the fat will rise to the surface.

FOR HEALTH FOOD BUFFS

The recipes here—diet, dairy, meatless, and herbal groups— are meant to prove soup can be all things to all people. You can, in fact, make a soup of anything you feel you should be taking in right now. The diet group will suggest ways other soup recipes can be reduced in calorie count. The dairy group shows how to use dairy products in soups—buttermilk, yogurt, sour cream. The cheese-based soups are protein-loaded meat substitutes, rich enough to satisfy for hours. The meatless soups are mostly based on dried legumes. If you are not a purist, you can use a chicken or beef bouillon cube to give flavor without including meat. But these flavorful legume soups have such a zesty, meaty flavor all on their own, they don't need that kind of help. (Most people know by now that the dried beans are a richer source of protein than peanut butter: not everybody knows it's a good idea to incorporate cheese, eggs, corn [corn meal muffins, for instance] and rice, into legume-based meals to enhance the amino acid methionine in the legumes.)

The herbal soups here are for fun. Mostly European, they are reminders of a time when herbs were our only medicine, and soups were considered the best remedy for almost everything, from a broken rib to a broken heart!

DIET SOUPS

Here are soups that will satisfy for hours and are very low in those rich ingredients dieters avoid. Onions are usually simmered, not sautéed, there are no thickeners, and cream is replaced by nonfat dry milk. And still they're very good!

ASPARAGUS BOUILLON—LEAN   Serves 3

To make Asparagus Bouillon you strain the solids from the broth, leaving a 15-calorie bouillon ideal for trimming calories.

1 pound asparagus	½ teaspoon dried borage
4½ cups water	Salt and pepper
1 small onion, chopped	

1. Remove tough, purple-white end of the asparagus, and 1 inch of the tip. Reserve tips. Chop the spears and place with tough ends, water, and the onion in a kettle over high heat. Cover, bring to a boil, reduce heat, and simmer 45 minutes. Add the borage, cover, and cook 15 minutes.
2. Strain out the solids and discard. Return broth to the kettle and add salt and pepper to taste.

To serve: Over high heat, bring broth back to a boil, add reserved asparagus tips, simmer 4 minutes, then ladle into bowls.

To make ahead: Complete through Step 2, then finish just before serving.

AVOCADO SOUP—LEAN   Serves 6

Be sure the avocados for this are dead ripe—very tender under pressure but not mushy to touch.

6 cups chicken broth, chilled
2 ripe avocados, peeled,
  seeded, sliced thin
¼ teaspoon coarse sea or
  kosher salt
6 thin lemon slices with
  rind, halved

3 tablespoons sherry,
  optional
½ cup minced parsley
Salt and pepper

1. Skim off and discard all fat from the surface of the broth.
2. Heat broth to boiling. Meanwhile, place avocados in soup bowls, sprinkle with salt, garnish with lemon slices. Stir sherry, if you wish, into broth, add parsley, and salt and pepper to taste. Remove broth from heat at once, and serve.

To serve: Ladle over avocado and lemon slices.

GAZPACHO WITH BROTH—LEAN   Serves 6

3 cups Chicken Broth—
  Lean, chilled (page 304)
3 medium cucumbers,
  peeled
1 small clove garlic, peeled
2 cups low-fat yogurt
3 tablespoons white vinegar
2 teaspoons salt
½ teaspoon pepper

4 ripe medium tomatoes
  (about 1 pound), peeled,
  chopped
½ cup minced scallions
½ cup chopped parsley
2 tablespoons minced fresh
  basil

1. Skim off and discard all fat from the surface of the broth.
2. Purée cucumbers and garlic with 1 cup broth in a blender or a food processor, 2 cups at a time. Turn into a large bowl and stir in remaining broth.
3. Place the yogurt in another bowl, and stir in the cucumber mixture, vinegar, salt, and pepper. Cover and chill 3 to 4 hours or overnight.

To serve: Ladle cucumber mixture into bowls and heap tomatoes into center of each. Garnish with scallions, parsley, and basil.

To make ahead: This tastes better if it is made the day before. Finish the preparation and chill the ingredients, but combine only minutes before serving.

BROTH-ON-THE-ROCKS

Serves 2

This is the fastest, easiest drink in town, and has only 11 calories! It's nutritious and tastes good, too! I use a clam juice that has 13 calories per 8-ounce bottle.

1 cup Chicken Broth—Lean (page 304) or 1 cup water with 1 chicken bouillon cube dissolved in it

1 cup bottled clam juice
1 teaspoon minced parsley

In a small saucepan over medium heat, combine the clam juice and chicken broth or water and bouillon cube. Heat just long enough to combine and stir in the parsley.

To serve: Pour into very tall glasses filled with ice cubes.

CHICKEN BROTH—LEAN

Makes 2 quarts

To have carcasses from two cooked chickens on hand to make this, store them in the freezer as they become available. Broth without bouillon cubes has about 9 calories per cup. Cubes add a touch more calories, but not enough to matter.

Carcasses of 2 chickens, cooked, with meat scraps and drippings from which all fat has been removed
1 small carrot, scraped
2 stalks celery and leaves
1 large onion
2 whole cloves

1 small bay leaf
1 teaspoon salt
½ teaspoon tarragon
¼ teaspoon dried thyme
4 peppercorns
3 quarts water
Chicken bouillon cubes
Lemon juice

1. In a large kettle over medium heat, combine all the ingredients except the bouillon cubes. Cover, bring to a boil, at once reduce heat, and simmer 3 to 4 hours.
2. Line a colander with 2 thicknesses of cheesecloth and strain broth through it. Allow the broth to cool, then refrigerate or freeze for future use.

To serve: Heat broth, adding a few grains from a crumbled bouillon cube as needed to enhance flavor. And/or add a little lemon juice.

CELERY SOUP—LEAN   Serves 6

Choose a celery head with some green to it for this. The flavor is stronger, but make sure the leaves are fine and appetizing; they provide much of the flavor.

2 quarts Chicken Broth—
Lean, chilled (page 304)
6 large stalks celery and
leaves, minced

1 thin slice onion
Salt and pepper
6 celery leaves

1. Skim off and discard all fat from the surface of the broth.
2. In a kettle over medium heat, bring broth to a boil, and add celery and onion. Simmer, uncovered, 30 minutes.
3. Purée in a blender or a food processor, 2 cups at a time, or press through a sieve. Return to the kettle and heat to boiling. Add salt and pepper to taste.

To serve: Ladle into bowls and garnish with celery leaves.

To make ahead: Complete through Step 2, then finish just before serving.

CREAM OF CAULIFLOWER SOUP
WITH CHEESE—LEAN   Serves 6 to 8

Most beef bouillon cubes report only 6 calories per serving, so use whatever brand you prefer.

4 cups cold water
½ head cauliflower, chopped
1 medium onion, chopped
4 beef bouillon cubes
1 cup nonfat dry milk
powder

4 ounces low-fat processed
cheese
Salt and pepper
2 tablespoons minced
parsley

1. In a saucepan over medium heat, bring 3 cups water to a rapid boil. Add the cauliflower, onion, and bouillon cubes; cover, reduce heat, and simmer 15 minutes. Stir milk powder into remaining 1 cup of cold water and add to the soup.
2. Purée in a blender or a food processor, 2 cups at a time, or press through a sieve. Return to medium heat and stir in cheese until it melts. Add salt and pepper to taste.

To serve: Ladle into bowls and garnish with parsley.

CREAM OF CHICKEN SOUP—LEAN   Serves 4

A cream soup can't be devoid of all calories, but this has only 72 per portion. Flour only contains 20 calories per tablespoon and mushrooms, though rich in nutrients, have practically no calories at all.

2 cups water
2 cups skim milk
4 chicken bouillon cubes
1 small clove garlic, whole
1 sprig fresh dill, or ⅛ teaspoon dried
½ cup minced celery

¼ cup minced onion
1 tablespoon all-purpose flour
⅛ teaspoon paprika
4 large mushroom caps, sliced thin
4 sprigs parsley

In a kettle over medium heat, bring all the ingredients except the mushroom slices and parsley sprigs to a boil. Reduce heat and simmer, uncovered, stirring often, until soup thickens, about 10 minutes. Stir in mushroom slices, turn off heat. Remove garlic clove.

To serve: Ladle into bowls and garnish with parsley sprigs.

To make ahead: May be made hours or a day ahead.

BORSCHT FOR DIETERS   Serves 6

Beet soup is a hearty dish. This one has all the fattening sour cream taken from its contents, and weighs in at about 25 calories per cup. Not bad!

4 medium beets, chopped
2 quarts boiling water
1 small onion, stuck with 2 whole cloves
1 teaspoon sugar

1 tablespoon lemon juice
Salt
4 Zucchini Flowers (page 41)

In a kettle over medium high heat, cook the beets in the water with the onion until the beets are tender, about 25 minutes. Remove the onion and discard. Add sugar, lemon juice, and salt to taste.

To serve: Ladle into bowls and garnish with Zucchini Flowers.

To make ahead: May be made hours or days ahead, and stored, covered, in the refrigerator.

FISH CHOWDER–LEAN   Serves 4

Here's a tasty fish chowder with all the calories (possible) gone. What's left comes to about 137 per cup.

1½ pounds haddock, flounder, or cod
2 cups cold water
1 small carrot, cut into thin rounds
½ small bay leaf
¼ teaspoon dried thyme
4 sprigs parsley
1-inch cube salt pork

1 medium onion, chopped
2 medium potatoes, chopped
1 quart skim milk
1 small egg yolk, lightly beaten
½ teaspoon cayenne
Salt and pepper
Paprika

1. In a kettle over medium heat, bring the fish and water to a boil with the carrot, bay, thyme, and parsley. Cover, reduce heat, and simmer 15 minutes. Remove from heat.
2. In a kettle over medium heat, render the fat from the salt pork, then discard crisped bits. Sauté the onion in the fat until browning lightly, about 10 minutes. Pour fish and broth into the kettle, add the potatoes and milk, cover, reduce heat, and simmer 20 minutes. Remove the bay leaf. Beat a little broth into the egg yolk, then stir back into the broth. Season with salt and pepper to taste, and reheat to just below boiling, but do not let boil.

To serve: Ladle into bowls and garnish with a little paprika.

CLAM CHOWDER—LEAN   Serves 4

Here is a quick and easy recipe for a clam chowder that makes a very filling dinner for very few calories—about 140 or 150.

¼ pound salt pork, chopped
½ teaspoon dried thyme
2 6-ounce cans chopped clams and liquor
1 quart skim milk

1 medium potato, chopped
1 medium onion, chopped
Salt and pepper
1 teaspoon minced parsley

In a kettle over medium heat, render the fat from the salt pork, then discard crisped bits. Add the thyme, clams and their liquor, the milk, potato and onion, cover, reduce heat, and simmer 20 minutes. Add salt and pepper to taste.

To serve: Ladle into bowls and garnish with parsley.

LETTUCE AND CHEESE CUP   Serves 4

Any lettuce, but especially oakleaf and other fluffy green lettuces, make this soup very good. Calorie count is around 130.

1 tablespoon butter
2 cups tightly packed shredded lettuce
1 small onion, minced
1 quart Chicken Broth— Lean (page 304)

2 small eggs
½ cup grated Parmesan cheese (about ¼ pound)
4 Zucchini Flowers (page 41)

1. In a kettle over medium heat, melt the butter and stir into it the lettuce and onion. Add the broth and cook 10 minutes, uncovered.
2. In a bowl beat the eggs and stir in the cheese. Whip the hot broth into the eggs, then return to low heat for a few minutes to heat through. Do not let boil.

To serve: Ladle into bowls and garnish with Zucchini Flowers.

MEATBALL SOUP—LEAN   Serves 8 to 10

This includes meat, but it is very lean ground beef. Divided among 8 diners, there would be about 180 calories per person— but that's not a lot if you make it a meal. Followed by salad with lemon juice and a low-calorie fresh fruit—medium-size peaches, pears, oranges, or tangerines at 50 to 60 calories each—Meatball Soup qualifies as diet food.

2 quarts Chicken Broth— Lean, chilled (page 304)
1 quart water
2 teaspoons sea or kosher salt
2 pounds spinach, chopped
1 head celery and leaves, chopped
1 medium onion, chopped
4 very ripe medium tomatoes (about 1 pound), chopped
16 ripe plum tomatoes (about 1 pound), chopped
8 peppercorns
1 small bay leaf

⅛ teaspoon dried thyme
1 pound very lean ground beef
¾ cup raw rice
1 egg white, beaten
1 teaspoon sea or kosher salt
⅛ teaspoon pepper
Salt and pepper
¼ pound mushrooms, sliced thin
1 tablespoon grated low-fat cheese
3 tablespoons chopped parsley

1. Skim off and discard all fat from the surface of the broth.
2. In a large kettle over high heat, bring water, broth, salt, vegetables, and herbs to a rapid boil. Cover, reduce heat, and simmer 1 hour.
3. In a food processor or a bowl, beat together beef, rice, egg white, salt, and pepper. Between your palms, roll meat into very small balls. Add to broth and cook 1 hour. About 5 minutes before broth is done, add mushroom slices. Add salt and pepper to taste.

To serve: Ladle into bowls and sprinkle with cheese and parsley.

To make ahead: May be cooked hours or days ahead, and stored in the refrigerator, but add mushroom slices, cheese, and parsley just before serving.

MUSHROOM BROTH—LEAN Serves 3

Takes 3 hours to cook, but the result is a clear, very low-calorie mushroom broth.

½ cup chopped dried
    mushrooms
2 quarts cold water
1 pound fresh mushrooms,
    chopped

1 large onion, chopped
½ teaspoon marjoram
Salt and pepper
1 tablespoon chopped chives

1. In a kettle over high heat, bring dried mushrooms and water to a boil, covered. Reduce heat and simmer 1 hour. Add fresh mushrooms and onion and simmer 1 hour.
2. Purée in a blender or a food processor, 2 cups at a time, or press through a sieve. Return to heat. Add marjoram and simmer 1 hour. Add salt and pepper to taste.

To serve: Ladle into bowls and garnish with chives.

Dividends: Leftovers are great for flavoring stews and gravies.

To make ahead: Keeps for days in the refrigerator.

MULLIGATAWNY—LEAN   Serves 4

This is not only a lean mulligatawny, it is also a fast one. Calorie count is around 29 per cup.

1 10-ounce can condensed tomato soup
1 10-ounce can condensed pea soup
1½ soup cans water
1 thin scallion and top, minced

½ teaspoon celery salt
½ teaspoon turmeric
½ teaspoon ground cumin
½ teaspoon curry powder
¼ teaspoon ground coriander

In a kettle over medium heat, combine all the ingredients, and stir as the soup heats. Simmer 8 minutes, covered.

To serve: Ladle into bowls.

ONION SOUP—LEAN   Serves 4

A skinny version of the other onion soups in this book. Here, since we've omitted bread and other calorie-rich ingredients, the count is about 44 per serving.

1 cup thinly sliced onion
2 tablespoons butter
4 beef bouillon cubes

1 quart water
Grated Parmesan cheese
Salt and pepper

In a kettle over medium heat, sauté the onion in the butter 10 minutes or until lightly browned. Add the bouillon cubes and the water, cover, reduce heat, and simmer 30 minutes. Stir in as little Parmesan cheese as possible without feeling cheated, and season with salt and pepper.

To serve: Ladle into bowls.

SNACKING BROTH—FAST   Serves 1

This will keep you out of trouble when you are tempted to snack fat while dieting. Cost—about 37 calories.

1 cup Chicken Broth—Lean (page 304)
½ teaspoon lemon juice
¼ teaspoon grated lemon rind

1 teaspoon grated Parmesan cheese
1 teaspoon minced parsley or chives

In a small kettle over medium heat, combine all the ingredients, and bring to a boil.

To serve: Ladle into a bowl and garnish with herbs.

Dividends: Just as good poured over a bowlful of rice.

SPINACH CUP—LEAN   Serves 4

Even with the touch of butter here, we still have only about 52 calories per cup.

1 small clove garlic, minced
1 tablespoon butter
1 thin scallion and top, minced
2 cups Chicken Broth—Lean (page 304)

1 10-ounce package frozen chopped spinach
Salt and pepper
Nutmeg

In a kettle over medium heat, sauté the garlic in the butter 2 minutes. Add the scallion and sauté 2 minutes. Stir in the broth, add the spinach, and cook until the spinach is done, about 5 to 8 minutes. Purée in a blender or a food processor, 2 cups at a time. Return to the kettle, add salt, pepper, and nutmeg to taste, and heat through.

To serve: Ladle into soup bowls.

To make ahead: May be made a day or two ahead, and keeps well. Cover, and store in the refrigerator.

JOGGER'S CREAM OF TOMATO SOUP—LEAN   Serves 3 to 4

Great chilled. If you do jog, make up a batch before you set out, chill it in the freezer, and have it ready to quench your thirst when you get home.

  2 cups tomato juice
  1 cup buttermilk
  1 tablespoon minced parsley

  Salt and pepper
  3 to 4 sprigs parsley

In a kettle over medium heat, bring tomato juice to a boil, and slowly stir in buttermilk. Sprinkle with parsley, add salt and pepper to taste, and simmer 1 minute more.

To serve: Ladle into bowls and garnish with parsley.

To make ahead: Keeps very well for a day or two.

TOMATO AND DILL SOUP—LEAN   Serves 6

There's a bit of oil in this soup, but when you divide it among 6, each portion includes a scant teaspoonful.

   1 large onion, chopped
   2 tablespoons olive oil
  12 ripe medium tomatoes
      (about 3 pounds),
      chopped
   3 tablespoons tomato paste

  1⅓ teaspoons dried dill
  3½ cups beef broth, chilled
   ¾ teaspoon salt
   1 tablespoon wine vinegar
   6 sprigs fresh dill
  Tabasco sauce

1. In a saucepan over medium heat, sauté the onion in the oil until lightly browned, about 10 minutes. Stir in tomatoes, tomato paste, and dill. Bring to boiling, stirring often. Reduce heat, cover, and simmer 15 minutes.
2. Purée in a blender or a food processor, 2 cups at a time, or press through a sieve. Return purée to kettle. Skim off and discard all fat from the surface of the broth. Over medium heat, stir the broth into the purée with the salt and wine vinegar. Simmer 1 minute.

To serve: Ladle into bowls, garnish with dill, and season with a dash of Tabasco sauce.

To make ahead: Keeps very well for several days in the refrigerator.

VEGETABLE SOUP—LEAN

Serves 4

This is a hearty soup concocted of fresh but inexpensive vegetables supermarkets offer all year round. Everything that makes vegetable soup fattening has been eliminated, but there's plenty left to flavor, and the soup satisfies the appetite and keeps you out of trouble. Portions count about 80 calories each.

2 medium carrots, chopped	¼ teaspoon dried oregano
2 large stalks celery, chopped	¼ teaspoon dried thyme
1 medium onion, chopped	1 teaspoon fresh basil, or ¼ teaspoon dried
2 10-ounce cans stewed tomatoes	Salt and pepper
2 cups cold water	1 tablespoon minced parsley
2 beef bouillon cubes	

In a large kettle over medium heat, bring all ingredients except salt, pepper, and parsley, to a boil, covered. Reduce heat and simmer 1 hour. Add salt and pepper to taste.

To serve: Ladle into bowls and garnish with parsley.

Dividends: Use leftovers as a sauce for skinned chicken breasts, and lean meats, or boiled vegetables.

To make ahead: Keeps several days in the refrigerator.

FRESH VEGETABLE SOUP—LEAN

Serves 6

With that lean chicken broth on page 304, you can make this in minutes, and the calorie count is only 82 for a very satisfying bowl of soup.

1 quart Chicken Broth—Lean (page 304)	1 small onion, minced
3 cups mixed, fresh, minced vegetables, such as cabbage, carrots, green beans, cauliflower	1 small clove garlic, minced
	Salt and pepper
	Minced parsley

In a kettle over high heat, bring the broth to a boil, and stir in the vegetables and garlic. Reduce heat and boil, uncovered, 5 minutes, stirring often. Add salt and pepper to taste.

To serve: Ladle at once into bowls and garnish with parsley.

WATERCRESS SOUP—LEAN   Serves 4

This counts for about 32 calories per serving.

1 small bunch watercress, minced	1 small clove garlic, minced
1 teaspoon grated onion	3 cups Chicken Broth—Lean (page 304)
1 tablespoon butter	Salt and pepper

In a kettle over medium heat, sauté the watercress, onion, and garlic in the butter 10 minutes, stirring constantly. Add the broth, heat through, and add salt and pepper to taste.

To serve: Ladle into bowls.

DAIRY SOUPS

Soups based on dairy products are healthy, and hearty, easy on sour stomachs and tired dispositions. There's just one caution— *don't boil soup* after the addition of milk, sour cream, buttermilk, yogurt, etc. Heat to *just below boiling,* and watch closely even then to make sure the dairy product isn't curdling.

BUTTERMILK SOUP WITH BROCCOLI   Serves 4

This could be made with any green vegetable, but it is particularly good with cauliflower, or as here, with broccoli.

½ cup chopped onion	¼ teaspoon curry powder
½ cup chopped green pepper	1½ cups buttermilk
3 cups chopped broccoli	1 cup half-and-half
1½ cups water	Salt and pepper
1 teaspoon salt	4 raw broccoli florets

1. In a saucepan over medium heat, simmer the onion, pepper, and broccoli with the water, salt, and curry powder, covered, until broccoli stem pieces are tender, about 10 minutes.
2. Purée in a blender or a food processor, 2 cups at a time, or press through a sieve. Return purée to the kettle over low heat. Stir in buttermilk and half-and-half; add salt and pepper to taste. Heat to just below boiling.

To serve: Ladle into bowls and garnish with broccoli florets.

To make ahead: Complete through the cooking, then finish just before serving.

BUTTERMILK PARTY SOUP WITH RUMCAKES   Serves 6

A Danish delight—chilled, sweet buttermilk soup for festive occasions.

1 stick sweet butter	½ teaspoon grated lemon
¼ cup sugar	rind
2 cups instant oatmeal	2 teaspoons strained lemon
¼ cup white corn syrup	juice
½ cup golden seedless raisins	1 teaspoon vanilla
¼ cup white rum	1 quart buttermilk
3 egg yolks	½ cup heavy cream
½ cup sugar	

1. In a saucepan over medium heat, melt the butter and stir in the sugar. When the mixture bubbles, after about 30 seconds, stir in the oatmeal and reduce heat. Cook 8 minutes, stirring constantly. Oatmeal will become golden brown; when it does, stir in the corn syrup. Butter a small cookie sheet, and drop oatmeal onto it by teaspoonfuls, crowding the cakes. Chill 6 hours.
2. Place raisins in rum in a cup and allow to soak. Stir now and then.

To serve: With an electric beater on high, beat the egg yolks until thick and lemon-colored. Little by little add the sugar and beat until the yolks whiten. Add lemon rind and juice, and vanilla. By hand, fold in the buttermilk and cream. Pour into a tureen. Place cakes around the tureen and press soaked raisins into the tops of the cakes. Dribble remaining rum onto the soup.

SOUR CREAM SOUP   Serves 8

This is a gala dish from Mexico.

12 scallions, chopped
1 small garlic clove, minced
1 sweet green pepper, chopped
2 tablespoons butter
2 quarts sour cream
½ cup milk

⅛ teaspoon prepared or dry mustard
Salt and pepper
½ pound Muenster cheese, grated
1 cup Croutons, Sautéed in Butter (page 33)

In a kettle over medium heat, sauté the scallions, garlic, and pepper in the butter until the scallions begin to be translucent, 5 to 7 minutes. Stir in the sour cream, milk, and mustard, add salt and pepper to taste, and heat to just below boiling. Remove from heat and stir in the cheese until it begins to melt.

To serve: Ladle into bowls and garnish with croutons.

CANADIAN CHEDDAR CHEESE SOUP   Serves 6

Any of the cheddars can be used for this, but the mild type is most popular. About one-quarter pound of cheese, grated, makes one cup.

2 large slices bacon
1 large onion, minced
1 medium carrot, grated
1 small clove garlic, minced
2 tablespoons all-purpose flour
½ teaspoon dry mustard

1 teaspoon paprika
4 cups chicken broth
1 cup milk
1 cup grated cheddar cheese
Salt and pepper
1 tablespoon minced dill or parsley

1. In a saucepan over medium heat, fry the bacon until crisp. Lower heat so fat does not burn, and remove bacon. Place on paper towel to drain, and reserve.
2. Sauté the onion, carrot, and garlic in the fat until the onion becomes translucent, about 5 minutes. Stir in the flour, mustard, and paprika. Beating constantly, add the broth and milk; cook, stirring, until bubbly. Add cheese and stir until melted. Do not allow to boil. Add salt and pepper to taste.

To serve: Laddle into bowls, crumble reserved bacon over the soup, and garnish with minced herbs.

Dividends: Leftovers make nice sauce for noodles or macaroni.

To make ahead: Complete through addition of milk, then finish just before serving.

CREAM OF GRUYÈRE SOUP   Serves 4

This is a so-rich cheese soup, called The King's Soup in Europe. Jarlsberg cheese can be used instead of Gruyère, but it won't be quite right.

4 cups chicken broth	3 tablespoons butter
½ cup water	2 egg yolks
1 package Swiss onion soup mix and dip mix	¼ cup dry white wine
⅛ teaspoon ground mace	½ cup grated Gruyère cheese
2 cups milk	Salt and pepper
4 tablespoons instant mashed potato powder	1 tablespoon minced parsley
	1 cup Croutons, Sautéed in Butter (page 33)

1. In a kettle over medium heat, bring the broth and water to a boil and stir in the soup mix. Add mace, lower the heat, and simmer, uncovered, 15 minutes. Purée in a blender or a food processor, 2 cups at a time, or press through a sieve. Return to the kettle over medium heat and stir in the milk, potato powder, and butter.
2. In a small bowl beat the egg yolks until thick and lemon-colored. Stir in 1 cup hot purée, then return mixture to the kettle. Stirring, heat to just below boiling, adding the wine, cheese, salt and pepper to taste.

To serve: Ladle into bowls and garnish with parsley and croutons.

Dividends: Nice sauce for noodles.

To make ahead: Complete through step 1, then finish just before serving.

CHEESE MILK TOAST   Serves 4

This is a cozy, comforting dish for stormy nights when you're not very hungry. Emmenthaler cheese is that golden, big-holed cheese we call Swiss. A good substitute is Norwegian Jarlsberg, which is blander but very good and easy to find.

1 quart milk	1 cup grated Emmenthaler
¼ teaspoon salt	cheese
Pinch pepper	2 tablespoons butter
4 slices white bread, toasted, cut into triangles	¼ teaspoon grated nutmeg

1. In a kettle over medium heat, scald the milk with the salt and pepper.
2. Turn broiler to high. Divide the toast triangles among 4 oven-proof bowls, sprinkle cheese over the toast, and pass under the broiler just long enough for the cheese to start to melt at the edges.
3. In a small saucepan over medium heat, melt the butter and when it begins to brown, stir once, and remove from heat.

To serve: Ladle scalded milk over melting cheese, sprinkle with nutmeg, and drizzle with brown butter.

YOGURT SOUP WITH SPINACH   Serves 4

Beet greens are traditional in this dish as it is made in Egypt, its land of origin. However, spinach leaves are almost as good—and generally are easier to come by. A similar soup to serve cold appears in Chapter 10.

1 small onion, minced	¾ cup raw rice
2 tablespoons butter	5 cups cold water
1 pound spinach leaves, washed, coarse stems removed	1 teaspoon salt
	⅛ teaspoon pepper
	2 cups yogurt
4 scallions, chopped	1 small clove garlic, crushed
1 teaspoon turmeric	

1. In a saucepan over medium heat, sauté the onion in the butter until lightly browned, about 10 minutes. Toss spinach leaves with the onions in the saucepan, and cook, stirring, until they wilt. Sprinkle the turmeric, the rice, and ¾ of the scallions

over the spinach, and pour in the water with the salt and pepper. Bring to a boil, cover, reduce heat, and simmer 15 minutes or until rice is just tender.
2. In a bowl beat the yogurt with the garlic. Stir the yogurt into the broth, and remove from heat.

To serve: Ladle into bowls and garnish with reserved scallions.

To make ahead: Complete through Step 1, then finish just before serving.

YOGURT AND LEEK SOUP   Serves 6 to 8

Nice hot or cold. You can make this with onions, too. A calorie saver.

4 medium leeks, sliced	2 teaspoons salt
4 medium potatoes, chopped	⅛ teaspoon paprika
2 tablespoons corn oil	1 cup yogurt
6 cups Chicken Broth—	2 tablespoons minced chives
Lean, chilled (page 304)	

1. In a saucepan over medium heat, sauté the leeks and potatoes in the oil until leeks begin to be translucent, about 10 minutes. Skim off and discard all fat from the surface of the broth. Stir the broth, salt, and paprika into the leek mixture; reduce heat and simmer, covered, 30 minutes.
2. Purée in a blender or a food processor, 2 cups at a time, or press through a sieve. Return to kettle over low heat. Stir in yogurt, and heat to just below boiling.

To serve: Ladle into bowls and garnish with chives.

Dividends: Use leftovers to stretch soups, but don't boil when heating.

To make ahead: Complete through puréeing, then finish just before serving.

ICED YOGURT AND CUCUMBER SOUP   Serves 4

This exotic way with chilled yogurt is a variation on a Persian theme. You can crack the ice by putting it into a food processor very briefly. There's another version made with chicken broth on page 346.

1½ cups yogurt
1½ cups skim milk
¾ teaspoon salt
1 large cucumber, peeled, chopped
1 tablespoon minced onion

2 tablespoons minced fresh dill
3 tablespoons golden seedless raisins
4 ice cubes, cracked

Combine in a bowl yogurt, milk, and salt. Fold in cucumber, onion, dill, and raisins. Chill in the freezer.

To serve: Ladle into chilled bowls, stirring up raisins so each portion has some. Float a heaping teaspoon of cracked ice on the top of each portion.

To make ahead: May be made several hours ahead: if you do, chill in the refrigerator.

GET-WELL SOUPS

GET-WELL BROTH   Serves 1

A lot of thought used to be devoted in France to fattening up thin people in the days when plump was good—and there was attention paid to reviving flagging appetites, particularly after an illness. My family (and many others) had and has lots of faith in eggs. This recipe Madeleine Hériteau remembers from her childhood in Calais as standard after a bout of flu.

1 cup beef broth
2 egg yolks

Pinch minced parsley

To serve: Heat the broth in a small saucepan, then remove from heat and quickly beat the broth into the egg yolks. Garnish with a bit of parsley.

INVALID SOUP—FAST
Serves 1

1 egg
1 cup boiling beef broth
Worcestershire sauce

Salt and pepper
1 jigger red wine, optional

Beat the egg in a blender on low; with the blender still on low, pour broth, a little at a time, into the blender, then add Worcestershire, salt and pepper to taste, and wine if you wish. Reheat to just below boiling, and serve at once.

To serve: Pour into a large mug.

SOPS FOR THE INVALID—FAST
Serves 1

Long ago in Britain (and maybe still today!) this was the doctor's prescription when the patient was recovering and it was time to encourage him or her to eat a little.

1 cup milk
1 teaspoon sugar
Few grains salt

1 piece thick white bread,
toasted, buttered, cut into
triangles

In a kettle over medium heat, bring the milk, sugar, and salt to a boil, stir 1 minute, then turn off heat.

To serve: Place toast triangles in bowl and ladle the soup over them.

MAKE-YOU-HUNGRY BROTH
Serves 1

This recipe was meant to make you hungry if your appetite had fallen off.

1 cup beef broth
2 tablespoons dry red wine

To serve: Heat the broth, ladle it into a warm bowl, and stir in the wine.

MILK SOUP—SWEET COMFORT   Serves 2

This is what it calls itself, sweet comfort, just right for someone not up to par. It's nicest made with hand-cut noodles, but packaged noodles are faster, of course.

2 cups milk	1 tablespoon butter
1 cup water	½ cup egg noodles
½ tablespoon sugar	2 slices bread, toasted and
¼ teaspoon salt	buttered

In a large kettle over medium heat, bring the milk, water, sugar, and salt to a boil. Stir in the butter and add the noodles. Reduce heat, partially cover, and cook 8 to 12 minutes or until noodles are done. Stir often, as noodles tend to stick.

To serve: Ladle into bowls and serve toast on the side.

FATTENING PRUNE SOUP   Serves 2

Thinness is not a common malady in our country, but in Europe in decades past it was something to guard against. Here's an old-fashioned European remedy for it—one of those recipes that is as much fun to read as it is to eat.

1 cup old-fashioned oatmeal	20 pitted prunes
2½ cups water	½ teaspoon salt
¼ lemon with rind, sliced thin	1 cup heavy cream
	Sugar

1. In a large kettle over medium heat, add oatmeal and water. Bring to a boil. Cover partially, reduce heat, and cook 30 minutes, stirring occasionally. Strain; discard oatmeal. Add lemon, prunes, and salt. Cover and simmer 20 minutes.
2. Purée in a blender or a food processor, 2 cups at a time, or press through a sieve. Return to the kettle and stir in the cream. Heat slightly, and add sugar to taste.

To serve: Ladle into bowls.

MEATLESS SOUPS FOR ONE-DISH DINNERS

These are hearty soups that make a completely satisfying meal without meat. Most of these are based on dried legumes: kidney beans, lentils, black beans, split peas, etc. You will find other dried legume soups in Chapter 12, Fast and Slow-Cook Pots. The soups here could all be done in an electric slow-cooker, too. Chapter 12 explains how to adapt dried legume recipes to slow-pot cooking.

Don't, by the way, be uneasy that we aren't recommending soaking the beans overnight. You may if you wish, but the more popular method today is to bring the beans to boiling for 2 minutes in plenty of water, and then to cover and let them soak for an hour or two before cooking.

A bean pot should be a watched pot. The rate at which beans will absorb water is unpredictable. Just add more water if your broth is turning to purée.

BARLEY SOUP   Serves 6 to 8

A hearty but meatless soup from Middle Europe. Don't be tempted to add more barley than the recipe calls for.

¼ pound dried mushrooms	2 tablespoons pearl barley
2 cups lukewarm water	2 bay leaves
2 cups chopped onion	8 peppercorns, cracked
4 tablespoons butter	1 teaspoon salt
2 medium leeks, sliced thick	½ cup sour cream
2 medium carrots, sliced thick	2 tablespoons butter
	Salt and pepper
6 cups water	1 tablespoon chopped dill
3 medium potatoes, chopped	weed

1. In a small bowl soak mushrooms in water for a few hours or overnight. Slice the mushrooms into strips, discarding any tough parts. Reserve water.
2. In a saucepan over medium heat, sauté the onion in the butter until translucent, about 5 minutes. Reduce heat and add the leeks and carrots; stir and cook 10 minutes. Add the water, potatoes, barley, bay, peppercorns, salt, mushrooms and their water. Bring to a boil, cover, and lower heat until simmering. Simmer for 35 minutes or until barley is tender. Stir in sour cream and butter, and remove from heat.

To serve: Ladle into bowls and garnish with dill.

To make ahead: May be made hours or a day ahead.

RUTH MANNING'S BLACK BEAN SOUP   Serves 8

Ruth Manning and Peter Darmi are famous Manhattan florists
who practically live with their flowers. This soup frequently
cooks on a little two-burner stove at the back of their lovely shop
while Ruth and Peter make elegant flower arrangements for
New York's most glamorous hostesses. If you are a purist about
meat, make this with your favorite vegetable bouillon cubes.

2 cups dried black beans	2 tablespoons sherry, optional
6 cups cold water	
1 large onion, chopped	Salt and pepper
1 medium carrot, chopped	2 hard-boiled eggs, sliced
1 large stalk celery, chopped	8 thin lemon slices with rind
3 tablespoons butter or soy oil	
4 cups beef broth or vegetable bouillon	

1. In a kettle over high heat, bring beans and water to a rapid
   boil; cook 2 minutes. Turn off heat, cover, and let stand 1
   hour.
2. In a kettle over medium heat, sauté onion, carrot, and celery
   in butter or oil until onion begins to be translucent, 5 to 7
   minutes. Stir in beans, their water, and broth. Bring to a boil.
   Cover, reduce heat, and simmer 2 hours, stirring often. Add
   water if soup becomes too thick. Purée in blender or a food
   processor, 2 cups at a time, or press through a sieve. Stir in
   sherry if you wish, add salt and pepper to taste, and reheat.

To serve: Ladle into bowls and garnish with egg slices and lemon
slices.

Dividends: Leftovers are excellent combined with vegetable
soups.

To make ahead: Complete through Step 2, then finish just before
serving.

GARBANZO BEAN SOUP

Serves 6 to 8

Garbanzos are called chick peas here. They look a bit like filberts, and are especially popular in Spain and Portugal. The flavor is nutlike and when they're cooked, they're mealy.

2 cups dried garbanzo beans	1 tablespoon Worcestershire
3 quarts water	sauce
½ teaspoon dried rosemary	4 tablespoons tomato paste
3 tablespoons minced onion	⅛ teaspoon pepper
3 medium cloves garlic,	1 cup shell macaroni
crushed	1 cup water
3 tablespoons olive oil	Salt and pepper
1 teaspoon salt	1 tablespoon minced parsley
2 tablespoons minced hot	
green pepper	

1. In a kettle over high heat, bring the beans and water with the rosemary to a rapid boil. Reduce heat and cook 3 hours, covered, stirring often. Add more water if kettle dries out.
2. In a saucepan over medium heat, sauté the onion and garlic in the oil until the onion is translucent, about 5 to 6 minutes. Stir in the salt, hot pepper, Worcestershire, tomato paste, and pepper, and cook another few minutes. Scrape into the bean kettle and rinse the saucepan with a little of the cooking water from the beans. Bring the bean kettle to a boil over medium heat. Stir in macaroni and water, cover, and cook 20 minutes more. Add salt and pepper to taste.

To serve: Ladle into bowls.

Dividends: Great stretched with a little tomato juice.

To make ahead: May be made several hours or a day ahead.

CHILI WITHOUT CARNE   Serves 6 to 8

Sauté a pound of lean ground round with the onions in this recipe, and you'll have a chili soup *con carne*, with meat. The use of chocolate in a vegetable dish came to me as a surprise. It is common in Latin American cooking—and gives a special, very good flavor.

2 cups dried kidney beans	1½ teaspoons salt
2 quarts water	½ teaspoon dried thyme
1 cup chopped onion	½ teaspoon ground cumin
1 cup chopped green pepper	1 cup pitted green olives
2 large cloves garlic, minced	½ ounce unsweetened chocolate
4 tablespoons vegetable oil	1 8-ounce can tomato sauce
1 tablespoon chili powder	Salt and pepper

1. In a kettle over high heat, bring the beans and the water to a rapid boil, and cook 2 minutes. Turn off heat, cover, and let stand 1 hour.
2. In a saucepan over medium heat, sauté the onion, pepper, and garlic in the oil until the onion becomes translucent, about 5 to 6 minutes. Stir in the chili, salt, thyme, cumin, beans and water, scraping up pan juices. Bring to a boil, reduce heat, cover, and cook 2 hours, stirring often. Add water if soup becomes too thick. After 1 hour, add olives and chocolate. Stir in tomato sauce just before cooking is complete. Add salt and pepper to taste. Add more chili powder if you wish.

To serve: Ladle into bowls.

Dividends: Combines nicely with other vegetable soups.

To make ahead: May be made a day or two in advance.

SUCCOTASH CHOWDER WITH FRESH LIMAS   Serves 8

An old Yankee recipe meant to be made a day ahead. Halve the butter, if you wish. Frozen or dried limas can be used. If you wish to use dried limas, boil them for 2 minutes and let stand in the boiling water 1 hour before proceeding with the recipe.

12 ears sweet corn	1 stick butter
2 cups fresh limas	2 tablespoons instant mashed potato powder
6 cups water	
4 cups milk	Salt and pepper

1. Cut the corn kernels from the ears and reserve. Place corn cobs with lima beans and water in a kettle over high heat. Bring to a boil, cover, reduce heat, and simmer 1 hour.
2. Remove corn cobs, scrape any kernels clinging to the cobs into the kettle, then discard the cobs. Add milk, butter, potato powder, salt and pepper to taste, and cut corn to kettle. Simmer 20 minutes, stirring. Add more milk if soup is too thick. Allow to cool, and let stand 1 day, covered, in the refrigerator before serving.

To serve: Ladle into bowls.

Dividends: Delicious stretched with a little milk.

To make ahead: This must be made the day before.

RED LENTIL CHOWDER

Serves 4

Lentils come in red, gold, green, and brown, and I am always surprised to see how similar they are—and taste—once cooked. They cook much more quickly than most dried beans, by the way, and are remarkably meaty-tasting and nutritious.

¾ cup dried red lentils	½ cup milk
6 cups water	½ cup nonfat dry milk
1 teaspoon salt	powder
½ cup minced carrot	Salt and pepper
¼ cup minced celery	1 cup croutons
⅛ teaspoon drained oregano	

1. In a kettle over medium heat, bring lentils and water with salt to a rapid boil. Reduce heat, cover, and simmer 20 to 30 minutes, or until lentils are falling apart. Add more water if mixture seems too thick. Stir in carrot, celery, and oregano. Cover and simmer 10 minutes.
2. Purée in a blender or a food processor, 2 cups at a time, or press through a sieve. Pour milk into kettle, and whisk in milk powder. Stir in purée, and heat to just below boiling. Add salt and pepper to taste.

To serve: Ladle into bowls and garnish with croutons.

Dividends: Nice extender for gravy.

To make ahead: May be made hours or a day ahead.

BLOND LENTIL SOUP   Serves 4

This recipe has a richer flavor than the preceding lentil recipe. Shallots look and taste like a cross between garlic and a small onion. If you have none, add a little extra garlic.

3 large stalks celery and leaves, cut into large chunks	2 tablespoons butter
	1 teaspoon grated lemon rind
	1 small bay leaf
1 large onion, peeled, halved	1 cup dried blond lentils
5 medium carrots, chopped	Juice of 1 small lemon, strained
6 cups water	
1 large onion, chopped	4 sprigs basil, bruised
3 shallots, minced, optional	Salt and pepper
2 or 3 large cloves garlic, minced	

1. In a kettle over medium heat, combine celery and leaves, onion, carrots, and water. Bring to a boil, cover, reduce heat slightly, and cook until carrots are tender. Remove and discard celery pieces and onion. Purée broth in a blender or a food processor, 2 cups at a time, or press through a sieve.
2. In the kettle over medium heat, sauté the onion, shallots if used, and garlic in the butter until the onion is lightly browned, about 10 minutes. Turn purée into the kettle. Turn heat to medium. Add lemon rind, bay, and lentils. Bring to a boil, cover, reduce heat, and simmer 40 to 60 minutes, stirring often and adding more water as it evaporates. Stir in lemon juice and basil sprigs; add salt and pepper to taste.

To serve: Ladle into bowls, apportioning 1 basil sprig to each bowl.

Dividends: Excellent reheated with cream as a stretcher.

To make ahead: Complete several hours or a day ahead, but add basil and lemon juice just before serving.

POOR MAN'S SPLIT PEA SOUP   Serves 4

It's called "poor man's" soup because there's no meat in it. The recipe dates back to the last century. It comes from the Winona area of Minnesota and was cooked in a big kettle over an open hearth. When strangers came to the door, it could be stretched to accommodate their needs by adding a little water.

2 cups dried yellow split peas
2 quarts water
2 bay leaves
⅛ teaspoon allspice

1 cup chopped potatoes
½ cup chopped onion
2 tablespoons butter
1 teaspoon salt
⅛ teaspoon pepper

1. In a kettle over high heat, bring peas and water to a rapid boil, cook 2 minutes, turn off heat, cover, and let stand 1 hour.
2. Return peas and water to medium heat, add bay leaves and allspice, cover and simmer until peas are soft, about 1 hour. Add potatoes, onions, butter, salt, and pepper, and cook until potatoes are tender, 30 to 35 minutes. Stir often. Add more water if soup becomes too thick. Add salt and pepper to taste.

To serve: Ladle into bowls.

Dividends: Leftovers are delicious—a very stretchable soup!

To make ahead: Tastes almost better made a day or two ahead.

LIMA PEA SOUP FAR EASTERN STYLE   Serves 3 to 4

A refreshing tropical approach to split peas.

½ cup dried green split peas
4 cups water
1 teaspoon salt
½ teaspoon mustard seed, crushed
½ teaspoon sugar

1 small hot green pepper, minced
1 tablespoon minced fresh coriander leaves
½ cup strained lime juice

1. In a kettle over high heat, bring the peas and water to a rapid boil. Cook 2 minutes, turn off heat, cover, and let stand 1 hour.
2. Return peas and water to medium heat. Add the salt, mustard seed, sugar, and pepper. Cover, lower heat, and simmer 1 hour or until peas are tender. Purée in a blender or a food processor, 2 cups at a time, or press through a sieve.
3. Return purée to the kettle, and reheat briefly with coriander leaves and lime juice.

To serve: Ladle into bowls.

To make ahead: Complete through Step 2, then finish just before serving.

FRESH MUSHROOM BISQUE DINNER   Serves 4

½ pound mushrooms,
  chopped
2 medium onions, chopped
½ stick butter
3 cups chicken broth
1 cup milk
4 tablespoons instant
  mashed potato powder

1 teaspoon salt
⅛ teaspoon pepper
½ cup heavy cream
4 English muffins, toasted
  and buttered

1. In a saucepan over medium heat, sauté the mushrooms and onions in the butter until the onions become translucent, about 5 minutes. Purée in a blender or a food processor, with 1 cup broth, or press through a sieve.
2. Return purée to the kettle over medium heat, and stir in the rest of the broth, the milk, potato powder, salt and pepper. Simmer 3 minutes. Stir in the cream.

To serve: Ladle into bowls. Serve hot with buttered English muffins on the side.

Dividends: Nice added to pan drippings to make gravies.

TOMATO VEGETABLE SOUP FROM JUICE   Serves 4

3 cups tomato juice
⅛ teaspoon dried oregano
½ teaspoon salt
⅛ teaspoon pepper
2 scallions

3 medium stalks celery
1 large green pepper
3 medium carrots
1 cup milk
8 saltines, buttered

1. In a kettle over medium heat, combine tomato juice, oregano, salt, and pepper. Bring to a boil, cover, reduce heat, and simmer 4 to 5 minutes.
2. Cut the vegetables into chunks and place them in a food processor. Process until the vegetables are minced. Turn them into the broth, cover, and simmer 3 to 4 minutes. Add the milk, and heat to just below boiling.

To serve: Ladle into bowls and crumble 2 saltines into each.

HERBAL SOUPS

Here are a handful of soups strong in herbal flavors and romance. Sage Soup and Broth of Mixed Herbs date back to the last century.

BEAN SOUP FLAVORED WITH BAY   Serves 6

Navy beans are the small white kind, either round or kidney-shaped. The puréed potato and water added at the end of the cooking here thickens the soup. If you want to avoid the extra calories, just cook the soup a little longer and it will thicken without the potato.

2 cups dried navy beans	2 medium bay leaves
2½ quarts cold water	1 teaspoon salt
1 ham hock	¼ teaspoon pepper
1 large clove garlic, optional	1 medium potato, peeled
	1 cup water
3 medium onions, chopped	Salt and pepper
2 medium carrots, chopped	1 tablespoon minced
4 big celery stalks and leaves, chopped	parsley or chervil

1. In a kettle over high heat, bring beans and water to a rapid boil. Cook 2 minutes, turn off heat, cover, and let stand 1 hour.
2. Add ham hock, garlic if you wish, onions, carrots, celery, bay leaves, salt, and pepper. Bring to a boil over medium heat, cover, reduce heat, and simmer 1½ hours, stirring occasionally. Remove ham hock and bay leaves. Chop ham meat and return to kettle. Purée potato and water together and return to soup. Cook 30 minutes, covered, stirring often. Add water if the soup becomes too thick. Add salt and pepper to taste. Remove the garlic clove.

To serve: Ladle into bowls and garnish with minced herb.

Dividends: Thin with tomato sauce and you have a new soup.

To make ahead: Complete the day before—flavor improves with time.

BAKED GARLIC SOUP
Serves 6

This recipe is based on a prize-winning recipe called Joe's Baked Garlic Soup that won the judges' approval at the 1980 Garlic Town Festival. Garlic Town is Gilroy, California, a big truck farming and agricultural center in southeastern California.

2 10-ounce cans stewed tomatoes
1 16-ounce can cooked garbanzos and liquid
4 summer squash, sliced thin
2 large onions, sliced thin
1/2 green pepper, seeded, chopped
1 1/2 cups dry white wine
6 large cloves garlic, minced

1 small bay leaf
1 teaspoon dried basil
1/2 teaspoon paprika
3 tablespoons butter
1 1/2 cup grated Monterey Jack or Muenster cheese
1 cup grated Romano cheese
1 1/4 cups heavy cream

1. Preheat the oven to 375 degrees.
2. In a large baking dish layer the vegetables; pour over them the wine mixed with herbs. Dot with butter, cover, and bake 1 hour. Lower heat to 325 degrees. Stir in cheeses and cream, and bake, uncovered 15 minutes.

To serve: Ladle into bowls.

Dividends: Great reheated. Top with bread crumbs, dot with butter, and brown under the broiler.

To make ahead: Complete hours ahead through the initial baking, but add cheeses and cream and bake 15 minutes more just before serving.

PARSLEY SOUP
Serves 2 to 4

Save the parsley stems in the crisper. They're great minced into salads made with iceberg lettuce.

1 cup sour cream
1 cup heavy cream
2 large bunches parsley
2 tablespoons minced onion
1 small garlic clove, minced

2 tablespoons butter
2 cups chicken broth
1/2 cup dry white wine
1 teaspoon salt

1. In a small bowl place sour cream and stir in heavy cream. Cover and let rest at room temperature.
2. Remove stems from parsley and mince remainder; measure out 1½ cups, loosely packed, and reserve 2 tablespoons more.
3. In a saucepan over medium heat, sauté onion and garlic in the butter until the onion is translucent, about 5 minutes. Add the 1½ cups parsley and cook, stirring, 3 minutes. Pour in the chicken broth, cover, reduce heat, and simmer 10 minutes. Stir in wine and salt. Purée in a blender or a food processor, 2 cups at a time, or press through a sieve. Return purée to heat, bring to a boil, remove from heat and stir in ¾ of the cream mixture.

To serve: Ladle into bowls and garnish with remaining cream and reserved parsley.

Dividends: Great base for other soups.

SAGE BROTH   Serves 4

Dried sage is the flavor that dominates in poultry seasonings, pork stuffings, and most flavored crumbs and croutons—but fresh sage is required to make this Middle European broth. It was used as a winter drink.

3 cups water	2 tablespoons sugar
1 tablespoon grated lemon rind	Juice of 1 lemon, strained
	2 cups dry red wine
2 tablespoons minced fresh sage	4 sticks cinnamon

In a kettle over medium heat, bring water with rind and sage to a boil, cover, reduce heat, and simmer 30 minutes. Strain, discarding herbs. Return broth to kettle, turn heat to medium, stir in sugar, juice, and wine. Bring to a boil and cook, stirring, until sugar is all melted. Taste and add more sugar if desired.

To serve: Put 1 cinnamon stick into each of 4 large mugs and pour broth over the sticks.

BROTH OF MIXED HERBS

Serves 6

A European recipe dating back to the early years of the last century, this calls for fresh herbs. Choose tiny branch tips.

1 teaspoon marjoram leaves, packed
1 teaspoon thyme leaves, packed
1 tablespoon minced chives
1 teaspoon minced mint leaves
4 tablespoons sweet butter
1 tablespoon all-purpose flour

6 cups boiling water
1 teaspoon salt
3 egg yolks
¼ cup sour cream
Salt and pepper
3 slices white bread, toasted, crusts removed, cut into triangles
6 herb sprigs

1. In a saucepan over low heat, sauté the herbs in half the butter until they are wilted, 3 to 4 minutes. Stir in the flour. Remove from heat.
2. In a kettle over medium heat, place the water and salt, and simmer. In a small bowl beat the egg yolks until thick and lemon-colored. Stir in the sour cream, then 1 cup of the simmering salted water. Return the egg-cream mixture to the simmering water, and heat, stirring, to just below boiling. Whip in the remaining butter, then stir the whole mixture into the *roux* of herbs. Return to low heat and cook to just below boiling. Add salt and pepper to taste.

To serve: Ladle into bowls and top with a triangle of toast and an herb sprig.

Ten

THE DIVINE COLD SOUPS

Cold soups are divine on hot days—remarkably satisfying to flagging appetites but light as cream puffs. You surely know vichyssoise, gazpacho, and cold cucumber soup, but there are dozens more of these chilly taste treats available for a little cooking. All you need is the courage to experiment.

Vichyssoise is the most famous of the iced soups, subtly flavored with leeks and thickened with potatoes and heavy cream. Its hallmark is a garnish of chopped chives. The combination of cooked vegetables and cream used in vichyssoise can be used to develop other cold vegetable soups from leftovers. The recipe for Broccoli and Cheese Soup in this chapter will suggest some other ways to combine a chilled vegetable soup. The cheese in this recipe is cottage cheese, and many cold soups call for dairy products; yogurt is very popular in cold soups, as is buttermilk. (One of the cold cucumber recipes here calls for both buttermilk and yogurt.) Chilled Purée of Carrots, Dog Day Corn Soup, and Icy Pea Soup with Mint are variations on the basic cold vegetable theme.

Gazpacho is a piquant mix of flavors, Spanish in origin, combining tomatoes, onions, green peppers, and garlic. So popular has it become that I have counted at least half a hundred recipes in recent years. And its success is deserved. With these basic ingredients you can—and obviously cooks do—develop all sorts of variations. You can dilute gazpacho with wine or broth, you can gel it, freeze it, mash it, flavor it with any and every herb, and it comes up tasting pretty good. And that in itself is a lesson in soup making. Many vegetable (and fruit) medleys are good served cold. The Iced Spring Vegetable Soup recipe suggests other possibilities.

Then there are the glorious fruit soups. It was in Sweden that I first tasted a cold fruit soup, Rhubarb Soup. It's a bit like having dessert first, and on a hot day a little pampering is nice! Since my first spoonful of Rhubarb Soup I've collected many one-fruit and fruit-medley recipes, and you'll find many of them here. Almost any tart fruit makes a good soup, and the berries make delicious cold soups. What are they like? Think of canned cling peaches chopped in their juice, spiced with lemon juice, and laced with thick *crème fraîche*. Served with croissants, or the type of biscuit that is used to make old-fashioned strawberry shortcake, and with sweet butter, the cold fruit soups are like—heaven!

And finally, there are some very good cold fish soups. These are light but hearty soups that easily make a meal in themselves served with rolls, cheese, salad, and a dessert. You can develop a number of soups based on the recipes at the end of this chapter, using as main ingredients cooked leftovers of cold fish and shell-fish.

TURNING LEFTOVERS INTO CHILLED SOUPS

Any of the recipes for vegetable creams in Chapter 7 and in Chapter 5 can become a chilled summer cream. To the leftovers, add a quantity of icy heavy cream that suits your sense of taste, and add salt and pepper and a bit of fresh herb. Served set in a bowl of cracked ice, these make delicious first course fare for hot summer days.

TIMING COLD SOUPS

Nearly all cold soups must be planned for because they must be icy cold. In this chapter I have eliminated most remarks under *Dividends* and *To make ahead*. All the soups here are good made ahead and left over. To stretch a leftover cold soup to serve more people, add cold broth, milk, cream, or wine, and for the fruit soups try ginger ale, fruit juice—or champagne!

Before serving cold soups, stir them well. Heavier ingredients have a tendency to sink to the bottom during the chilling period.

PREPARING FRUITS FOR COLD SOUPS

In cold soup recipes, orchard fruits are peeled, cored or pitted, and chopped. Apricots and plums need not be peeled. When I call for chopped fruit, I assume you have a food processor that does it easily. If you don't have one, cut the fruit into medium slices. The reason we use chopped ingredients is that they cook more quickly, saving time, energy, and flavor.

Never soak berries. Stem them and wash them quickly. If sand remains in the bottom of the wash bowl, rewash quickly.

Cherries are pitted before using. There are little cherry pitters for sale in kitchen supply centers, and they are well worth the modest investment called for.

CREAM IN COLD SOUPS

Many of these soups call for a combination of sour and heavy cream. Just sour or just whipped or thickened cream would do instead. But the combination makes something resembling the *crème fraîche* and clotted cream found in Europe, and is mighty good in a cold soup.

To get the combination just right, stir the heavy cream into the sour cream so they are well combined. The cream will be thin. After a few hours at room temperature—depending on the temperature—it will thicken. At this point, cover the bowl and chill the cream. If it is to be served almost at once, place the bowl in the freezer or chill over cracked ice.

TO MAKE A COLD SOUP PRETTY

Herbs and other fresh garnishes are plentiful in summer. Don't be limited to the herbs suggested in these recipes. Tip sprigs of almost any herb will be good—borage, thyme, mint, savory, sweet marjoram, basil (wonderful with tomatoes), dill, fennel. A big pinch of minced green herb set afloat on a round of hard-boiled egg in the middle of a cold soup dresses it.

For cold fruit soups, berries and slices of lemon, orange, lime, or fruit all make attractive and delicious garnishes. A hint of mint leaf with one of these garnishes makes the soup even prettier.

In the most elegant restaurants, cold soups are served in crystal bowls set in silver bowls filled with cracked ice. You can duplicate this with a pair of bowls, or come close by serving cold soups in crystal bowls iced in the freezer.

WHAT TO SERVE WITH COLD SOUPS

For vegetables, meat, and fish soups served cold, rolls or crusty French bread, butter, creamy cheeses, light salads, and a sweet dessert are just right. These also are very good with light sandwiches—white bread and butter and cold chicken, for instance.

The sweet fruit soups are very nice with croissants or sweet rolls and sweet butter, a leafy pale salad, and tea.

COLD SOUP INSTEAD OF PARTY PUNCH

A sweet cold soup isn't a punch. It's much thicker and it is usually rather rich. However, cold soups can be used at parties in the way punch is used—that is, poured into a big clear bowl, garnished, and set in the center of a buffet table with cups around and a ladle for self-service. You can use it as a first course, or a main course, but it isn't instead of a drink, such as iced tea or coffee.

As a decorative device for a party in the warm weather, it is as attractive and every bit as good as jellied consommés (which you will find in Chapter 2) and aspics.

APPLE AND BEEF SOUP
Serves 4 to 6

Use the early green apples that are tart, or if you are making this in spring, look for Granny Smith apples. Half a cup of semi-sweet, chilled wine—a Graves, for instance—could be added as a variation.

4 medium-large apples, grated	1 teaspoon curry powder
1 large onion, chopped	1 tablespoon strained lemon juice
4 stalks celery, chopped	½ cup sour cream
3 tablespoons butter	1 tablespoon minced parsley
4 cups beef broth	

1. In a saucepan over medium heat, sauté apples, onion, and celery in butter 5 minutes. Cover, lower heat, and simmer 10 minutes. Stir occasionally to make sure the mixture isn't running out of liquid. Add the broth, curry powder, and lemon juice, and bring to a boil.
2. Purée in a blender or a food processor, or press through a sieve. Chill thoroughly—4 to 6 hours—before serving.

To serve: Ladle into chilled bowls and garnish with sour cream and parsley.

APRICOT SOUP   Serves 6

To make a quick version of this soup, start with two 16-ounce cans of apricots in syrup, and eliminate Step 1, except for addition of sherry and lemon juice. Blend, stir in 3 cups water and heat to boiling, then proceed with Step 2.

10 to 12 small apricots (1 pound), sliced and pitted	¼ cup dry sherry
	2 tablespoons cornstarch
	2 tablespoons cold water
6 cups water	Sugar
6 tablespoons sugar	½ cup sour cream
3 tablespoons strained lemon juice	½ pint heavy cream
	Pinch salt

1. In a kettle over medium high heat, place apricots, water, sugar, lemon juice, and salt. Bring to a boil, cover, lower heat, and simmer until apricots are tender, about 10 minutes. Add the sherry and lower heat.
2. In a small bowl combine cornstarch and water; stir into hot apricots until mixture thickens and clears, 2 to 3 minutes. Add sugar to taste. Blend. Chill, covered, 4 to 6 hours, or overnight.
3. In a small bowl place sour cream and stir in heavy cream. Cover and let rest at room temperature, then chill.

To serve: Ladle into soup bowls and pour a little cream in the center; stir outward in widening circles, creating a decorative spiral.

ICED PURÉE OF AVOCADO   Serves 4

Avocados must be soft (but not mushy) or they won't have enough flavor to make this soup as good as it can be. It is delicious!

1 large or 2 small ripe avocados	½ cup sour cream
	½ cup half-and-half
1 large thin slice onion	Salt
½ medium clove garlic	Sweet paprika
1 cup chicken broth	

Halve the avocado, remove the pit, and spoon the avocado meat into a blender or a food processor with the onion, garlic, and broth. Purée. Scrape purée into a small bowl and pour the sour cream and half-and-half over the avocado purée, sealing it from the air. Chill, covered, 4 to 6 hours or overnight.

To serve: Combine avocado and creams, add salt to taste, and ladle into crystal bowls set in cracked ice. Garnish with a dash of paprika.

AVOCADO AND TOMATO SOUP   Serves 8

3 large avocados
3 cups chicken broth
2 cloves garlic, sliced
1 tablespoon lemon juice
1 teaspoon salt
¼ teaspoon turmeric

1 cup heavy cream
1 large tomato, chopped
8 thin lemon slices
2 tablespoons chopped
  chives

Halve and pit the avocados. Scoop 1 at a time into the blender or food processor with 1 cup of chicken broth, and process with garlic, lemon juice, and salt. Scrape into a refrigerator container with a tight lid. Stir in turmeric, cream, and chopped tomato. Cover and chill thoroughly—4 to 6 hours or overnight—before serving.

To serve: Ladle into soup bowls and garnish with a slice of lemon and a bit of chopped chive.

BANANA-APPLE SOUP   Serves 4

A curry-colored concoction whose ingredients no one will be able to guess.

1 medium potato, chopped
1 small onion, chopped
1 green apple, cored, chopped
1 large banana, peeled,
  chopped
1 small heart of celery and
  leaves, chopped
2 tablespoons minced chives

2 cups All-Purpose White
  Stock (page 45) or chicken
  broth
1 cup heavy cream
1 tablespoon butter
1 teaspoon turmeric
Salt and pepper

In a large kettle over medium high heat, combine potato, onion, apple, banana, celery, and broth. Cover, lower heat, and simmer until potato is soft, 20 to 30 minutes. Stir in cream, butter, turmeric, and add salt and pepper to taste. Chill thoroughly—4 to 6 hours or overnight—then purée in a blender or a food processor, 2 cups at a time, or press through a sieve.

To serve: Ladle into soup bowls and garnish with chives.

COLD BEER SOUP OR HANGOVER STEW   Serves 6

I have little love for beer soups, but this one is a classic. The flavor depends on the beer. If it isn't of good quality, imported, the soup will be awful.

1½ quarts imported beer   ¼ cup confectioners sugar
½ quart dry white wine   6 poached eggs
½ stick cinnamon   Saltines

1. In a large kettle over medium high heat, place the beer and bring to just below boiling.
2. In another kettle, place the wine, cinnamon, and sugar, and heat to just below boiling. Combine beer and wine in a large refrigerator bowl, cover, and chill thoroughly in the freezer or over cracked ice.

To serve: Ladle into 6 very large mugs and float a poached egg on top of each portion. Serve with saltines.

ICY BEET SOUP   Serves 4 to 6

This very quick version of borscht is delicious, and it is made from canned vegetables!

1 16-ounce can whole small   ½ teaspoon salt
   beets and liquid   ⅛ teaspoon pepper
2 large slices onion   1 cup sour cream
3 cups beef broth   Salt and pepper
2 tablespoons firmly packed   ½ large cucumber, peeled,
   dark brown sugar   chopped
2 tablespoons strained
   lemon juice

Purée beets with their juice in a blender or a food processor, along with slices of onion. Combine with the broth in a small saucepan over medium heat, and stir in sugar, lemon juice, salt, and pepper. Simmer, uncovered, 3 to 4 minutes. Allow to cool. Combine with sour cream, add salt and pepper to taste, and chill thoroughly—4 to 6 hours or overnight—before serving.

To serve: Ladle into soup bowls and garnish with cucumber.

BROCCOLI AND CHEESE SOUP   Serves 6

You may use frozen broccoli to make this. It's almost as good as fresh leftovers!

½ cup chopped onion
¼ cup chopped celery
6 cups chicken broth
2 cups cooked broccoli
1 cup cottage cheese

Salt and pepper
2 tablespoons chopped
  chives
6 cherry tomatoes

Purée the onion, celery, and 1 cup of broth in a blender or a food processor. Turn purée into a small saucepan over medium heat, and simmer 5 minutes. Return to the blender or food processor with the broccoli, and process 1 minute, adding as much broth as the container will hold, then turn mixture and remaining broth into a refrigerator dish with a tight lid. Stir in cottage cheese; and salt and pepper to taste. Cover and chill 4 to 6 hours or overnight.

To serve: Ladle into soup bowls and garnish with chives and halved cherry tomatoes.

CHILLED PURÉE OF CARROTS   Serves 6

Purée of carrot soup is called *Crème Crécy* by the French. Escoffier, the master chef, made it working only with the outer, orangy part of the carrot, which is apt to be sweetest. I just use a bag of supermarket carrots, but it's very good.

1 large onion, chopped
1 pound carrots, peeled,
  sliced thin
4 tablespoons butter
4 cups All-Purpose White
  Stock (page 45) or chicken
  broth

½ teaspoon curry powder
1 sprig fresh thyme or ¼
  teaspoon dried
½ teaspoon sugar
½ cup sour cream
½ cup heavy cream
Sprigs fresh thyme, optional

1. In a large saucepan over medium low heat, sauté onion and carrots in the butter, covered, for 20 minutes. Stir now and then to make sure carrots are not browning. Add broth, curry, thyme, and sugar. Cover and cook until carrots are very tender.
2. Purée in a blender or a food processor, 2 cups at a time, or press through a sieve. Combine sour and heavy creams, and stir into the purée. Cover and chill 4 to 6 hours or overnight.

To serve: Ladle into soup bowls and garnish with sprigs of fresh thyme if you wish.

CHERRY PIE SOUP   Serves 6

Here's a delicious chilled soup to serve at an elegant party.

1 can cherry pie filling
1 cup canned pineapple chunks
1 cup semisweet white wine, such as a Graves
½ cup pineapple canning liquid

½ teaspoon grated lemon rind
⅛ teaspoon cinnamon
Pinch salt, optional
1 cup whipped cream

Place the pie filling in the blender with the pineapple and purée. Turn into a serving bowl and stir in wine, juice, lemon rind, cinnamon, and a bit of salt if you wish. Refrigerate 4 to 6 hours or chill in the freezer if you're in a big hurry.

To serve: Ladle into soup bowls and garnish with a dollop of whipped cream.

CHERRY SOUP HUNGARIAN STYLE   Serves 4 to 6

This is made with sweet cherries, but more common is the cherry soup made with sour cherries.

2 16-ounce cans pitted sweet cherries and juice
1 cup sour cream

1 tablespoon cream sherry
Sugar

Strain cherries into the mixing bowl of a food processor. Reserve half a dozen whole cherries and chop the rest. Stir the juice into the sour cream with the sherry and sugar to taste. Combine with the cherries, and chill 4 to 6 hours or overnight.

To serve: Ladle into soup bowls and garnish with reserved whole cherries.

SOUR CHERRY SOUP FROM SCRATCH   Serves 4 to 6

Pitting cherries is a work of love that stains your fingers—unless you have one of those pitting gadgets. But this old-fashioned version of icy cherry soup is worth making an effort for.

2 pounds sour cherries, pitted
½ cup sugar
¼ teaspoon cinnamon
4 cups water
⅛ teaspoon salt

½ teaspoon grated lemon rind
2 tablespoons cornstarch
2 tablespoons cold water
1 cup heavy cream
¼ cup dry Bordeaux red

1. In a large kettle over medium heat, combine cherries, sugar, cinnamon, water, and salt. Cover and simmer 20 to 30 minutes, or until cherries are very soft. Strain cherries; reserve liquid. Purée the cherries in a blender or a food processor, and return to the liquid with the lemon rind.
2. In a small bowl combine the cornstarch and the water, and stir into the cherries. Cook until mixture thickens a little. Chill thoroughly—4 to 6 hours, or overnight.

To serve: Ladle into soup bowls and stir a portion of the cream and wine into each bowl.

DOG DAY CORN SOUP   Serves 6

Wonderfully easy and delicious for hot, hot days!

1 16-ounce can cream style corn
2 cups chicken broth
1 teaspoon curry powder or turmeric

1 scallion
1 cup heavy cream
Salt and pepper
2 tablespoons slivered green pepper

In a kettle over medium high heat, simmer corn, broth, curry or turmeric, and scallion 5 minutes, covered. Purée in a blender or a food processor, 2 cups at a time. Turn into a refrigerator dish with a tight lid, stir in cream, add salt and pepper to taste, cover, and chill 4 to 6 hours or overnight.

To serve: Ladle into soup bowls and garnish with slivers of green pepper.

TANGY CUCUMBER AND BUTTERMILK SOUP   Serves 6 to 8

You can make this in minutes, and it is wonderfully refreshing and energizing! Grate the cucumbers very fine.

4 large cucumbers, peeled, seeded, grated
1 tablespoon minced chives
1 tablespoon minced fresh dill
3 tablespoons brown sugar

1½ teaspoons Maille or other fine prepared mustard
½ pint sour cream
1 quart buttermilk
Salt

In a large refrigerator bowl with a lid, combine cucumbers, chives, dill, sugar, and mustard. Stir in sour cream, then mix in buttermilk. Add salt to taste, cover, and chill 4 to 6 hours or overnight.

To serve: Ladle into soup bowls.

CUCUMBER AND YOGURT SOUP   Serves 6

Here's a variation with yogurt instead of buttermilk. To dress it up, add ½ cup currants or seedless raisins before chilling.

4 large cucumbers, peeled, seeded, grated
1 large clove garlic, crushed
2 cups chicken broth

2 cups yogurt
Salt and pepper
2 tablespoons chives

In a large refrigerator bowl with a lid, combine cucumbers, garlic, broth, and yogurt. Add salt and pepper to taste. Cover and chill 4 to 6 hours or overnight.

To serve: Ladle into soup bowls and garnish with chives.

CUCUMBER SOUP WITH MINT   Serves 6

Save leftover mashed potatoes to make this one, and slice cucumbers paper thin.

2 large cucumbers, peeled, sliced

1 small clove garlic, minced
4 scallions, chopped fine

½ cup water
1 teaspoon salt
1 cup mashed potatoes
1 tablespoon minced fresh
  mint

4 cups chicken broth
1 cup light cream
Salt and pepper
Sprigs fresh mint

1. In a kettle over medium high heat, place cucumber, garlic, scallions, water, and salt. Bring to a boil, cover, lower heat, and simmer until cucumbers are tender, about 15 minutes. Add the potatoes and mint, and purée in a blender or a food processor, 2 cups at a time, or press through a sieve.
2. Turn purée into a large refrigerator bowl with a lid, and stir in chicken broth and cream. Add salt and pepper to taste. Cover and chill 4 to 6 hours or overnight.

To serve: Ladle into soup bowls and garnish with mint sprigs.

COLD FISH SOUP   Serves 8

Leftover cooked white fish, such as halibut, cod, flounder, and even luxury shellfish, like lobster, makes very good cold soup done this way. Just skip cooking the fish as described below.

2 cups milk
1 small bay leaf
¼ teaspoon dried thyme
1 pound white fish fillets

6 cups *Potage Bonne Femme*
  (page 203)
Chopped chives

1. In a kettle over medium heat, place milk, bay, and thyme; bring to a boil. Add fish and cook, uncovered, 8 to 10 minutes. Remove bay.
2. Place fish and milk in a blender or a food processor, and purée 2 cups at a time. Or break fish apart with a fork. Return to kettle over medium high heat and stir in *Potage Bonne Femme*. Bring to a boil, remove from heat, and chill, covered, 4 to 6 hours.

To serve: Ladle into soup bowls and garnish with chives.

FRESH FRUIT MEDLEY FOR A PARTY   Serves 8 to 10

This is served in Israel hot with boiled potatoes, but its origins are in northern Europe, where it is served cold with cream, as here. Add fruit juice if soup is too thick.

2 large yellow pears, peeled, cored, chopped	6 apricots, pitted, chopped
	Juice of ½ lemon, strained
2 large Granny Smith or other tart green apples, peeled, cored, chopped	Pinch salt
	½ to 1 cup sugar
6 purple plums or green-gages, pitted, chopped	½ cup small fruit; pitted cherries or seeded grapes, halved, or berries, whole
2 oranges, peeled, sliced thin, seeded	½ cup sour cream
	1 teaspoon cinnamon

In a large kettle over medium high heat, place pears, apples, apricots, plums or greengages, oranges, lemon juice, and salt. Bring to a boil, cover, lower heat, and simmer 10 minutes or until fruits are all tender. Add ½ cup of sugar, taste, and add more if desired. Add small fruit, and simmer, covered, 5 minutes. Chill, covered, 4 to 6 hours or overnight.

To serve: Ladle into soup bowls and garnish with spoonfuls of sour cream and a dusting of cinnamon.

TANGY FRUIT MEDLEY WITH WINE   Serves 4 to 6

Combine any plentiful fruits, but try to pair them, sweet and sour. Cherries, peaches, apricots, plums, mangos, grapes, tart apples—anything goes! Riesling, Rhine, Moselle, and champagne are all suitable wines.

3 cups pitted, chopped fruit	1 cup cake crumbs or crumbled pound cake
2 tablespoons strained lemon juice	
	Pinch ground cloves
¼ cup dry sherry	¼ teaspoon ground ginger
¼ cup dry white wine	¼ teaspoon cinnamon
⅓ to ½ cup sugar	1 cup light cream

1. In a large kettle over medium high heat, place chopped fruits, lemon juice, sherry, and wine. Bring to a boil, cover, lower heat, and simmer 10 minutes, or until fruits are tender. Add ⅓ cup sugar, taste, and add more if desired. Cook 5 minutes, then cool.

2. Purée in a blender or a food processor, or press 2 cups at a time through a sieve, adding cake crumbs, cloves, ginger, and cinnamon. Chill, covered, 4 to 6 hours.

To serve: Stir in cream and ladle into soup bowls.

GARLIC SOUP WITH MELON   Serves 4

This is of Spanish origin. To make it well you really need a mortar and pestle, or a small bowl with a rough interior. Select melon—cantaloupe, honeydew or crenshaw—according to fragrance. Sniff the ends, and press with your thumb; a meltingly flavorful fruit will yield a bit to pressure and give off a faint whiff of ripe-melon scent. Sometimes overripe half-melons are offered, plastic-wrapped, and these supply just about the amount of melon you need for this recipe. But don't be fooled—the major flavor here is garlic! Chop the almonds in the blender. It's easy.

3 large cloves garlic, peeled	¼ teaspoon pepper
¼ cup toasted almonds, chopped	4 cups chicken broth
	½ tablespoon wine vinegar
2 tablespoons olive oil	1 cup cubed ripe melon
2 slices white bread	1 tablespoon minced parsley
1 teaspoon salt	

Place the garlic in a rough-bottomed little bowl, and mash well. Mash the almonds into the garlic, and mix in the oil. Turn into a large saucepan over medium heat. Use a blender to make bread into crumbs or chunks, or cube it, and sauté in the oil mixture until bread is golden brown. Mash bread into oil, add salt and pepper, and stir in broth. Add vinegar and heat to boiling. Remove from heat, add melon, and chill, covered, 4 to 6 hours or overnight.

To serve: Ladle into soup bowls and garnish with parsley.

GAZPACHO SPANISH STYLE   Serves 6 to 8

This is an Andalusian version of the famous Spanish chilled vegetable soup served by smart hostesses. Plan to make it 24 hours ahead so it can be properly cold. Place the serving bowls in the freezer a couple of hours in advance so they'll be frosted, too.

3 tablespoons red wine vinegar	1 green bell pepper, seeded, chopped
2 large cloves garlic	1 large cucumber, peeled, seeded, chopped
¾ cup soft bread crumbs	
⅓ cup olive oil	1 cup tomato juice or sauce
6 to 8 large ripe tomatoes, seeded, chopped fine	Salt and pepper
	Sprigs fresh basil or parsley

Place the vinegar and garlic in a blender and purée. Place the bread crumbs in a small bowl, and stir in the vinegar and garlic mixture to make a soft paste. Combine oil, vegetables, and tomato juice or sauce and stir into the paste a little at a time. Add salt and pepper to taste. Chill 4 hours or overnight.

To serve: Ladle into chilled bowls and garnish with herb sprigs.

To make ahead: This is better prepared a day or two in advance so flavors can blend and soup can chill thoroughly.

GOOSEBERRY AND WINE SOUP   Serves 4 to 6

The parks in Ottawa, Canada, once were planted in gooseberry hedges, and I remember on boring, hot summer days the thrill of discovering ripe pink fruit among the green ovals that dotted the bushes. But green gooseberries are the right choice for making such traditional British dishes as Gooseberry Fool (dessert) and Gooseberry Sauce (for meats and game). The greenish fruits are sold by some small specialty markets.

1 pound stemmed gooseberries	½ cup sour cream
½ cup sugar	1 tablespoon all-purpose flour
2 lemon slices	Nasturtium blooms, optional
4 cups water	
½ to 1 cup Anjou wine, white	

1. Chop ¾ of the gooseberries; leave ¼ pound whole.
2. In a kettle over medium high heat, place gooseberries, sugar, lemon slices, water, and wine. Bring to a boil, cover, lower heat, and simmer until whole berries are soft, about 15 minutes.
3. In a small bowl combine sour cream and flour, and stir in 1 cup of hot fruit broth. Return to the kettle and over low heat, stir until the mixture thickens. Cover and chill 4 to 6 hours or overnight.

To serve: Ladle into soup bowls and garnish with flowers if you wish.

ORANGE AND RASPBERRY SOUP   Serves 6

This can be handled as a cocktail drink if you halve the quantity of raspberries and whipped cream.

 3 cups water
 1 stick cinnamon
 2 whole cloves
 ¼ cup strained lemon juice
 2 tablespoons cornstarch
 2 tablespoons cold water
 3 tablespoons sugar
 1 tablespoon butter
 Pinch salt

 1 teaspoon grated orange rind or ½ teaspoon grated lemon rind, optional
 1 cup raspberries
 1 16-ounce can frozen orange juice concentrate, thawed
 ½ cup heavy cream, whipped, sweetened

1. In a kettle over medium high heat, place water, cinnamon stick, cloves, and lemon juice. Bring to a boil, cover, lower heat, and simmer 5 minutes. Discard cinnamon stick and cloves, and lower heat.
2. In a small bowl combine cornstarch and water, and stir into hot broth, with sugar, until mixture thickens and clears, 2 to 3 minutes. Stir in butter, salt, rind, if you wish, and berries. Cook, uncovered, until fruit begins to look a little wilted, about 2 minutes. Chill, covered, 4 to 6 hours or overnight.

To serve: Stir orange juice concentrate into fruit soup. Ladle into soup bowls and garnish with sweetened whipped cream.

ORANGE AND TOMATO SOUP   Serves 6

This is also good when hot. Choose a really good eating orange to make the garnish: 1 sliced thin will yield at least 6 slices.

1 large scallion, white
   only, minced
2 tablespoons butter
4 cups tomato juice
2 teaspoons sugar
1 6-ounce can frozen orange
   juice concentrate, thawed

Salt and pepper
¼ cup sour cream
6 very thin slices unpeeled
   orange

In a kettle over medium heat, sauté scallion in butter until translucent, about 5 minutes. Stir in tomato juice and sugar, cover, and bring to boiling. Add orange juice concentrate, turn off heat, and stir until combined. Taste, and add salt and pepper if desired. Chill, covered, 4 to 6 hours or overnight.

To serve: Ladle into soup bowls and garnish with sour cream and orange slices.

CONSOMMÉ MADRILÈNE WITH ORANGES   Serves 4

1 8-ounce can mandarin
   oranges, drained
4 teaspoons cream sherry

4 cups hot *Consommé*
   Madrilène (page 59)
4 mint sprigs

Divide orange segments among 4 crystal consommé cups, reserving 8 segments. Divide sherry and *Consommé Madrilène* among the cups, stir briefly, then chill 4 to 6 hours or until consommé has jelled.

To serve: Garnish with reserved orange segments and mint.

MARCEL'S ICY CREAM OF PEA   Serves 6

This is *Papa chéri*'s one-minute summer soup—perfectly delicious and a boon on hot days.

1 17-ounce can peas
   and liquid
½ pint heavy cream

Salt and pepper
6 tiny mint sprigs

Purée the peas in a blender or a food processor, and turn into a bowl set over cracked ice. Stir in the cream, and add salt and pepper to taste. Chill thoroughly.

To serve: Ladle into consommé cups and serve set in bowls of cracked ice. Garnish each with a sprig of mint.

PEACHES AND CHAMPAGNE   Serves 6

The Swedes serve this as a soup or as a punch on Midsummer's Eve and at other summer festivals. It's a neat way to use up a bit of leftover champagne. Domestic champagne will do, and Riesling is an ideal wine to use in this recipe. To be really good, this soup must be made from peaches so ripe they are really fragrant and soft to touch. There's no cooking.

8 large, very ripe peaches (about 3 pounds)	½ cup sugar
2 tablespoons sugar	½ bottle champagne, iced
Pinch salt	½ bottle dry white wine, iced
2 teaspoons strained lemon juice	Sugar

1. Halve 3 peaches; remove and reserve pits. Slice peaches thin, sprinkle with 2 tablespoons of sugar, and set aside. Crack the 3 pits, remove the seeds, and scald seeds in boiling water 1 minute. Slip off skins and discard. Chop the seeds in a blender or in a food processor.
2. Add 5 pitted peaches, salt, lemon juice, and sugar to the blender or food processor, and process to make a purée.

To serve: Stir champagne into the peach purée (do not process). Place a portion of sliced sweetened peaches in each bowl, ladle in peach purée, and stir in a portion of wine. Taste and add a bit more sugar if desired.

PLUM AND PINEAPPLE SOUP   Serves 6

This soup doesn't benefit from a long chilling period, so you have to plan ahead a bit.

8 to 10 large ripe purple
   plums (about 1½–
   2 pounds), pitted
½ cup heavy cream

½ cup sour cream
3 cups chilled pineapple
   juice

1. Purée plums and pineapple juice in a blender or a food processor, 2 cups at a time. Cover and place in the refrigerator.
2. In a small bowl place sour cream and stir in heavy cream. Cover and let rest at room temperature. Shortly before serving, place in freezer to cool.

To serve: Ladle into soup bowls and stir a little cream into the center; stir outward in widening circles, creating a decorative spiral.

To make ahead: Purée and chill plums, and chill pineapple juice. Combine only 30 minutes before serving, then rechill.

RHUBARB SOUP   Serves 6

Once started, rhubarb grows like Topsy in most gardens, but it has only a brief season. When it's plentiful I save it, cut up in 2-cup lots, in the freezer, so it's available to make pies and lovely cold soups like this in summer.

2 cups rhubarb (3 to 5
   stalks), cut into 2-inch
   pieces
1 quart water
¼ to ½ cup sugar
Pinch salt

2 tablespoons cornstarch
2 tablespoons cold water
2 egg yolks
1 cup heavy cream, whipped,
   sweetened

1. In a kettle over medium high heat, place rhubarb and water. Bring to a boil, cover, lower heat, and simmer until rhubarb is very tender, about 10 to 15 minutes. Add sugar and salt, and cook, stirring, uncovered, 5 minutes. Beat lightly with a fork to break up rhubarb.
2. In a small bowl, combine cornstarch and water, then stir into hot broth until mixture thickens and begins to clear, 2 to 3 minutes.
3. In the bowl beat egg yolks until thick and lemon-colored. Stir

in 1 cup of hot broth, then return to the kettle. Heat to just below boiling. Chill, covered, 4 to 6 hours or overnight.

To serve: Ladle into soup bowls and stir in whipped cream.

RASPBERRY BROTH WITH WINE   Serves 4 to 6

When buying raspberries, be aware that the little boxes they sell these days for so much money don't contain a pint, but only half a pint of fruit! A faintly sweet Anjou is suitable for use in this recipe, as is leftover champagne, or ginger ale if not too sweet.

1 pint raspberries	1½ cups water
½ cup sugar	½ cup sour cream
1 teaspoon lemon juice	½ cup heavy cream
½ cup water	4 sprigs mint
½ cup wine	

1. Purée raspberries in a blender or a food processor, then mash purée through 2 thicknesses of cheesecloth, reserving liquid. Discard seeds.
2. In a small saucepan over medium high heat, combine sugar, lemon juice, and water, and bring to a boil. Cool, then stir in wine, water, and raspberry juice. Chill, covered, 4 to 6 hours or overnight.
3. In a small bowl place sour cream and stir in heavy cream. Cover and let rest at room temperature. Shortly before serving, place in freezer to cool.

To serve: Ladle into frosted glasses and stir in cream. Garnish with mint.

WILD RASPBERRY SOUP   Serves 4

The Scandinavians serve raspberries this way, as a soup to begin a meal. It is also a delicious dessert!

4 cups wild raspberries	½ to 1 cup sugar
(about ½ quart)	½ cup sour cream
1 ripe peach, peeled, pitted	

Purée berries and peach with the sugar in a blender or a food processor, 2 cups at a time. Chill, covered, 4 to 6 hours.

To serve: Ladle into soup bowls and garnish with sour cream.

SOUPE SÉNÉGALÈSE

Serves 6

This is an elegant cold curry France adopted from North Africa. There is another, more authentically North African version of this on page 207.

5 cups chicken broth	Salt and pepper
4 egg yolks	1 cup finely chopped cooked
2 teaspoons curry powder	chicken breast
1/8 teaspoon cayenne	3 to 4 tablespoons minced
1/4 teaspoon lemon juice	pimiento
2 cups heavy cream	

1. In a kettle over medium heat, bring the broth to a simmer.
2. In a bowl beat egg yolks until thick and lemon-colored. Add curry, cayenne, and lemon juice. Stir in the cream. Stir in 1 cup hot broth, then return the mixture to the kettle. Still stirring, heat to just below boiling. Add salt and pepper to taste. Refrigerate, covered, 3 to 4 hours or overnight.

To serve: Ladle into bowls, divide the chicken among them, and garnish with pimiento.

COLD SHRIMP BISQUE CREOLE STYLE

Serves 8

Some cooks like to sauté the peeled, deveined shrimp with a couple of ounces of brandy and flame them before puréeing. But to my mind that's gilding the lily.

2 tablespoons butter	2 tablespoons tomato paste
1 small onion, chopped	4 tablespoons butter
2 ripe medium tomatoes,	4 tablespoons all-purpose
peeled, seeded, chopped	flour
6 cups water	4 egg yolks
1 garlic clove, sliced	1 cup heavy cream
1 small bay leaf	Salt and pepper
1/4 teaspoon thyme	1 teaspoon filé powder,
1/2 lemon, sliced	optional
1 tablespoon salt	1/4 cup heavy cream, whipped
2 pounds raw shrimp	

1. In a saucepan over low heat, melt the butter and sauté the onion and tomatoes until the onion begins to be translucent, 5 to 7 minutes. Set aside.

2. In a kettle over high heat, place the water, garlic, bay, thyme, lemon, and salt. Bring to a boil, add shrimp, and when water returns to a boil, cover, lower heat, and simmer 3 minutes. Drain, reserving liquid, and shell and devein the shrimp. Reserve a few whole shrimp to serve as garnish. Purée the shrimp with the tomato paste in a blender or a food processor, adding a little liquid if needed.

3. In a saucepan over low heat, melt the butter and stir in the flour. Beating constantly, add the hot shrimp broth, and cook, stirring, until bubbly, 1 to 2 minutes. Combine in a blender or a food processor, 2 cups at a time, with the shrimp purée, and turn into the kettle. Stir in sautéed vegetables.

4. In a small bowl beat the egg yolks until thick and lemon-colored. Stir in the cream. Stir in 1 cup shrimp-vegetable mixture, then return to kettle. Heat to just below boiling. Add salt and pepper to taste. Stir in filé powder, if you wish and chill, covered, 4 to 6 hours or overnight.

To serve: Ladle into soup bowls and garnish with whipped cream and a few slivers of reserved whole shrimp.

SQUASH CREAM WITH HERBS   Serves 6

Crookneck or smooth yellow summer squash are equally good done this way, as are young zucchini.

2 large onions, chopped	2 large carrots, peeled, grated
3 tablespoons butter	
12 small summer squash, stemmed, sliced thin	1/4 teaspoon summer savory
	1/2 cup light cream
1 cup beef broth	Milk
1 cup water	Salt and pepper
6 medium potatoes, peeled, sliced thin	Sprigs fresh savory or parsley

1. In a large saucepan over medium high heat, sauté the onion in butter until translucent, about 5 minutes. Add squash and stir-fry 5 minutes. Add broth, water, potatoes, carrots, and savory. Cook, covered, 20 minutes or until carrots are tender.

2. Purée in a blender or a food processor, 2 cups at a time. Stir in cream, and add enough milk to thin to preferred consistency. Add salt and pepper to taste. Chill, covered, 4 to 6 hours or overnight.

To serve: Ladle into soup bowls and garnish with sprigs of herb.

COLD SORREL SOUP   Serves 4

1 recipe *Crème Germiny*
(Sorrel Soup with
Consommé, page 200)

Follow through Step 2, but reserve sour cream and whipped cream. Complete soup and chill, covered, 4 to 6 hours or overnight. Combine sour cream and whipped cream, cover, and chill.

To serve: Ladle into soup bowls and garnish with combined creams.

SPINACH FROST   Serves 6

This is quick to make, and elegant enough for a party.

1 10-ounce package frozen chopped spinach
½ cup water
1 quart half-and-half
4 chicken bouillon cubes
⅛ to ¼ cup dry white vermouth
1 teaspoon grated lemon rind
½ teaspoon ground mace or grated nutmeg
Salt and pepper
2 hard-boiled egg yolks

1. Cook the spinach in the water, following package directions, as briefly as possible. Purée in a blender or a food processor, or press through a sieve.
2. In a kettle over medium low heat, bring the cream with the bouillon cubes to just below boiling. Remove from heat. Stir in the puréed spinach, the vermouth, lemon rind, and mace or nutmeg. Chill, covered, 4 to 6 hours or overnight. Add salt and pepper to taste.

To serve: Ladle into crystal bowls set in cracked ice, and garnish by rubbing egg yolk through a sieve set over each bowl.

SPINACH SOUP WITH YOGURT—ICED   Serves 4 to 6

This is fast, easy, tasty, and super healthy! Nifty with hot biscuits for a summer lunch. A similar soup to serve hot appears in Chapter 9, page 318.

1 medium onion, chopped
2 tablespoons butter
2 tablespoons all-purpose
  flour
1 10-ounce package frozen
  chopped spinach

4 cups hot beef broth
1 cup yogurt
Salt and pepper
Pinch grated nutmeg
4 lemon wedges

1. In a saucepan over medium heat, sauté the onion in the butter until translucent, about 5 minutes. Lower heat, and stir in flour. Beating constantly, add broth and cook, stirring, until bubbly, 1 to 2 minutes. Raise the heat to bring liquid to a slow simmer, and add the frozen spinach. Cover and cook until spinach is tender, 5 to 7 minutes.
2. Purée in a blender or a food processor, 2 cups at a time, and let cool. Stir in yogurt, add salt and pepper to taste, and nutmeg, and chill, covered, 4 to 6 hours or overnight.

To serve: Ladle into soup bowls and garnish with lemon wedges.

ELEGANT COLD SPINACH SOUP   Serves 4 to 6

This is the elaborate, elegant, costly, and very good version of chilled spinach soup!

1 10-ounce package frozen
  leaf spinach
2 cups water
1 teaspoon salt
¼ teaspoon pepper
1 teaspoon brown sugar
Pinch grated nutmeg
1 tablespoon strained lemon
  juice

2 egg yolks
2 cups light cream
1 hard-boiled egg, sliced,
  optional
¼ small cucumber, sliced
  very thin
½ cup sour cream

1. In a kettle over medium high heat, place spinach, water, salt, pepper, sugar, nutmeg, and lemon juice. Bring to a boil, cover, lower heat, and simmer until spinach is tender, 5 to 7 minutes. Purée in a blender or a food processor, 2 cups at a time. Return purée to kettle.
2. In a small bowl, beat egg yolks until thick and lemon-colored. Stir in the cream. Stir in 1 cup of purée, then return to kettle. Heat to just below boiling. Chill, covered, 4 to 6 hours or overnight.

To serve: Ladle into soup bowls and garnish with egg slices if you wish, and cucumber slices, and dollops of sour cream.

STRAWBERRY SOUP AND YOGURT   Serves 6 to 8

This is thick, creamy, pure heaven! Don't soak berries—just wash lightly.

2 pints strawbberries,
    hulled, washed
½ cup sugar
1 cup water
2 teaspoons strained lemon
    juice

1½ pints yogurt
1 cup heavy cream
Sugar
Sprigs fresh mint

1. Reserve 6 to 8 large perfect berries. Purée the rest in a blender or a food processor, 2 cups at a time.
2. In a large saucepan over medium high heat, simmer sugar, water, and lemon juice 10 minutes. Let cool.
3. Stir puréed berries into syrup, and fold in yogurt and cream. Add sugar if desired. Chill, covered, 4 to 6 hours.

To serve: Ladle into soup bowls and garnish with whole berries and mint sprigs.

STRAWBERRY SOUP WITH WINE   Serves 4

This is light, dry, heady with wine and fragrant with orange and lemon rind. A Rhine wine or a Moselle is perfect for this recipe.

2 pints strawberries,
    hulled, washed
½ cup sugar
1 cup water
1 tablespoon grated orange
    rind
1½ teaspoons grated lemon
    rind

1 tablespoon strained
    lemon juice
1 cup light dry white wine
    or May wine
½ cup sour cream

1. Purée the berries in a blender or a food processor, 2 cups at a time.
2. In a large saucepan over medium high heat, simmer sugar and water 10 minutes. Let cool.
3. Stir puréed berries into the syrup. Add grated orange and lemon rind, lemon juice, and wine. Chill, covered, 4 to 6 hours.

To serve: Ladle into soup bowls and garnish with sour cream.

ICED SPRING VEGETABLE SOUP   Serves 6 to 8

Tender tops of asparagus and broccoli are just right for this recipe. Follow the cooking sequence carefully, and try to have a lot of green showing when soup is done by not overcooking.

7 cups All-Purpose White Stock (page 45) or chicken broth	1 cup chopped broccoli florets
1 clove garlic, sliced	2 small zucchini, stemmed, sliced thin
¼ teaspoon dried thyme	12 thin asparagus stalks, green only, chopped
1 small bay leaf	
1 tablespoon salt	1 small head spring lettuce, shredded
¼ teaspoon pepper	
10 scallions, chopped	½ cup minced parsley
1 cup chopped green celery tops and leaves	Salt and pepper
1 cup fresh peas	2 hard-boiled eggs, sliced

1. In a large kettle over high heat, place broth, garlic, thyme, bay, salt, and pepper; bring to a rapid boil. One at a time, add the vegetables to boiling broth in the following sequence, allowing broth to return to a rapid boil before adding the next: scallions, celery, peas, broccoli, zucchini, asparagus. When broth returns to a boil after addition of the asparagus, cook 4 minutes, then add lettuce. Cook 2 minutes, then add ½ the parsley. Cook 1 minute and turn off heat. Strain vegetables, returning broth to kettle.
2. Purée vegetables in a blender or a food processor, 2 cups at a time, or press through a sieve, returning each batch to broth as it finishes. Stir, add salt and pepper to taste. Chill, covered, 4 to 6 hours or overnight.

To serve: Ladle into soup bowls. Sprinkle remaining minced parsley in the center of each bowl and garnish with floating rounds of hard-boiled egg.

QUICK TOMATO CREAM—CHILLED   Serves 4

Use the best brand of tomato soup you can find.

3 cups canned tomato soup	1 teaspoon soy sauce
2 teaspoons grated onion	Salt and pepper
3 teaspoons minced parsley	1 cup heavy cream
3 tablespoons minced celery	Juice of 3 limes

Combine all the ingredients except cream and lime juice. Stir into the cream. Chill, covered, 4 to 6 hours or overnight.

To serve: Stir in the lime juice and ladle into frosted glass bowls set in cracked ice.

Eleven

10-MINUTE SOUPS FOR
THE 21ST CENTURY

In a world where events seem to be speeding up in geometrical progressions, instant soups are a logical development. We aren't going to be able to hoist electric slow-cookers with us as we set off to colonize Saturn, but we'll need the comforts a cozy soup can bring when we get there. I'm betting freeze dried foods will inherit the future. The Oregon Freeze Dry Company is already producing shrimps and other delicious foods in freeze dried form for the NASA shuttle. However, until these reach my supermarket and my pocketbook, I'm making fast soups with frozen, canned, and powdered ingredients.

Can a soup made from convenience ingredients in ten minutes be as good as a soup straight from your garden and cooked ten hours? Almost. Sometimes. Maybe yes. Compare the vichyssoise in this chapter with the one from scratch in Chapter 5, and you decide. Guests have been remarkably complimentary about soups like Rich Cream of Tomato, Cream of Mushroom, Marcel's Borscht, Cream of Spinach, Beef Broth Family Style, Onion Soup, and others made from recipes in this chapter.

I find them excellent, but the real test is how kids feel. Kids don't kid about anything as serious as food. One thing about 10-Minute Soups that prejudices kids in their favor is that even young children can make them. Anyone you can trust at the stove and who can handle a blender can prepare them. The very youngest cooks can try the collection of recipes labeled especially for them. The flavors are mostly bland, just the thing a young cook can serve to visiting friends.

The section titled Comforting Broths for Cold Days, with the exception of two soups that have spirits in them, are good bets for young people, too. The Sandwich Soups and Meal Starters, and the group called One-Dish Dinner Soups are all very successful family soups. A little more sophisticated are the chilled soups, and those you may want to save for entertaining.

STOCKING A LARDER FOR FAST SOUP MAKING

You can make a soup from most anything—and in Chapter 8, we do. You can make a fast soup from almost anything, too, if you stock a larder with that in mind. Here are the ingredients I count on when I want to make soup fast, and haven't gone shopping especially with soup in mind:

BROTHS: The best broths are homemade. Chapter 2 suggests lots of types to make and freeze in 1-cup lots for use with soups.

If you don't have a freezerful of broth, use bouillon cubes or powders, or canned broths. The best are expensive: H. L. Gibbs Ltd. puts up a beef broth powder in a 3-ounce size that costs more than a pound and a quarter of butter, and three times as much as other commercial brands. Steero is my favorite among the nationally distributed inexpensive broth cubes and granules. I haven't found a vegetable bouillon cube I like.

College Inn and canned broths of similar quality are first-rate for use in soups. Sometimes you can find a buy in the very large cans; open and freeze what you don't use.

CREAM: Canned and dried ingredients often have a somewhat bitter flavor, but heavy cream can make it vanish and gives soups made with these ingredients all the goodness of from-scratch soups. It's expensive, but often right after holidays there are sales on pints of heavy cream. Buy and freeze; it keeps for months.

GARLIC: Fresh garlic minced into a fast soup can do wonders. Buy heads and keep in a cool, dry place. Garlic powder won't do the job.

HERBS: It's handy to have both dried and frozen herbs in your larder. Basic herbs to keep are parsley, thyme, bay (used extensively in French cooking), chervil, oregano, rosemary, fennel, basil (used often in Italian cooking), dill, and chives. The frozen herbs are used in garnishes as well as in cooking. Invest in fresh herbs when they appear on the market, stem, dry, mince finely, pack into a lock type plastic bag, and freeze.

ONION: Commercially prepared bagged frozen onion chips are too expensive to use when you can peel fresh onions in a moment and chop them in one minute more in a food processor. Instant minced onions, in both, are fine for fast soups, but like Knorr Swiss Onion Soupmix and Dip Mix, they taste better after passing through a blender. The reason for this is that the texture of the onion bits when reconstituted in water is not quite what we expect, and so, disappointing. Knorr Swiss Leek Soupmix is a good substitute for Onion Soupmix.

MUSHROOMS: Dried instant cream of mushroom soup mix (Nestlé's Souptime is a good one) is a powdered soup base with many uses. Just a tablespoon of cream of mushroom soup mix can save a soup whose flavor seems blah; it brings a meaty but gentle special something wherever it goes. Mix it into a cup of Knorr Leek Soupmix or Onion Soupmix: it does wonders!

THICKENERS: Fast soups need thickening as do slow soups. My favorite thickener is the potato—preferably old potatoes, which are grainy and thicken best. In fast soups, a wonderful thickening agent is instant mashed potatoes. It's available as powder or flakes, and you use one tablespoon per cup of liquid. I add one tablespoon of butter for each tablespoon of instant mashed potatoes. There are fewer calories than in whole potatoes, so we can afford that extra bit of butter.

Substitutes for a potato powder to thicken soups are potato pancake mix, which has a similar effect on the soup, and either potato starch or cornstarch, which thicken the soup but leave it clear and add no flavor. Use one tablespoon of each—the effect is about the same as instant mashed potatoes.

TOMATOES: Some of the best fast soups start with a can of stewed tomatoes or tomato sauce. Del Monte is my favorite brand of sauce, but house brands of stewed tomatoes are often excellent. Tomato paste—one tablespoon to three cups of broth—can be a substitute: Add minced green peppers, onion, garlic, and minced celery leaves to make something like instant stewed tomatoes.

Tomato ketchup sometimes can help replace tomatoes in a recipe, and so can bottled chili sauce. But use these sparingly.

VEGETABLES: Frozen mixed vegetables, and frozen broccoli, cauliflower, green beans (Italian style), and spinach make good soup materials. Canned mixed vegetables are fine for use in vegetable soups and minestrone. And never throw away a leftover vegetable. It will adapt to some one of the fast recipes or to recipes in Chapter 8.

WITH LOVE FROM THE KIDS

These are soups quite young children can make and love to eat. What they love better is making their own variations—adding animal crackers or alphabet noodles, or hot dog slices, and other comforting foods. The only caution is this: It's best very young cooks stand and stir what they are cooking until it is done. Young people have important things on their minds and tend to wander from the stove when there's any waiting to do.

PEANUT BUTTER SOUP   Serves 6

Peanut Butter Soup is an African invention kids take to like ducks to water. It's great with big meaty sandwiches on a cold Sunday night, or when they rush in for a quick lunch. (For children, omit wine.)

1 tablespoon minced scallion	Pinch grated nutmeg
2 tablespoons butter	2 cups hot milk
2 tablespoons all-purpose flour	2 cups light cream
1 teaspoon salt	1 cup creamy style peanut butter
¼ teaspoon curry powder	¼ cup tawny port, optional
	Whole peanuts, optional

In a saucepan over medium heat, sauté the scallion in the butter until translucent, about 5 minutes. Lower heat, stir in the flour, salt, curry, and nutmeg. Beating constantly, add the hot milk, and cook, stirring, until bubbly, 1 to 2 minutes. Stir in the cream, raise heat a little, and bring to a boil. Add peanut butter and continue to stir until blended. Stir in wine if you wish, and turn off heat.

To serve: Ladle into soup bowls and garnish with whole peanuts.

Dividends: Nice cold or reheated. Stretch with milk.

To make ahead: Keeps well, refrigerated, for several days.

RICH CREAM OF TOMATO SOUP—FAST   Serves 3

The Cream of Tomato Soup (page 174) is absolutely delicious—but this one is even better if you like a very rich tomato flavor. It takes about 2 minutes to make.

1 15-ounce can tomato sauce	Salt and pepper
1 cup heavy cream	Saltines

In a kettle over medium heat, combine tomato sauce with cream, add salt and pepper to taste, and heat to just below boiling.

To serve: Ladle into bowls and offer saltines on the side.

CORN 'N' CHEESE SOUP—FAST   Serves 3 to 4

1 16-ounce can cream style corn	⅛ teaspoon cayenne
1 teaspoon instant minced onion	6 tablespoons grated Muenster or Monterey Jack cheese
2 cups milk	1 tablespoon minced chives
⅛ teaspoon prepared mustard	4 slices white bread, toasted and buttered, cut into triangles
½ teaspoon salt	

In a kettle over medium heat, bring the corn and its liquid to a boil and stir in the onion, milk, mustard, salt, and cayenne. Lower heat and stir in the cheese. Cook 3 minutes, stirring.

To serve: Ladle into bowls, garnish with chives, and float toast triangles on top.

CORN CHOWDER—FAST   Serves 4

1 16-ounce can cream style corn	3 tablespoons instant mashed potato powder
1 thin slice onion, minced	2 tablespoons minced green pepper
3 cups milk	Salt and pepper
½ teaspoon salt	2 tablespoons butter
¼ teaspoon pepper	

In a kettle over medium heat, bring the corn, onion, milk, salt, and pepper to a slow boil. Stir in the potato powder and green pepper. Simmer 2 minutes. Add salt and pepper to taste.

To serve: Ladle into bowls and dot with butter.

TOMATO SOUP AND PEANUT BUTTER
CROUTONS—FAST   Serves 4

I owe this recipe to Cecily Brownstone and Harold A. Littledale. Cecily is the Food Editor for Associated Press, and when I was asking for her permission to use her version of Mrs. Roger's Cream of Peanut Soup, she recalled that Harold, a mutual friend, loved toast with peanut butter and tomatoes ladled over the top. It's a nifty combination.

4 slices white bread, toasted, buttered, and spread with peanut butter

1 recipe Cream of Tomato Soup (any style)

To serve: Ladle hot soup into bowls and spoon in peanut butter toast, cut into small squares.

TOMATO VEGETABLE CHOWDER—FAST   Serves 3 to 4

With a sandwich, this makes a great midday meal for kids—and they can make it themselves if they like!

1 8-ounce can tomato sauce
1 8-ounce can mixed vegetables and liquid
½ cup milk

½ cup heavy cream
Salt and pepper
½ cup small soup crackers or crumbled saltines

In a kettle over medium heat, combine tomato sauce with vegetables and their liquid, and heat to boiling. Stir in milk and cream, and add salt and pepper to taste.

To serve: Ladle into cups and garnish with Oysterettes or crumbled saltines.

WATERCRESS SOUP   Serves 6

This soup is quick and very easy—an ideal way to perk up a meal for unexpected guests. Just heat the veal broth—or it could be chicken broth or beef broth—and add the cress!

½ bunch watercress
6 cups veal broth

1. Wash the watercress, remove the tip leaves from the stems and reserve. Chop the remaining watercress into ¼-inch lengths.
2. In a kettle over medium heat, heat the broth to simmer, and add the chopped watercress stems. Simmer 5 minutes.

To serve: Just before serving, add reserved leaf tips, stir the soup once or twice, then ladle into soup bowls.

COMFORTING BROTHS FOR COLD DAYS

The milky soups seem particularly comforting to children on bad days, while the recipes with spirits seem to help older people to perk up. All of these are old-fashioned approaches to quick nourishment.

BEEF BOUILLON SHIP STYLE—FAST   Serves 4

6 teaspoons Bovril
4 cups boiling water
Sea Toast

Over medium heat in a kettle combine Bovril and water, bring to a boil, and remove from heat.

To serve: Ladle into mugs and serve with Sea Toast on the side.

BEEF BROTH FAMILY STYLE—FAST   Serves 4

4 cups beef broth
1 small clove garlic, sliced
2 tablespoons butter

4 thick slices stale French bread
1 tablespoon minced parsley

In a kettle over medium heat, combine broth and garlic. Bring to a boil, then turn off heat. Remove the garlic slices.

To serve: Spread the butter over the bread and place the slices in the bottom of the bowls. Ladle the soup into the bowls and garnish with parsley.

SHERRY SOUP   Serves 4

4 cups chicken broth
4 tablespoons instant mashed potato powder
2 egg yolks
2 tablespoons dry sherry

$\frac{1}{2}$ cup heavy cream
Salt and pepper
1 fresh mushroom cap, sliced very thin

1. In a kettle over medium heat, bring the broth to a boil. Stir in the potato powder. Cook 3 minutes.
2. In a small bowl beat the egg yolks until thick and lemon-colored. Stir in 1 cup of hot broth, then return to the kettle, stirring. Add the sherry, heavy cream, salt and pepper to taste, and the mushroom slices. Heat to just below boiling, but be sure not to let boil.

To serve: Ladle into soup bowls.

ONE-DISH DINNER SOUPS—FAST

Easy soups for teen-agers to make. They are recipes most families enjoy and are very simple. Add biscuits or corn muffins (from a mix), a hearty salad, cheese, fruit, hot chocolate, and the meal is not only very fast, but very satisfying.

CREAM OF CHEDDAR SOUP—FAST   Serves 4 to 6

4 cups chicken broth
½ cup water
1 package Swiss onion soup mix and dip mix
1 small carrot, minced
1 small stalk celery and leaves, minced
1 cup milk
4 tablespoons instant mashed potato powder
1 cup grated mild cheddar cheese
3 tablespoons butter
Salt and pepper
½ cup Croutons, Sautéed in Butter (page 33)

1. In a kettle over medium heat, bring the broth and water to a boil and stir in the Soupmix. Add carrot and celery, lower heat, and simmer, uncovered, 15 minutes.
2. Purée in a blender or a food processor, 2 cups at a time, or press through a sieve. Return to the kettle and stir in the milk. When it is simmering, stir in the potato powder and cheddar. Cook 3 minutes, stirring constantly. Stir in the butter and heat to just below boiling. Add salt and pepper to taste.

To serve: Ladle into bowls and garnish with croutons.

CHILI SOUP—FAST
Serves 4

You can improve this fast soup by adding leftover cooked beans, small chunks of cooked steak or beef, raw, diced green peppers, or minced celery. The brand I use is Old El Paso Chili with Beans. Serve this with corn muffins. They enhance the nutritional value of the beans, and they taste wonderful with chili.

1 15-ounce can chili with beans	¼ ounce unsweetened chocolate (halve a
3 cups beef broth	½-ounce square)
2 tablespoons butter	4 tablespoons minced onion

In a kettle over medium heat, combine chili with broth and chocolate. Stir until chocolate is melted, then simmer 3 minutes, uncovered.

To serve: Ladle into bowls and divide butter among them. Pass the onions.

CHILI AND CHEESE SOUP—FAST
Serves 4

1 recipe Chili Soup—Fast	2 tablespoons chopped chives
½ cup grated American processed cheese	

Complete recipe for Chili Soup—Fast, stir in the cheese, and heat until cheese begins to melt.

To serve: Ladle into bowls and garnish with chives. Omit minced raw onion if you wish.

ONION SOUP—FAST
Serves 4

The best onion soup is easy to make from scratch and takes little time. But here's a super-easy and quick recipe that's not bad at all.

4 cups beef broth	4 slices French bread, toasted
4 tablespoons instant minced onion	4 heaping tablespoons grated Jarlsberg or Swiss cheese
2 tablespoons butter	

1. In a kettle over medium heat, bring the broth to a boil, add the onion and butter, and simmer together 3 minutes.
2. Place 1 slice of toast in the bottom of 4 individual ovenproof soup crocks or bowls, sprinkle cheese over each piece of toast, and divide the broth among them. Place crocks on a cookie sheet and set under a preheated broiler until the cheese bubbles.

To serve: Set the soup crocks on small service plates.

PEA SOUP AND HOT DOGS—FAST

Serves 3 to 4

1 10-ounce can condensed
  split pea soup
1 cup chicken broth
1 cup water
⅛ teaspoon dried savory

⅛ teaspoon marjoram
2 frankfurters, sliced thin
Salt and pepper
½ cup croutons

In a kettle over medium heat, combine soup, broth, water, savory, and marjoram. Bring to a boil, add frankfurter slices, cover, reduce heat, and cook 5 minutes. Add salt and pepper to taste.

To serve: Ladle into bowls and garnish with croutons.

PEA SOUP WITH HAM—FAST

Serves 4

1 20-ounce can green
  split pea soup
½-pound slice smoked ham,
  cut into 1-inch cubes

1½ cups water
1 cup croutons

In a kettle over medium heat, bring the soup to a boil. Stir in the ham and the water. Simmer, uncovered, 10 minutes.

To serve: Ladle into bowls and garnish with croutons.

SPAGHETTI SOUP—FAST   Serves 4

1 15-ounce jar spaghetti sauce flavored with meat	3 tablespoons butter
1 small clove garlic, minced	2 tablespoons grated Parmesan cheese
3 cups beef broth	1 tablespoon minced chervil or parsley
1/4 cup raw broken spaghetti pieces	

1. In a kettle over medium heat, combine spaghetti sauce with garlic and broth. Bring to a boil, add spaghetti, reduce heat, and simmer, uncovered, 12 minutes or until spaghetti is tender. Stir often—spaghetti tends to stick to bottom.
2. Stir in butter and Parmesan cheese, and cook 1 minute, uncovered.

To serve: Ladle into bowls and garnish with chervil or parsley.

SPINACH AND EGG SOUP—FAST   Serves 4

1 recipe Cream of Spinach— Fast (page 382)	4 slices white bread, toasted, buttered, cut into cubes
4 eggs	

1. Complete recipe for Cream of Spinach Soup—Fast.
2. Over low heat, break the eggs onto the soup surface, 1 in each corner of the kettle. Cover and cook 3 minutes or until egg white has become opaque.

To serve: Ladle soup carefully into bowls, with 1 egg per bowl. Garnish with toast cubes.

ONE-DISH DINNER SOUPS WITH SEAFOOD

Soups are a wonderful way to use up leftover fish. And—soups made with canned fish favorites, like tuna, can be very tasty. Fish canned in water, not oil, is the right choice for soup-making.

CLAM AND CHICKEN CHOWDER   Serves 8

5 cups chicken broth
3 cups bottled clam juice
1 10½-ounce can clams, minced, and liquor

⅛ teaspoon dried thyme
Salt and pepper
½ pint heavy cream, whipped

In a kettle over medium heat, bring all the ingredients but the salt and pepper and the cream to a simmer. Simmer, covered, 5 minutes. Add salt and pepper to taste.

To serve: Ladle into bowls and garnish with cream.

MANHATTAN CLAM CHOWDER—FAST   Serves 4

1 6½-ounce can chopped clams and liquor
1 10½-ounce can condensed vegetable soup
1 soup can cold water
¼ cup finely minced celery

¼ small bay leaf
⅛ teaspoon dried thyme
¼ cup cream, any kind
Salt and pepper
2 tablespoons butter

In a kettle over medium heat, bring all ingredients but the salt and pepper and butter to a simmer. Simmer, covered, 5 minutes. Add salt and pepper to taste.

To serve: Ladle into bowls and divide butter among them.

LOBSTER CREAM—FAST   Serves 6

1 10-ounce can condensed tomato soup
1 10-ounce can condensed pea soup
2 10-ounce cans chicken consommé

½ pound shredded cooked lobster meat
Dry sherry
Salt and pepper

In a kettle over medium heat, combine all the ingredients except sherry and seasonings, and bring to a boil. Remove from heat, stir in sherry to taste, and add salt and pepper to taste.

To serve: Ladle into bowls.

SALMON BISQUE—FAST   Serves 4

1 7- to 8-ounce can red
  salmon and liquid
4 tablespoons butter
4 tablespoons all-purpose
  flour
4 cups milk, scalded

Salt and pepper
1/8 teaspoon grated nutmeg
1/2 tablespoon strained lemon
  juice
1 tablespoon minced parsley

1. Place salmon in a small bowl, remove bones and skin, and mash with liquid.
2. In a saucepan over low heat, melt the butter and stir in the flour. Stir in the fish. Beating constantly, add the scalded milk, and cook, stirring, until bubbly. Season with salt and pepper and nutmeg. Stir in lemon juice and let stand, covered, one hour.

To serve: Reheat to just below boiling, then ladle into bowls and garnish with parsley.

SHRIMP BISQUE—FAST   Serves 4

4 cups milk
1 6- to 7-ounce can tiny
  shrimp and liquid
1/2 teaspoon dried thyme
4 tablespoons instant
  mashed potato powder

1 tablespoon dry sherry
Salt and pepper
2 tablespoons butter
1/2 cup Croutons, Sautéed in
  Butter (page 33)

1. In a kettle over medium heat, bring the milk, shrimp with their liquid, and the thyme to a slow boil. Stir in the potato powder and simmer 3 minutes. Stir in the sherry, and add salt and pepper to taste.
2. Purée in a blender or a food processor, 2 cups at a time or press through a sieve.

To serve: Ladle into bowls, divide the butter among them, and garnish with croutons.

TUNA FISH CHOWDER—FAST   Serves 4 to 6

1 10¾-ounce can condensed
   cream of mushroom soup
1 cup cold water
1 thin slice onion
2 cups milk
1 6½- or 7-ounce can tuna
   (packed in water) and
   liquid

1 tablespoon butter
Salt and pepper
1 teaspoon white wine
   vinegar
1 tablespoon minced chives

In a kettle over medium heat, bring the mushroom soup, water, and onion to a slow boil. Stir in the milk, tuna and its liquid, and butter. Add salt and pepper to taste. Simmer 2 minutes. Stir in the vinegar.

To serve: Ladle into bowls and garnish with minced chives.

SANDWICH SOUPS AND MEAL STARTERS

The recipes here produce a group of creamy vegetable soups ideal to serve as a first course for family dinners but so elegant, you can count on them to make an impression on guests who pride themselves on their taste in food. So fast to make and so easy, they're perfect to serve with sandwiches for lunch.

MARCEL'S BORSCHT—FAST   Serves 4 to 6

4 cups beef broth
1 16-ounce can sliced beets
   and liquid
1 tablespoon butter
½ teaspoon salt

1 teaspoon light brown
   sugar
1 tablespoon white vinegar
4 to 6 tablespoons sour cream

1. In a kettle over medium heat, bring the broth to a boil and add the beets with their liquid. Simmer 5 minutes. Add butter, salt, sugar, and vinegar, and simmer 10 minutes.
2. Purée in a blender or a food processor, 2 cups at a time or press through a sieve.

To serve: Ladle into bowls and garnish each with a tablespoon of sour cream swirled into the center.

CREAM OF BROCCOLI—FAST
Serves 4 to 6

2 cups water
1 10-ounce package frozen chopped broccoli
1 teaspoon salt
1 thin slice onion
4 cups milk
4 tablespoons instant mashed potato powder
1½ teaspoons salt
⅛ teaspoon grated nutmeg
2 tablespoons butter
2 slices American processed cheese, optional
Salt and pepper

1. In a kettle over medium heat, bring the water to a boil and add the broccoli, salt, and onion. Cook 10 minutes, then purée in a blender or a food processor, 2 cups at a time, or press through a sieve.
2. Pour the milk into the kettle and bring to a simmer. Stir in the potato powder, salt, and nutmeg. Simmer 3 minutes. Stir in the puréed broccoli, the butter, and the cheese if you wish. Add salt and pepper to taste.

To serve: Ladle into bowls.

CREAM OF GREEN BEAN SOUP—FAST
Serves 4 to 6

4 cups water
1 package Swiss onion soup mix and dip mix
1 10-ounce package frozen green beans
1 cup milk
6 tablespoons instant mashed potato powder
2 teaspoons salt
¼ teaspoon pepper
½ teaspoon dried dill
1 cup heavy cream, optional
Salt and pepper
½ cup Croutons, Sautéed in Butter (page 33)

1. In a kettle over medium heat, bring the water to a boil. Add the onion soup mix and the beans. Cook, uncovered, 15 minutes.
2. Purée in a blender or a food processor, 2 cups at a time, or press through a sieve. Return to the kettle over medium heat. Add the milk, and stir in the potato powder, salt, pepper, and dill. Cook 3 minutes. Add the cream, if you wish, and salt and pepper to taste.

To serve: Ladle into bowls and garnish with croutons.

CREAM OF CARROT SOUP—FAST   Serves 4 to 6

4 cups water
1 package Swiss onion soup mix and dip mix
3 medium carrots, sliced thin
1 teaspoon salt
1/8 teaspoon pepper
1/8 teaspoon dried thyme

1 cup milk
4 tablespoons instant mashed potato powder
3 tablespoons butter
2 tablespoons minced parsley

1. In a kettle over medium heat, bring the water to a boil. Add the soup mix, the carrots, salt, pepper, and thyme. Lower heat and simmer, uncovered, 15 minutes.
2. Purée in a blender or a food processor, 2 cups at a time, or press through a sieve. Return to the kettle and stir in the milk. Stir in the potato powder, and cook 3 minutes.

To serve: Ladle into bowls, dot with butter, and garnish with parsley.

CAULIFLOWER AND CHEESE SOUP—FAST   Serves 3 to 4

2 cups water
1/2 teaspoon salt
1/8 teaspoon paprika
1 thin slice onion
1/2 10-ounce package frozen cauliflower

1 1 1/4-ounce package cheese sauce mix
2 cups milk
1 cup heavy cream
1/8 teaspoon grated nutmeg
1 tablespoon minced parsley

1. In a kettle over medium heat, bring the water to a boil with the salt, paprika, and onion, then add the cauliflower. Simmer 10 minutes, uncovered. Strain, reserving the cooking liquid. Cut the cauliflower into tiny florets.
2. Turn the cheese sauce mix into a saucepan over low heat and stir in the milk. Stir in the cauliflower liquid and the florets, then the cream. Add the nutmeg, and heat to just below boiling.

To serve: Ladle into bowls and garnish with parsley.

CREAM OF CELERY SOUP—FAST
Serves 4

1 10¾-ounce can cream of celery soup
2 cups milk
1 large stalk celery and leaves, cut into 1-inch lengths

2 tablespoons butter
Salt and pepper
1 cup Croutons, Sautéed in Butter (page 33)

1. In a kettle over medium heat, bring the soup to a simmer. Stir in the milk and celery. Simmer 3 minutes, stirring.
2. Purée in a blender or a food processor, 2 cups at a time, or press through a sieve. Return to kettle, stir in butter, and add salt and pepper to taste. Reheat to just below boiling.

To serve: Ladle into bowls and garnish with croutons.

CREAM OF DILL SOUP—FAST
Serves 4 to 6

4 cups chicken broth
2 tablespoons minced fresh dill
1 teaspoon salt
⅛ teaspoon pepper
1 cup milk

4 tablespoons instant mashed potato powder
½ cup heavy cream
2 tablespoons butter
4 sprigs fresh dill

In a kettle over medium heat, bring the broth to a boil with the dill, salt, and pepper, and simmer 10 minutes. Stir in the milk and the potato powder. Cook 3 minutes. Stir in the cream and the butter.

To serve: Ladle into bowls and garnish with dill sprigs.

MINESTRONE WITH BEANS AND NOODLES—FAST
Serves 6 to 8

1 cup water
1 clove garlic, minced
2 tablespoons olive oil
½ teaspoon dried basil
¼ cup raw broken spaghetti pieces or alphabet noodles
1 cup beef broth
Salt and pepper

2 10-ounce cans stewed tomatoes
1 8-ounce can mixed vegetables and liquid
1 8½-ounce can baby lima beans or kidney beans
½ cup grated Parmesan cheese

In a kettle over medium heat, bring water to a boil with garlic, oil, and basil. Add spaghetti or noodles. Simmer 5 minutes, uncovered. Add broth, tomatoes, vegetables, and beans. Cook 5 minutes, covered. Add salt and pepper to taste.

To serve: Ladle into bowls and sprinkle with Parmesan cheese.

CREAM OF MUSHROOM SOUP—FAST   Serves 4 to 6

4 cups water
¼ package Swiss onion soup mix and dip mix
1 cup milk
4 tablespoons instant mashed potato powder

3 packages dried cream of mushroom soup
3 tablespoons butter
1 cup heavy cream
Salt and pepper

1. In a kettle over medium heat, bring the water to a boil and stir in the soup mix. Lower heat and simmer, uncovered, 15 minutes. Purée in a blender or a food processor, 2 cups at a time.
2. Return purée to the kettle and stir in the milk. When it is simmering, stir in the potato powder and mushroom soup mix. Cook 3 minutes. Stir in the butter, and heat to just below boiling. Stir in the cream. Add salt and pepper to taste.

To serve: Ladle into bowls.

POTATO-CUCUMBER SOUP—FAST   Serves 6

6 cups chicken broth
1 small onion, chopped
1 cucumber, chopped
6 tablespoons instant mashed potato powder

Salt and pepper
1 bunch watercress, chopped
1 cup heavy cream
2 tablespoons butter

1. In a kettle over medium heat, bring the broth to a boil, stir in the onion and cucumber, and cook 3 minutes. Stir in the potato powder and cook 3 minutes. Add salt and pepper to taste.
2. Purée in a blender or a food processor, 2 cups at a time, or press through a sieve. Return purée to the kettle and bring to a boil, then stir in the chopped watercress. Turn off heat at once, and stir in the cream and the butter.

To serve: Ladle into soup bowls.

CREAM OF SPINACH SOUP—FAST   Serves 4 to 6

2 cups water
1 10-ounce package frozen
  chopped spinach
1 teaspoon salt
1 thin slice onion
4 cups milk

4 tablespoons instant mashed
  potato powder
1 teaspoon salt
1 package dried cream of
  mushroom soup
2 tablespoons butter

1. In a kettle over medium heat, bring the water to a boil and add the spinach, salt, and onion. Cook 10 minutes, then purée in a blender or a food processor, 2 cups at a time, or press through a sieve.
2. Pour the milk into the kettle and bring to a simmer. Stir in the potato powder, salt, and mushroom soup mix. Simmer 3 minutes. Stir in the puréed spinach, then stir in the butter.

To serve: Ladle into bowls.

CLEAR TOMATO SOUP FOR A CROWD   Serves 12 to 14

This is a quickie soup to whip up for after-ski parties (serve hot) or for after-sun parties (serve cold).

2 24-ounce cans beef
  consommé
2 large onions, chopped
½ cup chili sauce
¾ cup catsup
2 10-ounce cans stewed
  tomatoes

1 teaspoon Tabasco sauce
½ tablespoon paprika
1½ teaspoons salt
¼ teaspoon pepper
½ cup whipped cream
Basil sprigs

In a large kettle over medium heat, simmer all the ingredients except the cream and basil.

To serve: Pour into a tureen and garnish with whipped cream and basil sprigs.

Dividends: Leftover soup makes a good base for a new soup including leftover vegetables.

To make ahead: Make a day ahead, and add cream and basil just before serving.

CREAM OF TOMATO SOUP—FAST   Serves 4

2 10-ounce cans stewed   Salt and pepper
  tomatoes   Crackers
1⅓ cups heavy cream

Purée tomatoes in a blender or a food processor, 2 cups at a time, or press through a sieve. Turn into a kettle over medium heat and bring to a simmer. Add the cream and simmer 1 minute. Add salt and pepper to taste.

To serve: Ladle into bowls and serve crackers on the side.

CREAM OF ZUCCHINI SOUP—FAST   Serves 4 to 6

4 cups water   ¼ teaspoon pepper
1 package Swiss onion soup   1 small clove garlic, finely
  mix and dip mix   minced
1 10-ounce package frozen   1 cup beef broth, optional
  zucchini   Salt and pepper
1 cup milk   ½ cup Croutons, Sautéed in
6 tablespoons instant   Butter (page 33)
  mashed potato powder
2 teaspoons salt

1. In a kettle over medium heat, bring the water to a boil. Add the onion soup mix and the zucchini. Cook, uncovered, 15 minutes. Purée in a blender or a food processor, 2 cups at a time, or press through a sieve.
2. Return purée to the kettle over medium heat. Add the milk and stir in the potato powder, salt, pepper, and garlic. Cook 3 minutes. Add the broth if you wish; add salt and pepper to taste.

To serve: Ladle into bowls and garnish with croutons.

CHILLED AND EASY

These chilled soups are meant to be put together in minutes. That means there's little cooling time. If no cooking is involved, the soups will be cooler if you start with chilled ingredients. Where some cooking is required, most are cooled by processing in a blender with ice cubes: use big cubes (as opposed to chips of ice) from a regular ice tray.

Many of these recipes suggest cooling in the freezer. The assumption being made is that the soup will be in the freezer some minutes, but not long enough to freeze. If you have hours of chilling time, cool the soup in the refrigerator instead of the freezer.

APRICOT AND ORANGE SOUP—FAST   Serves 4

This resembles the Apricot Soup recipe in the chapter on chilled soups, but it is made with canned fruit, and substitutes orange juice for the dry sherry.

¼ cup sour cream	1 tablespoon strained lemon
¼ cup heavy cream	juice
1 16- to 17-ounce can apricot	1 cup orange juice
halves and syrup	Sugar
1 tablespoon potato starch	4 ice cubes
or cornstarch	Grated orange rind
1 tablespoon cold water	

1. In a small bowl place sour cream and stir in heavy cream. Cover and let rest at room temperature.
2. In a kettle over medium heat, strain the fruit syrup, reserving the fruit. Bring the syrup to a simmer. In a small bowl combine starch and cold water, and stir into syrup until mixture thickens and clears, 2 to 3 minutes. Add juices, and sugar to taste. Turn off heat. Turn apricot halves into the syrup and beat lightly with a fork to break them up a little. Add ice cubes and stir until they are dissolved. Add more orange juice if needed. Place in freezer until chilled.

To serve: Ladle into bowls and pour a little cream into the center; stir outward in widening circles to create a decorative spiral. Sprinkle orange rind into each bowl as a garnish.

BANANA-ORANGE SOUP—FAST   Serves 4

Ripe bananas are speckled with brown spots. Choose carefully!

1 tablespoon potato starch or cornstarch	1/8 teaspoon ground mace
1 tablespoon cold water	5 ripe bananas, peeled
3 cups milk	1 cup heavy cream
1/4 teaspoon salt	Brown sugar
1 tablespoon grated orange rind	2 very thin slices unpeeled orange—halved

1. In a small bowl combine starch and water. In a kettle over medium heat, bring the milk to a simmer and stir in the starch mixture, the salt, rind, and mace.
2. Purée bananas in a blender. Stir into milk mixture, reduce heat, and simmer, stirring, 5 minutes. Remove from heat and stir in cream. Add brown sugar to taste. Chill in freezer.

To serve: Ladle into bowls and garnish with orange slices.

CORN AND TOMATO COCKTAIL—FAST   Serves 4 to 6

1 16-ounce can stewed tomatoes	8 ice cubes
1 16-ounce can cream style corn	Salt and pepper
	1 cup heavy cream
1 tablespoon instant minced onion	4 to 6 sprigs fresh dill or parsley
3 tablespoons instant mashed potato powder	4 to 6 slim celery sticks

1. In a kettle over medium heat, combine tomatoes and corn with onion, and bring to a boil. Cook 3 minutes. Stir in potato powder.
2. Process with ice cubes in a blender or a food processor, 2 cups at a time. Add salt and pepper to taste. Stir in heavy cream. Chill in freezer.

To serve: Ladle into tall frosted glasses and garnish with dill or parsley sprigs. Put a celery stick into each glass as a stirrer.

RUSSIAN CUCUMBER AND BEET SOUP—FAST · Serves 6

3 cups veal or chicken broth
5 tablespoons minced dill pickle
1 16-ounce can sliced beets and liquid
1 tablespoon honey
4 ice cubes
1 tablespoon strained lemon juice, optional

Salt and pepper
1½ cups sour cream
1 medium cucumber, peeled, chopped
2 hard-boiled eggs, sliced
1 tablespoon minced fresh dill

1. In a kettle over medium heat, bring the broth to a boil with the pickle. Add the beets, sliced, and their liquid. Simmer 3 minutes and turn off heat. Stir in the honey and ice cubes.
2. Purée in a blender or a food processor (with ice), 2 cups at a time, or mash through a sieve (without ice). Add lemon juice, if you wish, and salt and pepper to taste. Chill in freezer.

To serve: Ladle into bowls. Spoon sour cream into the center of each bowl and stir a little outward. Mound cucumber around plate rims and garnish with sliced eggs and dill.

CUCUMBER AND PEA SOUP—FAST · Serves 4 to 6

2 medium cucumbers, peeled if waxed
1 medium clove garlic, sliced
1 11¼-ounce can condensed split pea soup

1½ cups veal or chicken broth
Salt and pepper
1 cup sour cream
4 to 6 sprigs fresh mint

Combine cucumber, garlic, pea soup, and broth in a blender or a food processor, and process 2 cups at a time until well blended. Season with salt and pepper to taste. Chill in freezer.

To serve: Ladle into bowls and stir in sour cream until blended. Garnish each bowl with a sprig of mint.

CURRIED SOUP—FAST

Serves 6 to 8

1¼ cups beef broth
1 11¼-ounce can condensed split pea soup
1 tablespoon curry powder
1 10-ounce can tomato madrilene
4 ice cubes

2 cups half-and-half
1 tablespoon strained lemon juice
Salt and pepper
2 large tart apples, chopped

In a kettle over medium heat, combine broth, pea soup, and curry. Bring to a boil, lower heat, and simmer 3 minutes. Remove from heat. Add madrilene and ice cubes, and stir until melted. Stir in half-and-half and lemon juice. Add salt and pepper to taste. Chill in freezer.

To serve: Divide chopped apples among soup bowls and ladle soup over them.

GAZPACHO—FAST

Serves 4

1 16-ounce can stewed tomatoes
2 medium cucumbers, sliced, peeled if waxed
3 anchovy fillets
12 pitted black olives
4 cloves garlic, sliced
⅛ teaspoon ground cumin

3 tablespoons vinegar
⅓ cup olive oil
1 tablespoon minced parsley
1 sprig fresh thyme, or ⅛ teaspoon dried
2 scallions
1 tablespoon strained lemon juice

Chop in a food processor, 2 cups at a time, all the ingredients except the lemon juice. Turn into a large salad bowl and toss ingredients, then chill in freezer.

To serve: Ladle into chilled cups and sprinkle a few drops of lemon juice on each before serving.

VEGETABLE COCKTAIL—FAST   Serves 6

1 20-ounce can green
  split pea soup
2 6-ounce cans mixed
  vegetable juice
1 large stalk celery and
  leaves, chopped

1 teaspoon salt
3 teaspoons sugar
8 ice cubes
1 tablespoon chopped chives

1. In a kettle over medium heat combine pea soup, juice, celery and leaves, salt, and sugar. Bring to a boil, reduce heat, and simmer, uncovered, 10 minutes. Remove from heat.
2. Process with ice cubes in a blender or a food processor, 2 cups at a time. Chill in freezer.

To serve: Ladle into tall frosted glasses and garnish with chives.

VICHYSSOISE—FAST   Serves 6

This "fast" vichyssoise is so good you can serve it to your gourmet friends. It's almost as delicious as vichyssoise made from scratch.

1 package Swiss onion soup
  mix and dip mix
4½ cups water
4 tablespoons instant
  mashed potato powder
4 tablespoons butter

1 cup milk
1 cup heavy cream
Salt and pepper
2 tablespoons chopped
  chives

1. In a kettle over medium heat, combine onion soup mix with water and bring to a boil. Lower heat and simmer, uncovered, 15 minutes. Stir in the potato powder and cook 3 minutes. Stir in the butter and heat to just below boiling.
2. Purée in a blender or a food processor, 2 cups at a time, with the milk and the cream. Add salt and pepper to taste. Chill in freezer.

To serve: Ladle into bowls and garnish with chives.

Twelve

FAST-AND SLOW-COOK POTS

A pressure cooker, a slow-cook electric pot, and a big dutch oven are all very handy for the soup cook. Onions, vegetables, and meats sauté very well in the bottom of a dutch oven, and it also is a good slow-cooker—an ideal combination for soup making. The pressure cooker can be used to make stocks and broths rapidly—half an hour to an hour from start to finish, as compared to 4 to 6 hours by ordinary cookpots, and 10 to 12 hours by slow-cook pot. A slow-cook pot does the thick main-course and bean soups beautifully, and you don't have to be there to watch it.

I was intrigued to learn through testing that each of these pots produces a soup that tastes a little different, even if the same ingredients are used. Because of the boiling action, soup produced in the pressure cooker and in the dutch oven is rich, thick, and reduced in quantity compared to the soup done in a slow-cook pot, which lets no steam escape and barely bubbles its contents. One recipe I tested in all three pots is Bean Soup Asturias, below. Prepared in an enameled dutch oven, at the end of three hours of cooking the soup was thick, flavorful, the beans disintegrated, and the most distinct flavor was salt pork and blood sausage. I had four generous servings.

Bean Soup Asturias took only one hour in a pressure cooker, and I had to add two more cups of water to make it liquid enough to be called a soup. I cooked it on rapid pressure, with the rocker going at a great rate. The flavor was rich, and the consistency nice and thick.

Cooked nine hours on Low in a slow-cook pot, Bean Soup Asturias was light, thin, and the flavor of the onions came through much more clearly than in either of the other tests.

ABOUT DUTCH OVENS

I am familiar with two types of dutch oven, and each comes in sizes from two to six or more quarts. A dutch oven is made of a heavy metal that disperses heat so that contents cook evenly and slowly. My mother's dutch oven, called a *cocotte* in French, was made of cast iron and she used it mostly for stews—but never stews with tomatoes as the acid seemed to develop an unpleasant flavor in contact with metal. In larger sizes, the cast-iron dutch oven is really too heavy to handle. I use a dutch oven made of stainless steel covered with flowered porcelain, pretty enough to bring to the table. It's Sanko Ware, and the 8-quart size does a beautiful job with soup in big batches, and stock.

You do have to keep an eye on the contents of a dutch oven

however; thick soups may catch on the bottom and burn if left for a very long time without stirring.

ABOUT SLOW-COOK ELECTRIC POTS

Soups cooking on Low in a slow-cook electric earthenware pot don't have to be watched. Little if any steam escapes, so broth is more plentiful, thinner, and either more elegant or more tasteless, depending on what you are making. For the gourmet who has a job outside the home, it's the best way to have from-scratch meals ready to go when dinnertime rolls around. (I wrote a whole cookbook on the subject: *The Best of Electric Crockery Cooking.*) However, while it's a good method for making many soups, it's not the best way to make all soups. In a slow-cooker, vegetables darken. Among brands I have tried, and which have stood the test of time, are the Rival Crock-Pot—I recommend the 4- to 5-quart size for soup—and the Sunbeam Crocker-Cooker, 4½-quart size. If you have an electric, stainless steel all-purpose slow-cooker, it will make great soups and, like a dutch oven, allows you to sauté ingredients beautifully before you add the liquid to make it into soup. However, I find that these, like the dutch oven, tend to burn on the bottom, especially bean and other thick soups, unless watched.

ABOUT PRESSURE COOKERS

Betty Wenstadt, Home Economist with the National Presto Industries, uses a pressure cooker for everything. Betty uses her cooker for stocks and broths and then uses the broths as the base for vegetable soups made with either cooked or raw chopped vegetables. The basic principles evident in a reading of Betty's broth recipes can be applied to making the broths in Chapter 2. However, there are a number of things *not* to do in a pressure cooker:

Do not fill a pressure cooker more than two-thirds full when making soups.

Do not cook soup in it that includes raw rice—indeed, *any* rice. Nor split peas, nor grains, like barley. These will foam up, make masses of froth, and can clog the vent.

Bean soups may be prepared in a cooker, but only if the beans have been soaked in water to cover (3 cups for 1 cup beans, and pour off the leftover water before the next step in the recipe) plus 2 tablespoons oil and 1½ teaspoons salt. The oil and the salt keep the bean jackets on. The other way you can cook a bean soup in the pressure cooker is illustrated by the recipe below for Bean Soup Asturias—Pressure Cooker Method I, and that is by including fat and salt in with the beans when you start the cooking. (Betty doesn't really feel comfortable with this, however.)

Behind these cautions is the fact that fine particles that foam up can clog the pressure cooker vent. (It's easier to follow instructions than it is to try to figure out how serious a problem a clogged pressure cooker vent can present.)

When you make bean soup in a pressure cooker, do expect to stop the cooking and check the beans after twenty minutes. Let the steam pressure fall of itself, uncover the beans, and test for doneness. If necessary, continue cooking another three to five minutes.

Because broth and bean soups require long cooking, they are among the soups you might consider making in a pressure cooker. They're good.

TRY YOUR OWN
FAST- AND SLOW-POT TESTS

Here are four recipes I developed for Bean Soup Asturias as a result of testing this dish in the fast and slow pots described above.

The dutch oven method for making Bean Soup Asturias follows the basic principles used in planning the recipes for most of the soups in this book. Compare this method with the three others here for cooking the same soup in a slow-cook electric pot and in a pressure cooker, and you will understand how to adapt recipes to the slow- and fast-cooking containers.

**BEAN SOUP ASTURIAS—DUTCH OVEN
METHOD**   Serves 10

This is a main-course soup. I consider the blood sausage optional because not everyone likes it, and the soup is hearty enough without it. I discard the salt pork when the cooking is over, but taste it first; you might prefer to return it, or a small portion of it, to the soup. I tested this in a 4½-quart dutch oven and did not soak the beans nor in any way pretreat them before I started the cooking.

2	cups dry navy beans	1	16-ounce can whole tomatoes and liquid
12	cups water		
1	2-by-5-inch piece salt pork, 1 inch thick	2	morcilla (Spanish blood sausage), cut into ¼-inch slices, optional
1	very large clove garlic, minced	1	large potato, chopped
1	teaspoon salt		Salt and pepper
2	pork chops, center cut loin (about ½ pound, boneless)		

1. In a large kettle or a dutch oven over high heat, combine the beans, water, salt pork, garlic, salt, and chops. Cover, bring to a boil, reduce heat, and simmer 2 hours.
2. Add the tomatoes, sausage, and potato; cook 20 minutes or until potato is tender. Discard salt pork; break chops into bits and return to soup. Season with salt and pepper to taste.

To serve: Ladle into bowls.

To make ahead: Wonderfully good made the day before.

BEAN SOUP ASTURIAS—SLOW-COOK POT METHOD

Serves 10

1 recipe Bean Soup Asturias
 —Dutch Oven Method, but
 use only 10 cups water

1. In a large kettle over high heat, combine beans, salt pork, and water. Cover, bring to a boil, and boil 1 minute.
2. In an electric slow-cook pot on Low, place the garlic, salt, and pork chops; pour the beans and water over them. Cover and cook undisturbed 8 to 12 hours.
3. Turn the heat to High. Add the tomatoes, sausage, and potato to the pot, cover, and cook 20 to 30 minutes or until potato is tender. Discard salt pork. Break pork chops into bits and return to soup. Season with salt and pepper to taste.

To serve: Ladle into soup plates.

To make ahead: Cook overnight through Step 2, then complete Step 3 in the morning or shortly before serving.

BEAN SOUP ASTURIAS—PRESSURE
COOKER METHOD I

Serves 4 to 6

Beans are unsoaked in this recipe. It works because the pork fat and the salt keep bean skins intact. I've halved the quantity of beans for the small cooker (4½-quart size), but increased the proportion of water because it seems to lose a lot of water during the cooking.

1 cup dry navy beans
8 quarts water
1 2-by-5-inch piece salt pork, ½ inch thick
1 medium clove garlic, minced
1 pork chop, center cut loin, (about ¼ pound, boneless)

1 cup whole tomatoes and liquid
1 morcilla (Spanish blood sausage), optional
1 medium potato, chopped
Salt and pepper

1. In a pressure cooker over medium high heat, combine the beans, 6 cups water, salt pork, garlic, and pork chop. Cover and heat until the rocker begins to move gently. Reduce heat enough to maintain a gentle rocking. Cook 30 minutes. Turn off heat and allow the pressure to drop of itself. Open the pot and add the remaining water, or enough of it to bring the pot to half-full. If the beans need more cooking, pressure cook another 3 to 5 minutes.
2. Add tomatoes, sausage, and potato, and cook over low heat, uncovered, 20 to 30 minutes. Discard the salt pork. Slice the sausage into ¼-inch pieces, break the chop into bits and return meat to soup. Season with salt and pepper to taste, and add a little more water if needed.

To serve: Ladle into big soup plates.

To make ahead: Excellent made the day before.

BEAN SOUP ASTURIAS—PRESSURE
COOKER METHOD II

Serves 4 to 6

This method is the basic approach to making bean soups in a pressure cooker, with beans soaked 8 hours or overnight with water to cover (3 cups to 1 cup dry beans), 2 tablespoons oil, and 1½ teaspoons salt.

1 cup dry navy beans	1 pork chop, center cut
3 cups water	loin, (about ¼ pound,
2 tablespoons oil	boneless)
1½ teaspoons salt	1 cup whole tomatoes and
8 cups water	liquid
1 2-by-5-inch piece salt	1 morcilla (Spanish blood
pork, ½ inch thick	sausage), optional
1 medium clove garlic,	1 medium potato, chopped
minced	Salt and pepper

1. In a small bowl combine beans, water, oil, and salt; soak 8 hours or overnight. Check and add more water if level falls below bean tops.
2. Drain beans and discard water. In a pressure cooker over medium high heat, combine the soaked beans, 6 cups water, salt pork, garlic, and pork chop. Cover and heat until rocker begins to move gently. Reduce heat enough to maintain a gentle rocking. Cook 20 minutes. Turn off heat and allow the pressure to drop of itself. Open the pot and add the remaining water, the tomatoes, sausage, and potato. Cook over low heat, uncovered, 20 to 30 minutes. Discard the salt pork. Slice the sausage into ¼-inch pieces, break the chop into bits. Season with salt and pepper to taste, and add a little more water if needed.

To serve: Ladle into big soup plates.

To make ahead: Excellent made the day before.

BEAN AND MUSTARD GREEN SOUP— PRESSURE COOKER METHOD

Serves 10

This is *Caldo Gallego*, a very thick, main-course Spanish soup, another illustration of the use of a pressure cooker in speeding up soup cooking. I've quartered the quantity of mustard greens that is used in the Spanish recipe and eliminated a ham hock, as I found these ingredients strong.

1 cup dry navy beans	stemmed, or 1 10-ounce
3 cups water	package frozen greens
2 tablespoons oil	2 strips meaty bacon,
1½ teaspoons salt	chopped
10 cups water	¾ cup minced onion
1 2-by-5-inch piece salt	¾ cup minced green pepper
pork, ½ inch thick	1 large clove garlic, minced
2 pork chops, center cut	2 cups chopped potato
loin, (about ½ pound)	3 to 4 chorizo sausages
¼ pound fresh, tender	Salt and pepper
turnip or mustard greens,	

1. In a small bowl combine beans, water, oil, and salt; soak 8 hours or overnight. Check and add more water if level falls below bean tops.
2. Drain beans and discard water. In a pressure cooker over medium high heat, combine soaked beans, 6 cups water, salt pork, and pork chops. Cover and heat until rocker begins to move gently. Reduce heat enough to maintain gentle rocking. Cook 20 minutes. Turn off heat and allow the pressure to drop of itself. Open the pot and add the remaining water and the greens. Cook, uncovered, over low heat 30 minutes.
3. Meanwhile, in a large skillet over medium heat, sauté the bacon until crisp, about 5 to 10 minutes. Add the onion, green pepper, and garlic, and cook until the onion is becoming translucent. Scrape into the cooker with the potato and chorizos. Cover and cook over low heat 45 minutes. After 35 minutes remove the sausages, prick them all over, and return to the cooker. Stir occasionally and add more water if needed. Lift out the sausages and pork; slice the sausages; cut the pork and salt pork to bits, and return meats to the cooker. Skim excess fat from the soup surface. Season with salt and pepper to taste, and heat through before serving.

To serve: Ladle into big bowls.

PRESSURE COOKER BROTHS

The recipes below are for 4-quart pressure cookers, as are those above. They yield about 1½ quarts of broth, well flavored. Betty Wenstadt, at Presto, uses the type of cooker called a canner, with a capacity of 13 quarts (some go up to 22-quart capacity) to make big batches of broth so there will be lots for freezing for future use. That's the size pressure cooker you would need to make the high-yield recipes for broths in Chapter 2, the type containing lots of bones and other ingredients. The timing for cooking big batches in large cookers is, surprisingly, about the same as for the beef and chicken broth recipes given below. You start the timing when the rocker begins to move. In the bigger batches, it will take longer for the rocker to begin to move, especially if the ingredients are chilled from the refrigerator.

CHICKEN BROTH—PRESSURE COOKER METHOD
Makes 1½ quarts

This is Betty Wenstadt's method for making chicken broth, fast.

2 pounds cut-up chicken (or wings, backs, necks)	1 medium carrot, chopped
1 teaspoon salt	1 small onion, chopped
1 medium stalk celery, chopped	6 cups water
	2 eggs, optional

1. In the pressure cooker over medium high heat, combine all the ingredients except the eggs, cover, and heat until the rocker begins to move gently. Reduce heat enough to maintain gentle rocking. Cook 15 minutes, then turn off heat and allow the pressure to drop of itself. Open the cooker. Strain through 2 thicknesses of cheesecloth. Refrigerate until the fat rises to the surface, then skim off the fat and discard. Use as directed in recipe of your choice.
2. If you wish to clarify the broth, return the cooker to high heat and bring broth to a boil. Break the eggs into a small bowl and crush the shells into the eggs. Stir the eggs into the boiling broth and cook 2 minutes, stirring. Turn off heat and let stand 20 minutes. Strain through 2 thicknesses of cheesecloth. Use broth as directed in recipes.

Dividends: Boiled chicken may be served hot with a little broth, or used cold in salads, or served with a vinaigrette dressing.

BEEF BROTH—PRESSURE COOKER
METHOD

Makes 1½ quarts

This is Betty Wenstadt's recipe. She turns the clarified broth into vegetable soups by adding 1 to 4 cups cooked or raw chopped vegetables. Betty dices vegetables; I chop them in a food processor. If you don't plan to make this broth into consommé, clarifying—the final step—isn't necessary.

1½ pounds lean beef (neck or stew meat), cut into 2-inch pieces	¼ cup diced carrot
	1 medium bay leaf
	1½ tablespoons salt
1 tablespoon oil	⅛ teaspoon pepper
6 cups water	1 teaspoon chopped parsley
½ cup diced onion	2 eggs, optional

1. In the pressure cooker over medium high heat, thoroughly brown the meat in the oil. Add remaining ingredients except the eggs. Cover and heat until the rocker begins to move gently. Reduce heat enough to maintain a gentle rocking. Cook 15 minutes, then turn off heat and allow the pressure to drop of itself. Open the cooker. Strain through 2 thicknesses of cheesecloth. Refrigerate until the fat rises to the surface, then skim off the fat and discard. Use as directed in recipe of your choice.
2. If you wish to clarify the broth, return the cooker to high heat, and bring broth to a boil. Break the eggs into a small bowl and crush the shells into the eggs. Stir the eggs into the boiling broth and cook 2 minutes, stirring. Turn off heat and let stand 20 minutes. Strain through 2 thicknesses of cheesecloth. Use broth as directed in recipes.

Dividends: Boiled beef and vegetables may be served as in Pot-au-Feu, hot or cold with a vinaigrette dressing or with a little hot broth.

SOME SLOW-COOKER BROTHS AND SOUPS

Long-cooking broths and soups that make main courses for a meal are good candidates for your slow-cook pot. Here is a representative handful from my book, *The Best of Electric Crockery Cooking*: they are reproduced here with permission of the book's publishers, Grosset & Dunlap, with my thanks.

BEEF BROTH—SLOW-COOK POT METHOD   Makes 2 quarts

The bones selected should have a lot of meat clinging to them.

2 pounds meaty beef and veal soup bones	2 teaspoons salt
	4 large sprigs parsley
2 tablespoons melted butter or beef drippings	½ teaspoon pepper
	2 quarts water
2 medium carrots, chopped	1 teaspoon dried thyme
2 medium onions, chopped	1 medium bay leaf
¼ pound salt pork	1 large clove garlic, chopped
2 large stalks celery, chopped	Coarse sea or kosher salt

1. Preheat the oven to 450 degrees.
2. Spread the bones in a large saucepan and sprinkle them with a little melted butter or drippings. Roast in the oven 30 to 40 minutes, until well colored. Turn the bones and the pan juices into the slow-cooker, along with the remaining ingredients, except the coarse salt. Cover and cook on Low for 10 to 12 hours.
3. Line a colander with 2 thicknesses of cheesecloth and strain the broth through it. Discard bones and herbs, and place the meat and vegetables in a bowl. Allow the remaining broth to cool, then refrigerate or freeze for future use.

Dividends: Serve the meat with the vegetables and a little degreased hot broth in a large soup plate. Pass coarse sea or kosher salt.

CHICKEN BROTH—SLOW-COOK POT
METHOD
Makes 2 quarts

2½ pounds cut-up chicken
  (or necks, backs, wing
  tips)
1 small onion, chopped
1 medium carrot, chopped
1 medium parsnip, cut up
2 medium cloves garlic,
  sliced

6 peppercorns
2 large sprigs parsley
1 medium bay leaf
½ teaspoon dried thyme
2 teaspoons salt
2 quarts water

1. Place all the ingredients in the slow-cooker. Cover and cook on Low for 10 to 12 hours.
2. Line a colander with 2 thicknesses of cheesecloth and strain the broth through it. Discard bony chicken parts and herbs. Scoop vegetables and meat into a bowl. Allow the remaining broth to cool, skim off and discard the fat on it, and refrigerate or freeze the broth for future use.

Dividends: Serve the meat with the vegetables and a little degreased hot broth in a large soup plate. Or save meat and use to make sandwiches or salad.

CALIFORNIA CHICKEN GUMBO
FOR A MOB
Serves 12 to 14

A good recipe for outdoor parties. A main-course soup.

¼ cup chicken fat
¼ cup diced ham
½ cup chopped celery
1 cup chopped onion
½ cup chopped green
  pepper
¼ cup raw rice
4 tablespoons all-purpose
  flour
2½ quarts chicken broth
1 cup drained sliced okra,
  fresh or canned

1 cup chopped tomatoes
2 tablespoons minced
  pimiento
2 pounds boneless chicken,
  diced
⅓ cup dried black-eyed
  peas, baby limas, or light
  red kidney beans
2 teaspoons salt
½ teaspoon pepper
2 tablespoons minced
  parsley or dill

In a large skillet over medium high heat, render the fat, and in it sauté the ham, celery, onion, and pepper until the onion begins to be translucent, about 10 minutes. Add the rice, and stir constantly for 5 minutes. Stir in the flour and at once pour in a cup of broth, scraping up the pan juices. Turn the contents of the skillet into the slow cooker, add remaining broth and all other ingredients, except the parsley or dill. Cover and cook on Low 10 or 12 hours.

To serve: Ladle into big soup plates and garnish with parsley or dill.

CHICKEN CHOWDER MARTHA'S VINEYARD STYLE

Serves 12

An old-fashioned New England recipe.

4 to 5 pound boiling fowl	2 medium onions, chopped
2 quarts water	4 cups chopped potato
1 medium bay leaf	4 cups milk, scalded
¼ teaspoon dried thyme	2 tablespoons butter or
3 whole cloves	margarine
1 teaspoon salt	Paprika or freshly grated
¼ pound salt pork	nutmeg

1. Place the fowl, water, bay, thyme, cloves, and salt in the slow-cooker. Cover and cook on Low for 7 to 9 hours. Skin the chicken pieces, and discard skin and bones. Mince the meat. Allow the broth to cool, then skim off and discard the fat on it.
2. In a kettle over medium high heat, render the fat from the salt pork. Discard the cracklings. Add the onion and cook until beginning to brown, 8 to 10 minutes. Add the chicken broth and the potato and simmer, uncovered, 20 minutes. Add minced chicken and simmer 10 minutes. Add the milk and butter, and serve when butter has melted.

To serve: Ladle into big soup plates. Garnish with paprika or nutmeg.

COACH HOUSE BLACK BEAN SOUP   Serves 8

This is an excellent recipe. If you want to make it in a regular pot instead of the slow-cooker, add cooked beans to ingredients in Step 2, cook 4 hours, then complete as directed here.

2 cups black beans	3 sprigs parsley
10 cups water	2 medium bay leaves
5 strips bacon, chopped	2 large cloves garlic, sliced
2 medium stalks celery, chopped	2 medium carrots, cut into large chunks
2 medium onions, chopped	2 medium parsnips, chopped
2 tablespoons all-purpose flour	¼ teaspoon pepper
	2 teaspoons salt
2 smoked ham hocks, or ham bone and rind	2 tablespoons Madeira
	2 hard-boiled eggs
3 pounds beef shin bones, cracked	8 thin lemon slices

1. In a kettle over high heat, combine beans and water. Cover, bring to a boil, boil 2 minutes, then turn off heat. Turn into a slow-cook pot on Low, and cover.
2. In the kettle over medium high heat, sauté the bacon 5 minutes. Add the celery and onions, and cook 5 minutes. Remove from heat and stir in the flour. Pour a little of the bean water into the kettle and scrape the kettle contents into the slow-cooker. Add ham hocks or bone and rind, beef bones, parsley, bay, garlic, vegetables, pepper, and salt. Cover and cook 8 to 12 hours.
3. Lift bones and hocks from soup; reserve meat, but discard bones and rind. Purée the soup in a blender or a food processor, 2 cups at a time, or press through a sieve. Return to the slow-cooker, and turn the heat to High. Dice the meat and return to the soup. Stir in the Madeira and heat through.

To serve: Pour into a tureen and grate the hard-boiled eggs into it. Float slices of lemon on the surface.

Dividends: Excellent reheated. Before you refrigerate, remove lemon slices.

To make ahead: Complete, but add Madeira, eggs, and lemon slices just before serving.

TURTLE SOUP   Serves 8

My Escoffier says to start this soup with a turtle that is nice and fleshy, weighing about 120 to 180 pounds, but there are easier ways to go about things. These days one can find turtle flesh frozen or canned, and in the islands, wise cooks buy it fresh and pounded, ready to cook. To make this in a regular kettle, use 10 cups of water and simmer 3 to 4 hours.

2 pounds turtle, cut into ½-inch pieces
2 medium onions, minced
2 medium stalks celery, minced
1 medium carrot, chopped
1 16-ounce can whole tomatoes
1 large bay leaf, crumbled
2 large sprigs parsley
1 pound beef soup bones, cracked
6 cups water
1½ teaspoons salt
¼ teaspoon pepper
2 tablespoons dry sherry
1 lemon, sliced very thin

Place all the ingredients except the sherry and lemon in a slow-cooker turned to Low. Cover and cook 8 to 12 hours or until the turtle is very tender. Strain through 2 thicknesses of cheesecloth. Dice the meat and return to the broth with marrow from the bones. Turn to High. Add the sherry and heat through.

To serve: Ladle into consommé cups, floating a very thin slice of lemon on top of each.

Note: Mock Turtle Soup recipes call for equal proportions of clam and beef broths, flavored with a pinch of thyme and marjoram, and a little sherry.

APPENDIX

Where to shop if you can't find it locally:

Cardullo's Gourmet Shop
6 Brattle Street
Cambridge, Mass. 12138
$5.00 minimum mail order plus
postage

Italian, Oriental

Casa Moneo Spanish Imports
210 West 14th Street
New York, N.Y. 10011
$15.00 minimum mail order plus
postage

Mexican, South American,
Puerto Rican

H. Roth & Son
1577 First Avenue
New York, N.Y. 10028
$5.00 minimum mail order

Middle Eastern, Russian,
Indian, Indonesian, Hungarian,
French

Kiehl Pharmacy
109 Third Avenue
New York, N.Y. 10003
$15.00 minimum mail order

Herbs

Mario Bosco Company
263 Bleeker Street
New York, N.Y. 10014
$25.00 minimum mail order

Italian

Wing Fat Company
35 Mott Street
New York, N.Y. 10013
$30.00 minimum mail order

Chinese, Japanese, Thai

Haig's Delicacies
441 Clement Street
San Francisco, California 94118
$10.00 minimum mail order

Indian

American Tea,
Coffee & Spice Company
1511 Champa Street
Denver, Colorado 80202
$5.00 minimum mail order

Greek, Middle Eastern,
Indian

Antone's   Indian, Hispanic
P.O. Box 3352
Houston, Texas 77001
$3.50 minimum mail order

Antone's Import Company   Indian, Hispanic
4234 Harry Hines Boulevard
Dallas, Texas 75219
$3.50 minimum mail order

Central Grocery   Herbs
923 Decatur Street
New Orleans, Louisiana 70116
$20.00 minimum mail order

MEMOS ON MEASUREMENTS—
Some useful tables and charts

Most of the world today measures according to the metric system.
The United States measures according to a system I was taught to call
"avoirdupois" which deals in pounds, ounces, pints and quarts instead
of in grams and liters. To confuse us all further, Britain and Canada
(now converted to the metric system) have a pound and a pint heavier
than ours in the U.S.

Fortunately, in soup-making, it is generally true that measurements
can be more relaxed than in cake-baking, and still produce good results.
Below are a few tables I have found helpful in making soups using
measurements from other lands.

Fahrenheit and Centigrade (Metric)
Oven Temperatures

Fahrenheit	Centigrade
500°	260°
450°	232°
400°	205°
350°	177°
325°	168°
275°	135°
225°	107°

Metric Equivalents

Weight

1 ounce	28.35 grams
3½ oz.	100 grams
1 pound (16 oz.)	453.59 grams
2.2 pounds (35½ oz.)	1 kilogram

Volume

1 teaspoon (⅙ oz.)	5 milliliters
1 tablespoon (3 tsp.)	15 milliliters
1 cup (8 oz.)	¼ liter
2 cups (1 pt.)	½ liter
4 cups (1 quart)	0.946 liter

Conversion Table

Inches to centimeters = multiply inches by 2.54
Centimeters to inches = multiply centimeters by .39

Ounces to grams = multiply ounces by 28.35
Grams to ounces = multiply grams by .035

Fahrenheit to centigrade = subtract 32 from the Fahrenheit temperature, multiply by 5, then divide by 9
Centigrade to Fahrenheit = multiply centigrade temperature by 9, divide by 5, and add 32

Equivalent Table

Ingredient	Weight	Measure
Dried beans	1 pound	2 cups +
Cheese, grated	½ pound	2 cups
Sour cream	16 ounces	2 cups
Garlic	1 large clove	1 tablespoon, minced
Meat	1 pound	2 cups, chopped
Mushrooms	1 pound	4 cups, sliced
Potatoes	1 pound	2 cups, grated
Tomatoes	1 large ripe tomato	1 cup, chopped

Can Sizes in Cups and Ounces

Can	Weight	Cups
6-ounce	6 ounces	¾ cup
8-ounce	8 ounces	1 cup
#1	9 ounces	1 cup
#1	10½ to 12 ounces	1¼ cup
#300	14 to 16 ounces	1¾ cups
#303	16 to 17 ounces	2 cups
#2	20 ounces	2½ cups
#2½	1 pound, 13 ounces	3½ cups
#3 (46 ounces)	3 pounds, 4 ounces	5¾ cups
#10	7 pounds +	12-13 cups

Liquid Ingredients

1 teaspoon = ⅙ fluid ounce = 5 grams = 5 milliliters
3 teaspoons = 1 tablespoon = ½ fluid ounce = 15 grams = 15 milliliters
2 tablespoons = ⅛ cup = 1 fluid ounce
8 tablespoons = ½ cup = ¼ pint = 4 fluid ounces
1 cup = ½ pint
2 cups = 1 pint
4 cups = 1 quart

Solid Ingredients

Ingredient	Ounces	Grams
Rice, 1 teaspoon	⅙ ounce	5 grams
Salt, 1 tablespoon	½ ounce	15 grams
Butter, 1 cup	8 ounces	240 grams
Dried beans, 2 cups	16 ounces (1 pound)	500 grams
Spices, 1 teaspoon	½ ounce	2½ grams
Grated cheese, 1 cup	4 ounces	100 grams
Flour, 1 tablespoon	½ ounce	15 grams

INDEX

ABOUT THE AUTHOR

JACQUELINE HÉRITEAU is the author of *Oriental Cooking the Fast Wok Way* and *The Best of Electric Crockery Cooking,* as well as numerous other cooking and gardening books. She is also a professional publicist and lives in New York City with her husband—author-painter Earl Hubbard—and the two youngest of her three children.